AF575967

Snapshots 1971–77

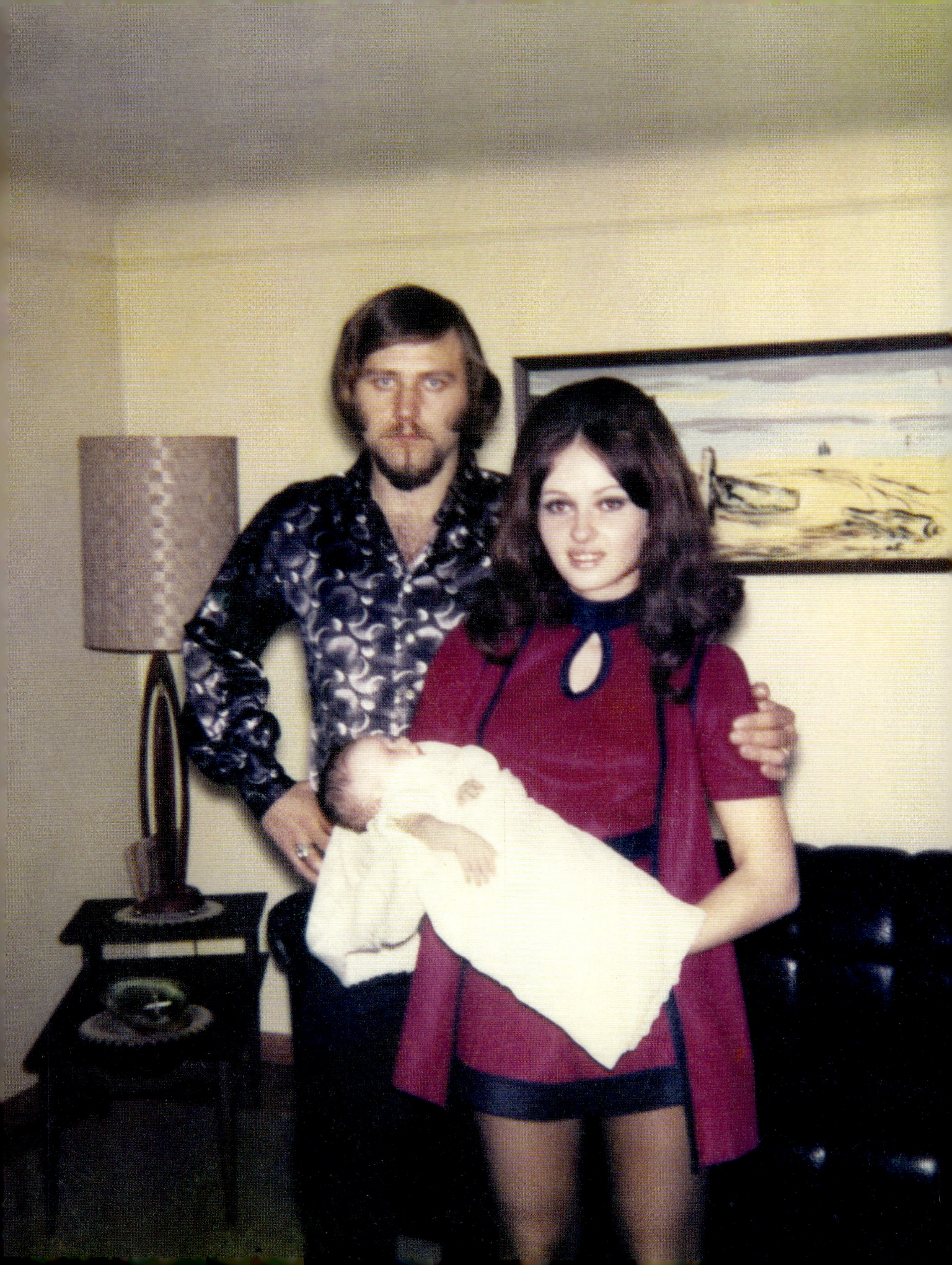

Snapshots 1971–77

Michael Lesy

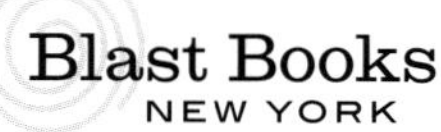

Blast Books
NEW YORK

For Nadia and Alex

Published by Blast Books, Inc.
P. O. Box 51, Cooper Station
New York, NY 10276-0051
www.blastbooks.com

Edited and designed by Laura Lindgren
Typeset in Optima Nova

ISBN: 978-0-922233-50-2 (alk. paper)

Library of Congress Control Number: 2021934705

Printed and bound in China

First Edition 2021

10 9 8 7 6 5 4 3 2 1

The How and Why of This Book

In 1971 my friend and I found most of the snapshots in this book in a dumpster behind a photo processing plant in San Francisco.*

My friend worked for the plant as a courier. His job was to drive a Harley all day around San Francisco, delivering snapshots to drugstores, picking up undeveloped film, and driving it back to the plant for processing.

He was a motorcycle worker bee.

The people at the plant were so busy, they barely noticed his comings and goings.

The result: No one stopped us when we walked through the plant late afternoons, went out the back door, and dug through the trash.

Every week, for four weeks during the summer, we took home whatever snapshots we found. They were in the trash because the machines that made them—duplicates, triplicates, quadruplicates—made them faster than the people on the line could stop them.

We guessed we took home seven thousand a week.

I'd spend days looking through them. Some I kept; most I threw out.

The process was mesmerizing—a drug experience without drugs.

---

* Also in this book are some sixty snapshots from Cleveland. Drugstores in Cleveland threw away unclaimed snapshots after several weeks of waiting for customers to pick them up. I never found out if the drugstores had an official time limit. I suspect that when they ran out of space to keep them behind the front counter, they threw the pictures into a bag and—once the bag was full—threw the bag away. The manager of one of the Cleveland drugstores happened to be a friend of a friend who knew I'd want them.

That image-induced drug experience was what I later (after many years of looking at larger and larger collections of images) described as a state of "dilated calm."* To be able look *at* and see *into* one image after another over the course of many hours, unflaggingly, as I looked at more and more images, was something I first learned while looking at all the snapshots from the processing plant in San Francisco.

When I returned to Wisconsin at the end of summer and began looking at archival images there, I used—with a more concrete purpose in mind—what I learned to do in San Francisco. I would use it again, over the course of my thirty-year scholarly career, to conduct research into larger and larger collections of archival images.

While my friend was out delivering snapshots and I was looking through other people's lives in pictures, the world was coming apart at the seams.

In 1971, these were the headlines:

> Army Lieutenant William Calley was convicted of killing—and ordering his men to kill—five hundred defenseless civilians—old men, women, and children—in the village of My Lai in Vietnam. Calley's superiors were exonerated.
>
> Three of Charles Manson's devotees were convicted of killing, at Manson's command, seven people—people they didn't know—in their homes in L.A. One of the victims was a woman—Sharon Tate, a movie star—who was eight and a half months pregnant.

* By 2017 I could look at an archival collection of more than 500,000 images six hours a day, five days a week, for three months, without burning out. I described this process, this state of dilated calm, in the introduction to my book *Looking Backward* (W. W. Norton, 2017).

The *New York Times* published excerpts from classified documents that their author, Daniel Ellsberg, had removed from the Pentagon. The documents described the U.S. government's conduct of the war in Vietnam and the way the government—from presidents on down—had lied to the American people about it.

Heavily armed New York state troopers quelled the uprising of Attica State Prison. Inmates had seized the prison after they learned that the Black Panther George Jackson (who'd been convicted of robbery and murder) had been killed while trying to escape from San Quentin. Dozens of people—inmates and guards—died during the uprising and the fighting that followed.

Apollo 14 landed on the moon. Alan Shepard, the mission's commander, celebrated the occasion by hitting two golf balls an unearthly distance across the lunar surface.

While Shepard played golf on the moon and the war in Vietnam got worse, people went to the movies. In the movies, they dreamed with their eyes open.

They dreamed nightmares.

Four films premiered that year:

A Clockwork Orange (advertised as "being the adventures of a young man whose principal interests are rape, ultra-violence, and Beethoven").

The French Connection (about a sophisticated ring of heroin smugglers and two tough New York City police detectives).

Dirty Harry (about a heavily armed San Francisco police detective who conducted himself as if he were judge, jury, and executioner).

Straw Dogs (about violence and rape in a small English village).

Back in Madison, Wisconsin, I resumed my life as an American history graduate student—and an aspiring documentary photographer.

Every day I asked myself the same question:

How and why had the U.S. gotten itself into such terrible trouble?

As a photographer, I carried a 35mm, single-lens reflex camera with me when I walked through the world. The French photographer Cartier-Bresson and the American photographer Walker Evans were my inspirations. Bresson's *Decisive Moment*, The Museum of Modern Art's *Family of Man*, and an anthology of Farm Security Administration photographs made during the Great Depression were on my shelf.

As a graduate student, I began researching a collection of photographs made in the small town of Black River Falls, Wisconsin, between the last decade of the nineteenth century and the first decade of the twentieth.

Many of them were studio portraits. Economic depression and epidemic disease lay behind the eyes of the people in the photographs.

As I looked at their faces, as I read about their lives, I thought about my family—and I thought about my past.

My mother's mother had been an indentured servant in the Ukraine. In America, the man who became her husband bought out her contract so he could marry her. She bore him seven children, one after the other.

My father's family came from a small town outside of Warsaw. His father owned a cobbler's shop. When my father was six, his father died and the family became paupers. Now and then, after school, Polish boys chased him through the fields, like dogs chasing a rabbit.

In 1921 my father's family immigrated to America and moved to Cleveland.

Back in Poland, after World War II started, the SS herded everyone living in my father's town into the town's big wooden synagogue. First, they forced them to scrape off the synagogue's frescoes of the Creation with their fingernails. Then they locked the doors and burned everyone alive.

In America, my father became a doctor.
A relative of my mother introduced her to him.
Their marriage lasted sixty years.

My parents waited until the end of the war in Europe before they tried to have a family. I was their only child.

They saved their money and sent me to the best private school in Cleveland that was willing to admit Jews. The Holocaust had made the school more tolerant.

I learned Latin and German. I read what I was told to read: Dickens and de Maupassant and O'Henry.

The only things that stayed with me were the hymns we sang in chapel before class. There were two I never forgot. They became beacons.

This is how one began:

"Glorious things of thee are spoken, Zion, city of our God. He whose word cannot be broken formed thee for his own abode."

It was written by John Newton, the same man who wrote "Amazing Grace."

The other hymn I remembered was written by the poet James Russell Lowell:

"Once to every man and nation comes the moment to decide, In the strife of Truth with Falsehood, for the good or evil side . . . Then it is the brave man chooses, while the coward stands aside. . . ."

I didn't know when I sang those hymns, that John Newton had been a slave trader before he converted, or that James Russell Lowell had been an abolitionist.

What I did know, though, when I stood and sang with everyone else, was that Jesus had been a Jew and that when I had to make a choice between truth and falsehood, I would make the right choice. I would be brave.

When the time came to go to college, I went to Columbia. During my first year I had to read excerpts from books Columbia considered "the foundation stones of contemporary civilization."

St. Augustine's *City of God* took its place next to the hymns I once sang. Together, they lit my path through the world.

Augustine said that there were two kinds of love in the world.

He said people who lived in the City of Man loved earthly things. They believed that owning things would make them happy—if not forever, then long enough for them to acquire more things, other things, better things. Since everyone wanted the same things, people fought each other. Desire, dread, envy, and sorrow swept through them.

Augustine admitted that the people who lived in City of Man were capable of love but, he said, they loved the wrong things.

The right kind of love, the *true* kind of love, said Augustine, was the love of Heaven. People in the City of God lived inside their faith. They believed when they died, they would live again in the Heavenly Jerusalem. They would live in the Light, and they would live in it forever.

I wanted to believe that, but I had my doubts.

In chapel, after we sang hymns, we would recite "The Lord's Prayer" together. I still remember the words—and I still love them.

But at Columbia, after Augustine, I was assigned Hobbes.

Hobbes's description of life—lived without moral law*—as "solitary, poor, nasty, brutish, and short" made sense to me. It made as much sense as "Do unto others as you would have them do unto you."

I found a place for the Hobbes next to the Augustine and the hymns I used to sing. Hobbes, to me, was a warning light: I'd been born in 1945—just as the dead were being counted.

I mention all this as a way to explain why, fifty years later, I still have the snapshots in this book.

In 1971 I felt—and still feel—like a stranger in a strange land. I was—and I am—appalled and amazed by this country. I was—and remain—deeply curious.

* The SS, however, claimed its conduct was a law unto itself.

Looking through the snapshots, fresh from the trash, was like being blasted by a firehose of information, soaked and pinned to the wall by it. It was intimate, domestic, close-up information that I could never have known otherwise.

I realized something important: the people who made the pictures were insiders, not outsiders. I also understood that the people *behind* the camera made, without intending to, pictures of themselves.

Seen through the eyes of an outsider like me, the snapshots looked in four directions at once: out at the subject, back at the photographer, inward at their assumptions and beliefs, and then out, beyond them, at the world in which they thought they lived.

I took hundreds and hundreds of snapshots with me when I went back to Wisconsin from San Francisco. I understood them as forming an archive—an archive of the present.

Fifty years later, everything and nothing has changed.

In Wisconsin, I kept looking through the Black River Falls archival photographs until I'd memorized them.* Then I began to conduct myself like a conventional historian: I studied state and federal census data and read and reread microfilm copies of the local paper.

Eventually, I met an elderly woman who had served as the town's historian for decades. She knew everything about the place, the high and low of it, its official history and its unofficial one. I conducted long

* The photo-archival process of looking *and* remembering—that image-induced drug experience without drugs state of mind—was the same as looking at the snapshots in San Francisco, but reaching back into a time long gone.

interviews with her in her dining room, tape-recorded them, transcribed them, and sent her the transcripts. I wanted to be sure I'd quoted her correctly.*

To all this information, I added public health records, case histories of local people who'd been committed to the state mental hospital—and excerpts from short stories and novels about the Midwest that had been published during the time I was investigating.

I edited everything together—texts and transcripts, news articles and scenes from short stories—as if I were editing a movie. The results were taped-together pages of quotations intercut with copies of archival photographs—a collage of words and pictures—a fugue of images and stories about the town, the region, and the state it was in.

I made two copies of this book-length collage.

One I submitted to my thesis committee. The other I submitted to a publisher.

My committee was skeptical of my methods and my findings. The use of archival photographs as primary documents baffled and alarmed them. They were academics who only believed in words.

Book reviewers in the United States, the United Kingdom, and western Europe thought otherwise.

"The poetry of history" was how one reviewer described what I'd made. My PhD committee wasn't entirely convinced—half its members thought I'd found a new way to tell history; half thought I was a fraud—the academic equivalent of a counterfeiter.

Eventually, the committee granted me a PhD—with great misgivings.

---

* She was outraged when she read them. "I forbid you to quote me! You don't have to live here—I do!" I obeyed her: once I fact-checked what she'd said, I paraphrased her words and attributed them to two different, anonymous sources.

My book, *Wisconsin Death Trip*, sold well. My publisher went on to publish more of my books. For the next twenty years, from one book to the next, I traveled throughout the United States giving lectures, each illustrated with hundreds of archival images.

I don't remember when I made color slides of the snapshots I'd found in San Francisco. Now and then in my travels, I'd show them to audiences. When the lights came back on, we'd talk about what they'd seen. Were they art? Were they documents? And if so, what did they document?

When I showed the images, I was careful not to try to over explain them. I'd point out gestures, glances, postures, settings. For the San Francisco snapshots, unlike the Wisconsin images, I had no accounts of events to go along with them. I'd make hints and prompt people to look and then look again.

The purpose of those slide shows—and now the purpose of this book—was to show images whose meanings appear obvious, but which are riddles with more than one answer.

How to Read the Snapshots in This Book

One of my teachers told me that cameras were no different from pencils: they can write poems as easily as they can write shopping lists.

The snapshots in this book do both.

Looked at individually, as visual documents, they reveal—or allude to—the hopes, fears, and desires of the people who made them. Sometimes snapshots tell the truth, sometimes they lie, sometimes they do both.

Looked at in large numbers—in batches of a dozen or a hundred or a thousand—they line up like bits of colored glass in a kaleidoscope and form patterns . . . patterns of shared belief, patterns of shared meaning.

Seen in one way, snapshots can be read as social and historical documents.

Seen in another way, they can be read as psychological documents—as tableaux/enactments/emblems whose meanings are hidden *and* obvious.

If they are seen as social, historical, *and* psychological documents—and if they are seen in large batches—snapshots can reveal the collective consciousness of very large groups of people.

Whether looked at singly or in multiples, snapshots have to be deciphered. What they leave out is often as important as what they leave in; what they emphasize and what they minimize can be equally revealing.

As visual/social/psychological documents, snapshots provoke a variety of responses—some objective, some subjective—from the people who look at them.

Even the simplest image may require multiple viewings.

A Word of Advice

Snap judgments followed by second thoughts are built into the structure of this book.

—M.L.

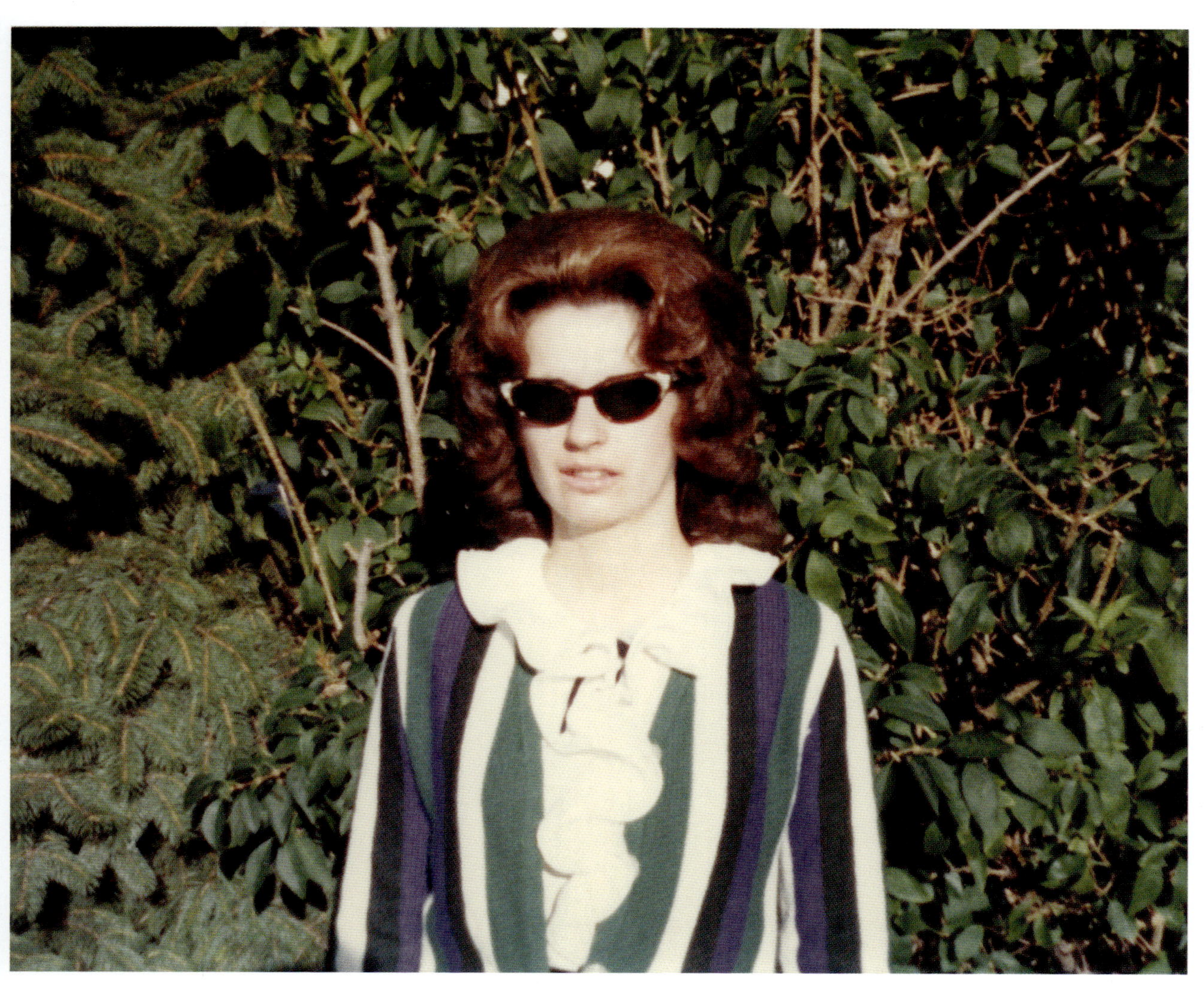

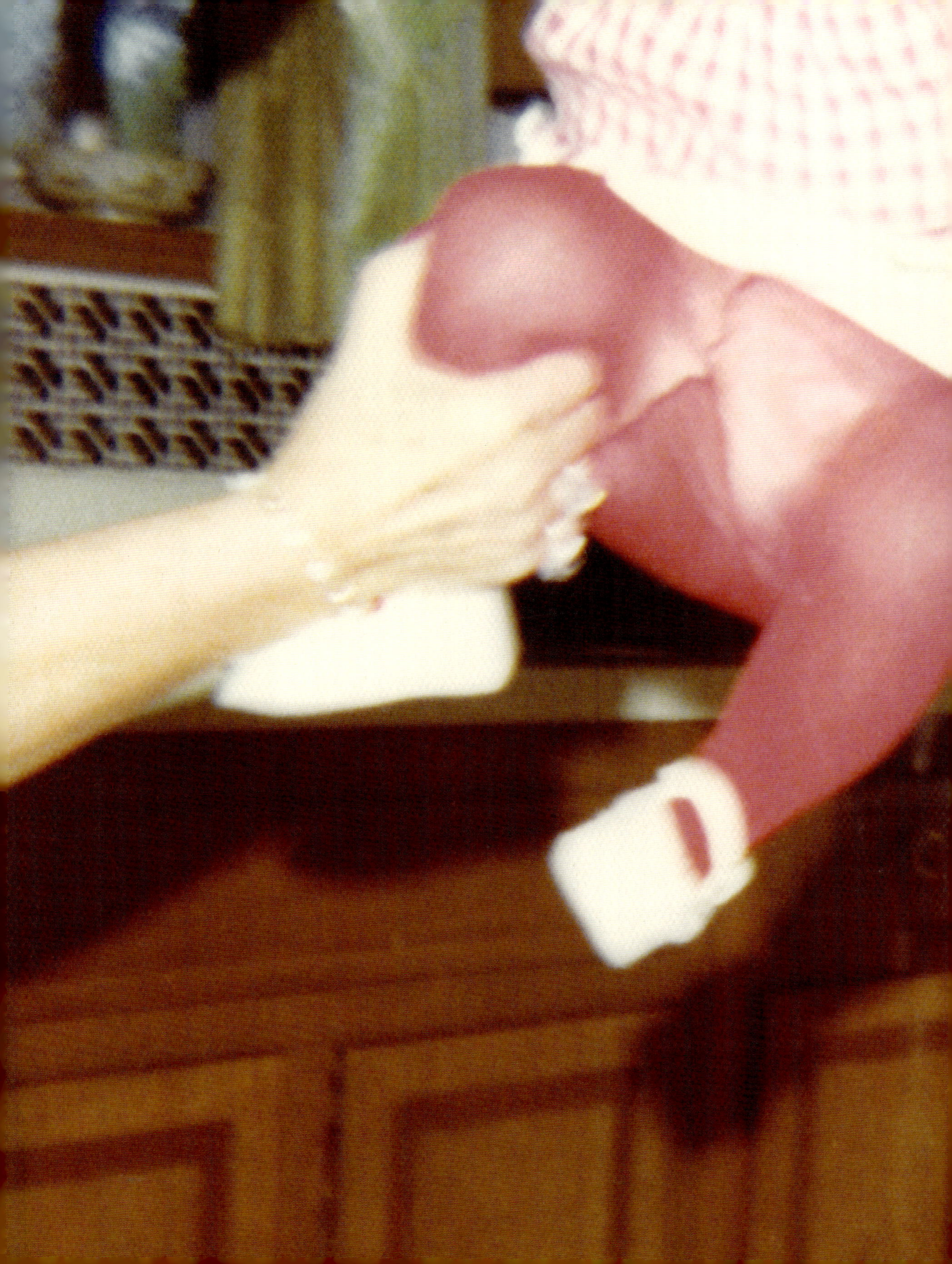

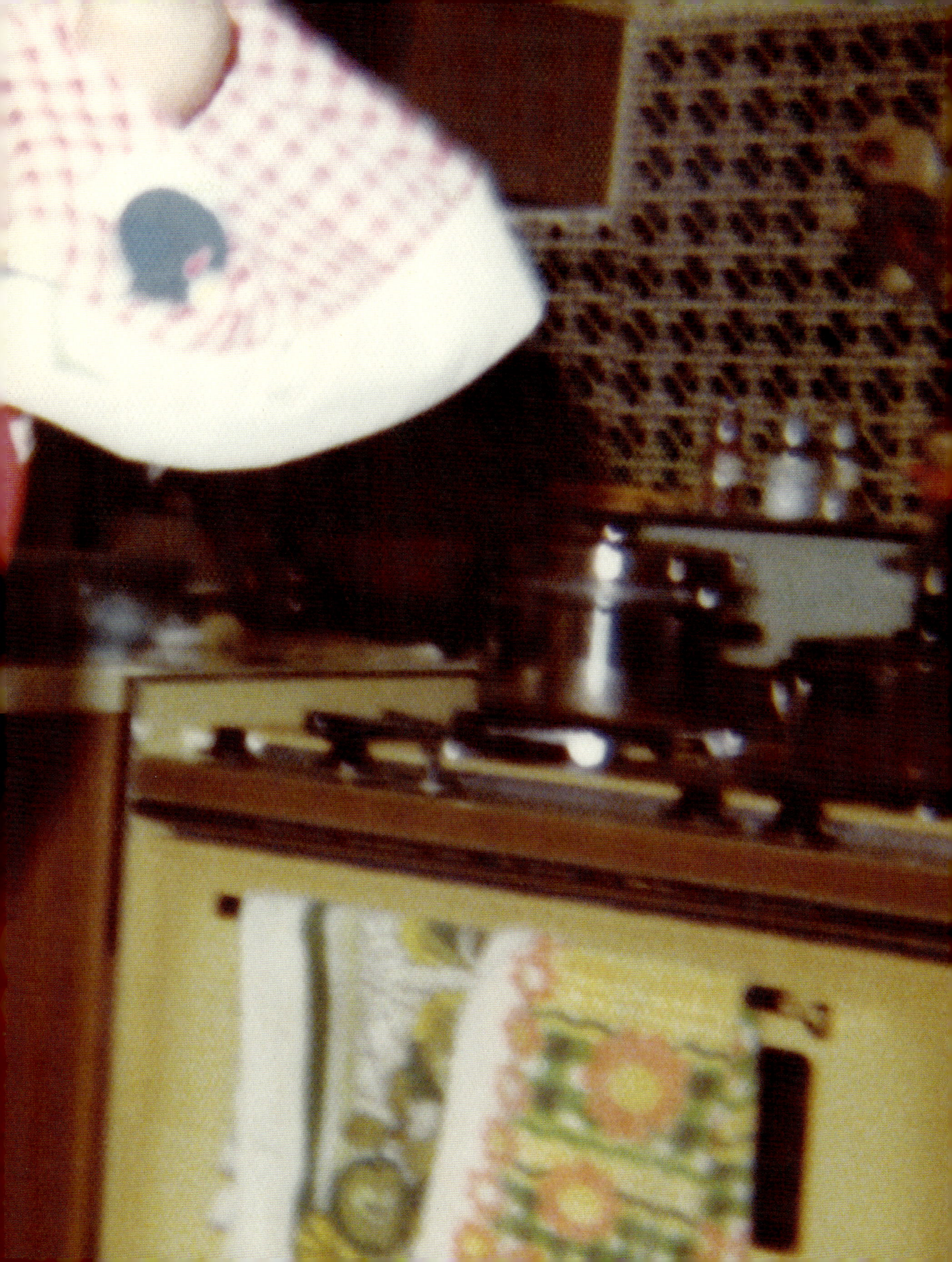

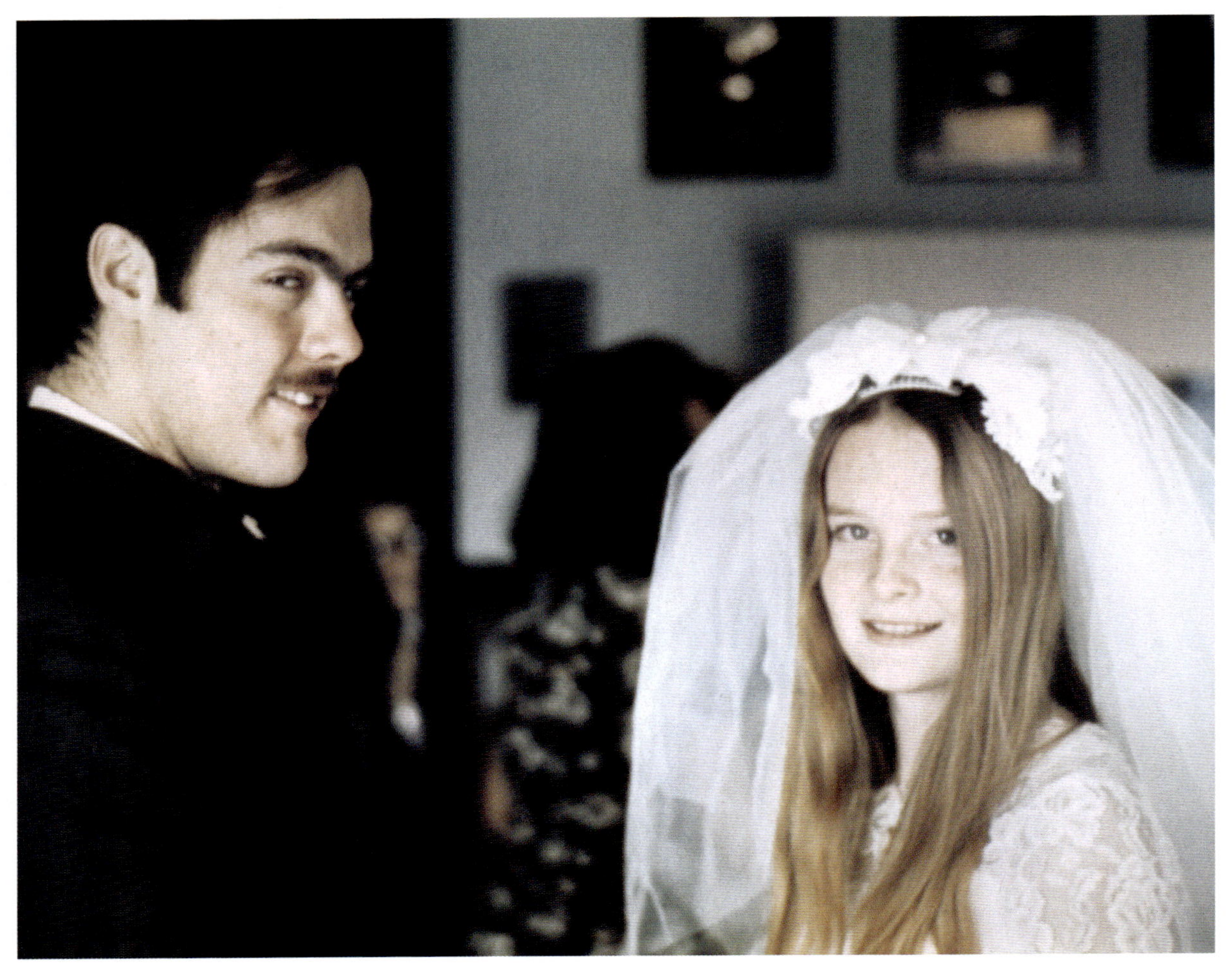

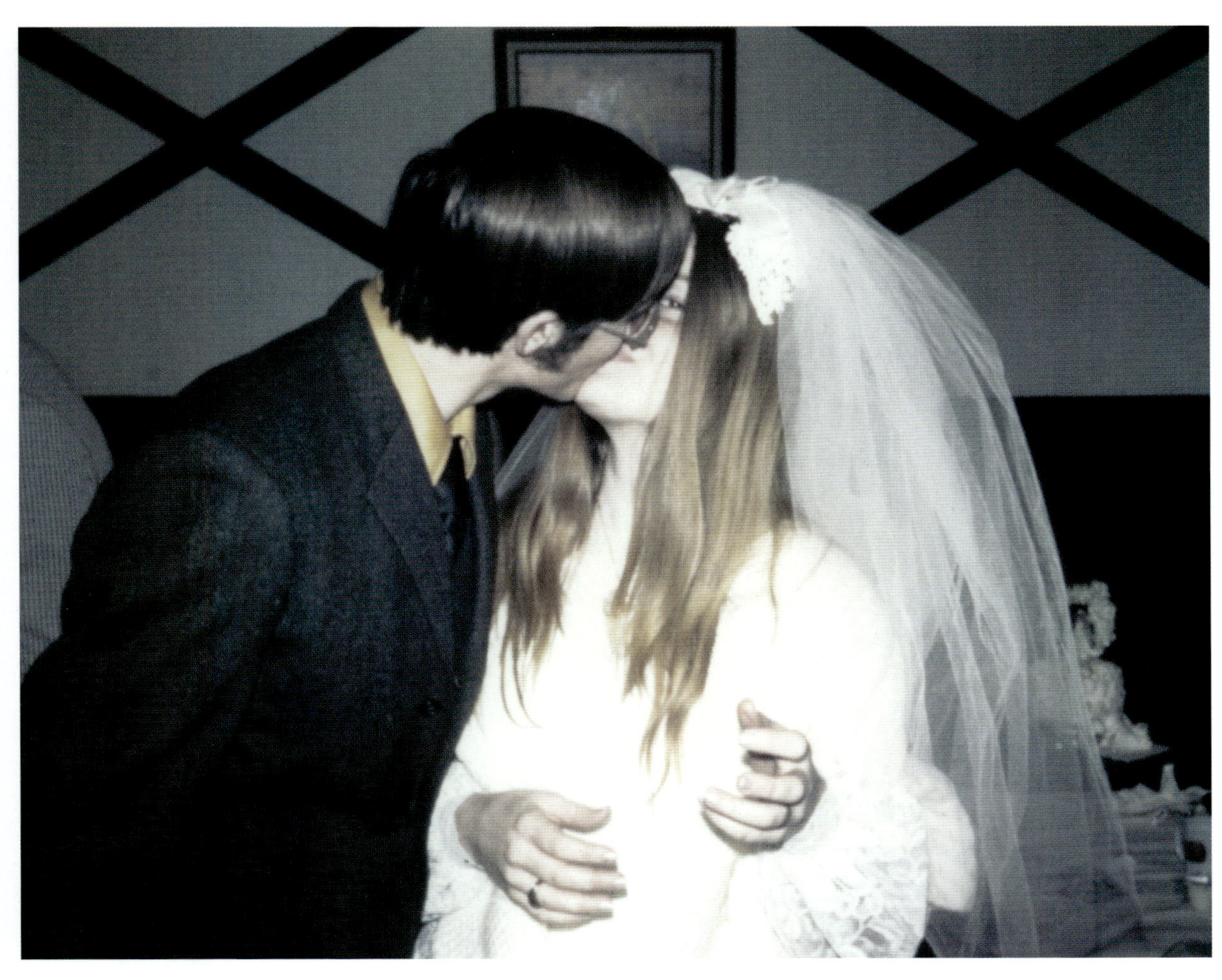

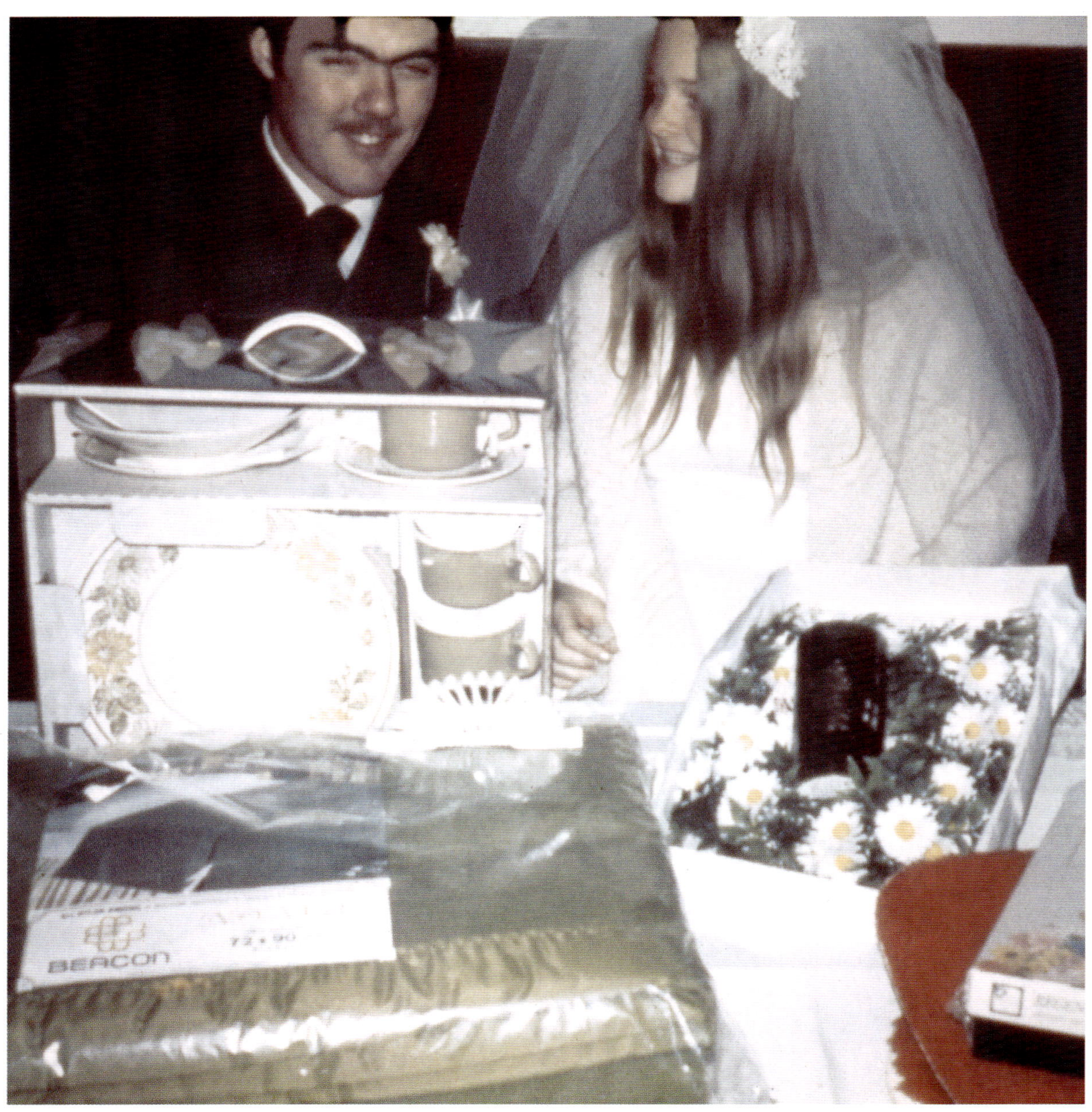
BEACON
72 x 90

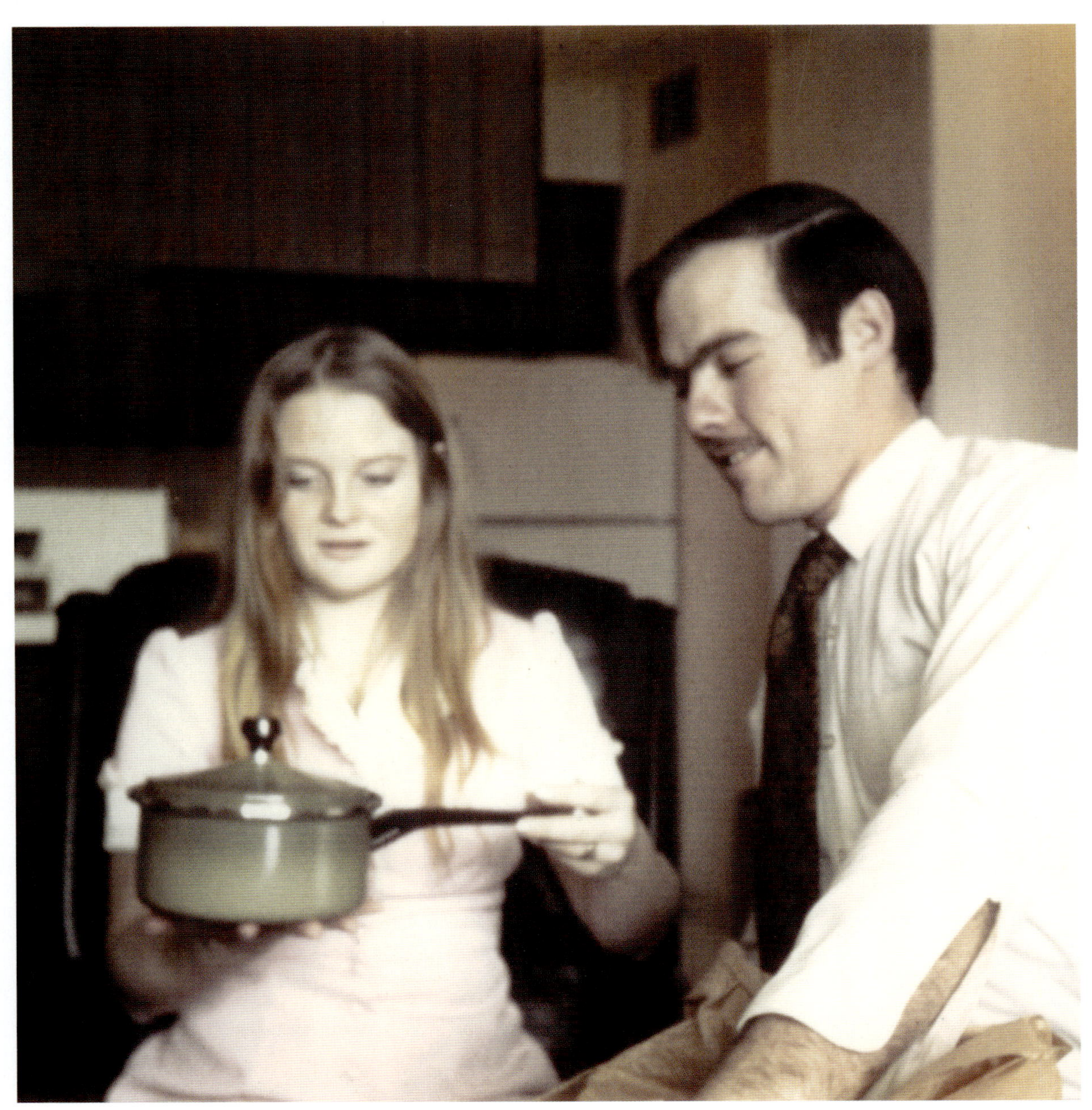

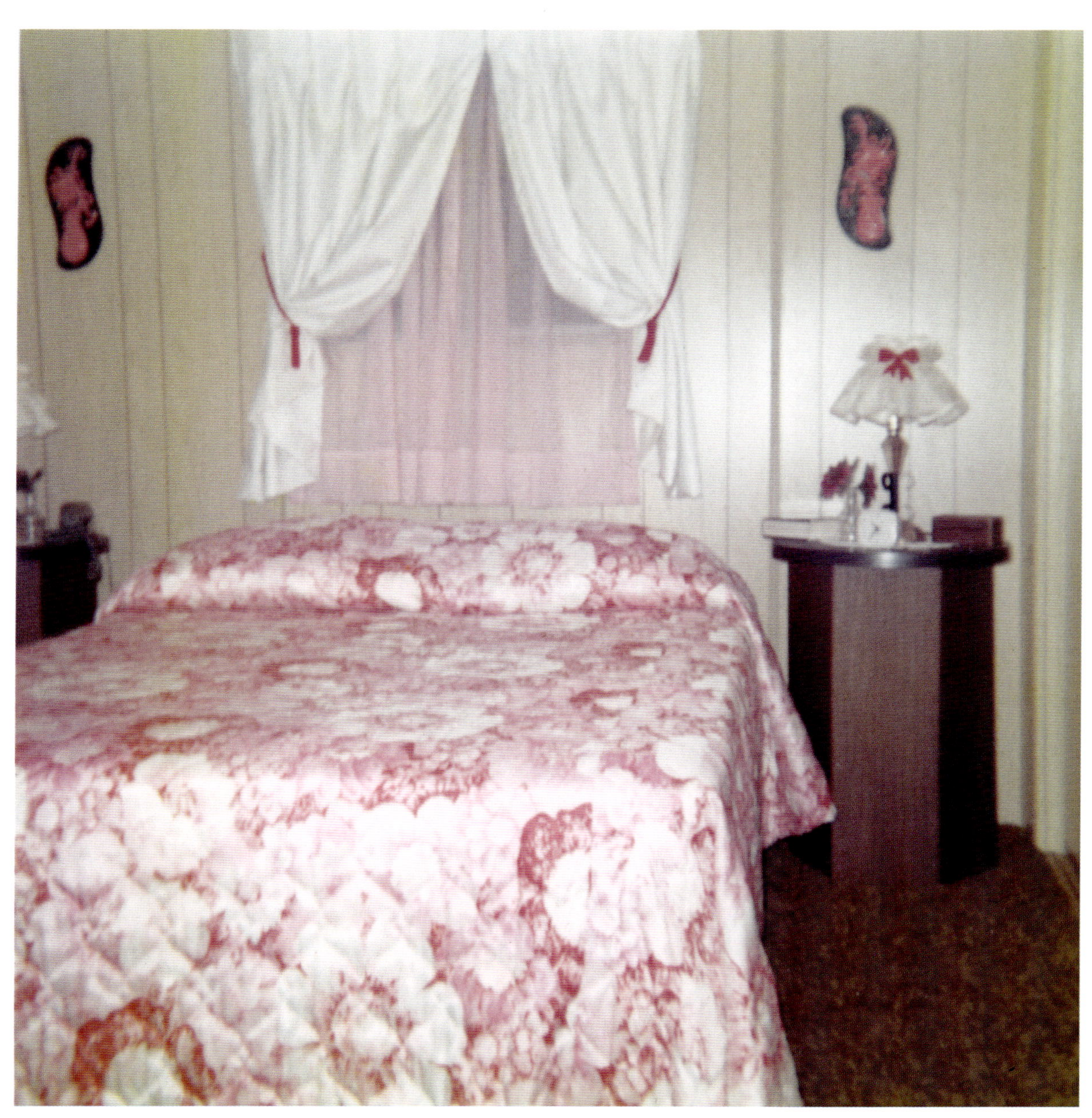

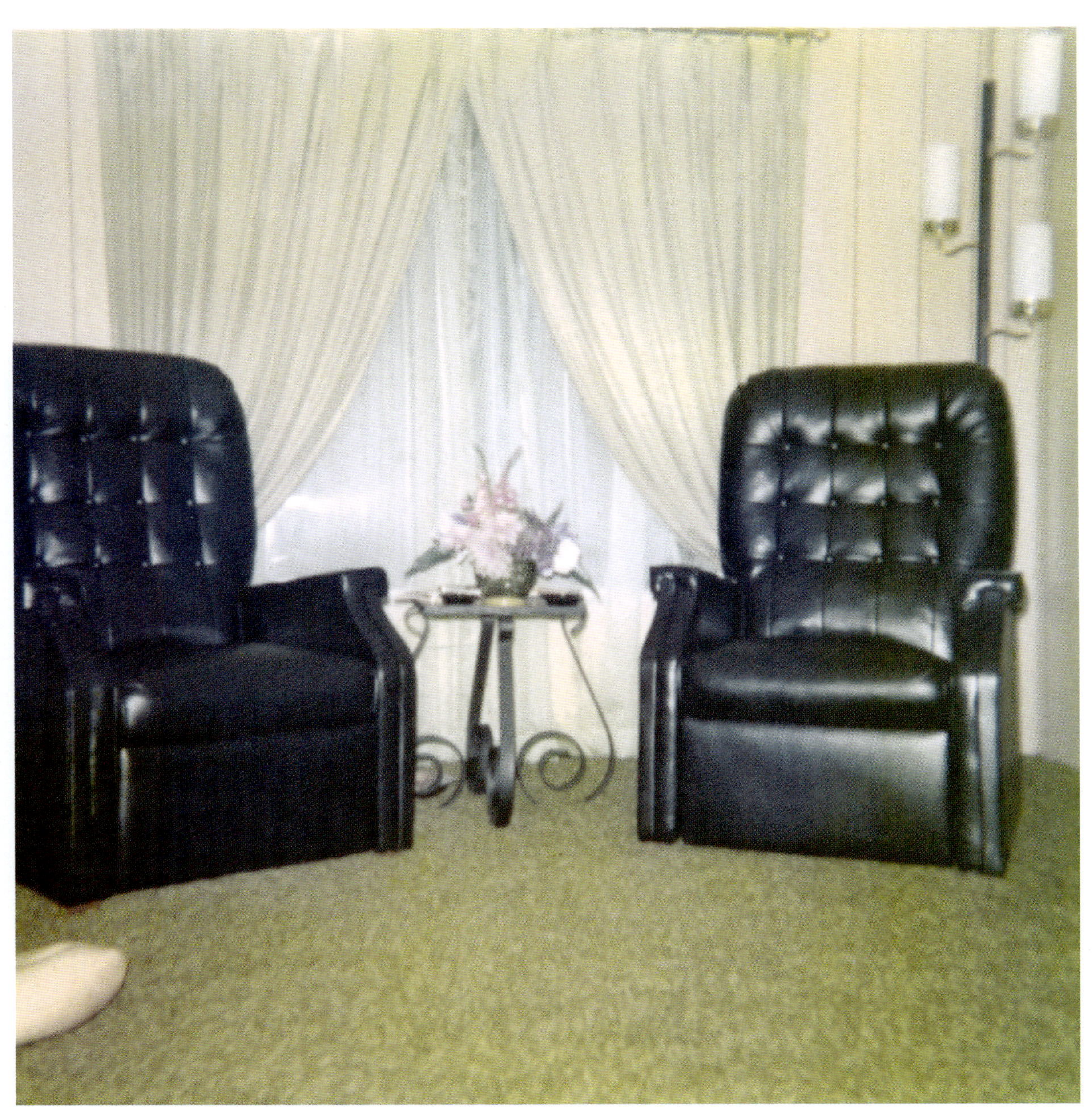

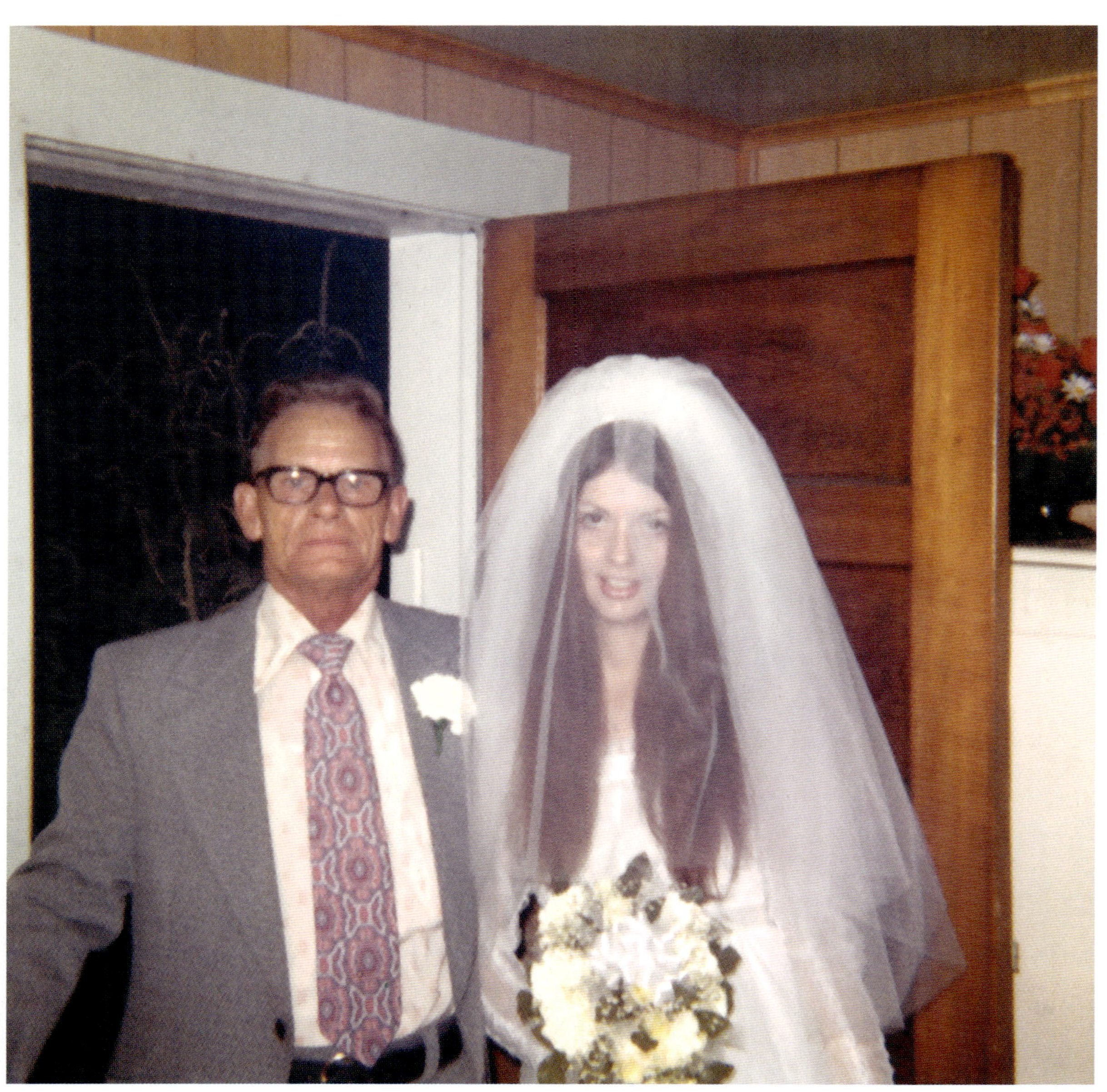

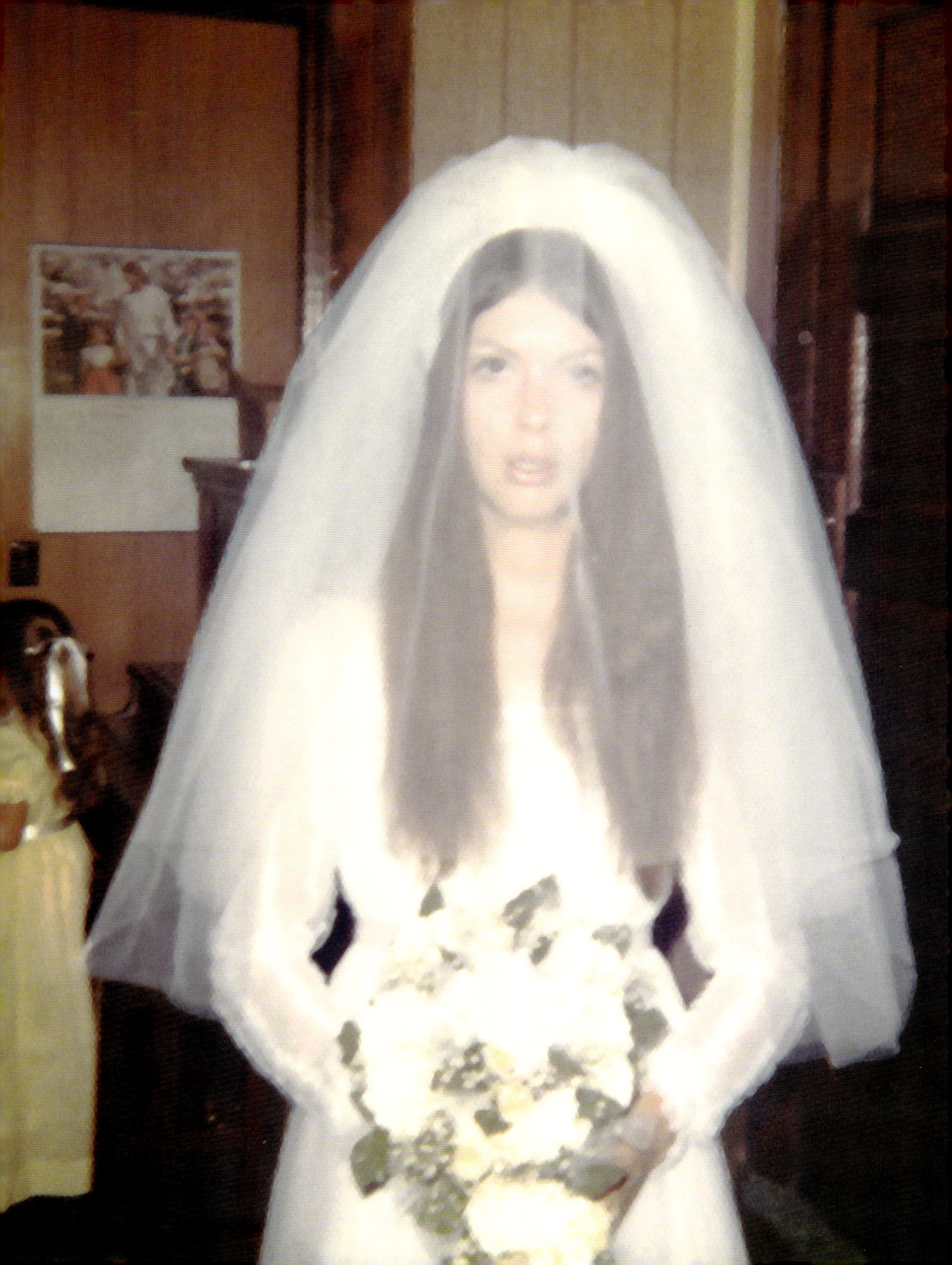

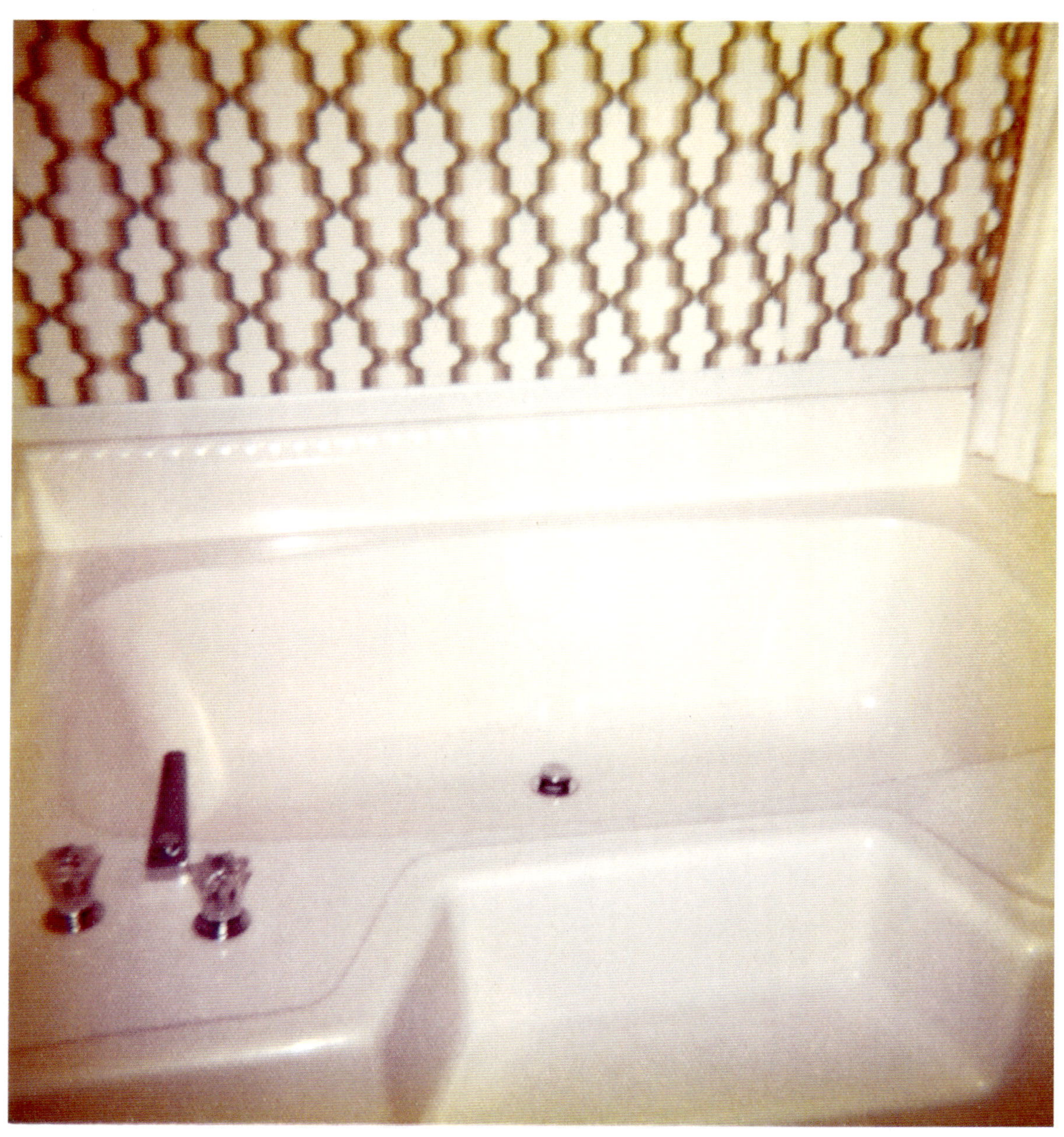

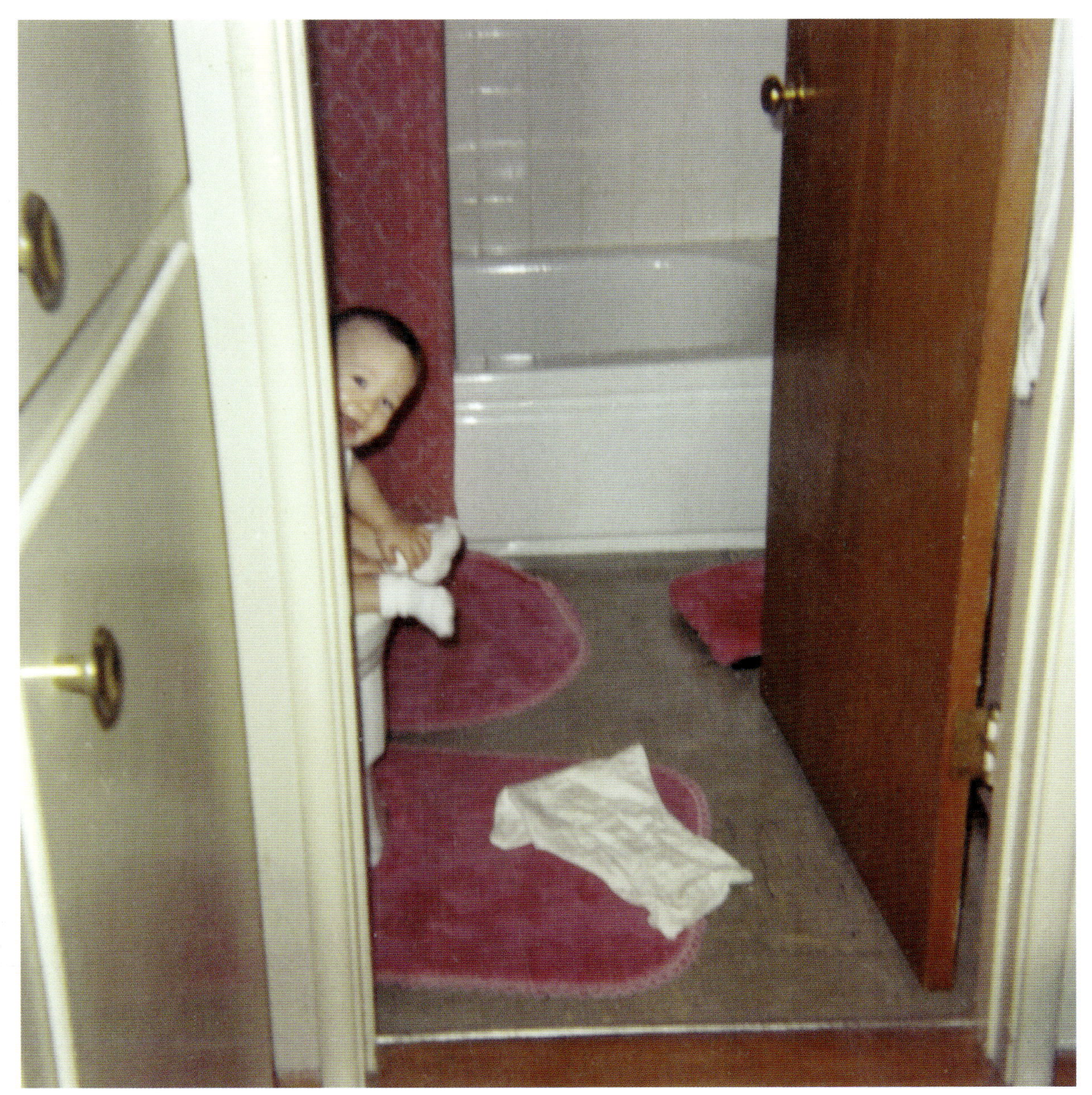

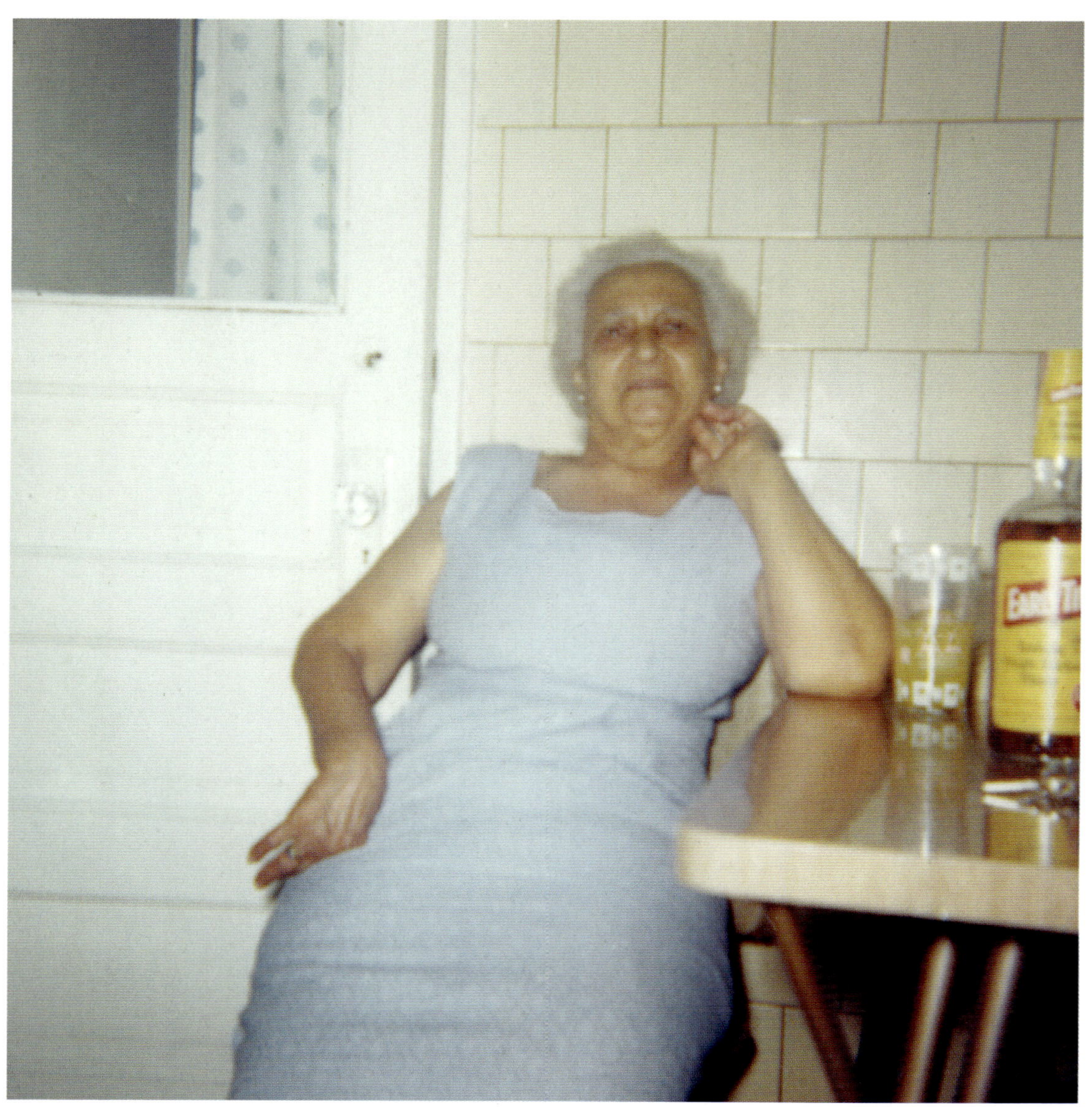

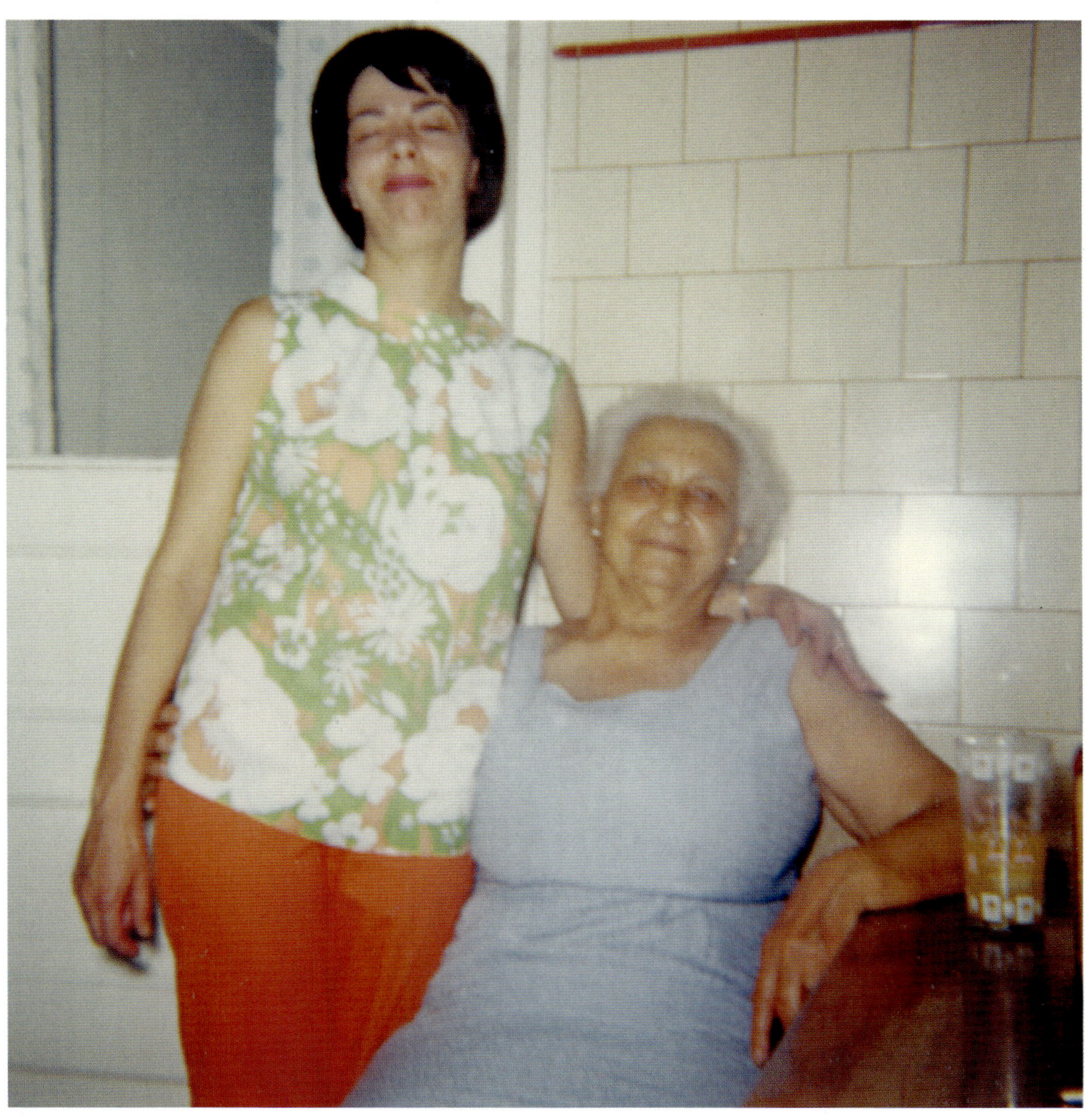

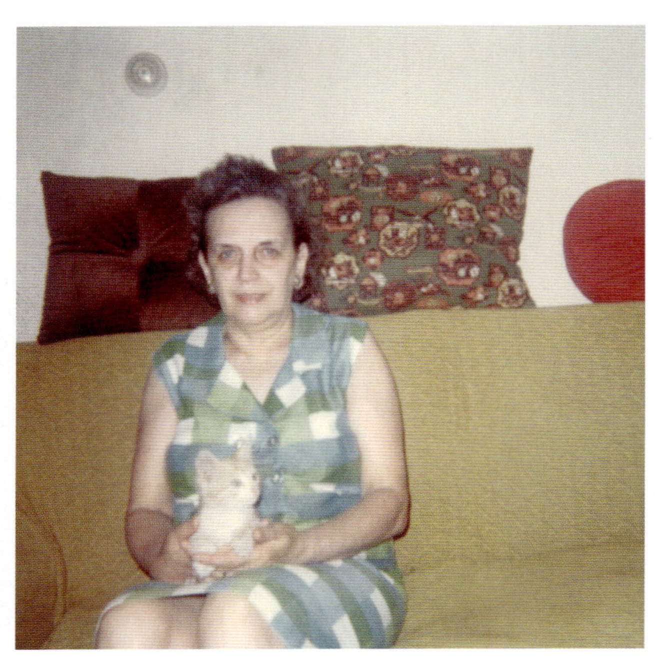

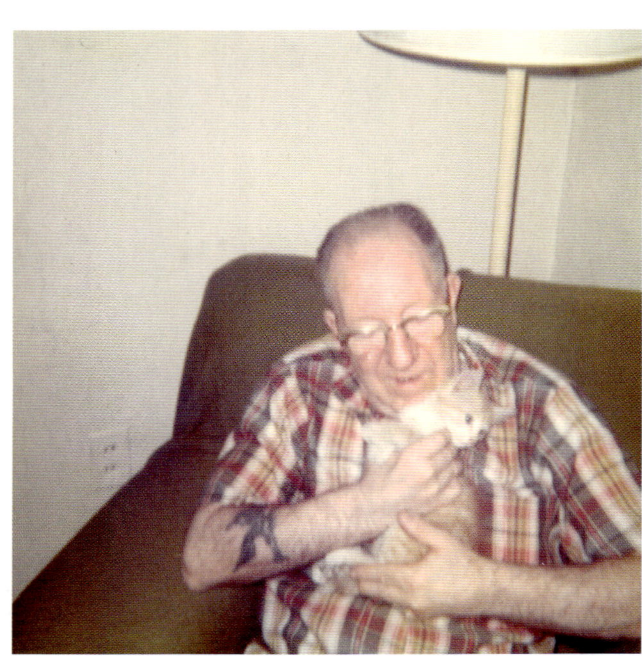

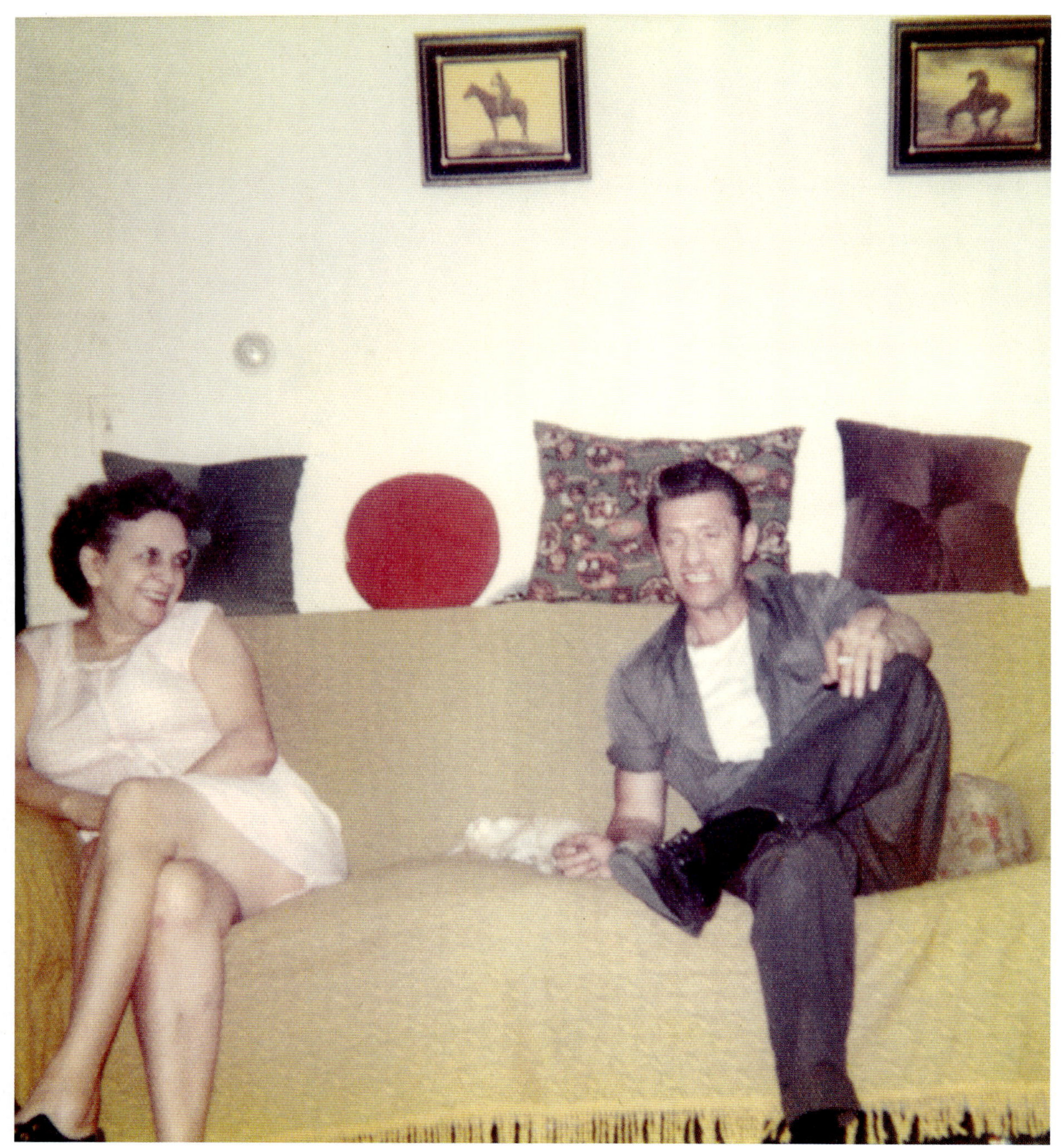

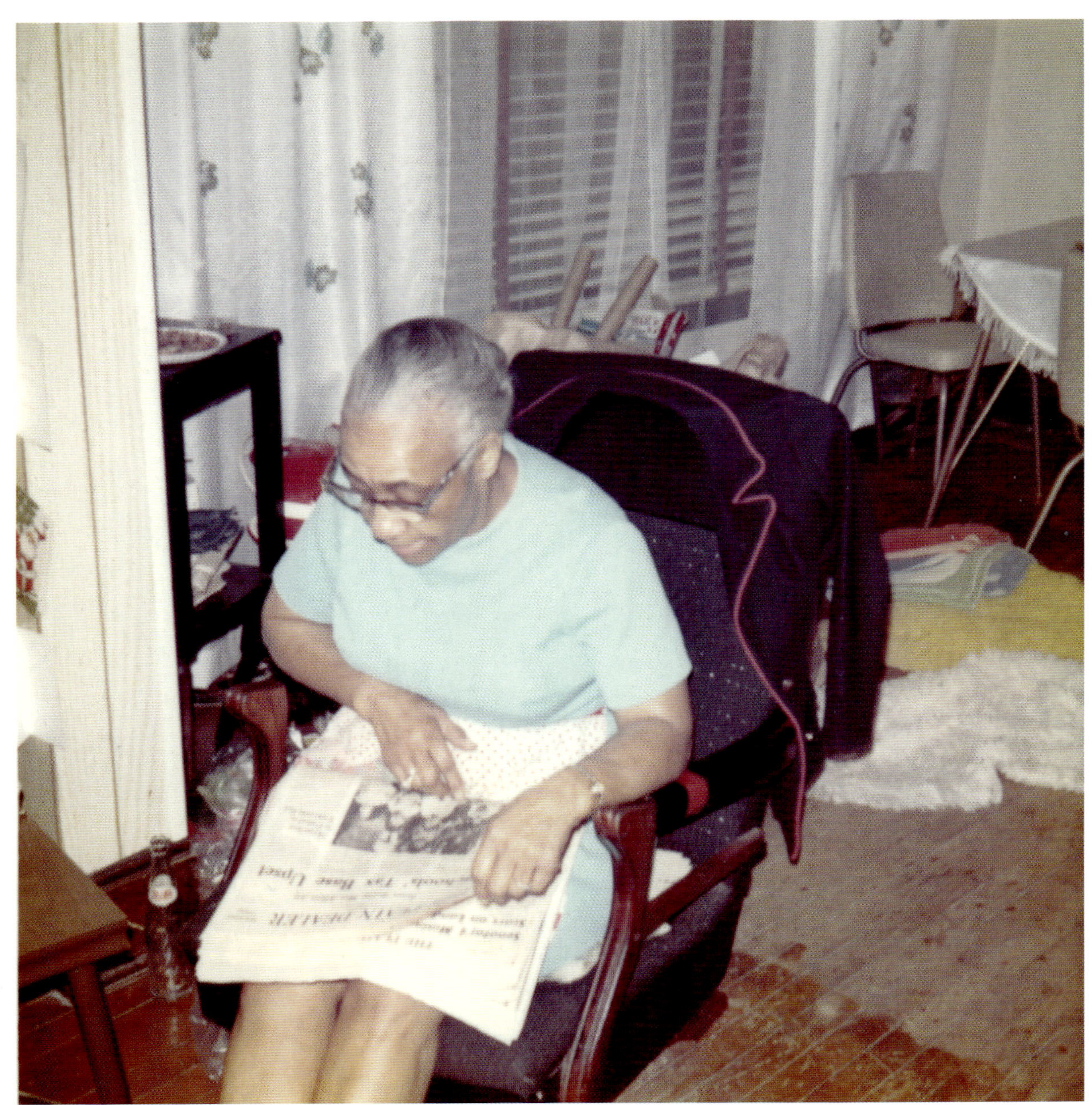

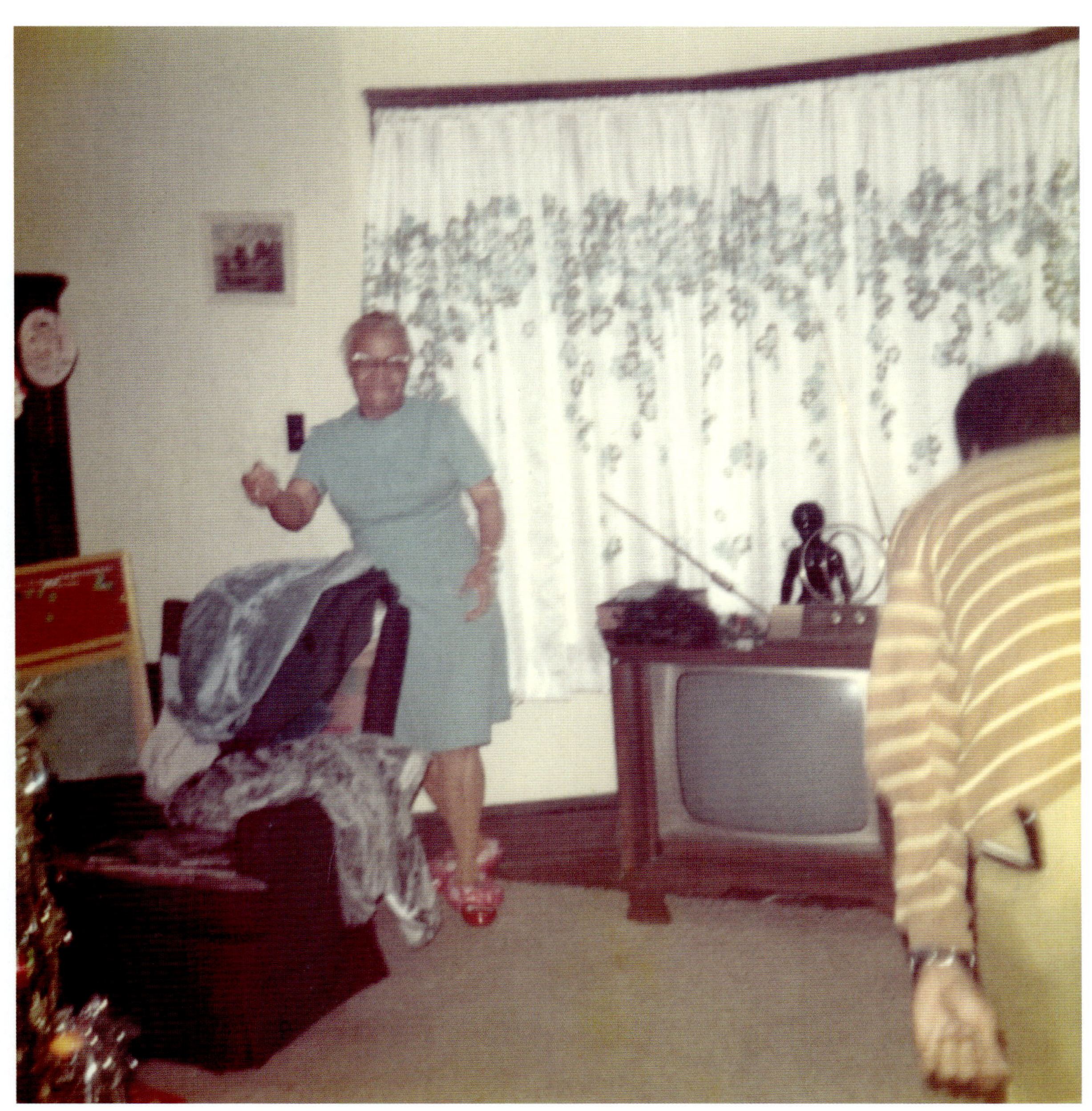

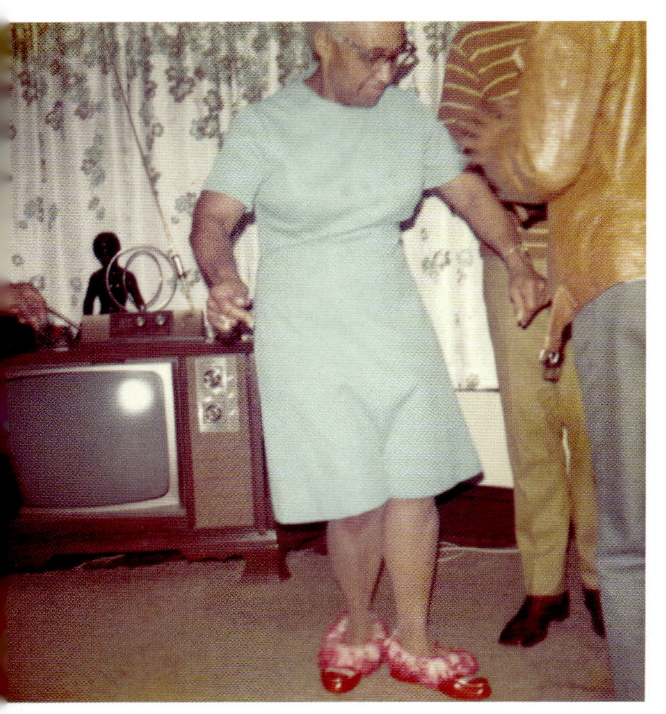
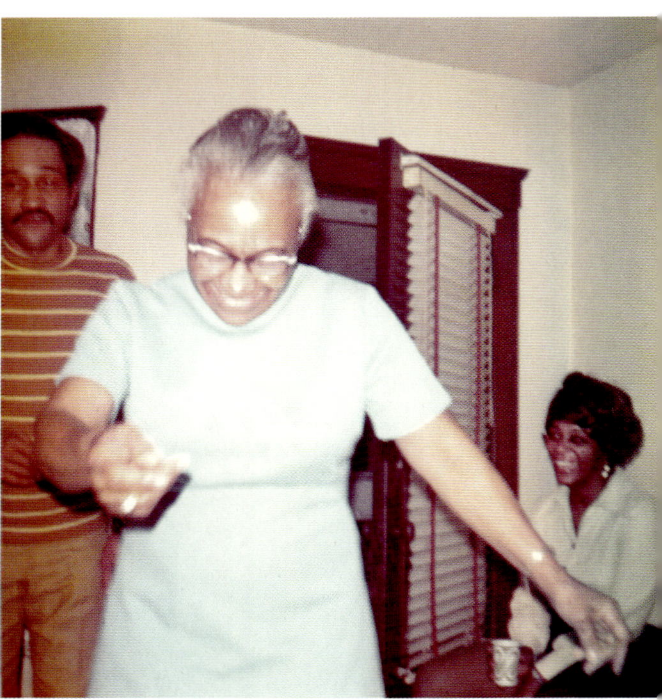

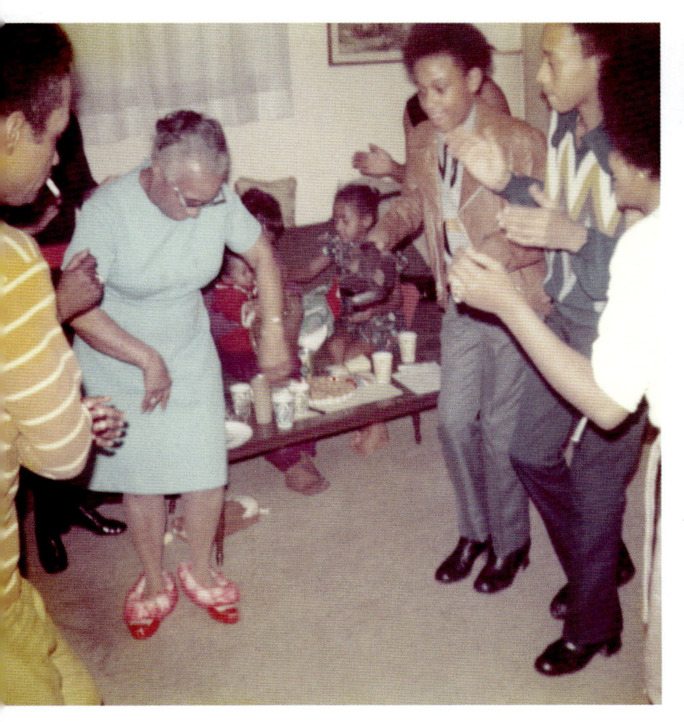

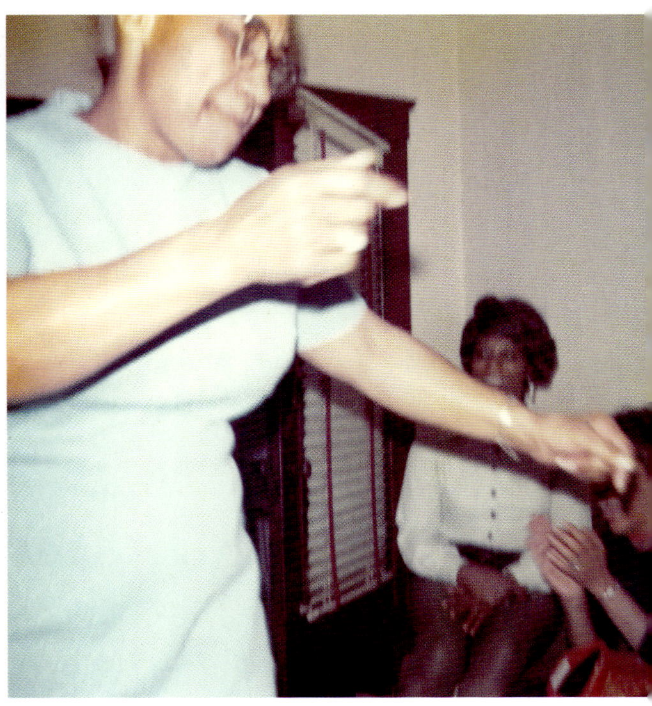

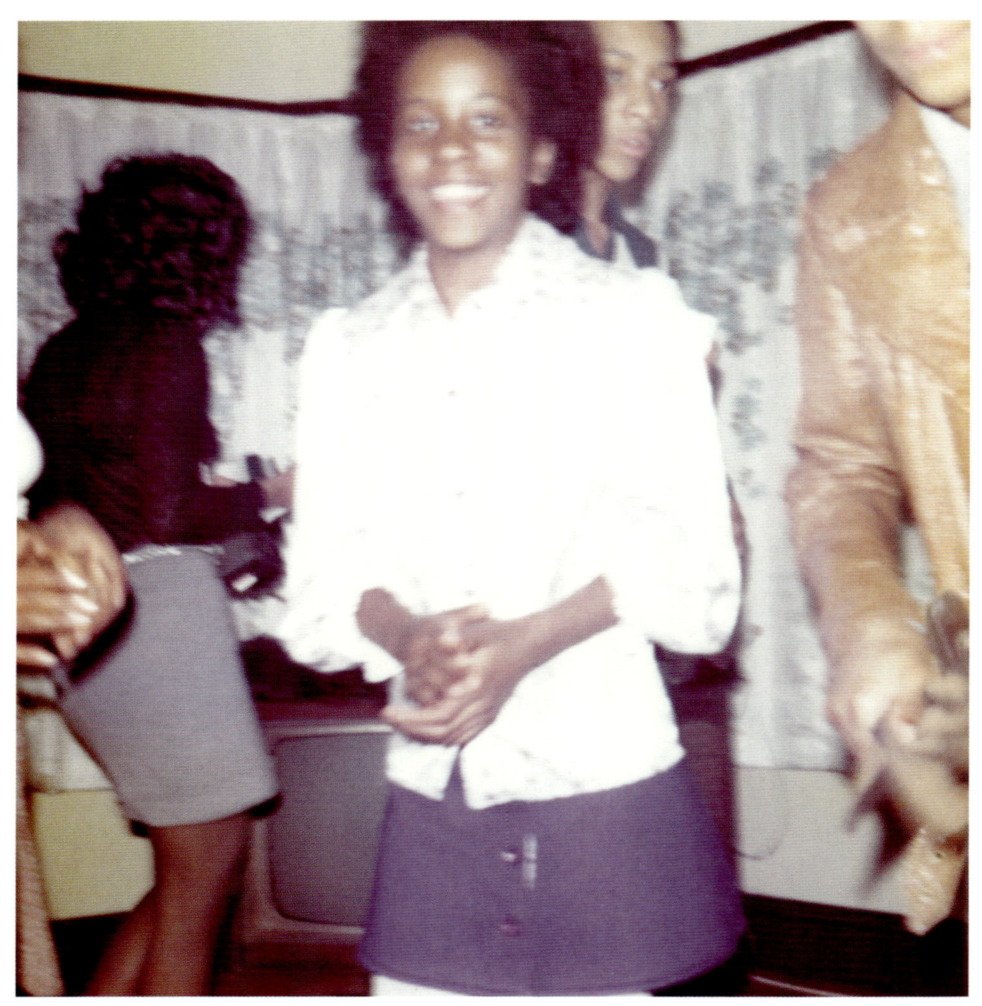

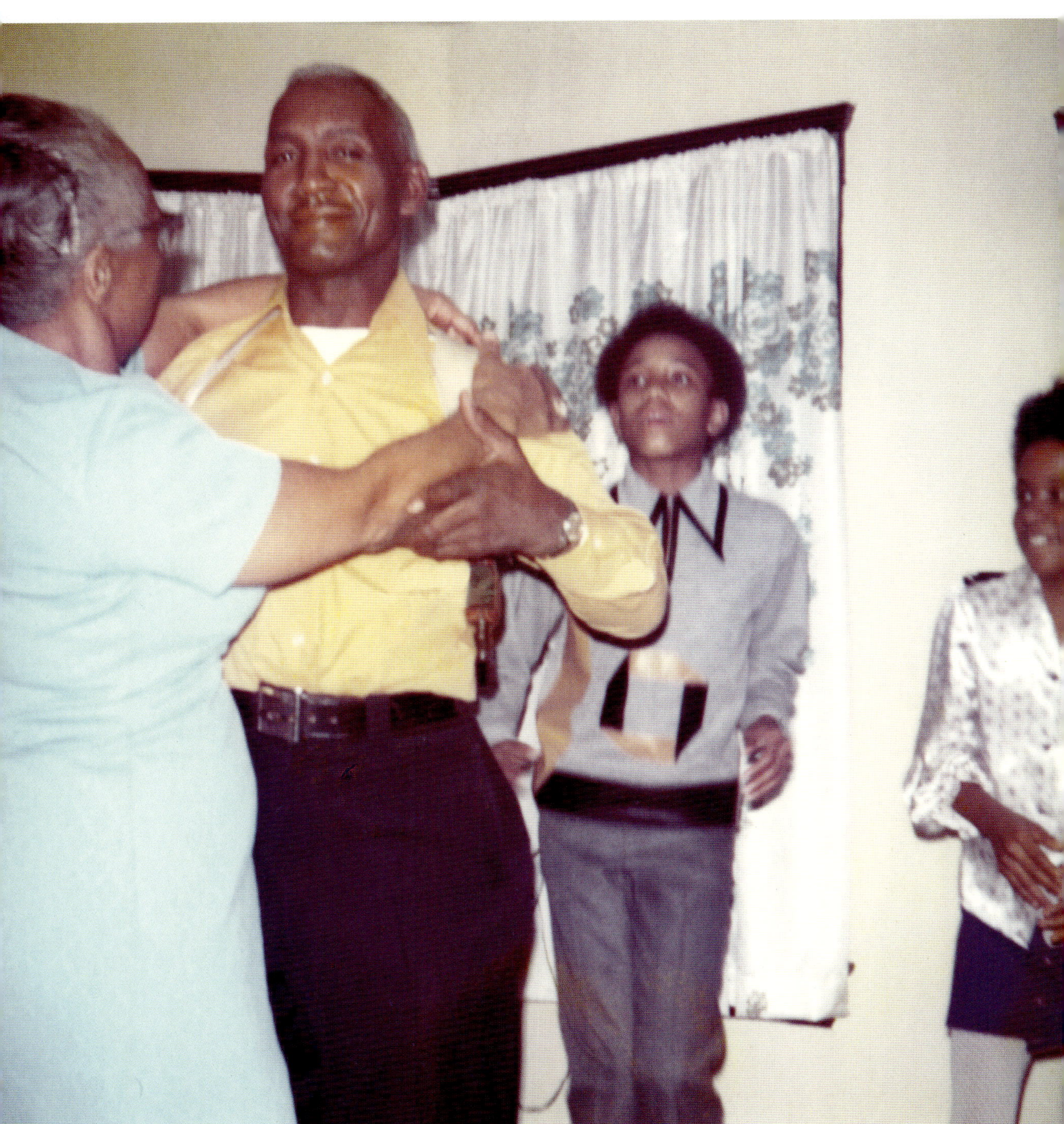

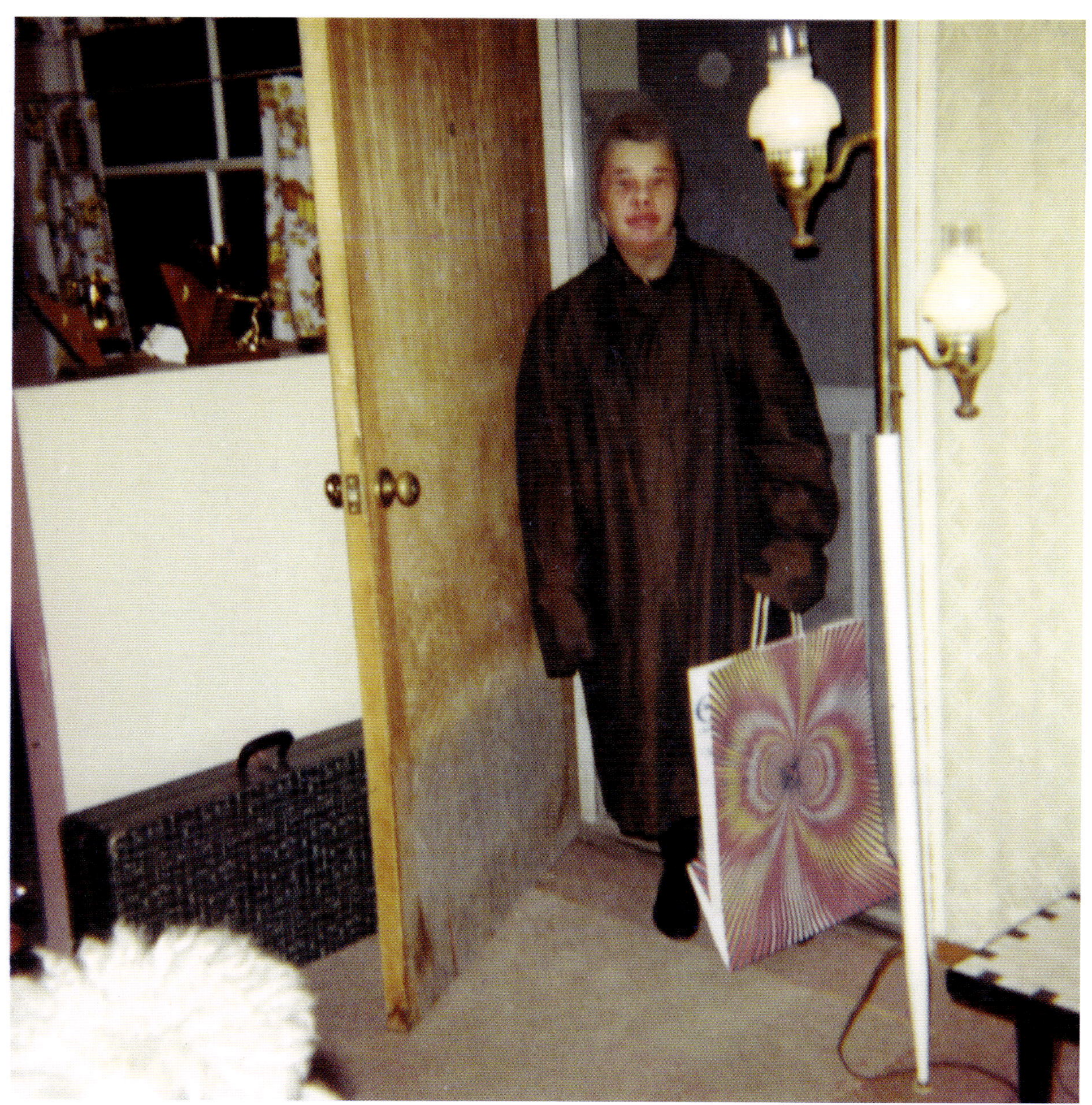

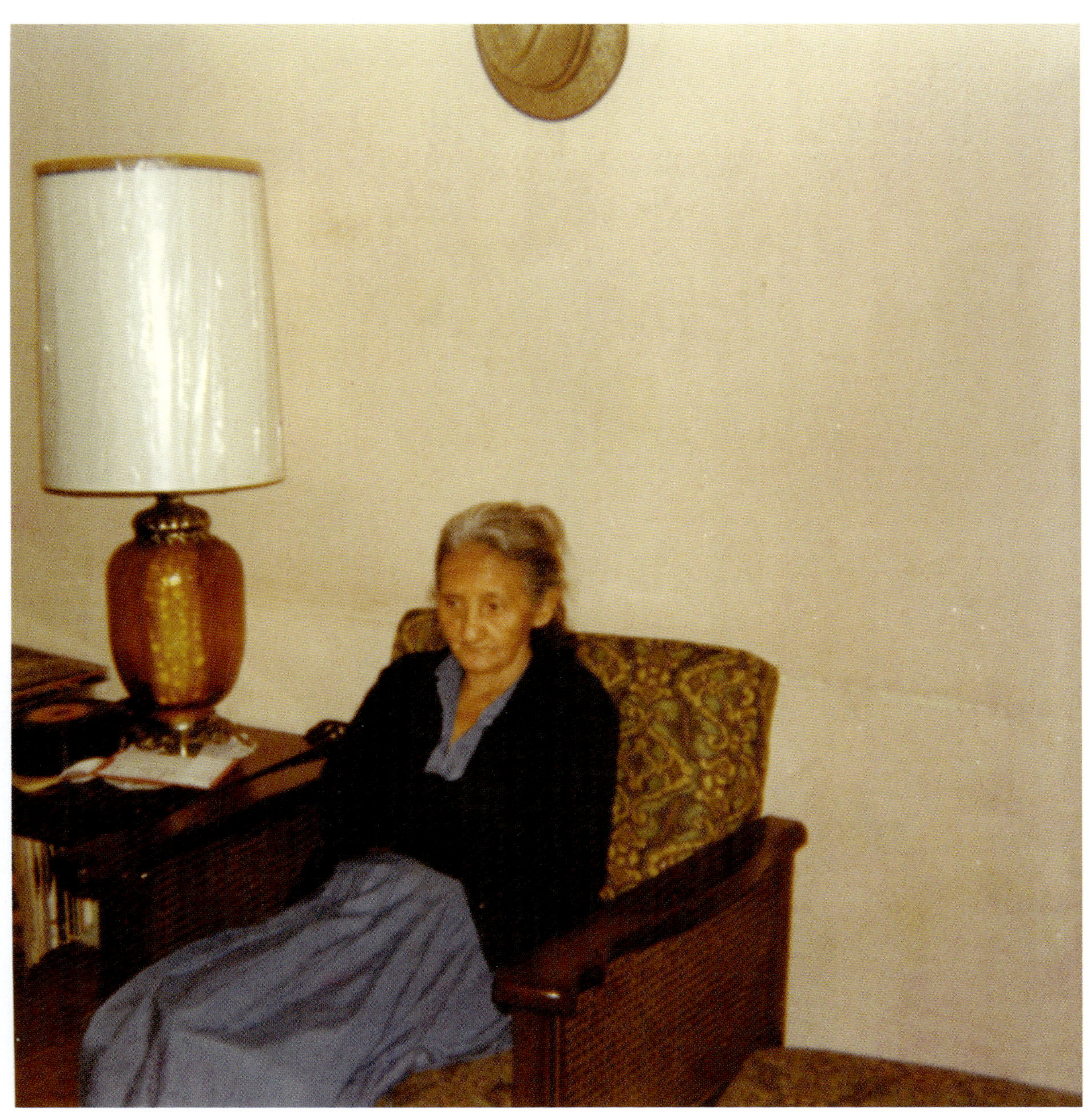

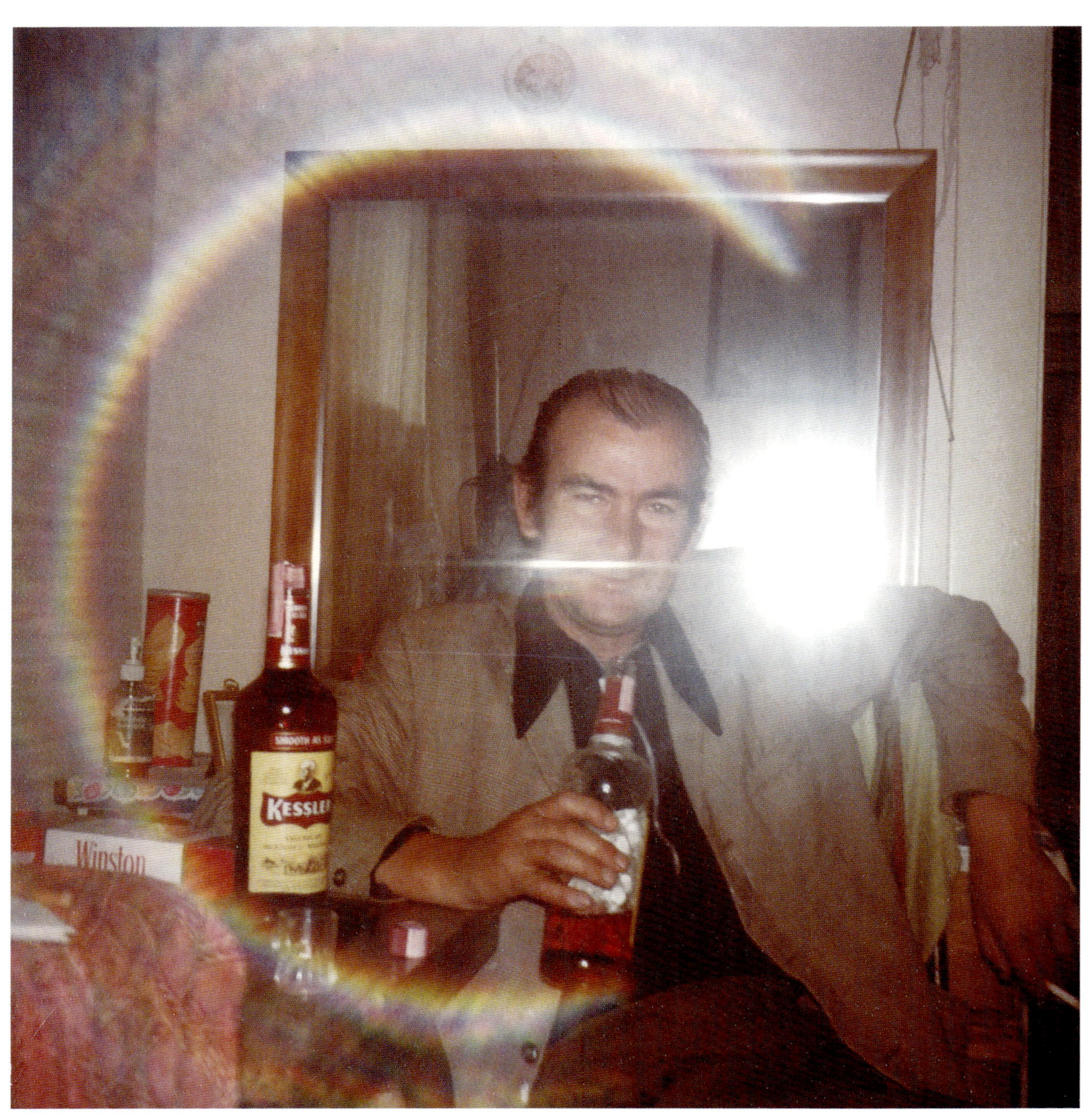
Winston

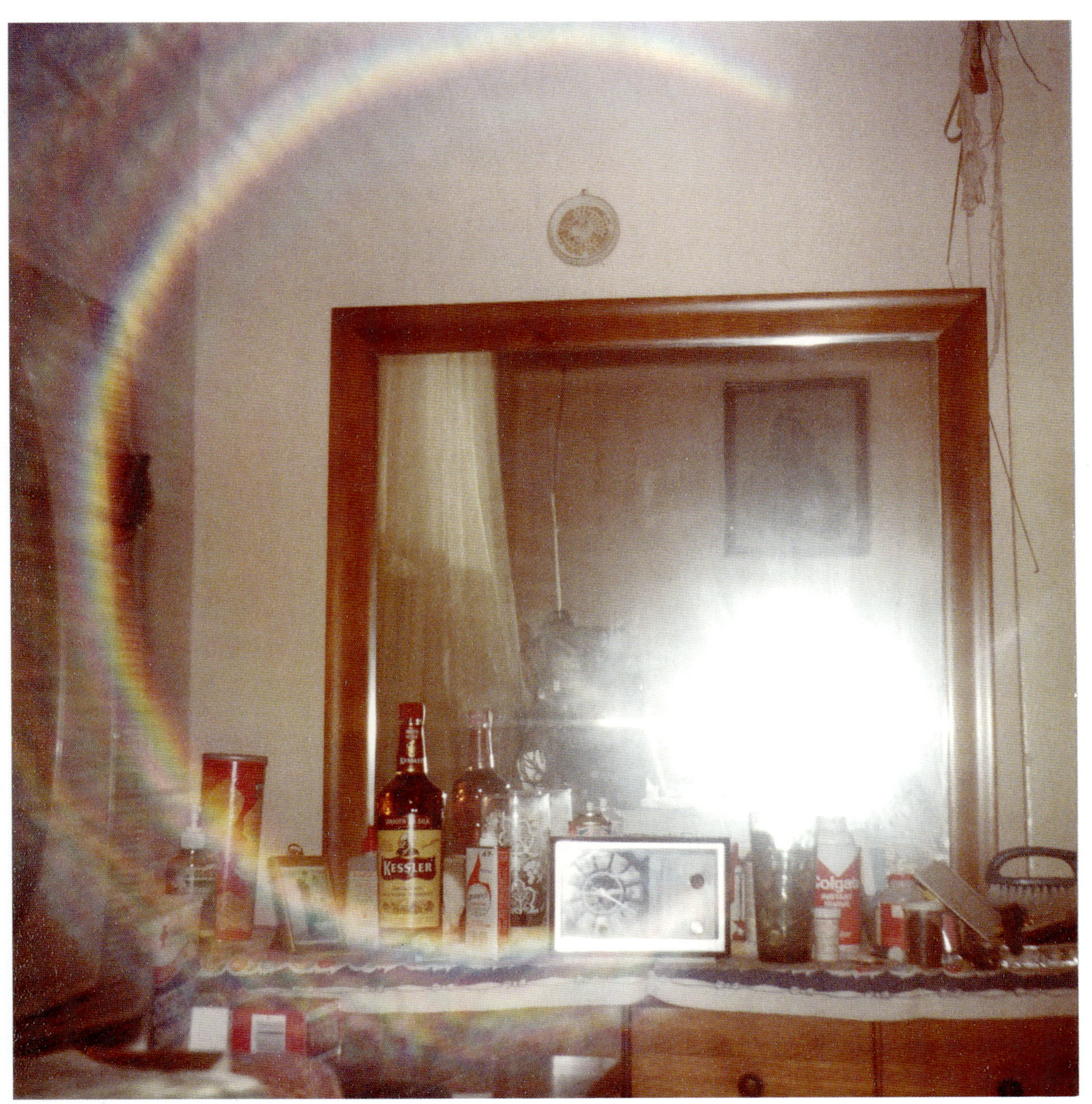
KESSLER

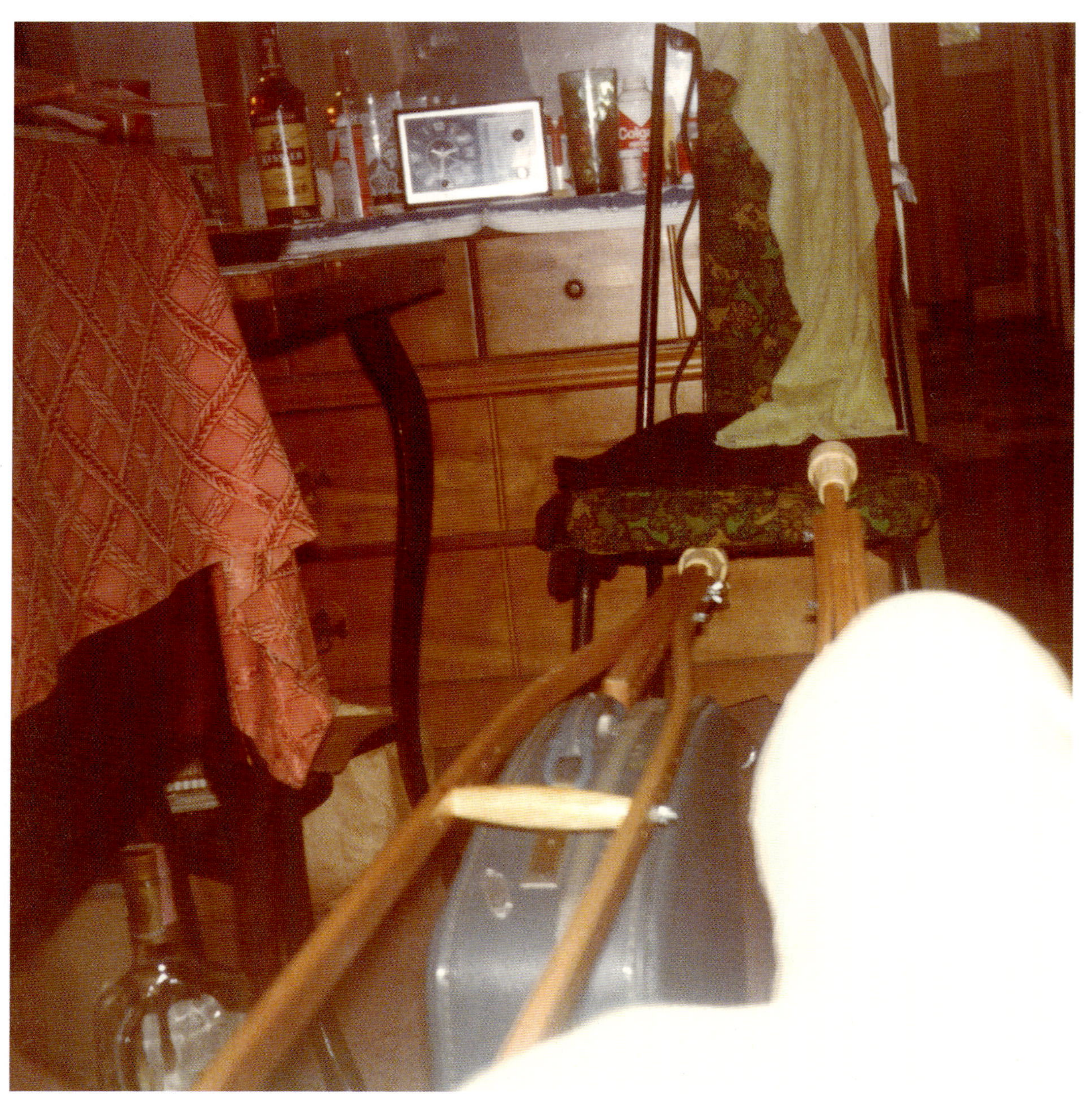

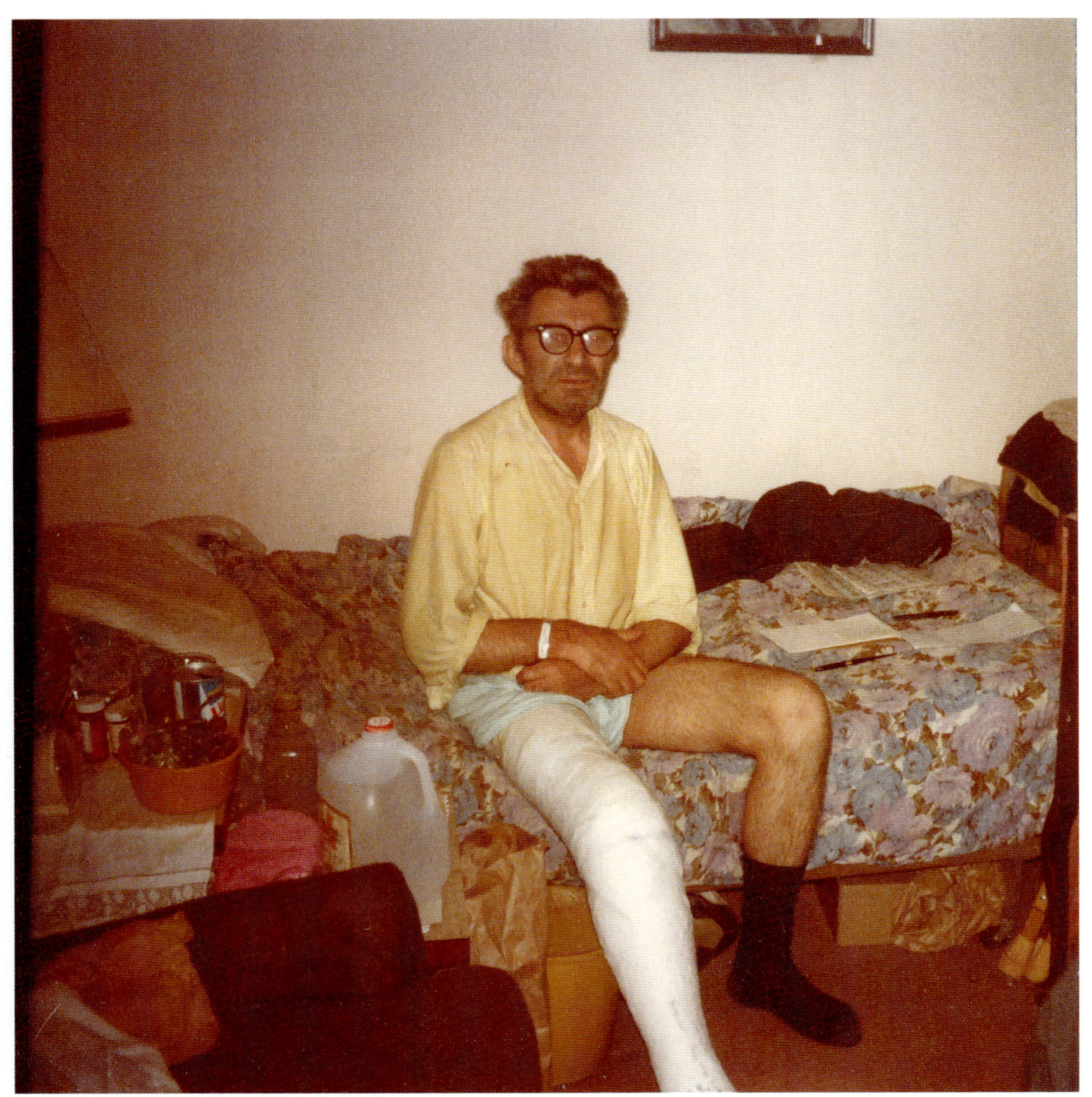

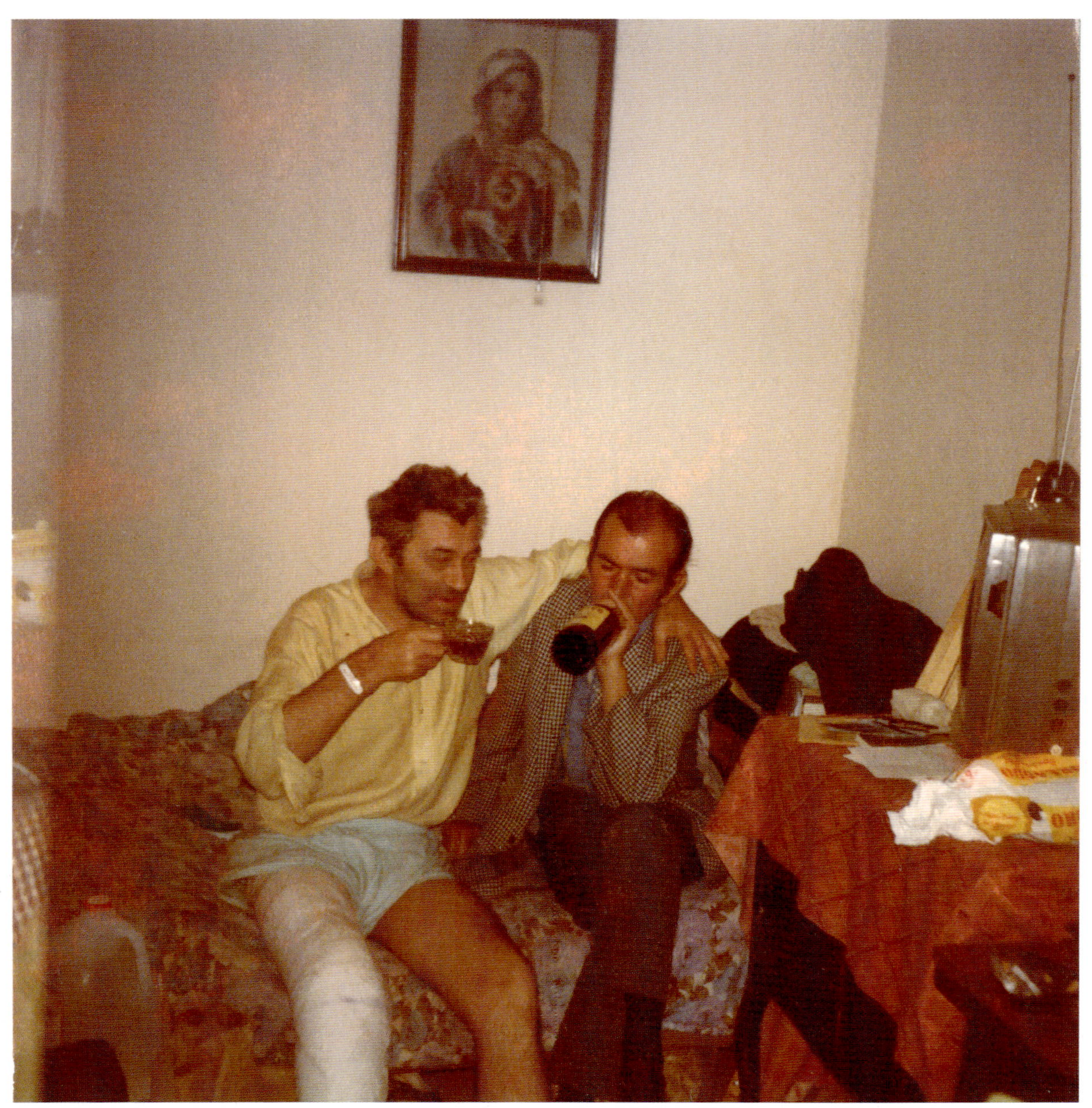

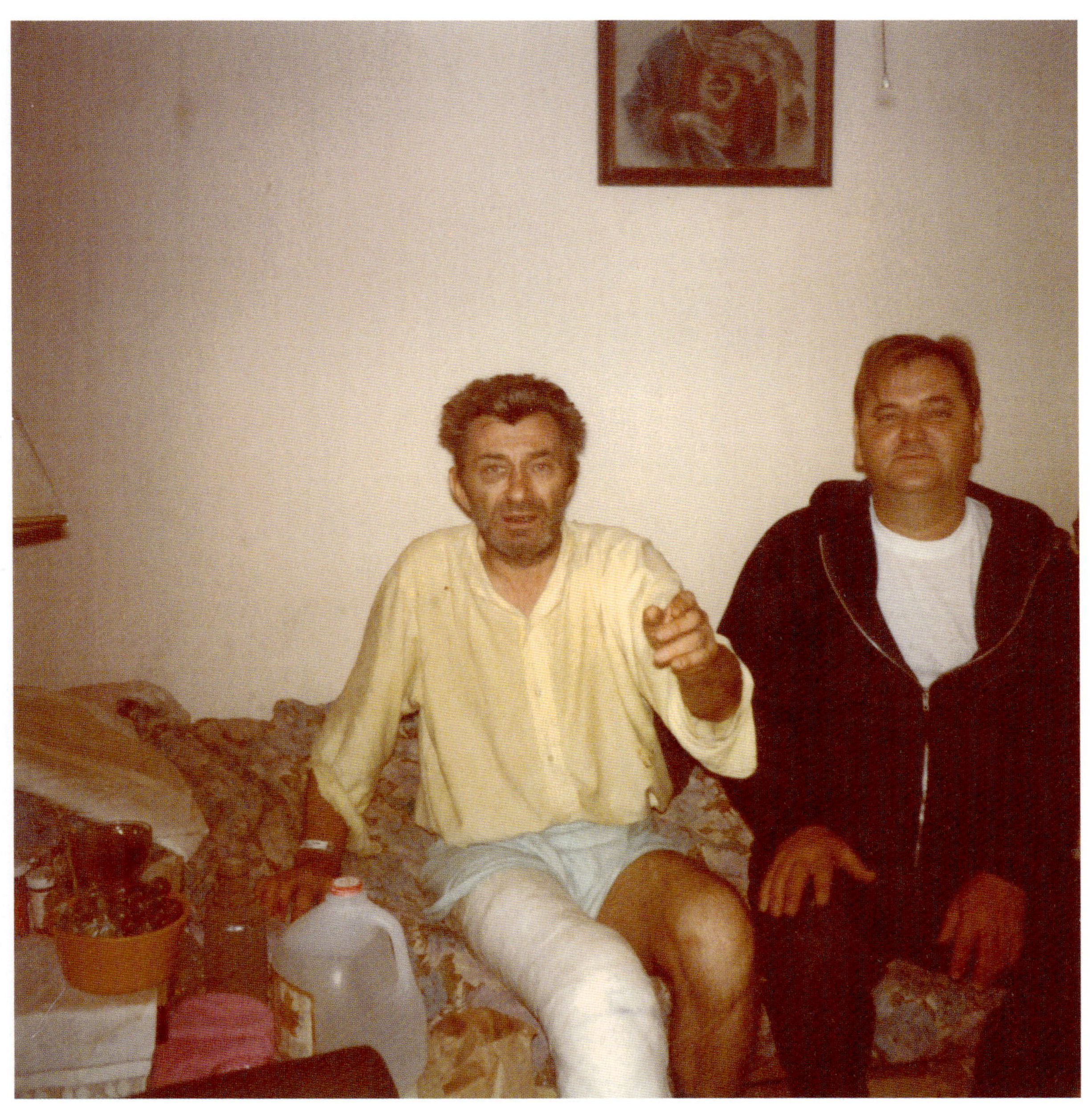

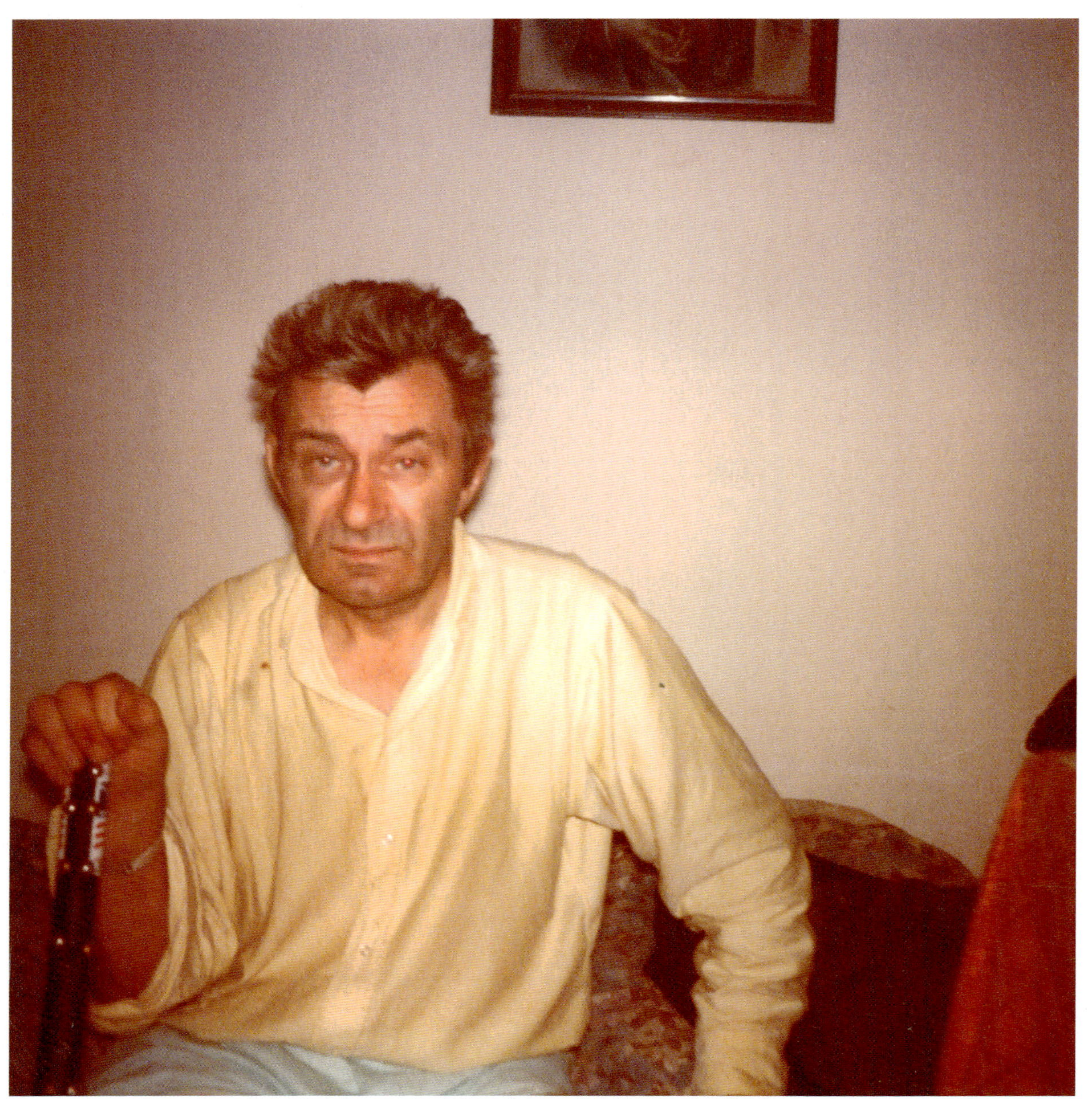

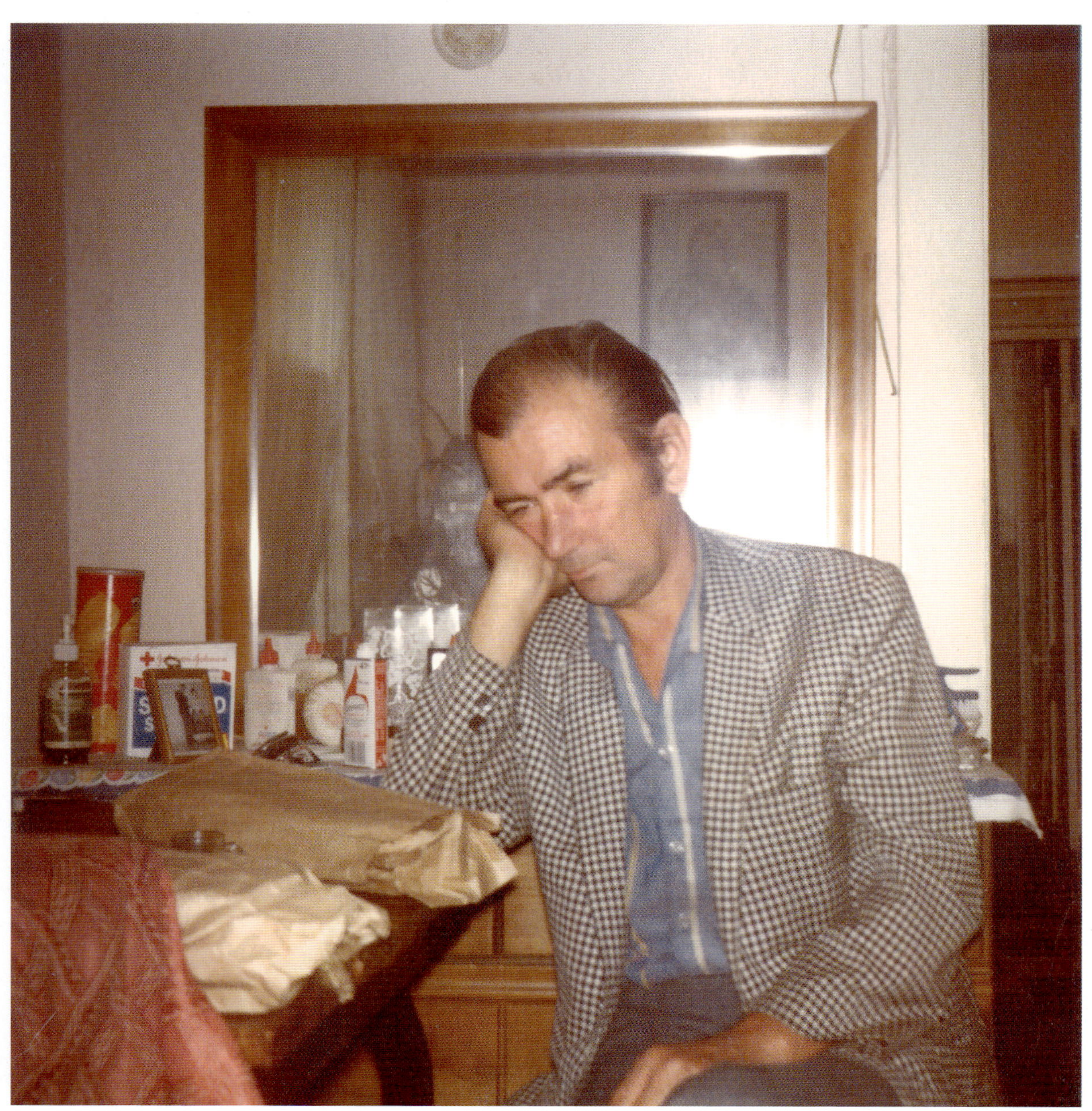

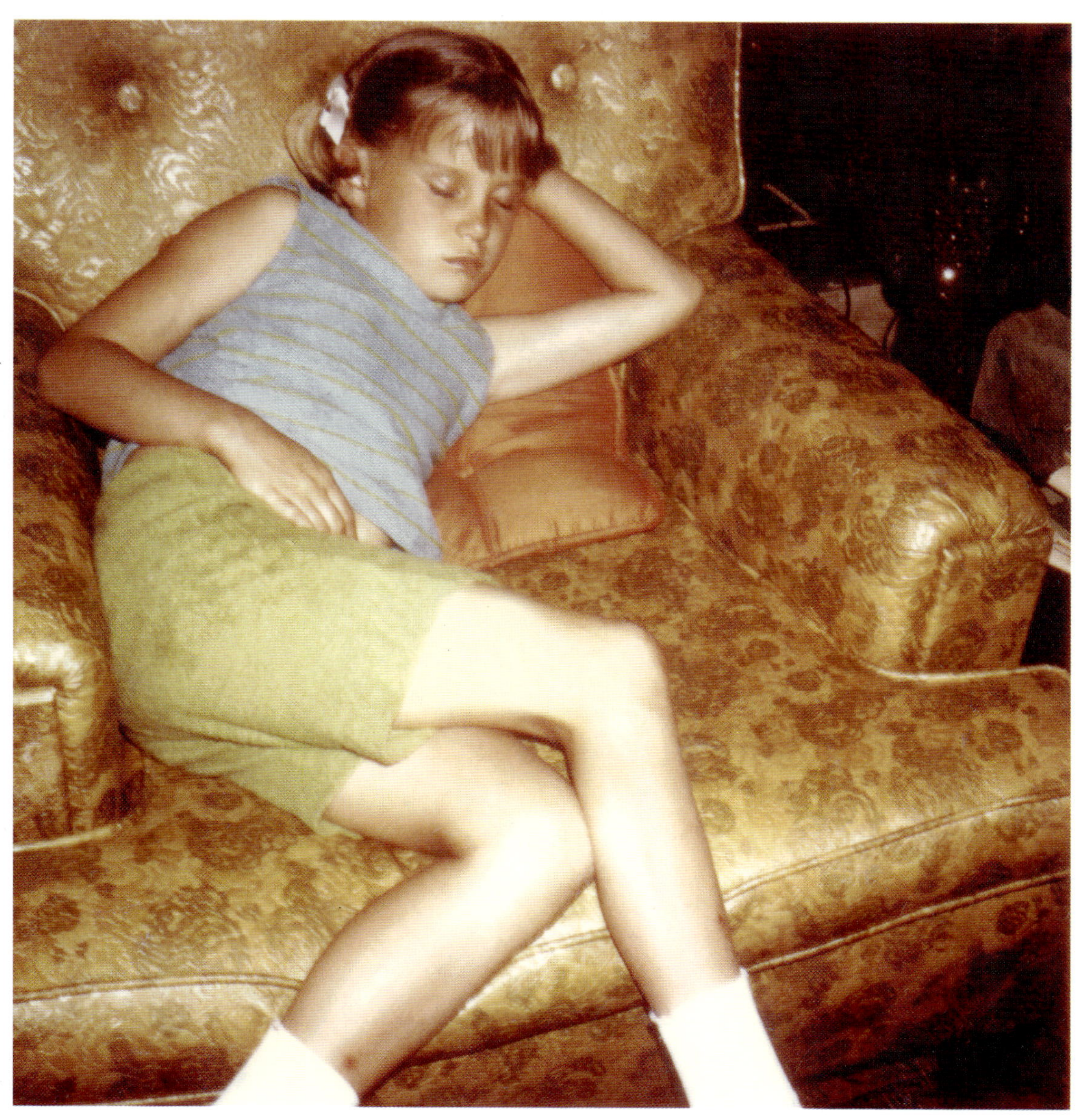

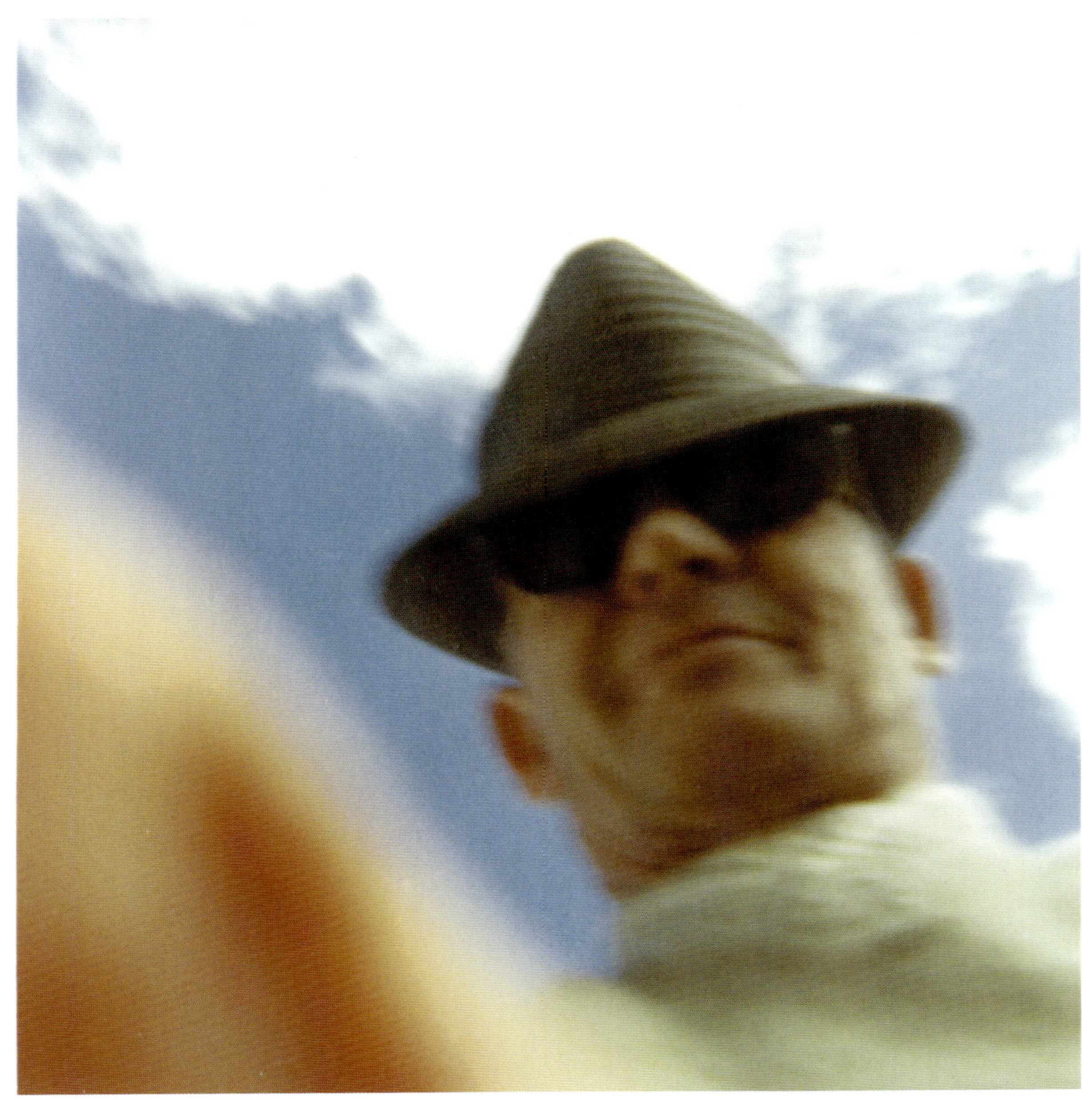

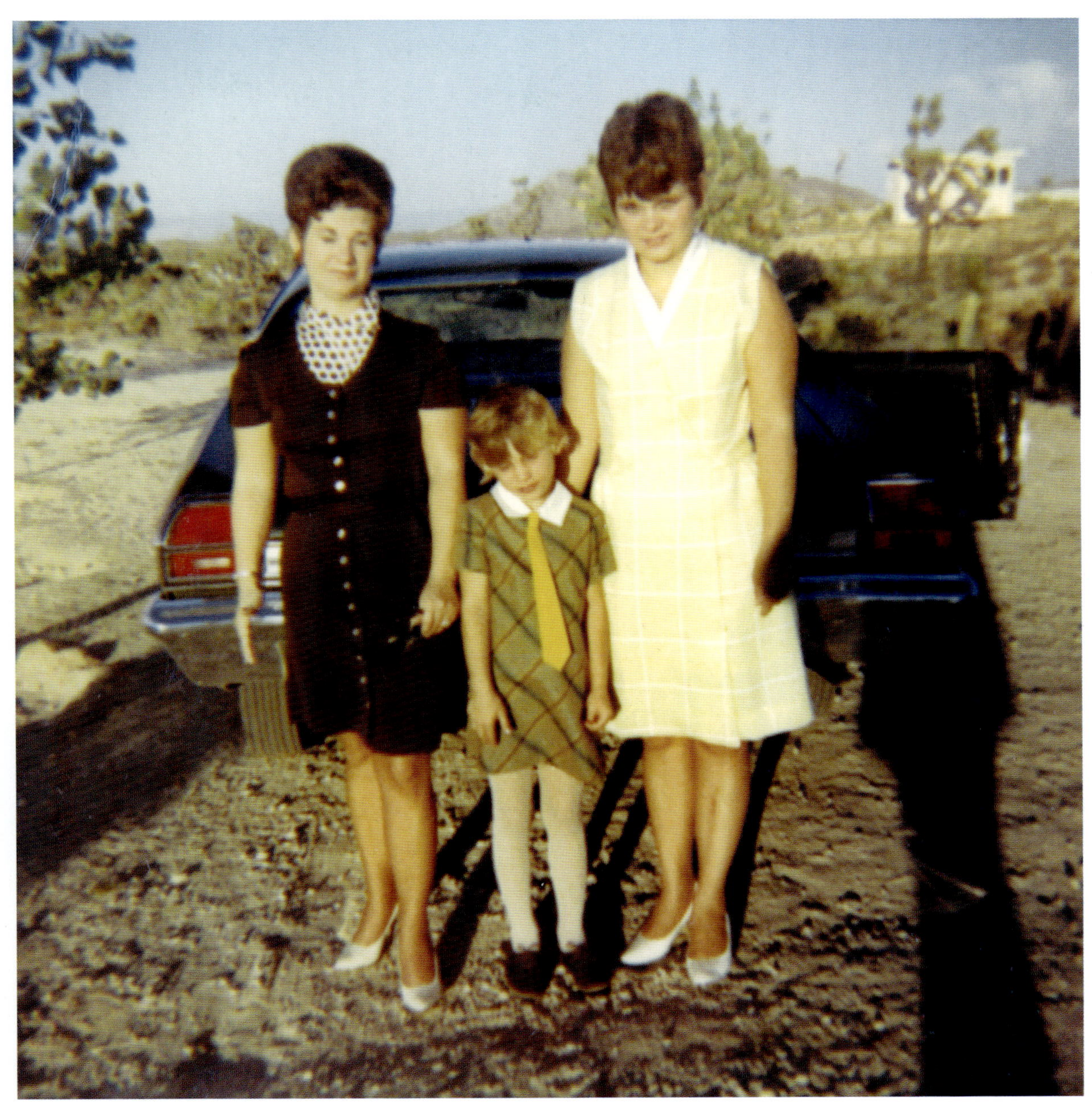

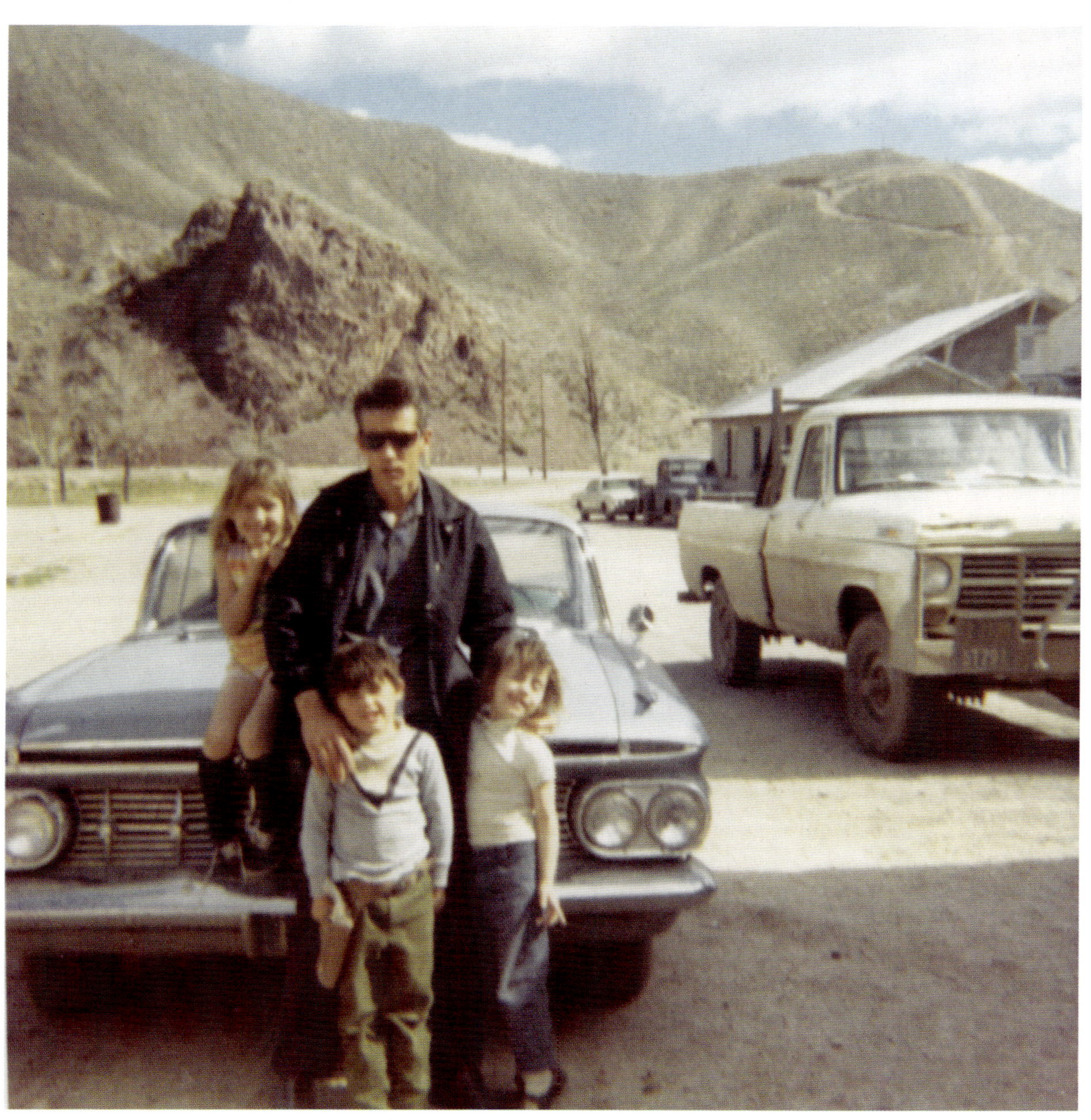

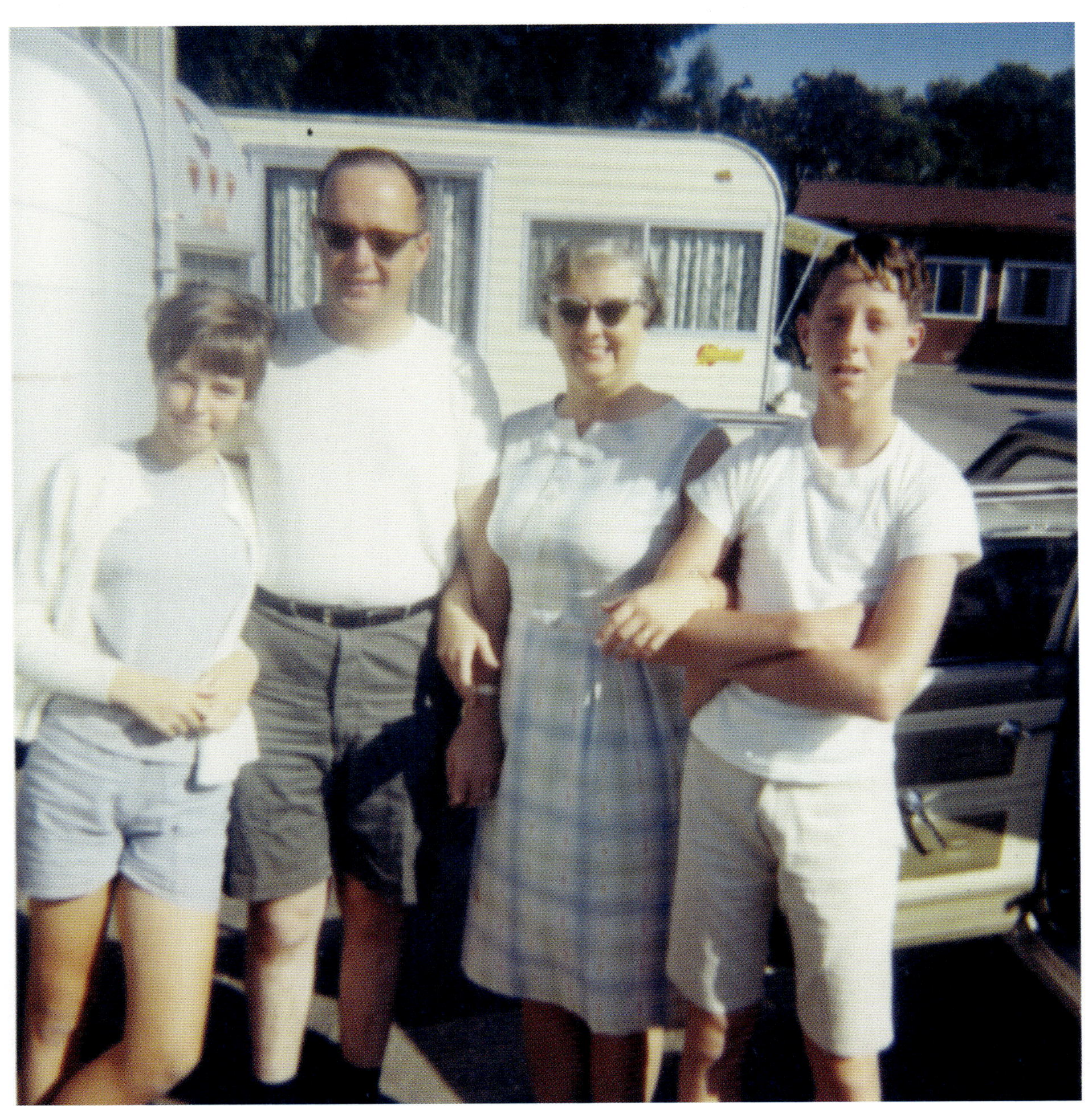

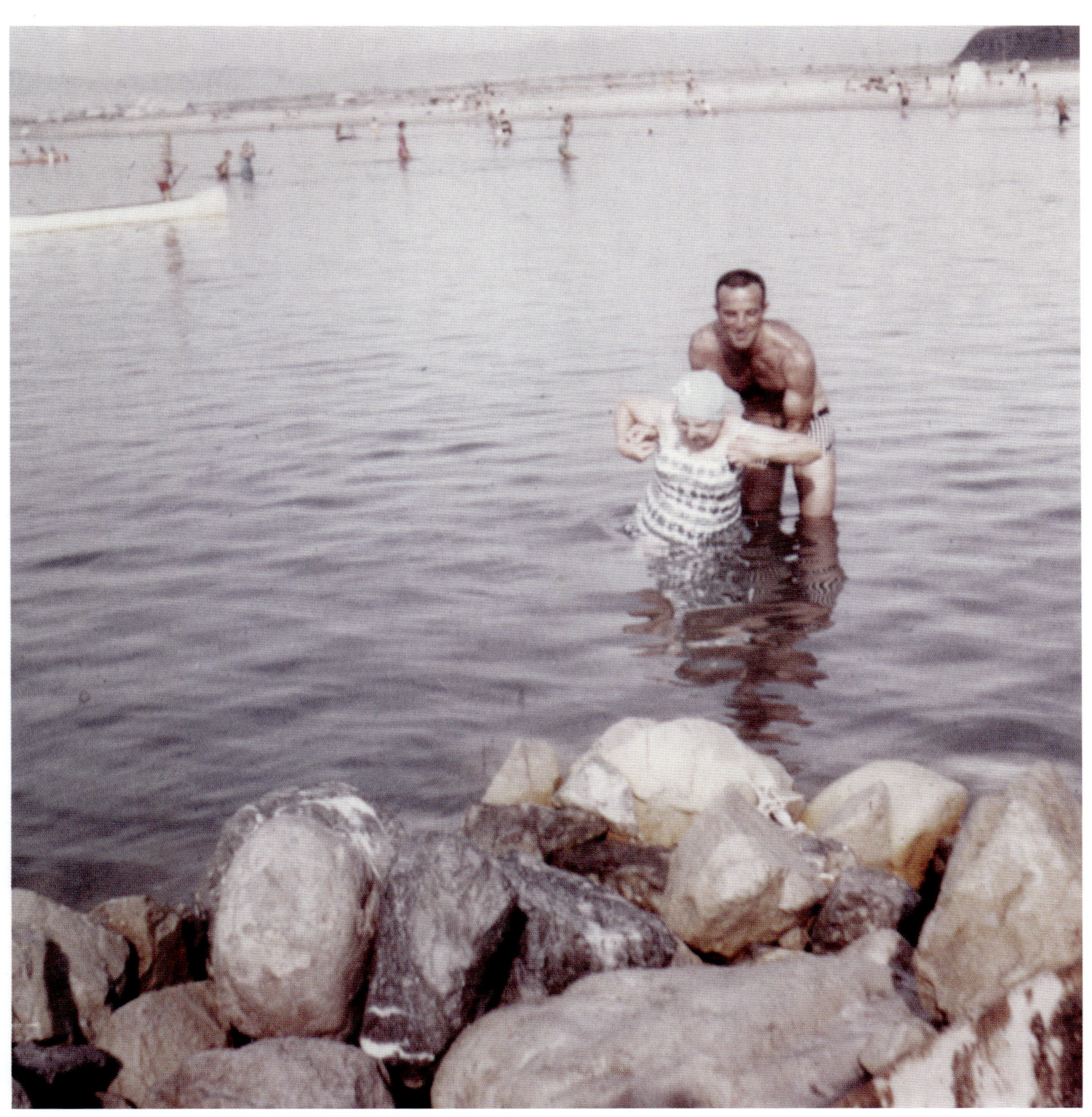

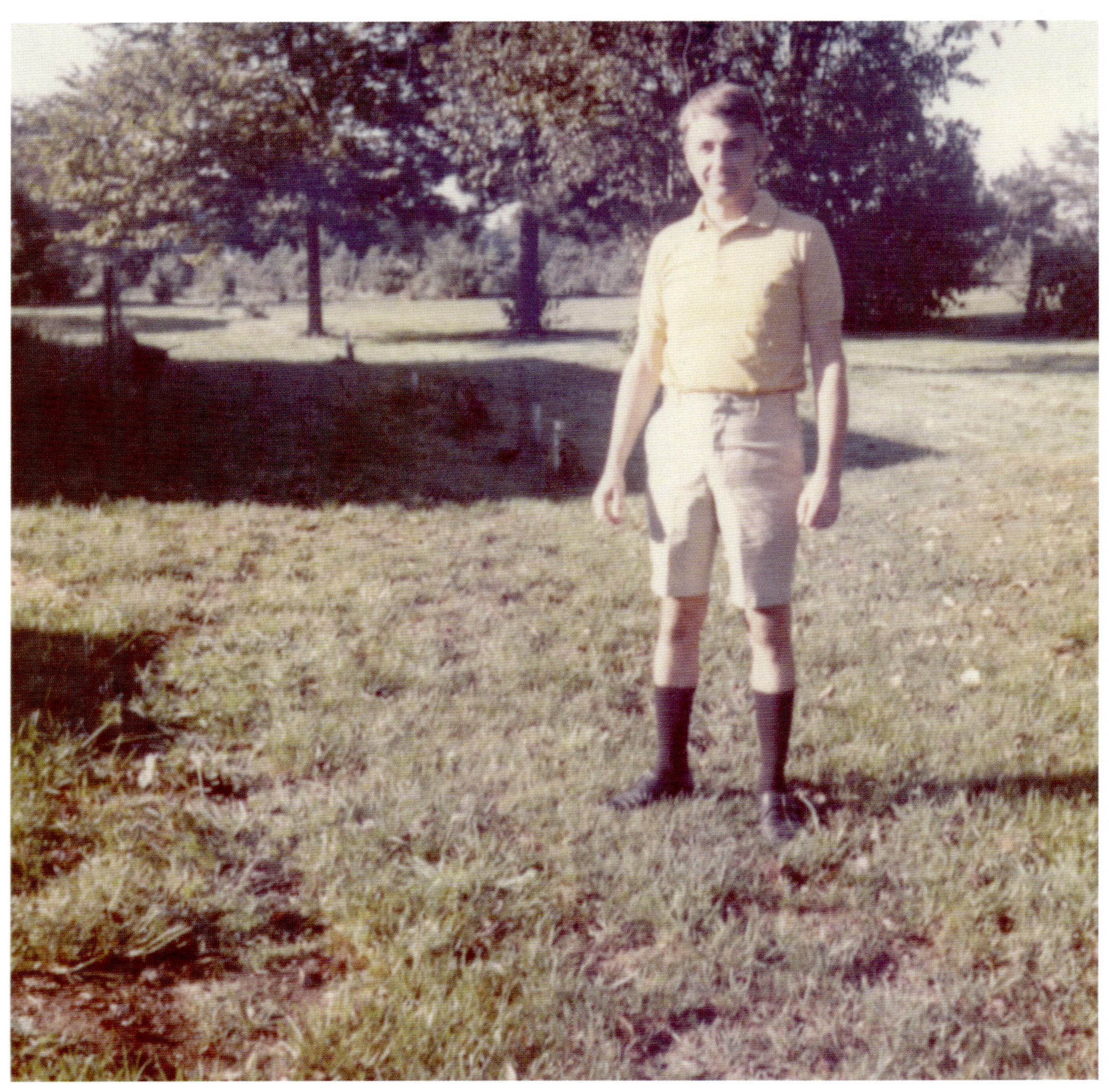

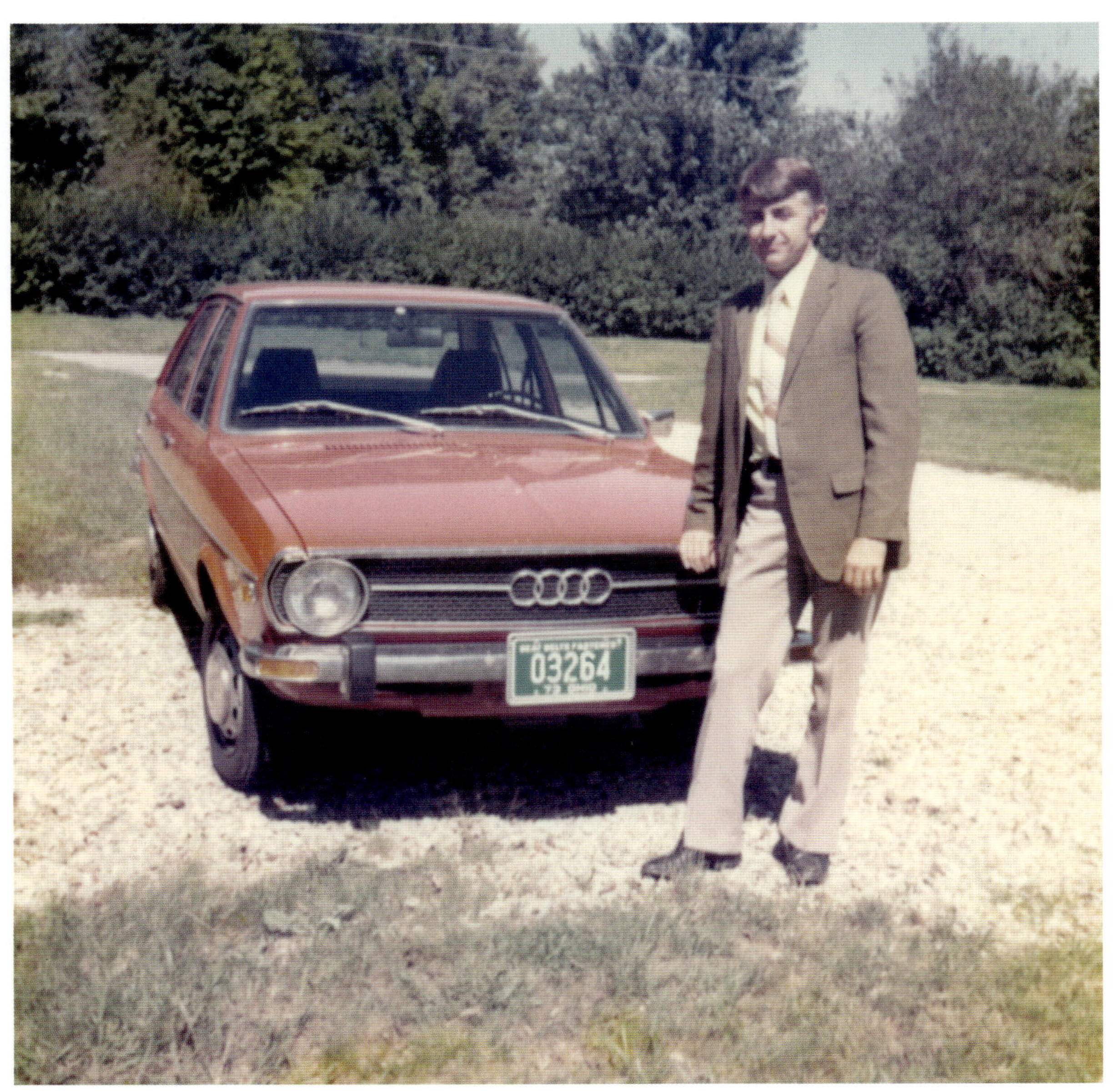
03264

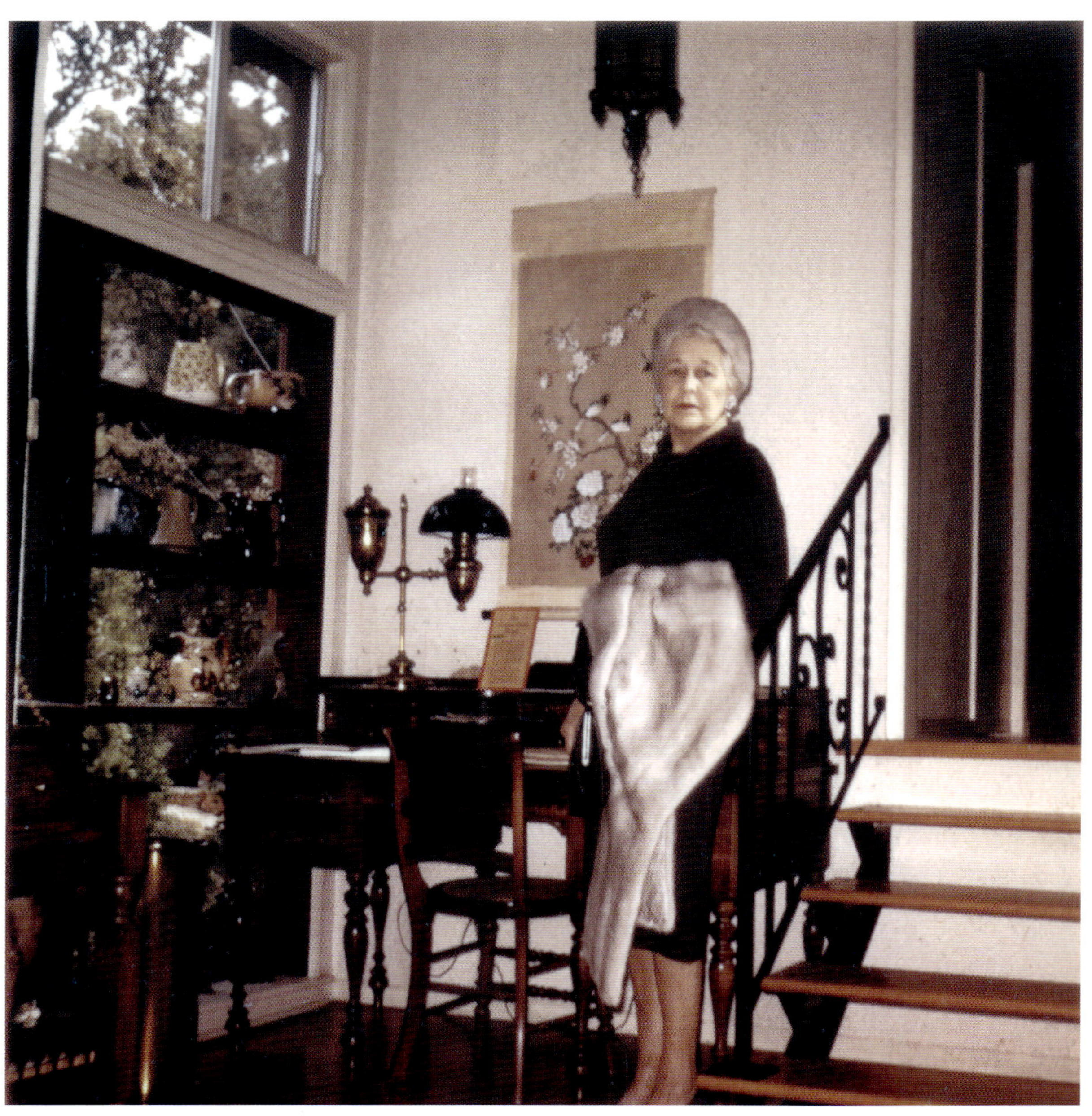

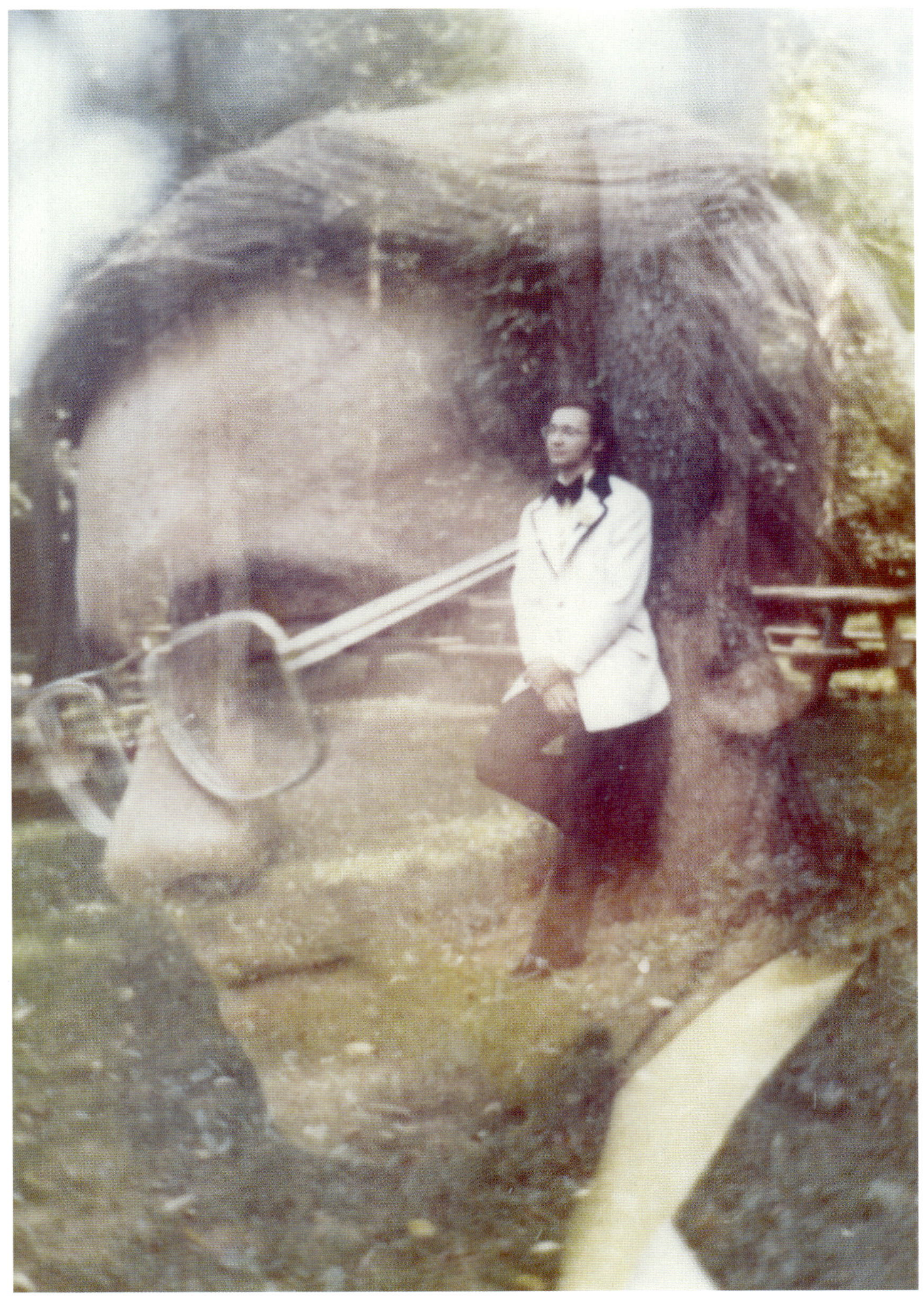

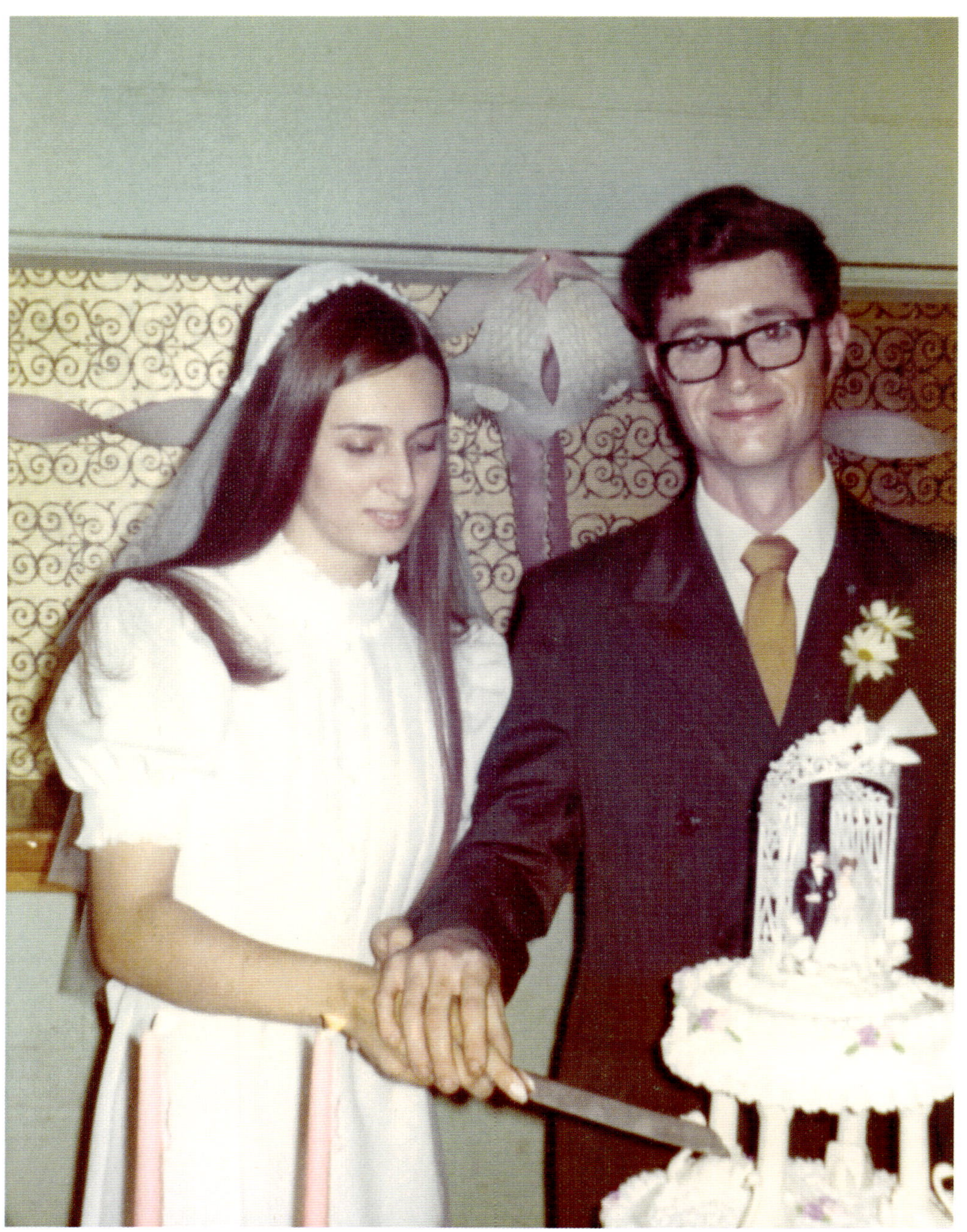

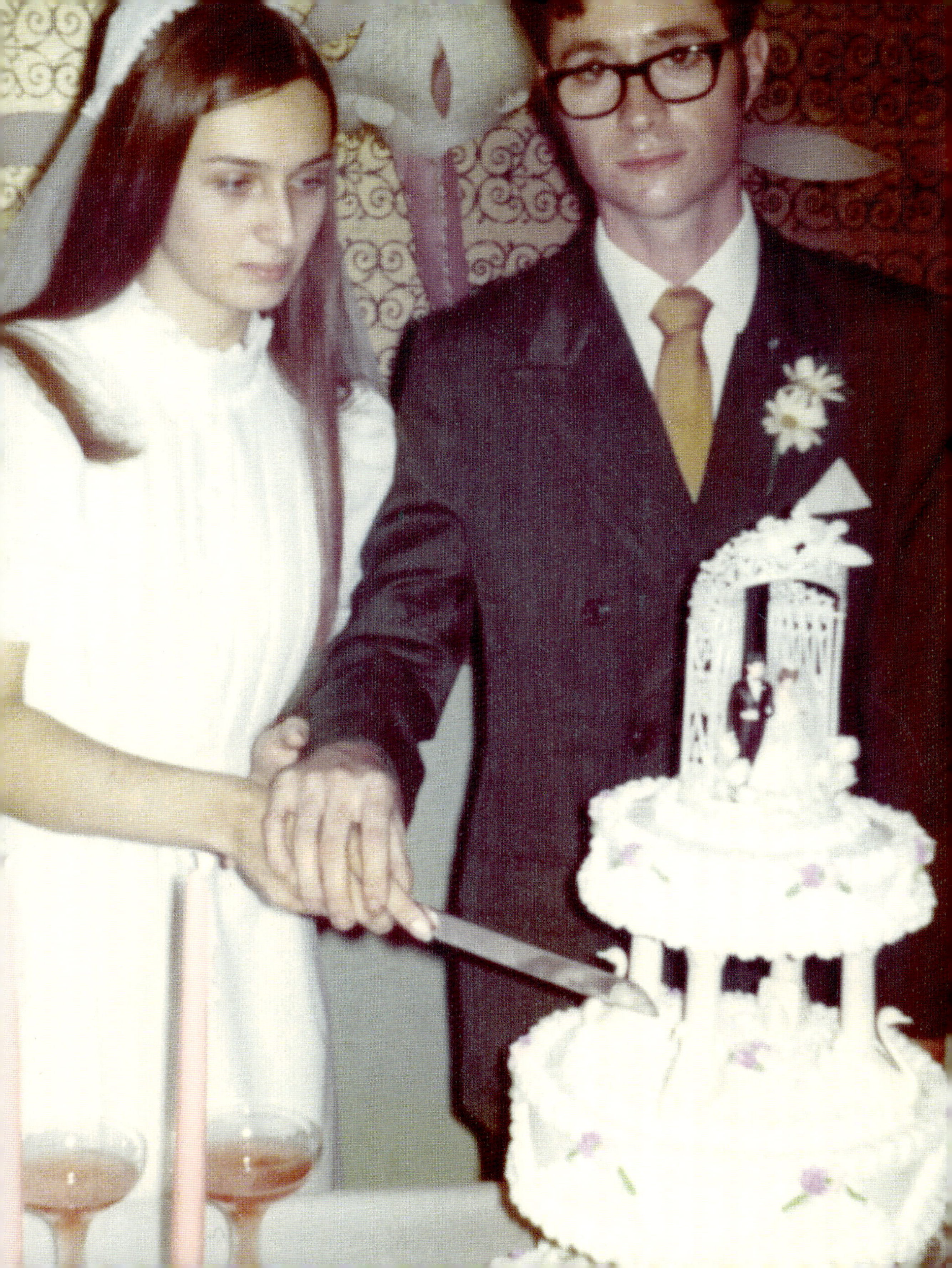

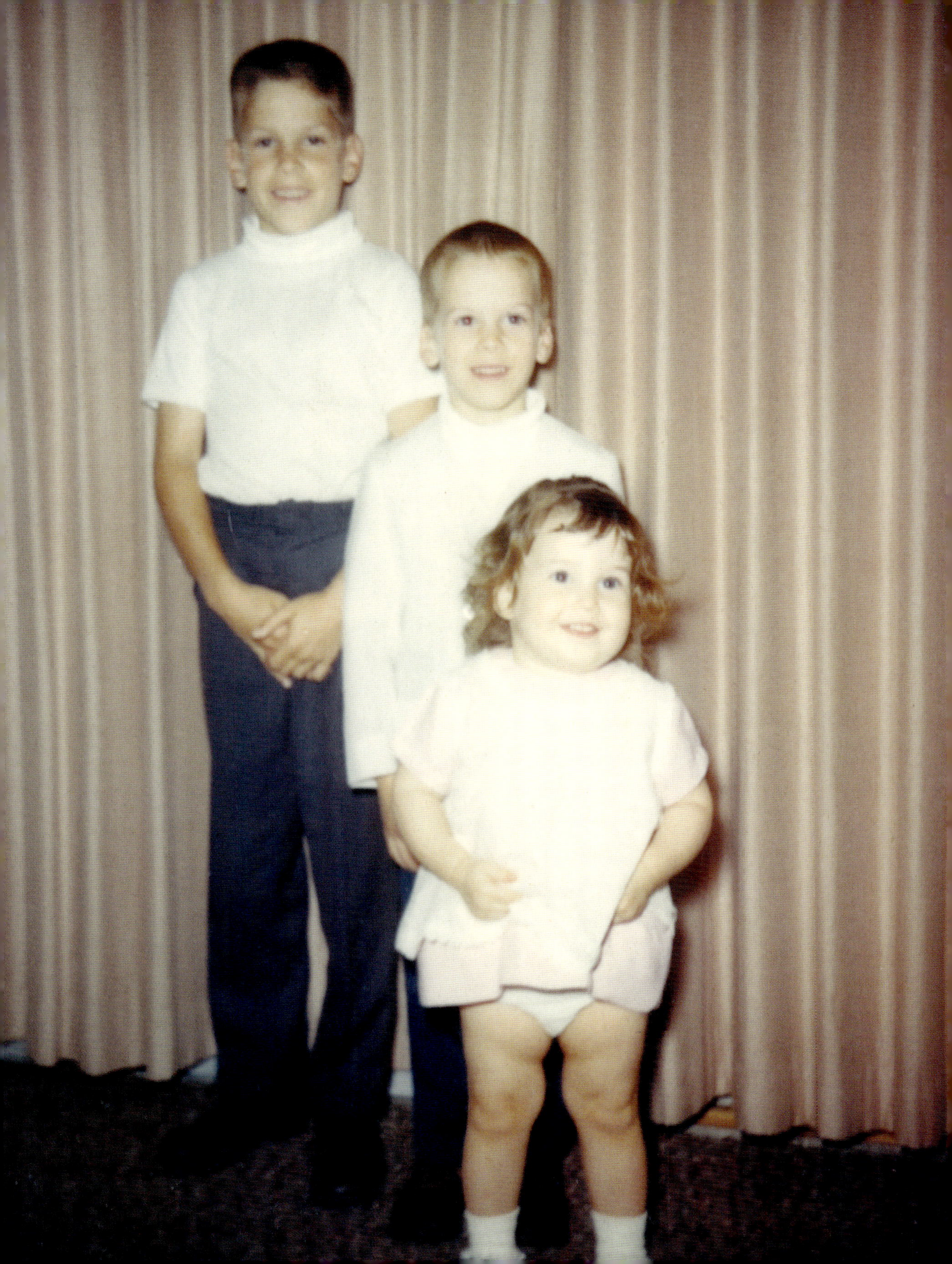

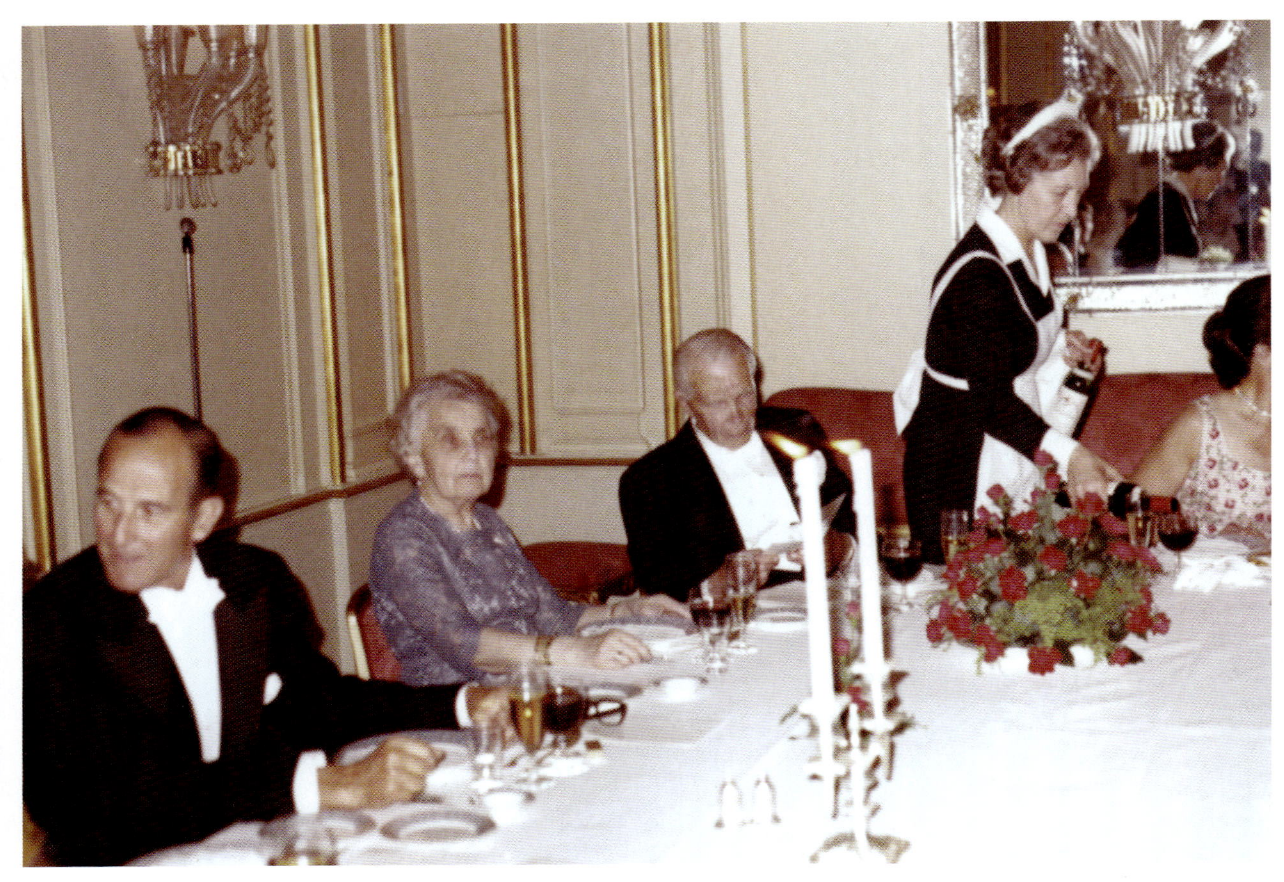

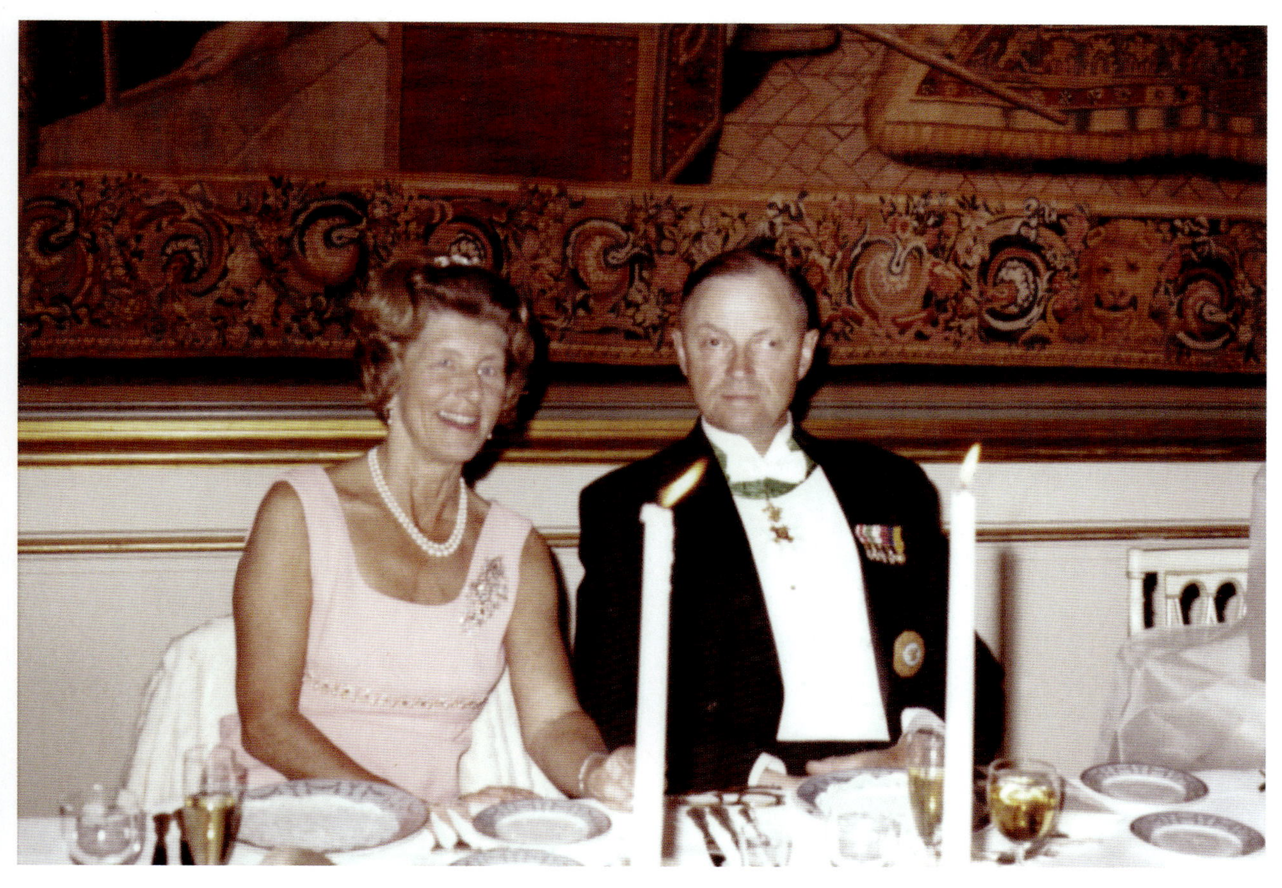

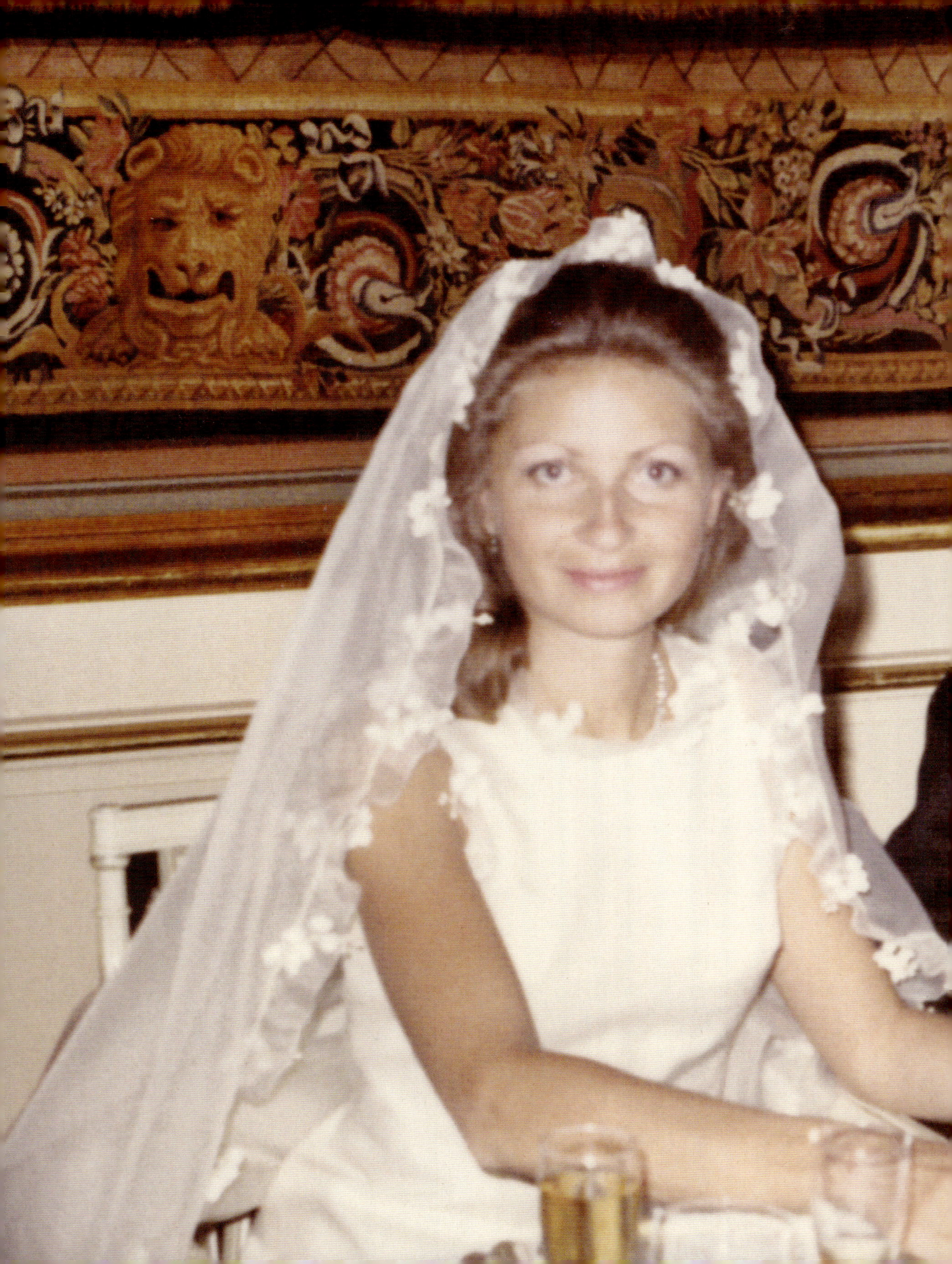

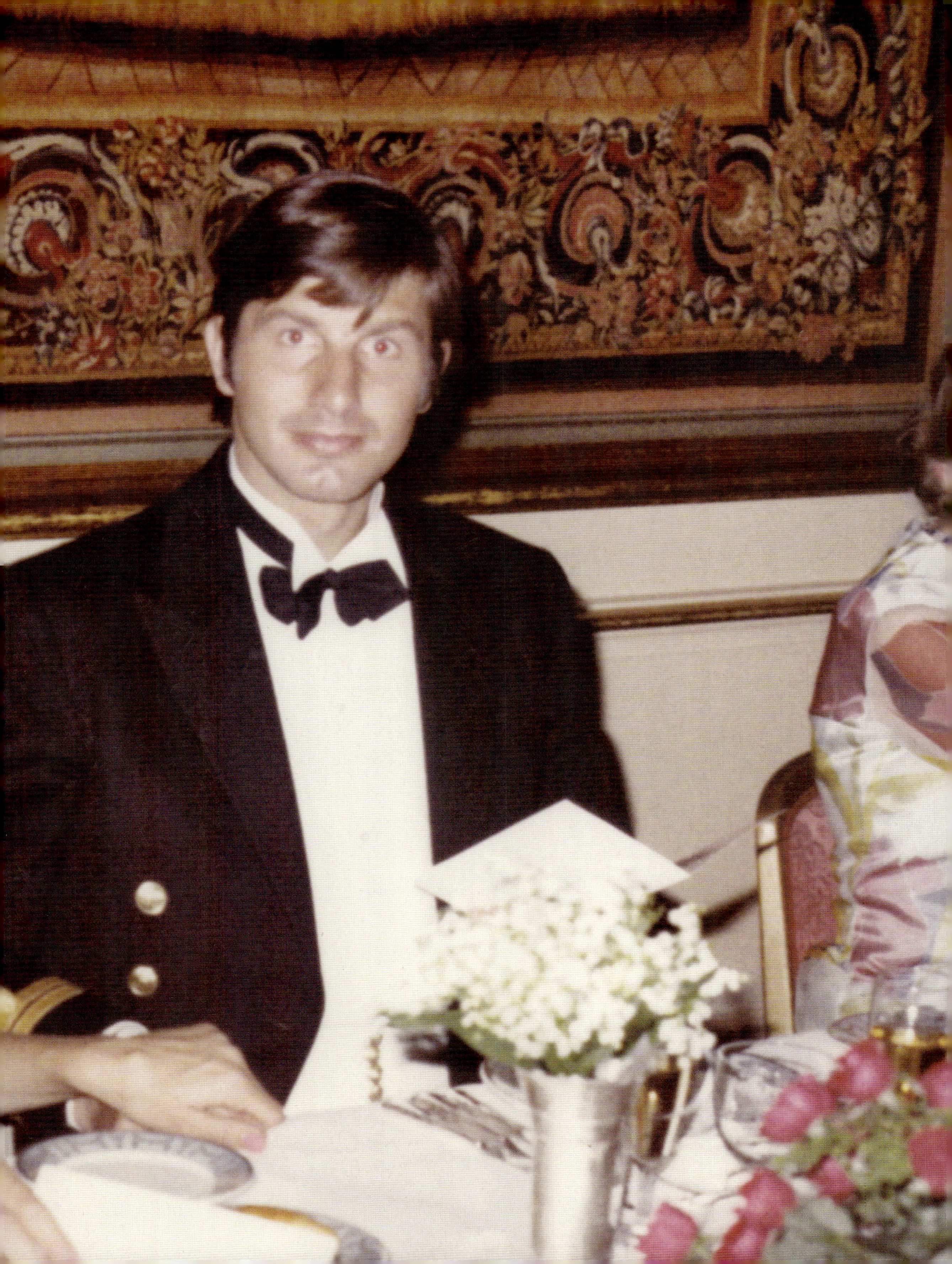

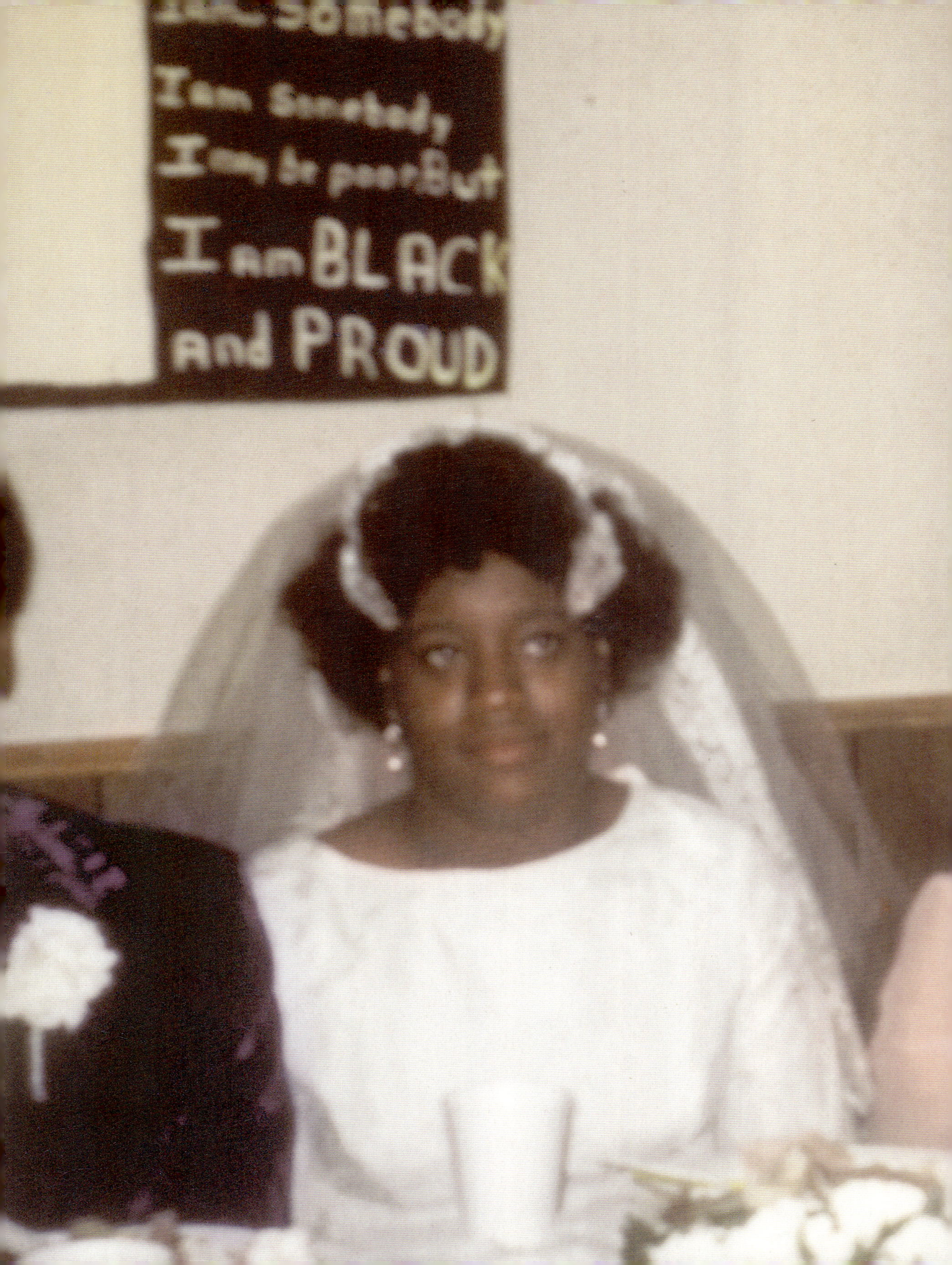

somebody
I am Somebody
I may be poor But
I am BLACK
and PROUD

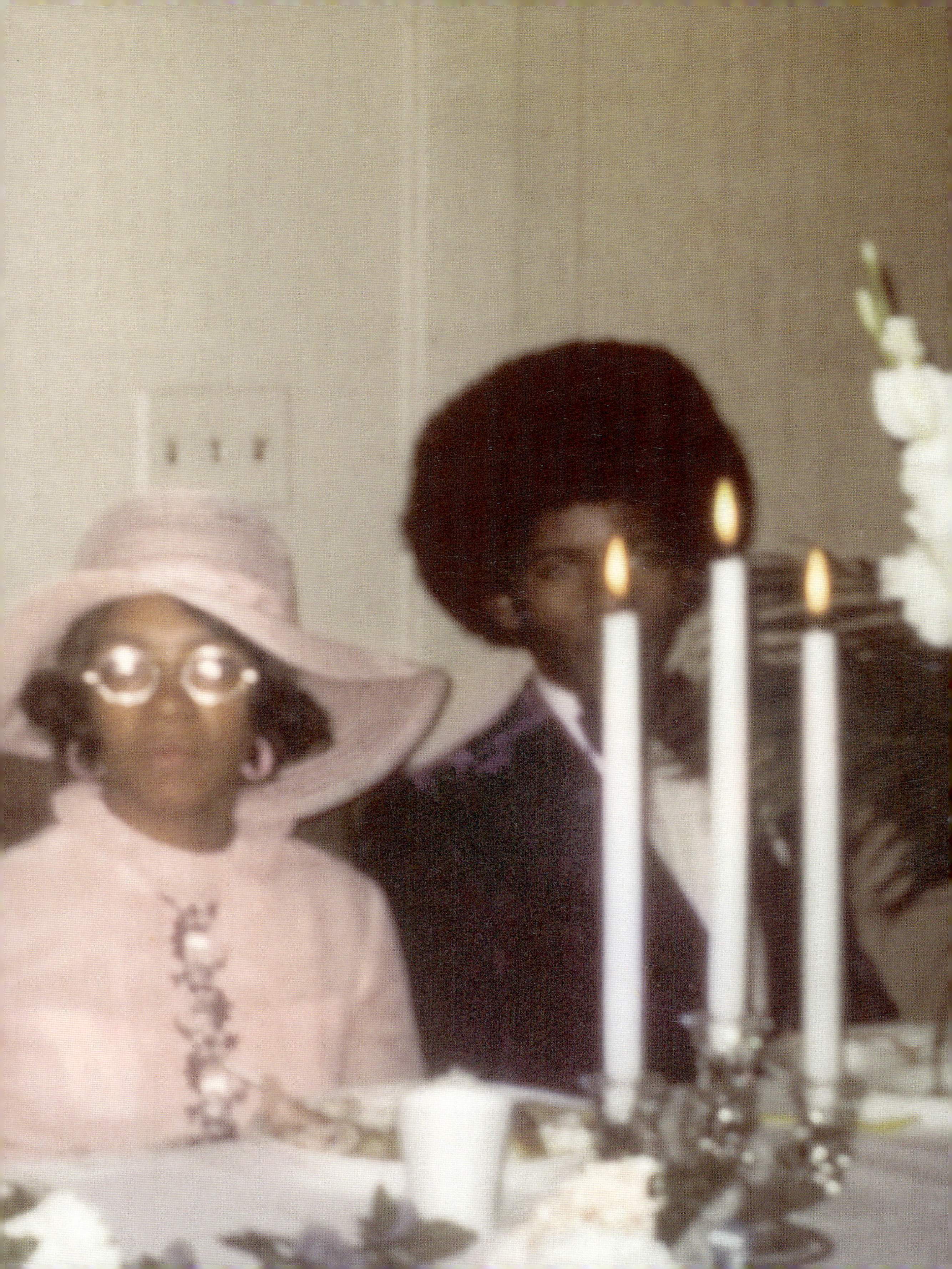

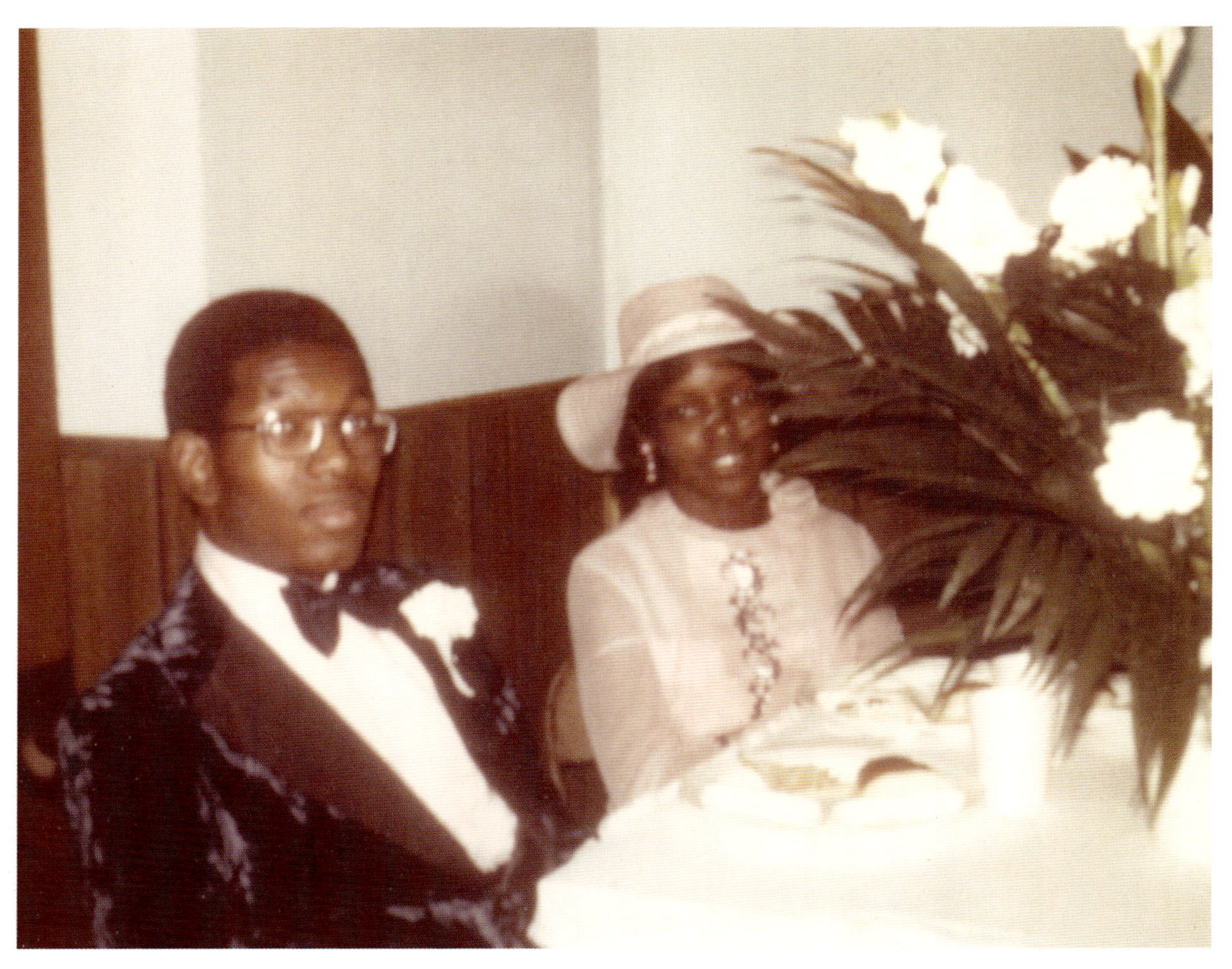

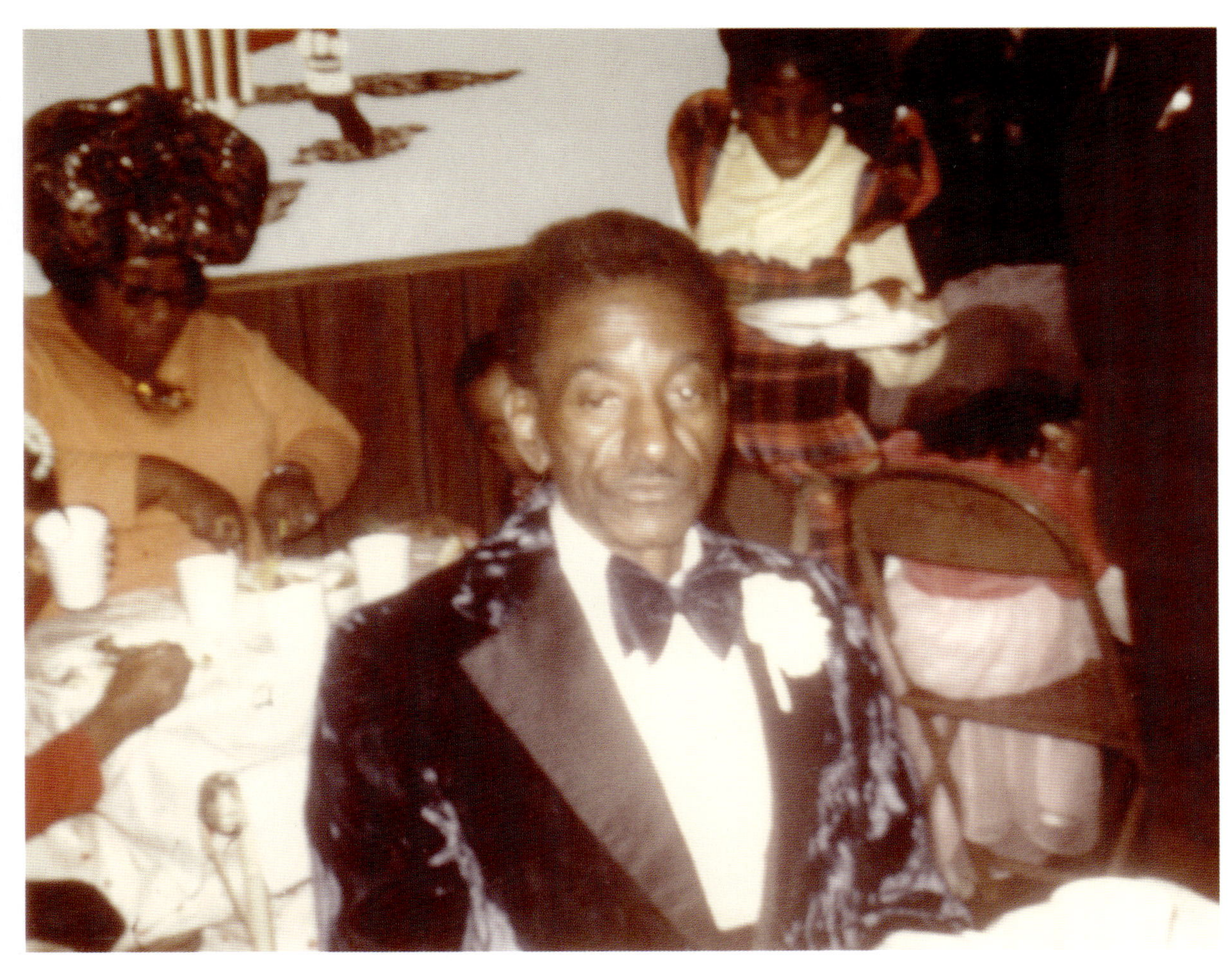

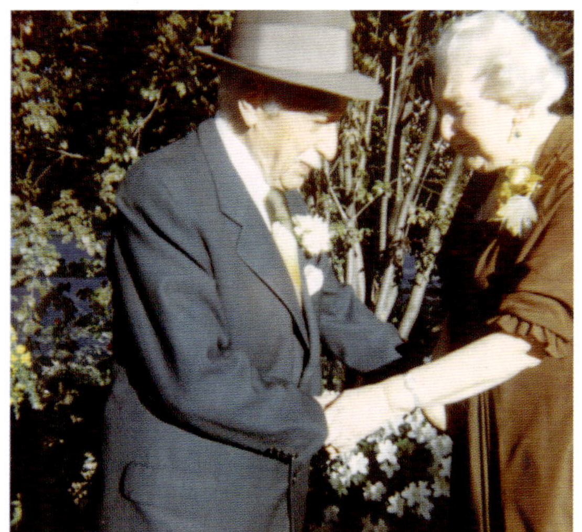

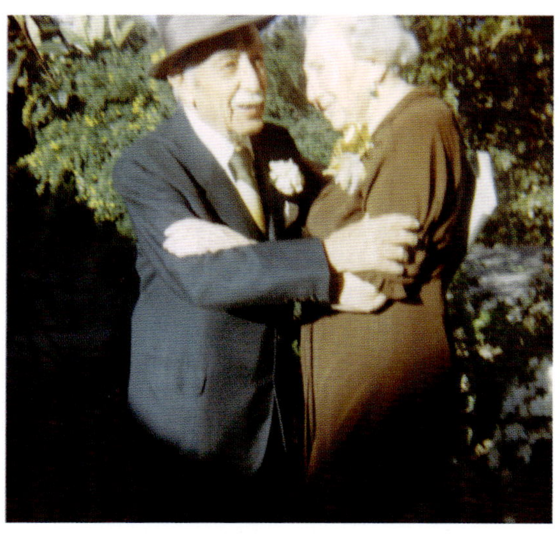

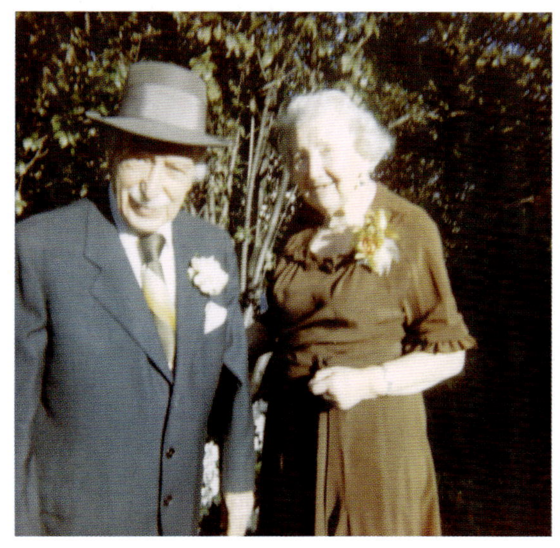

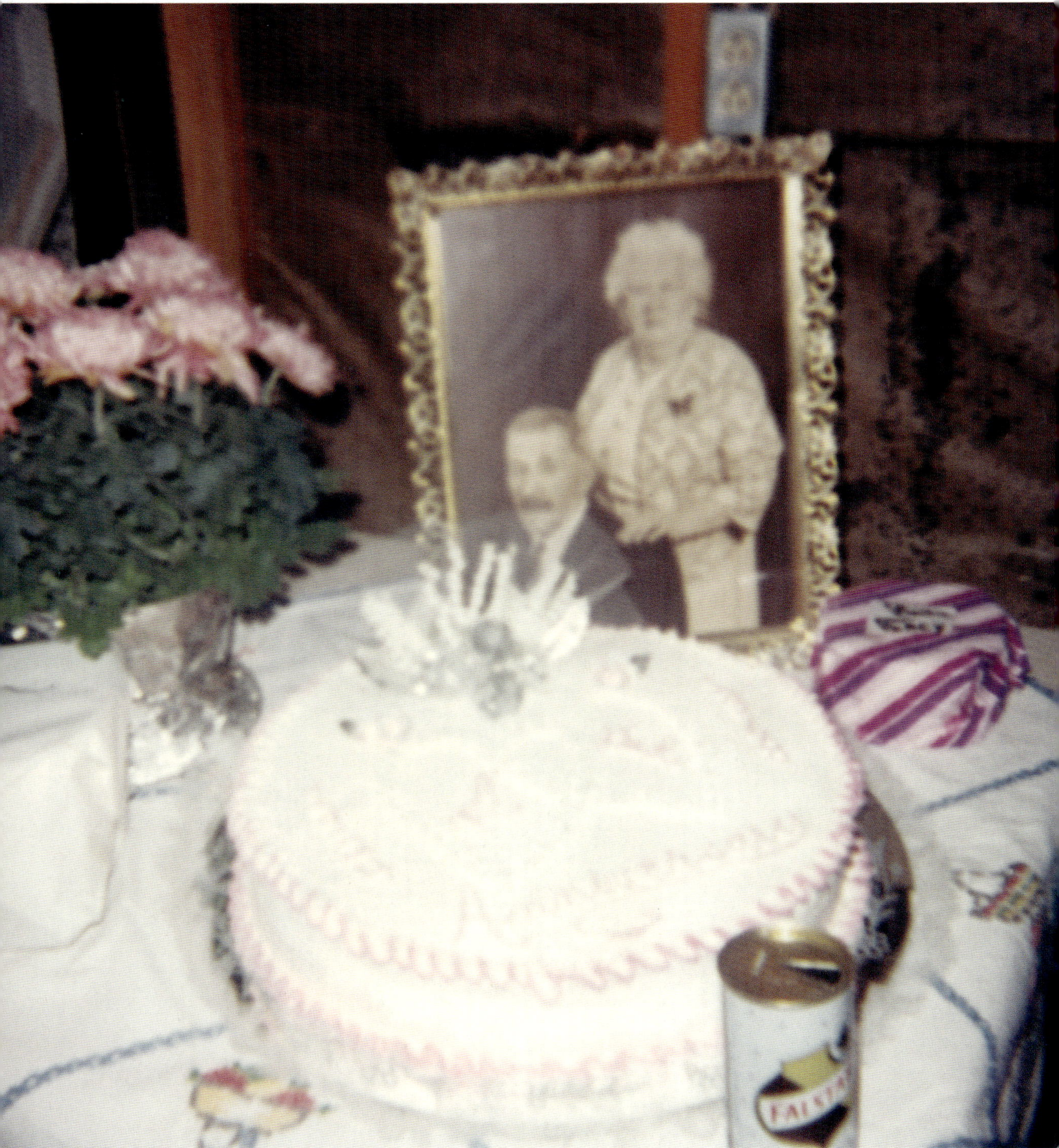

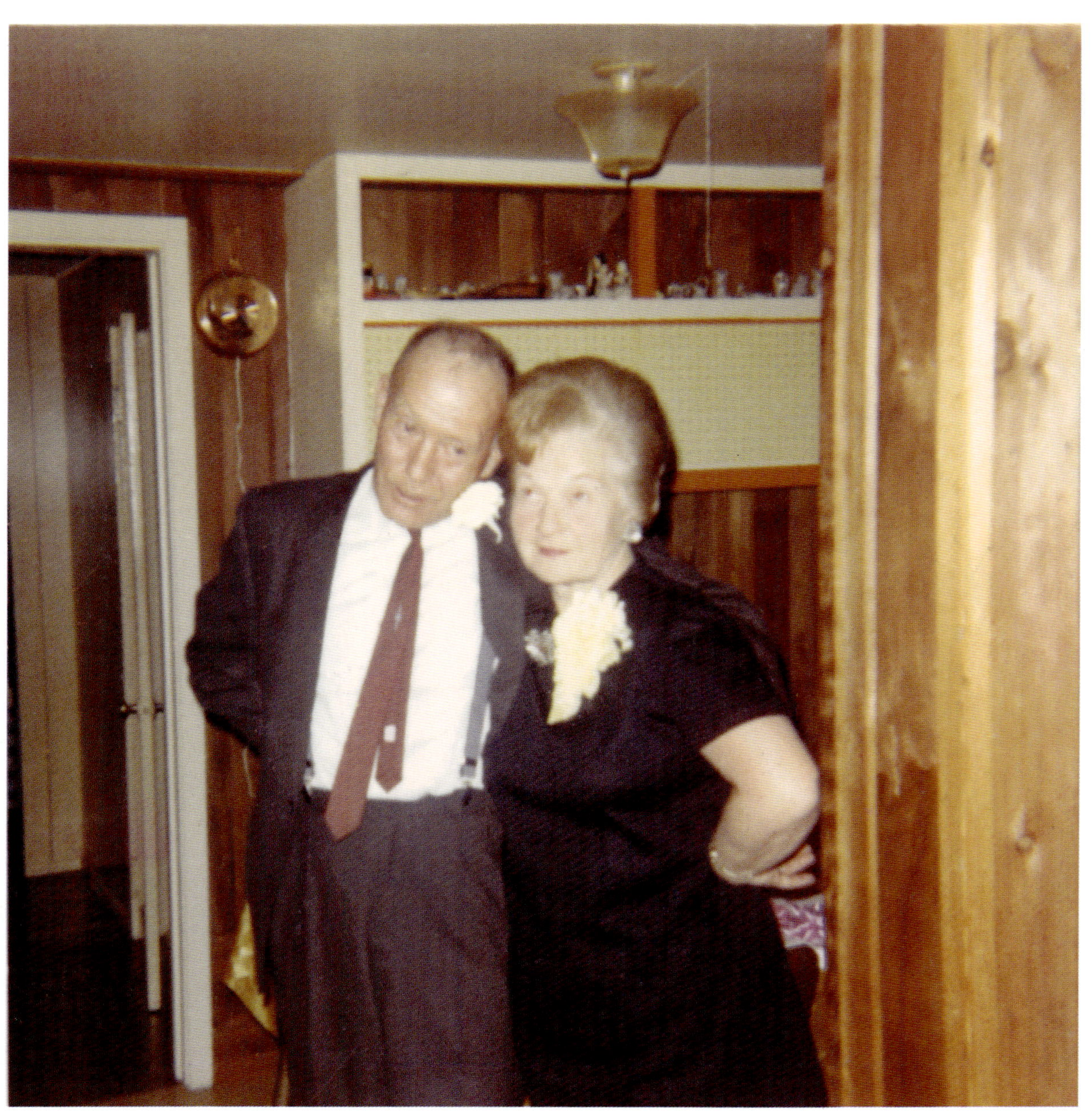

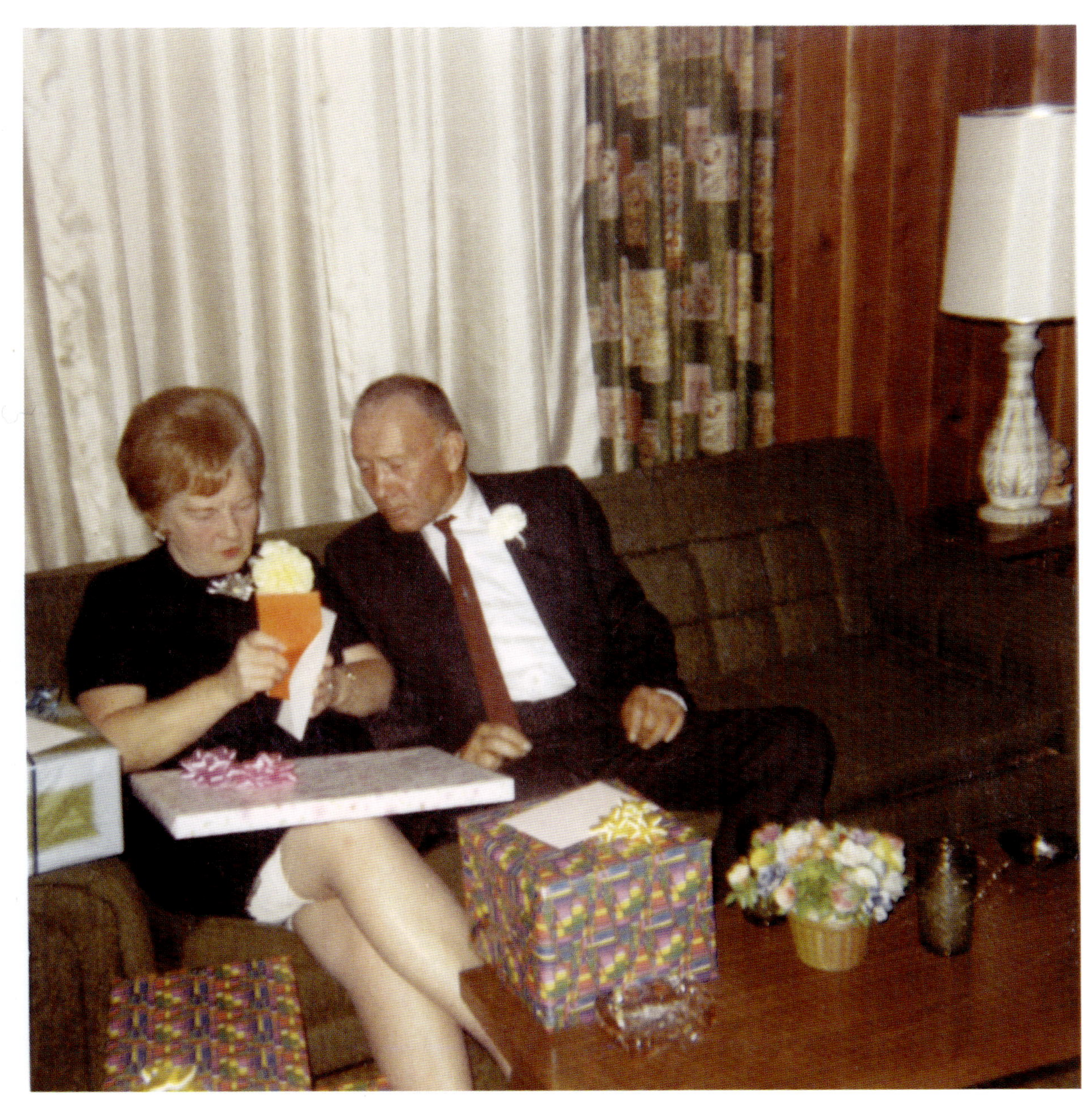

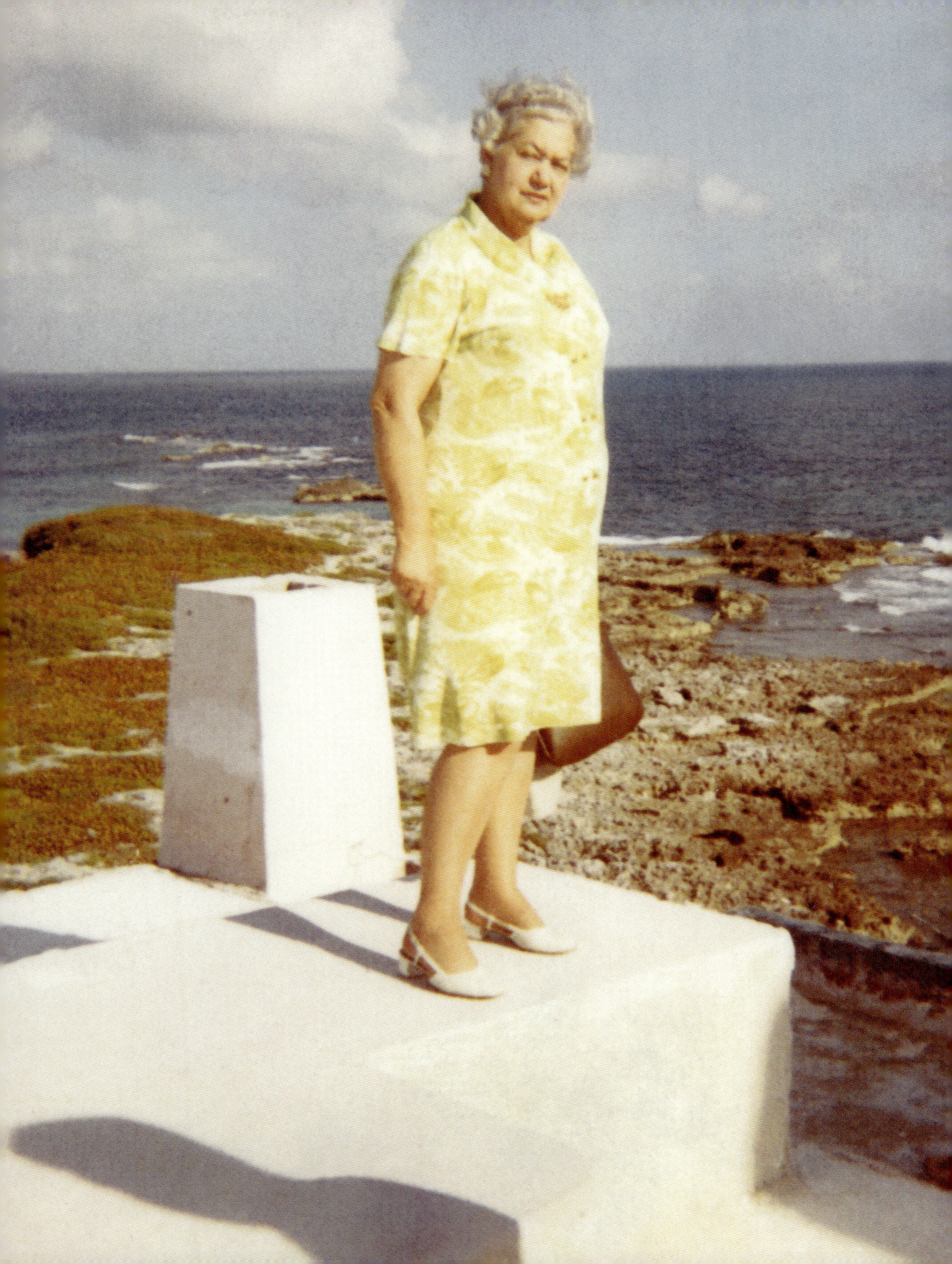

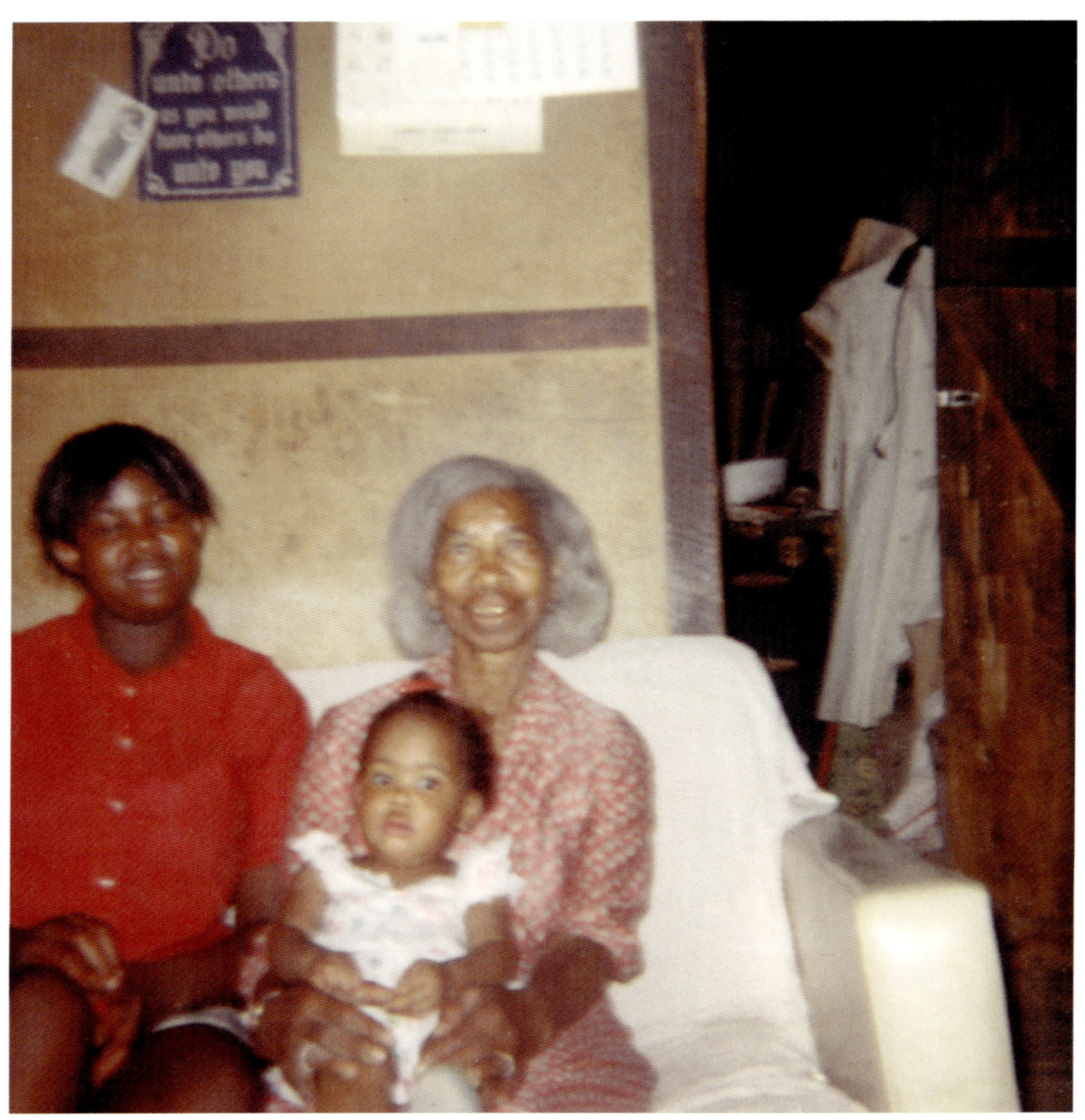
Do
unto others
as you would
have others do
unto you

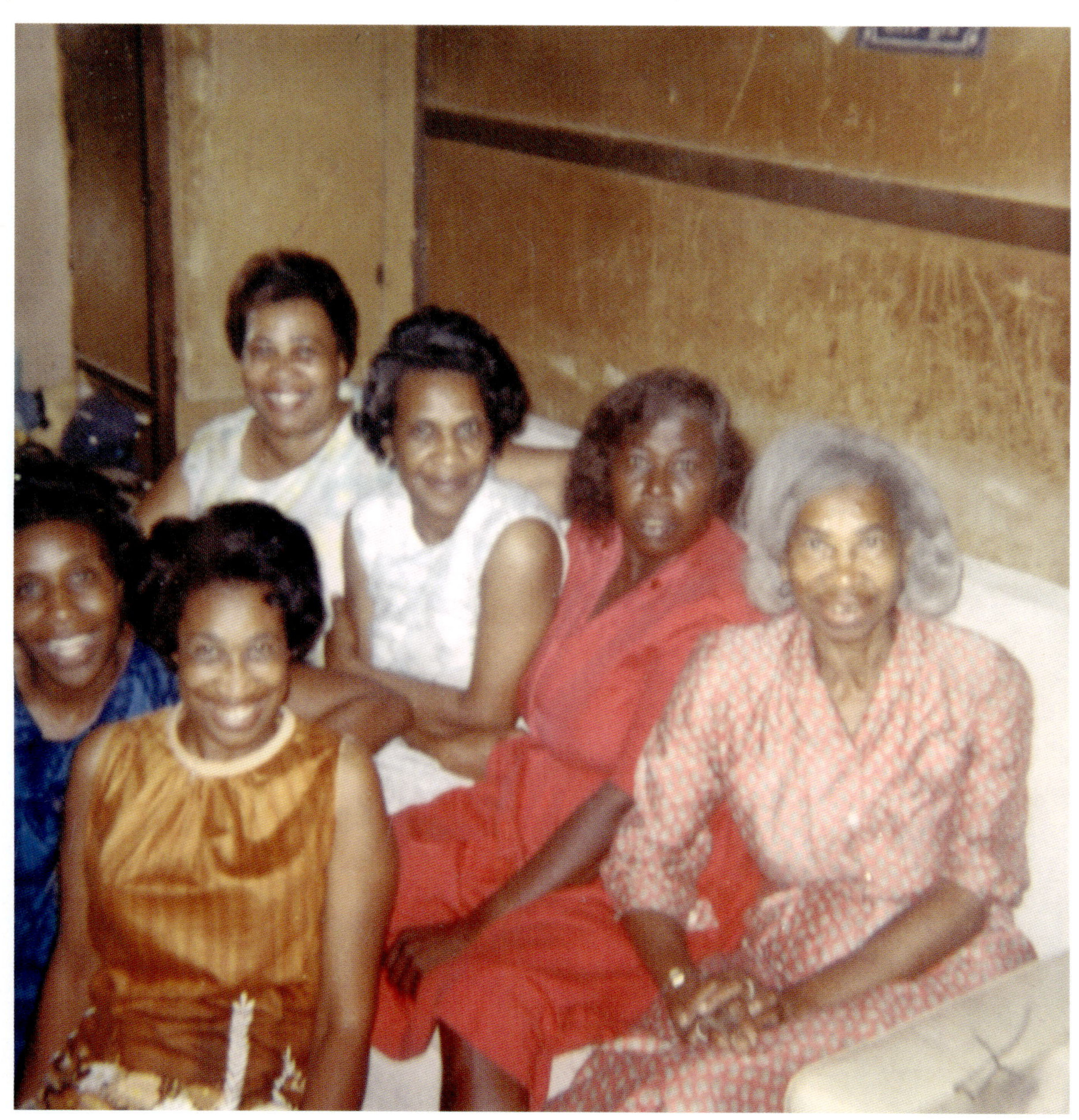

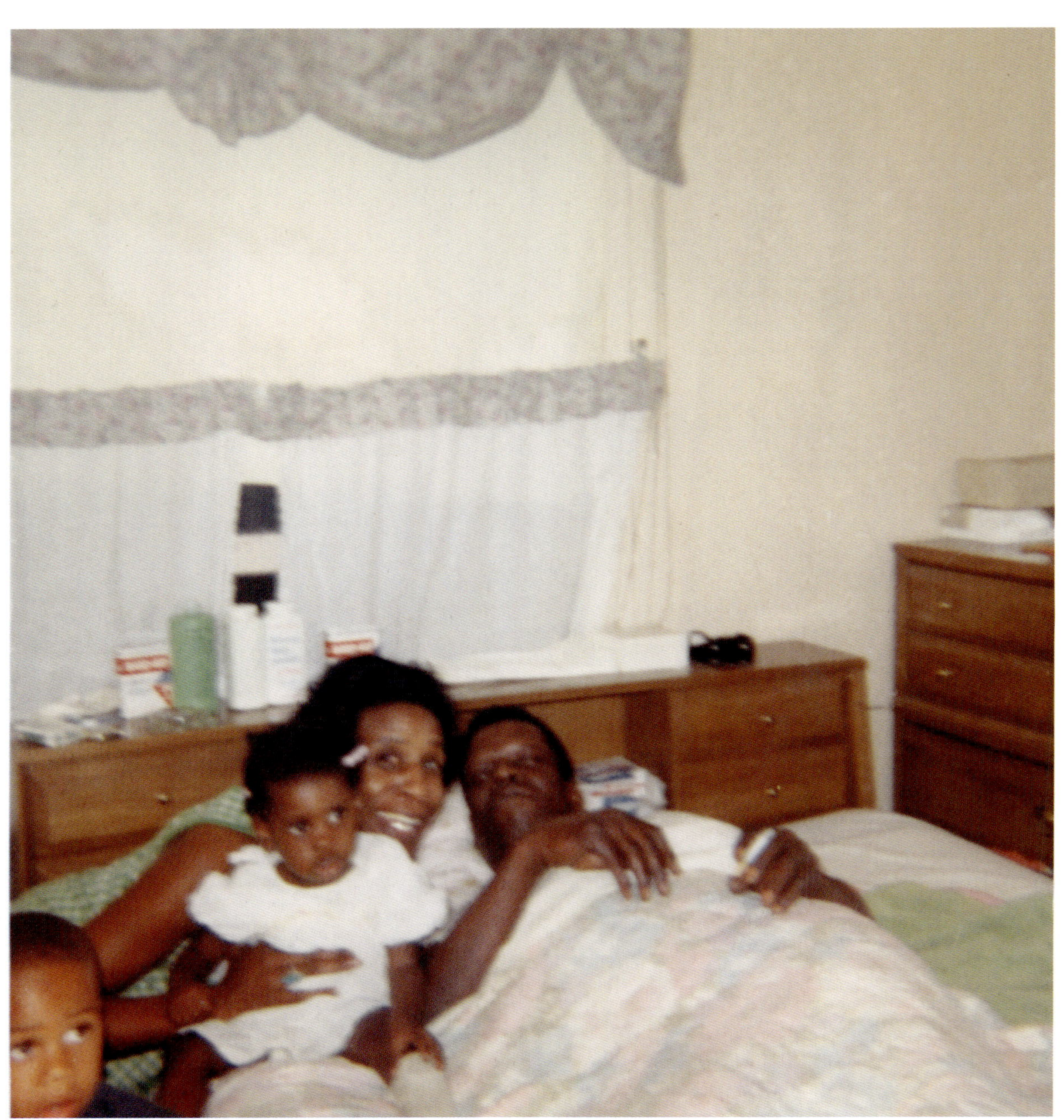

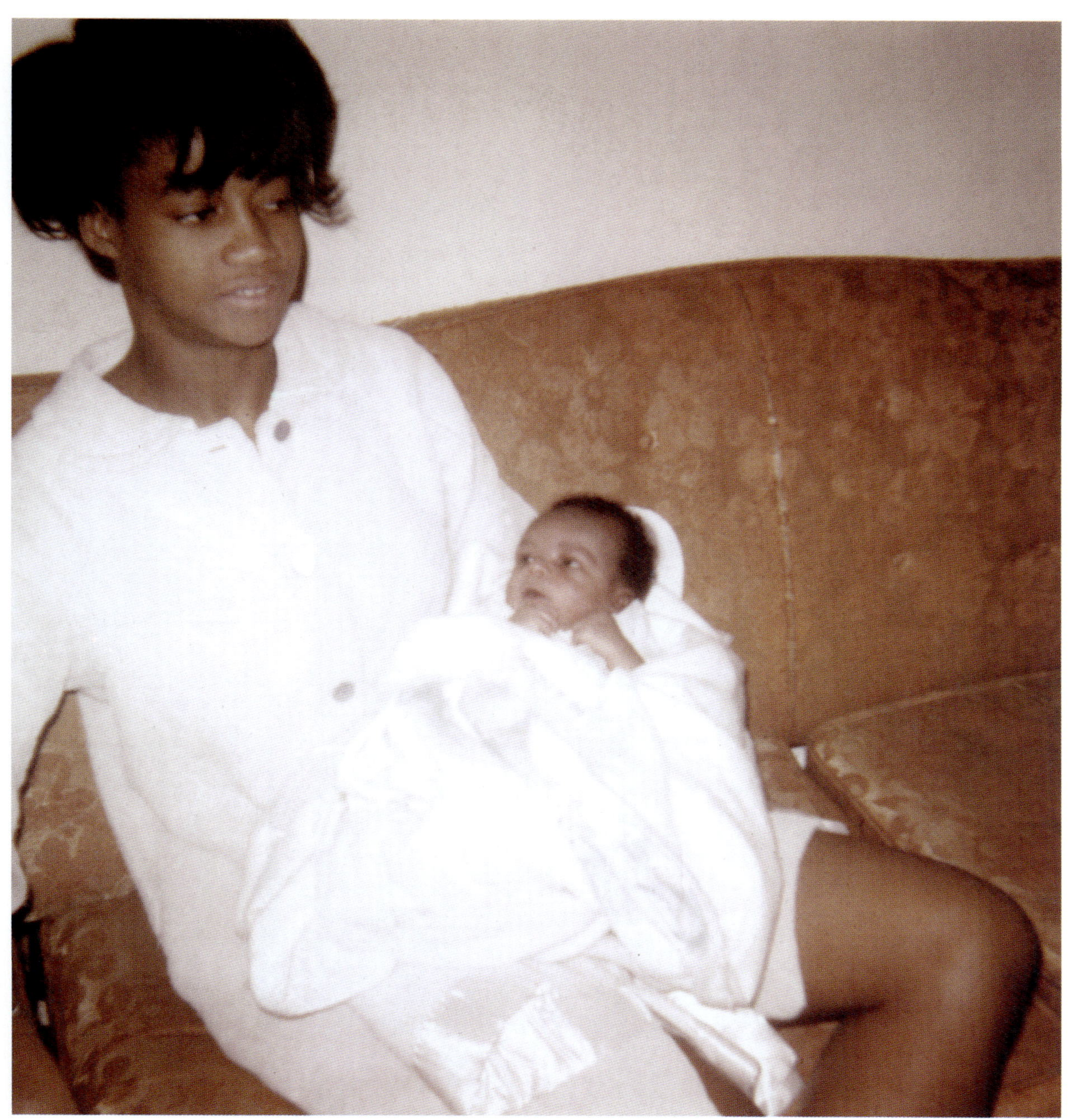

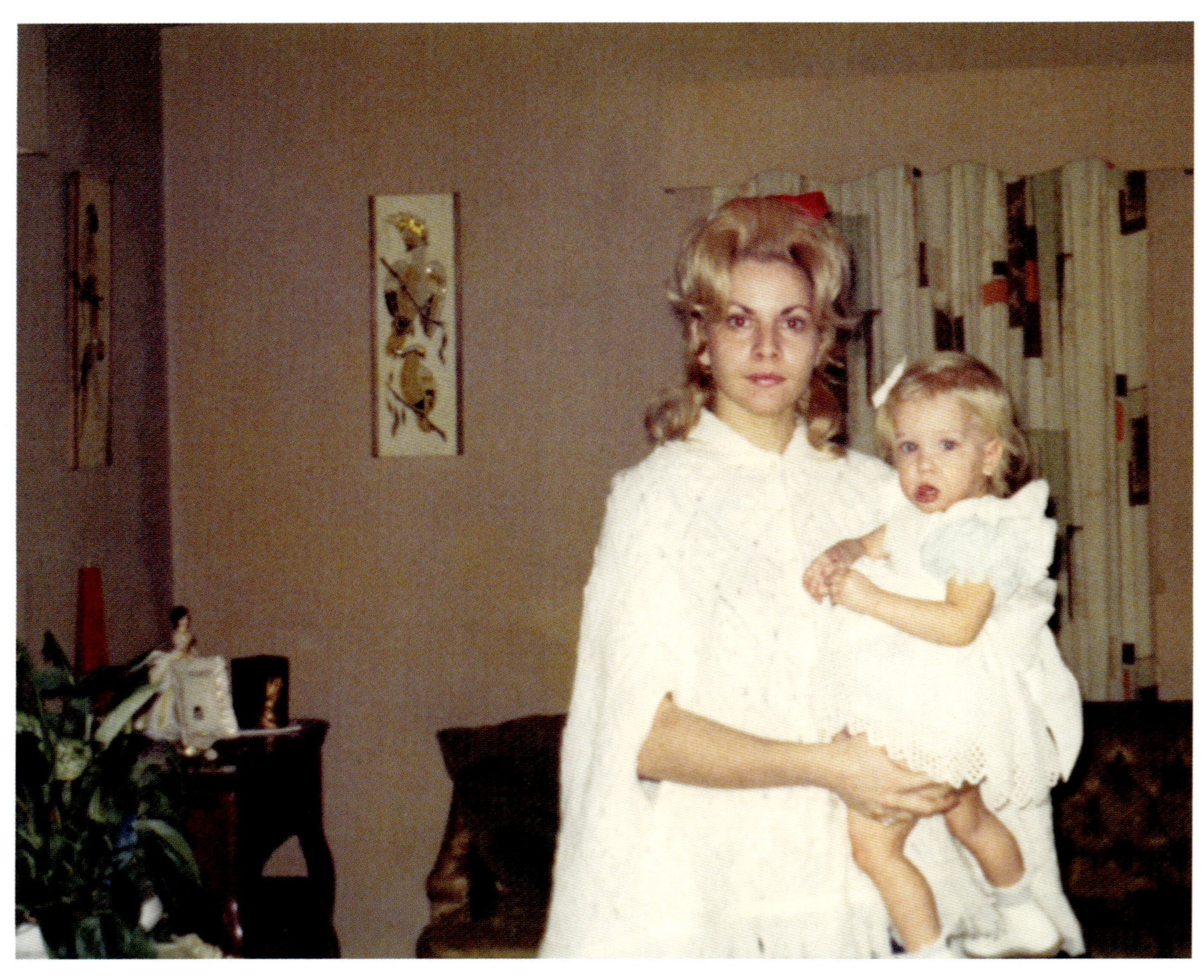

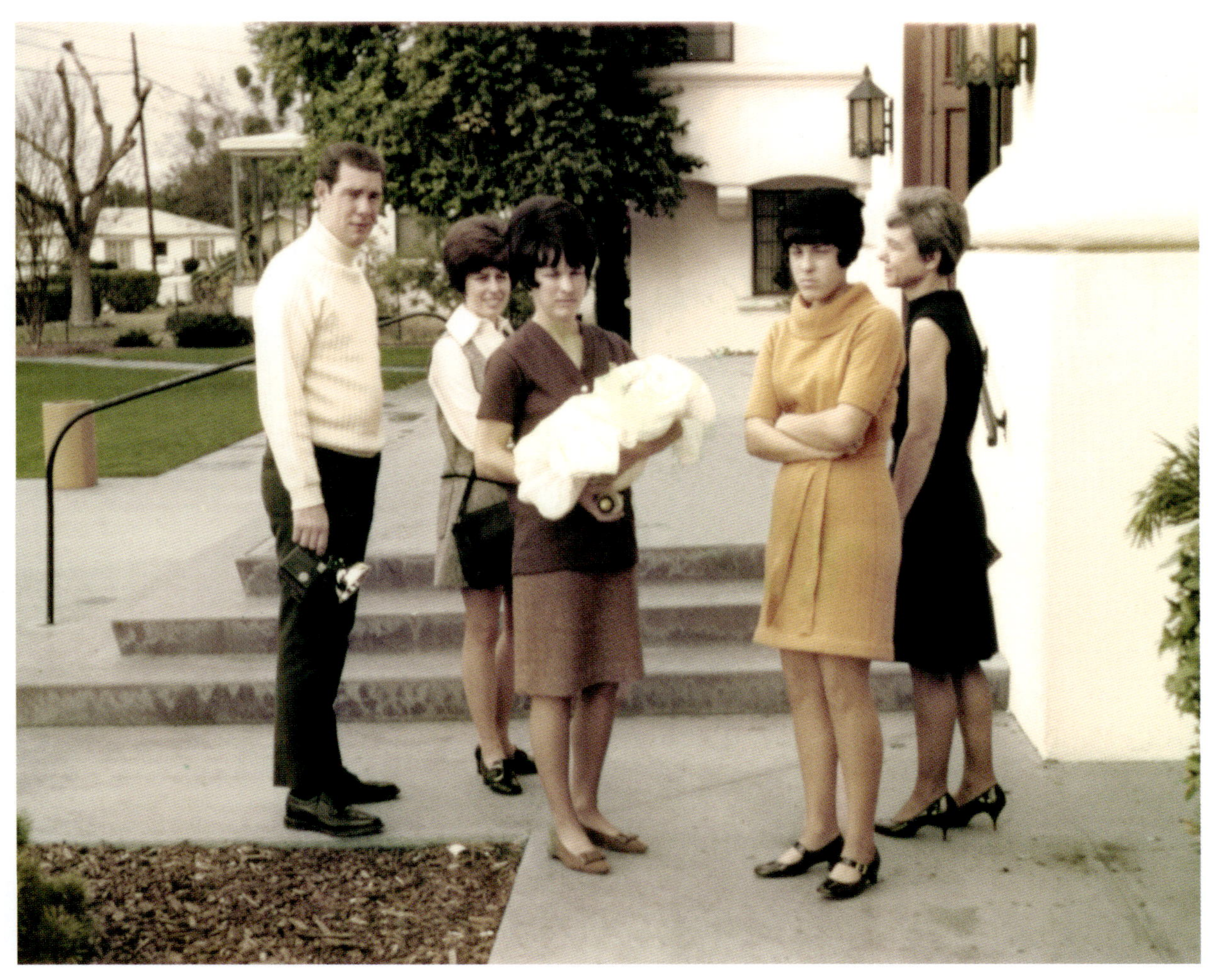

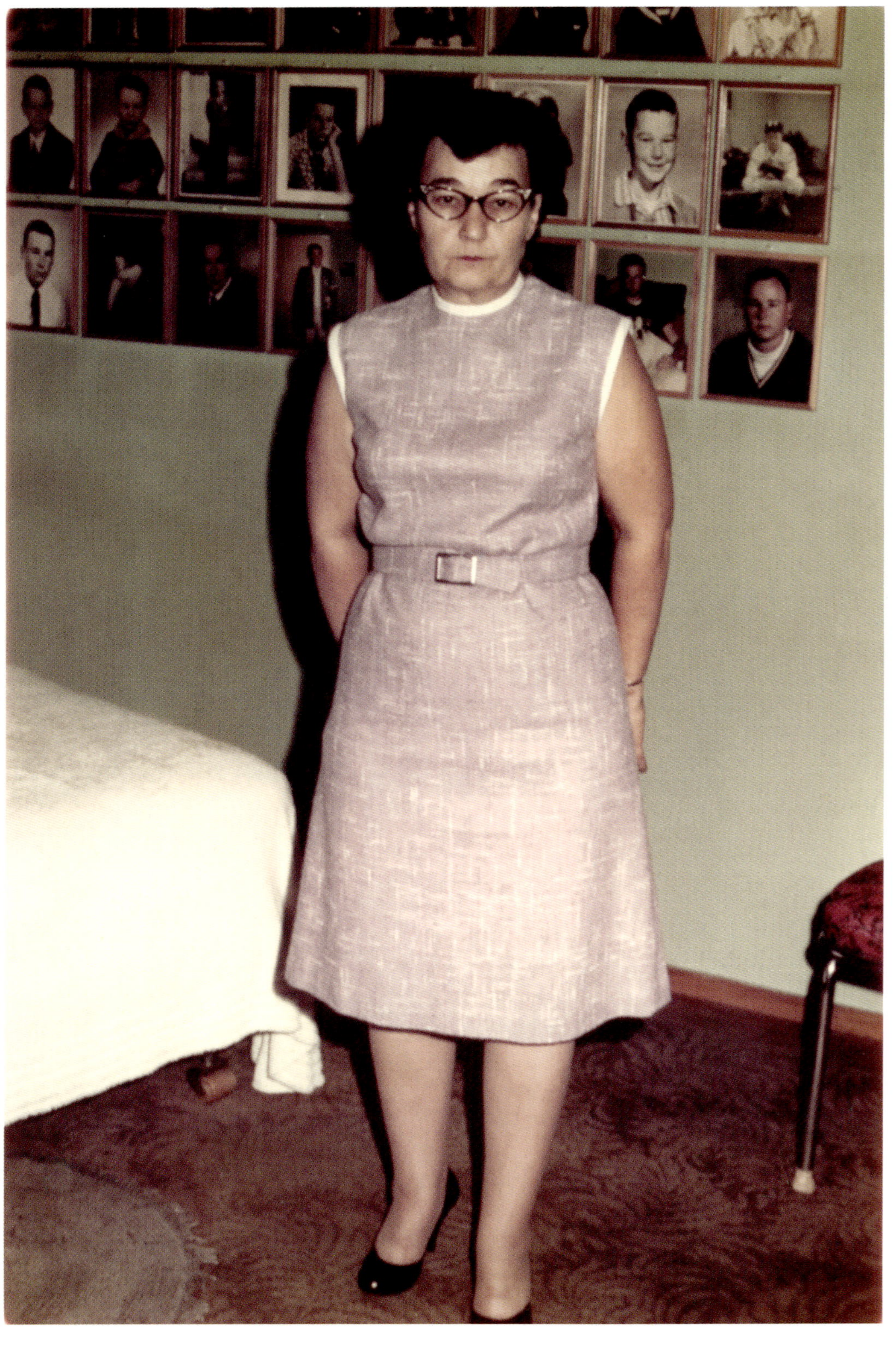

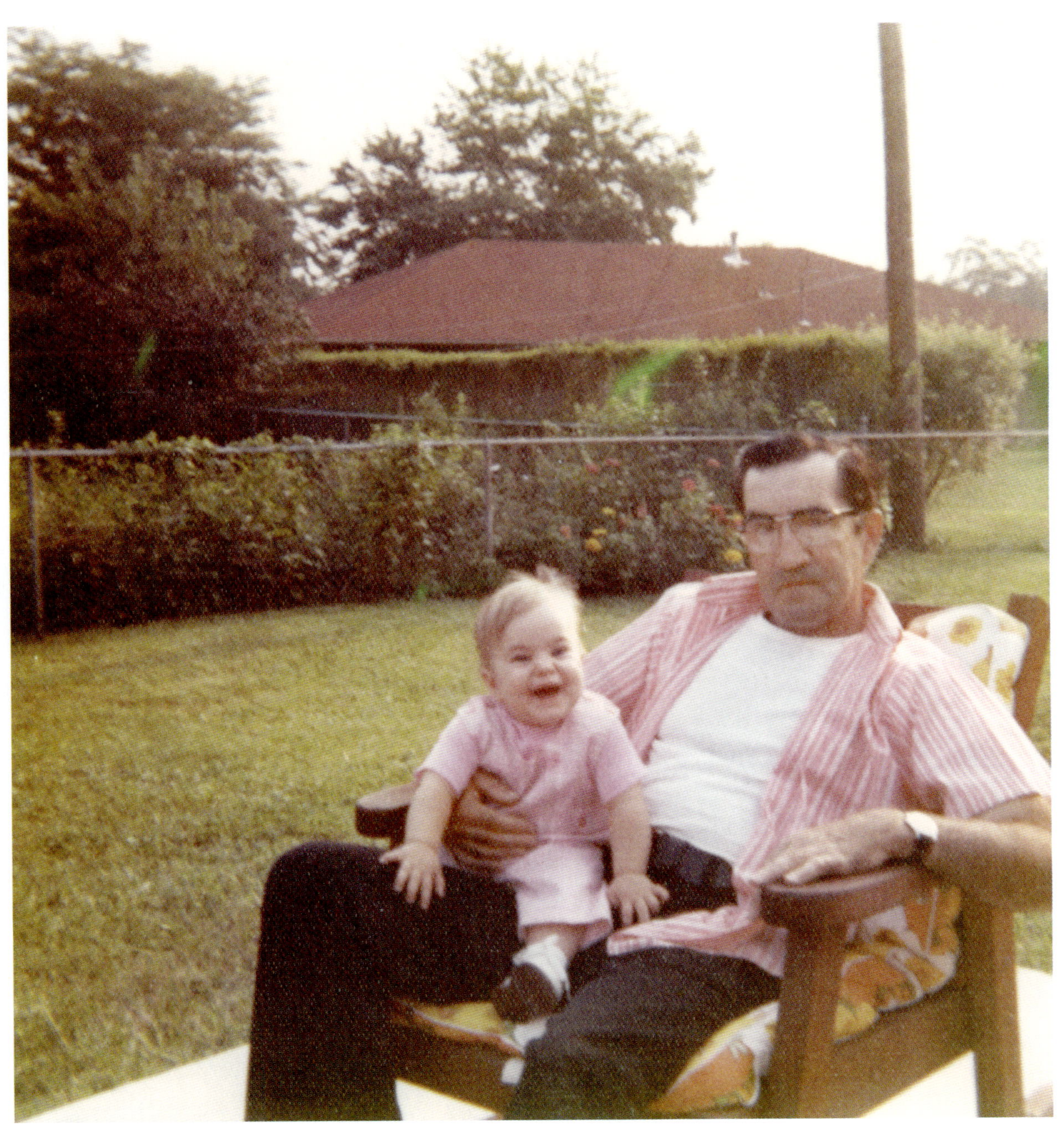

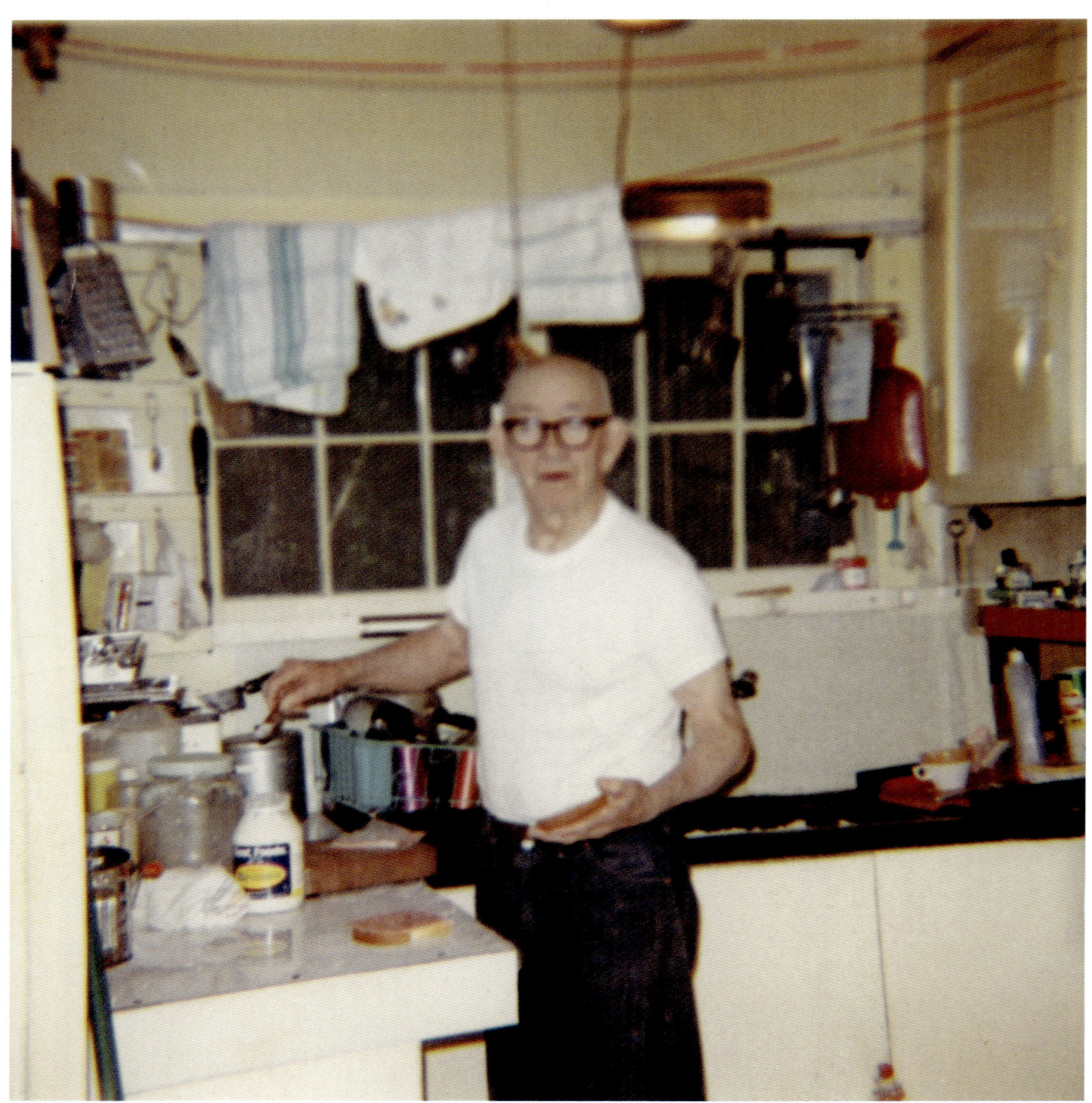

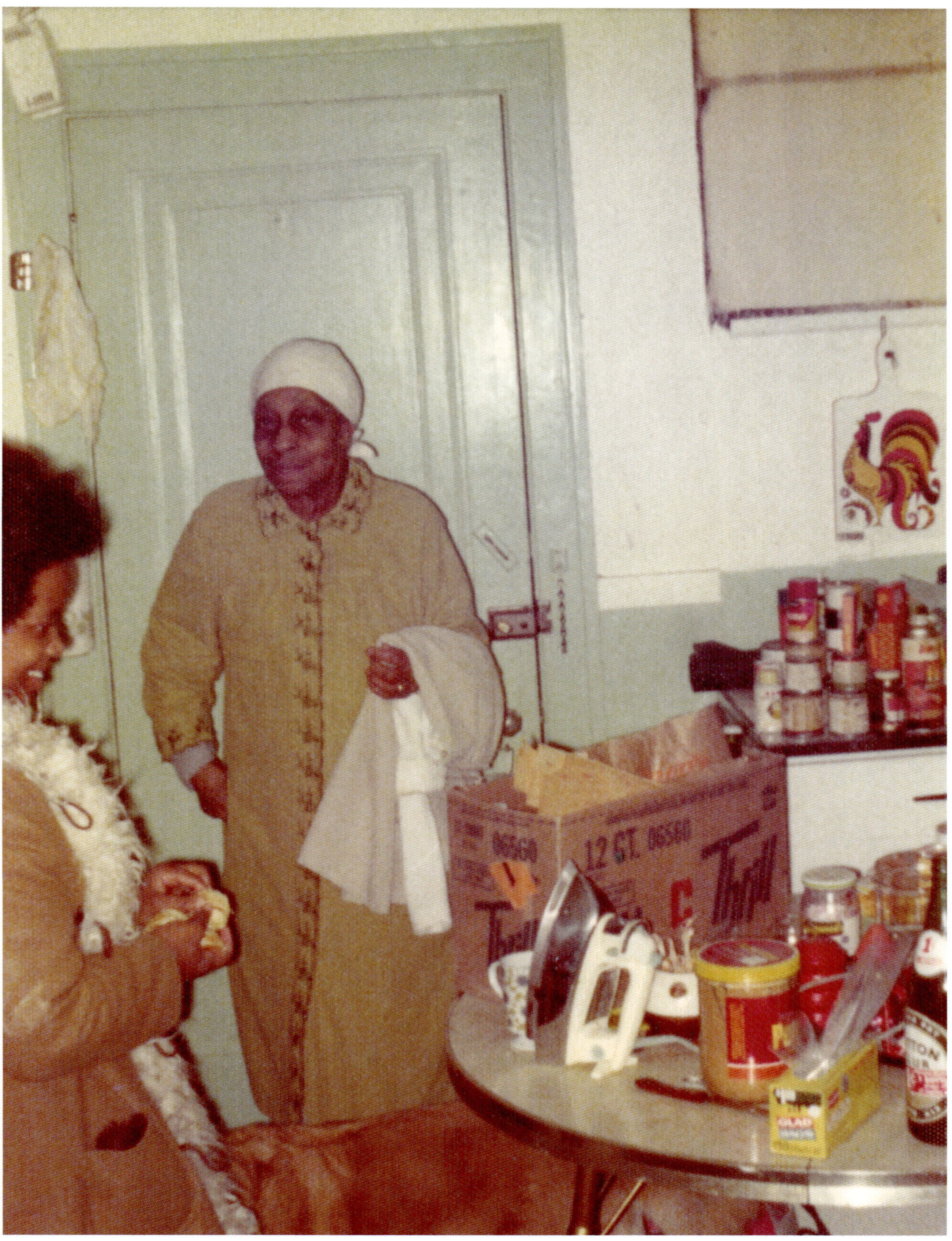
12 QT. 06560
Thrill

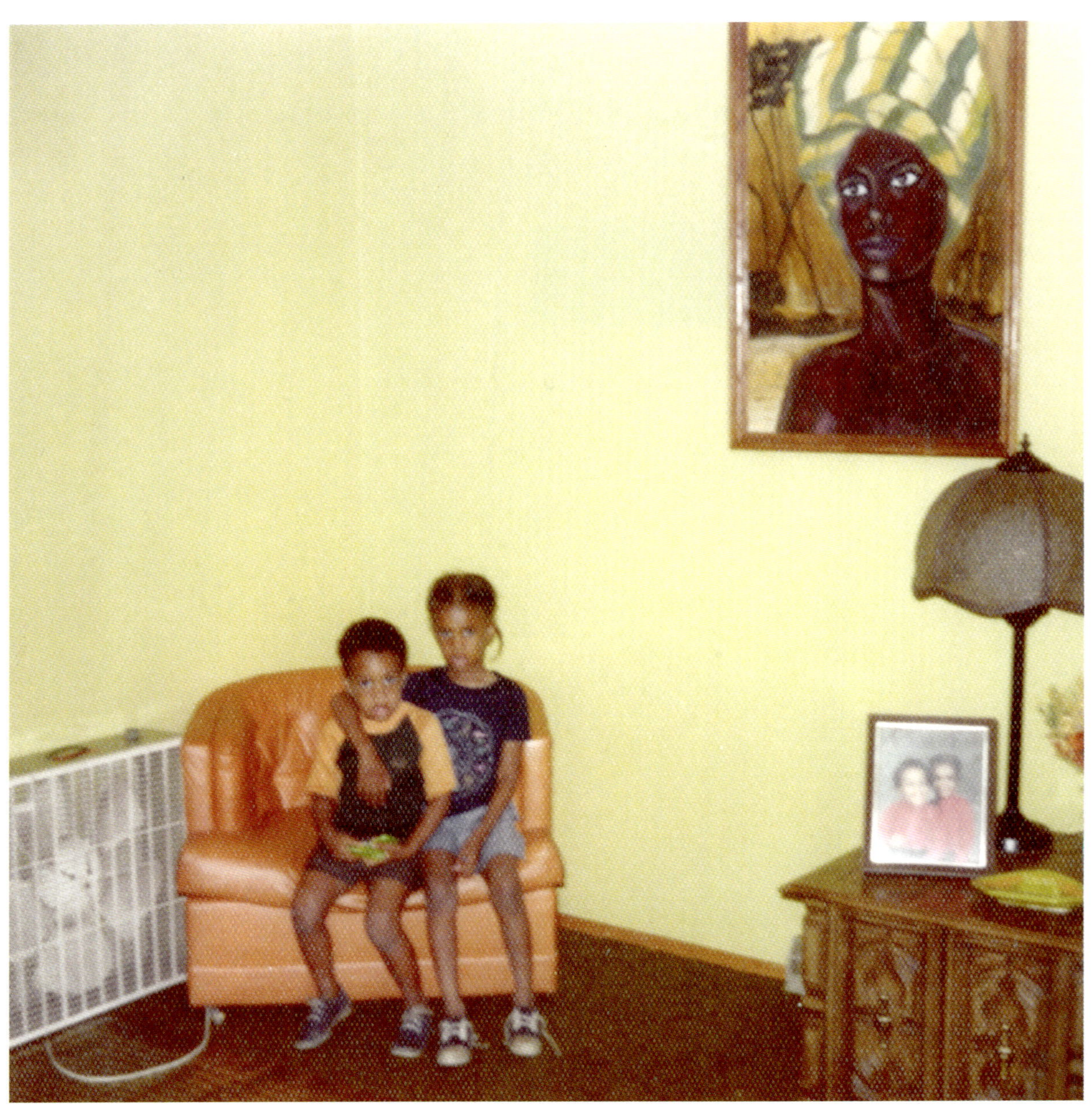

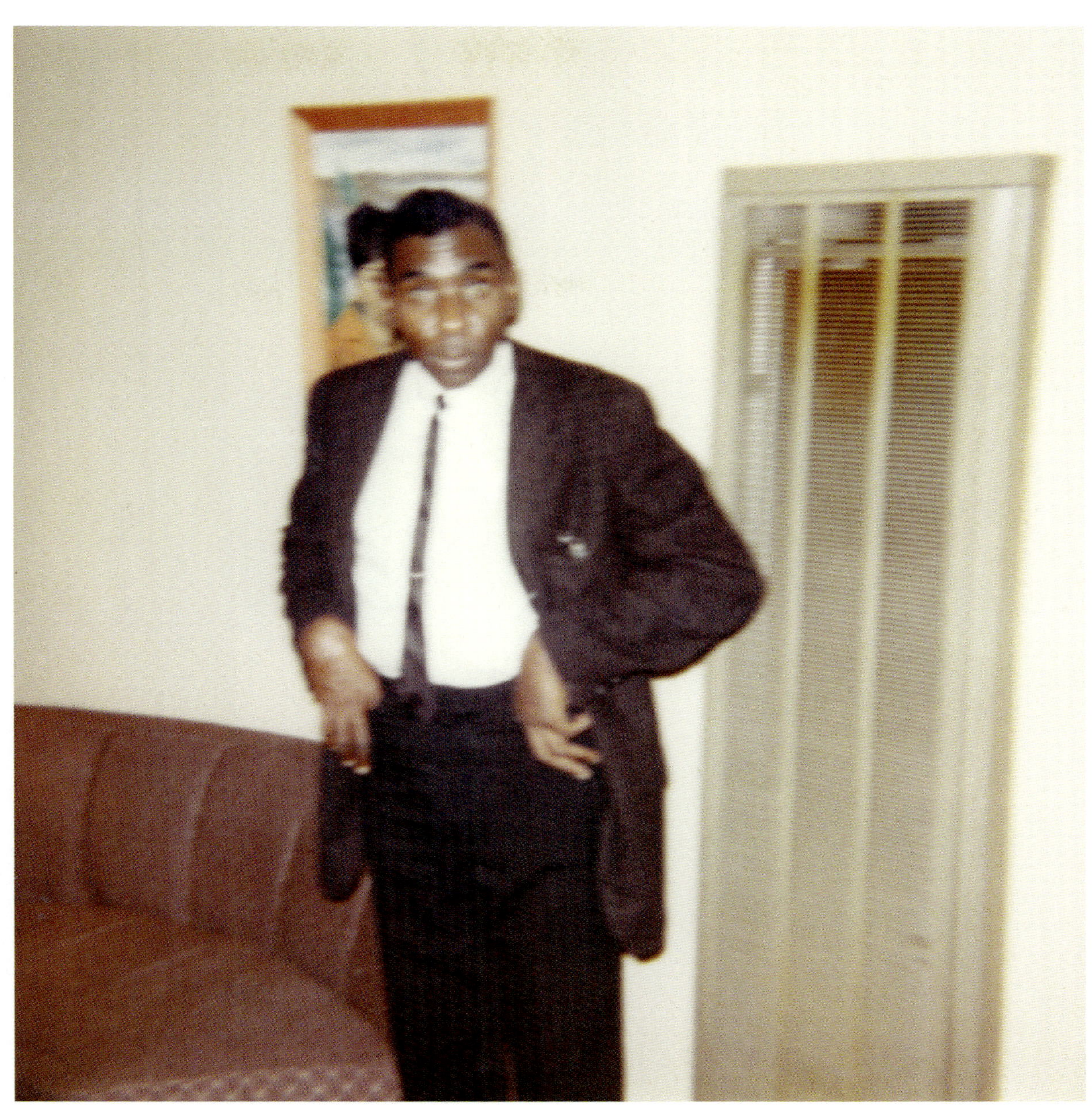

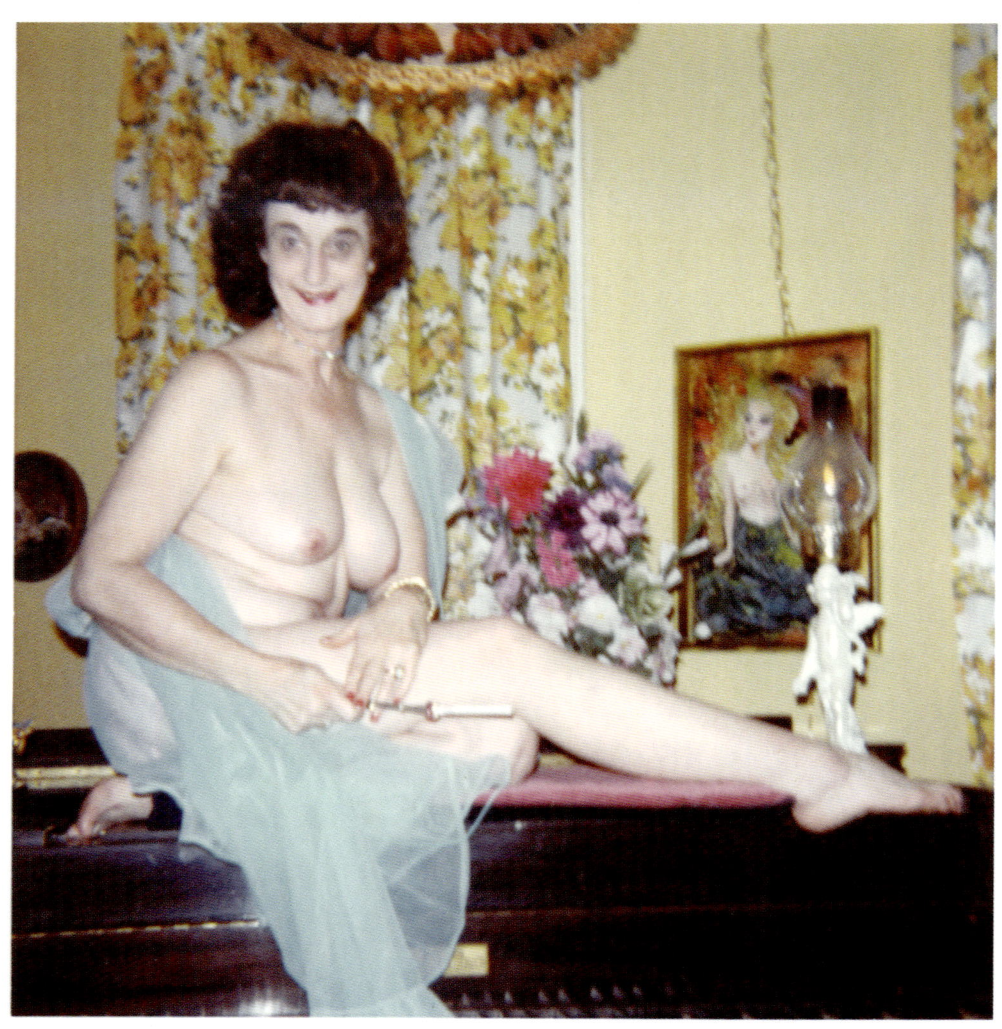

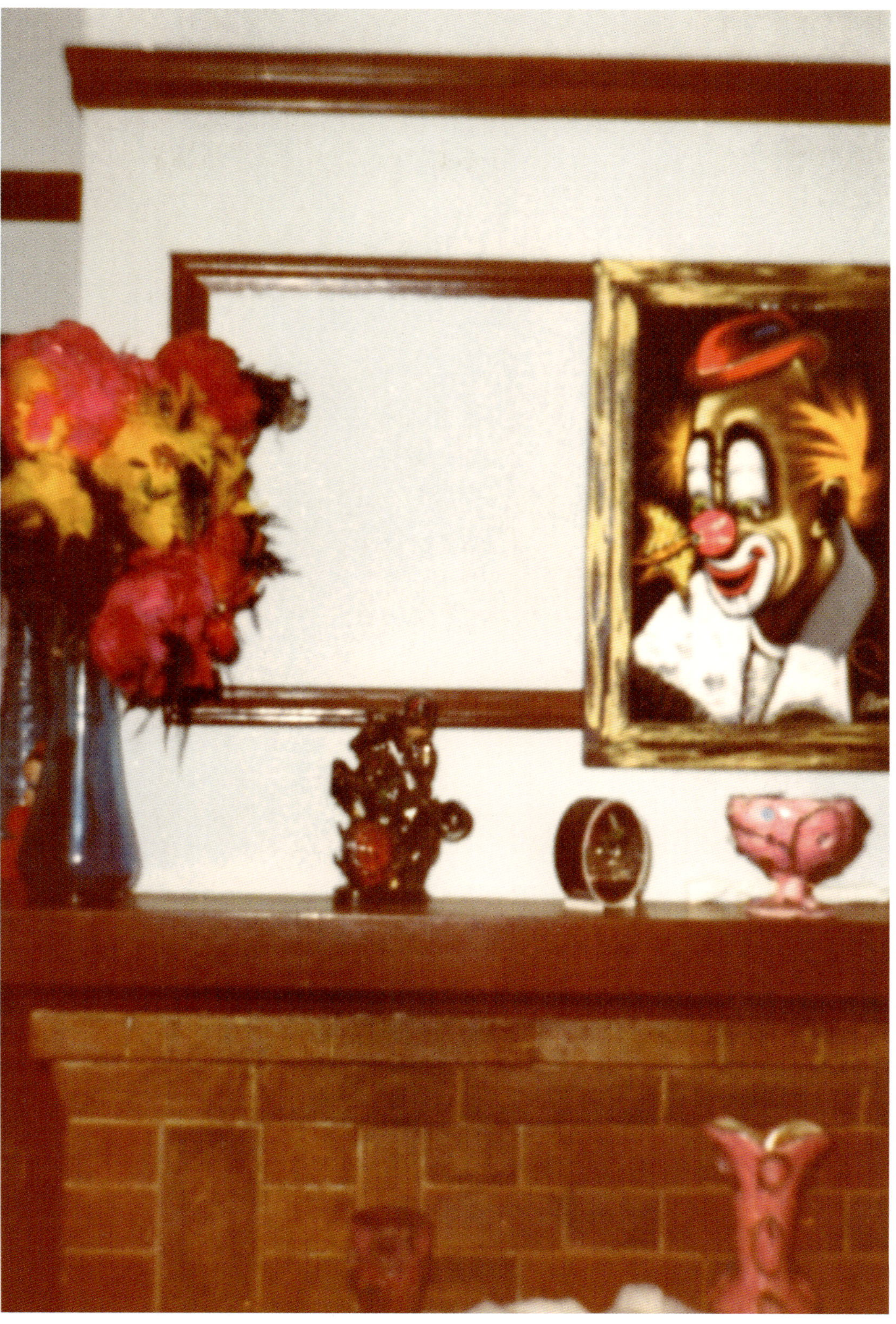

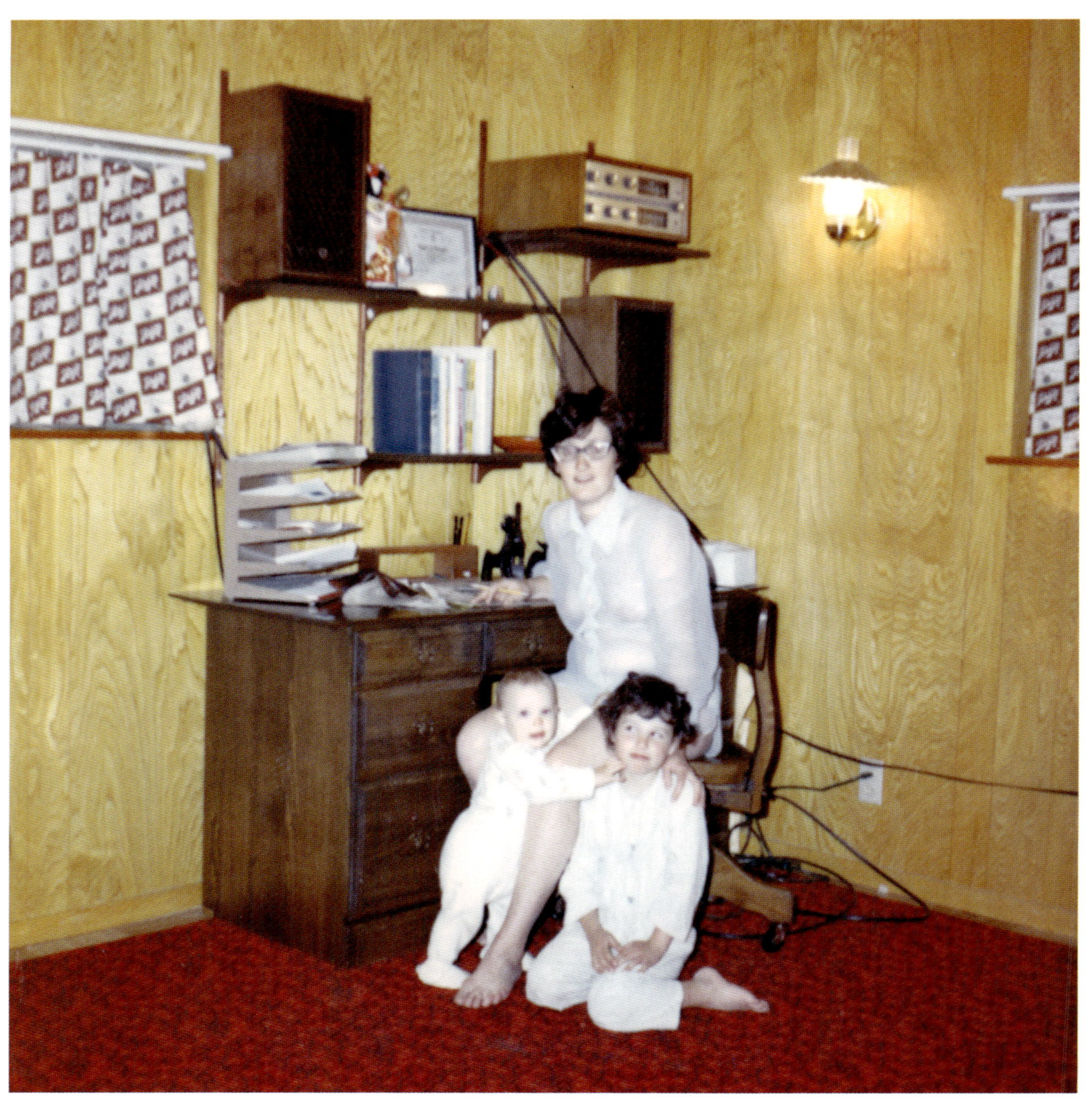

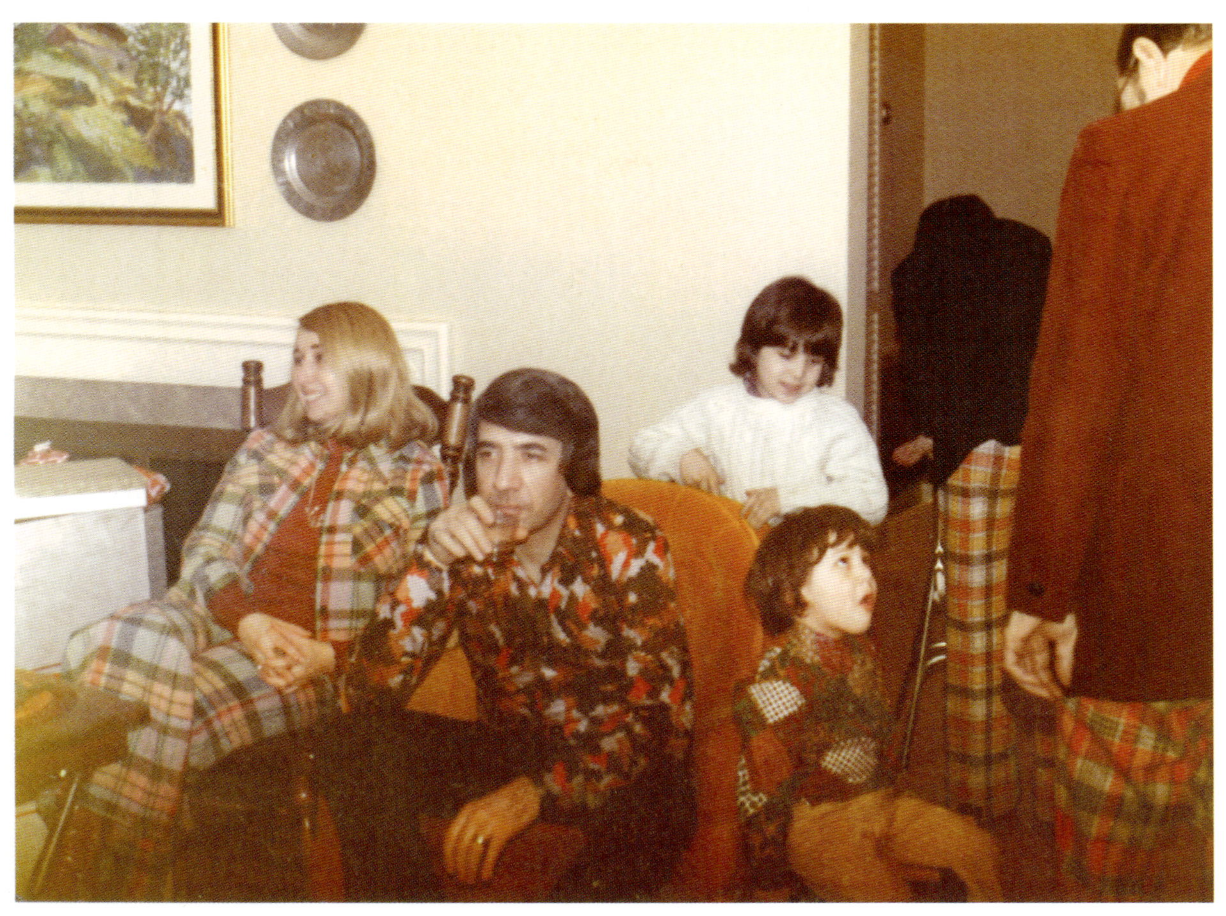

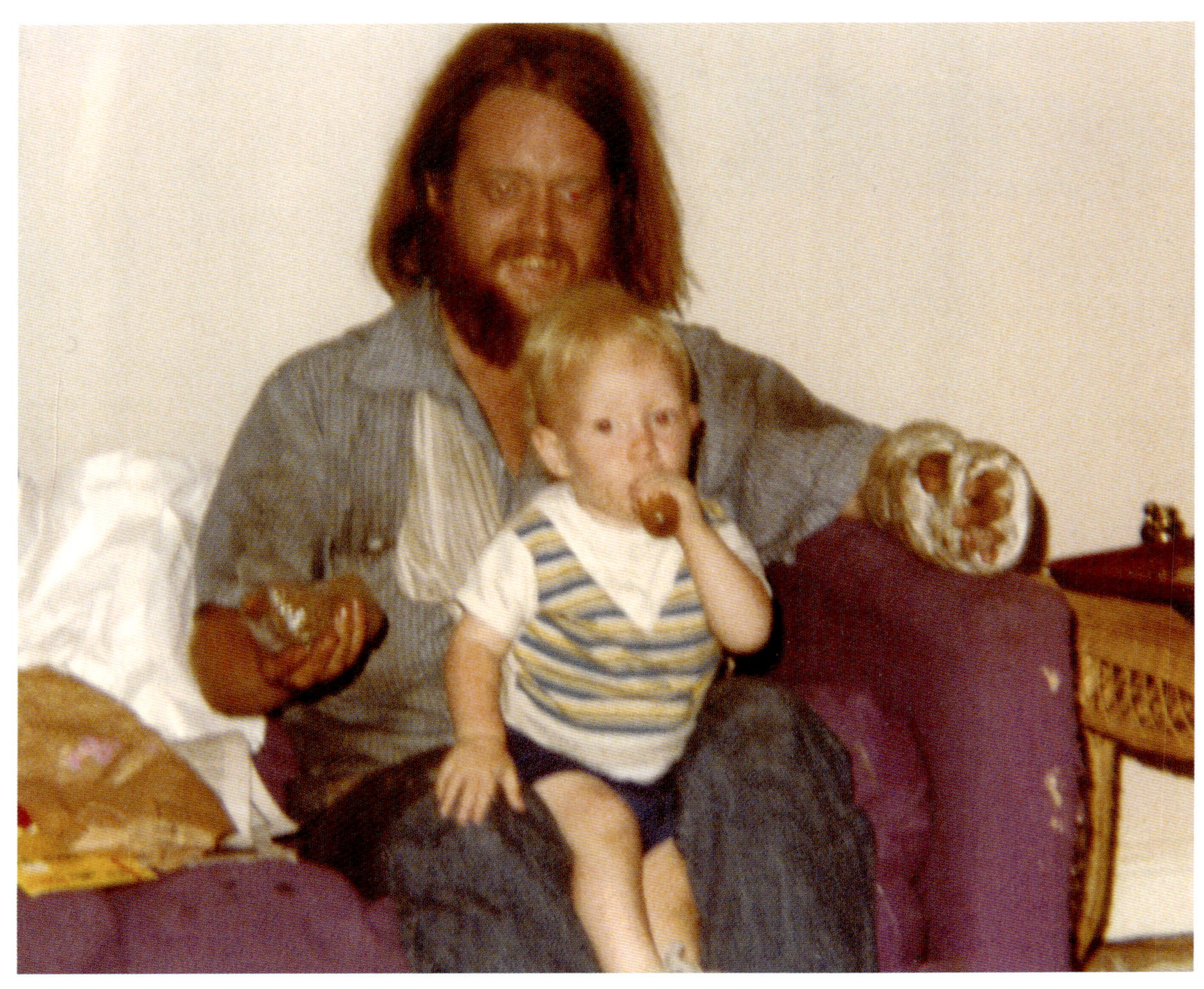

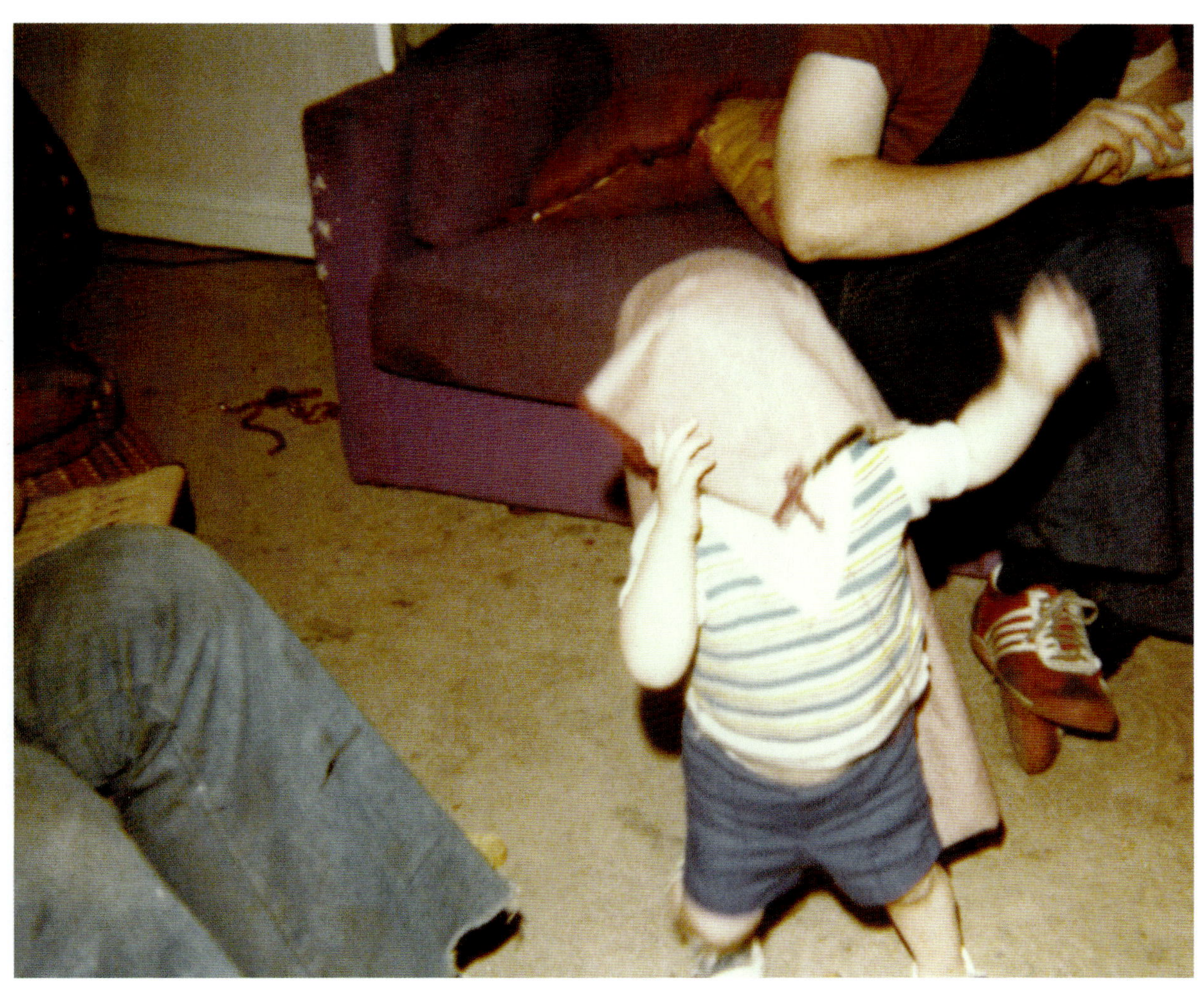

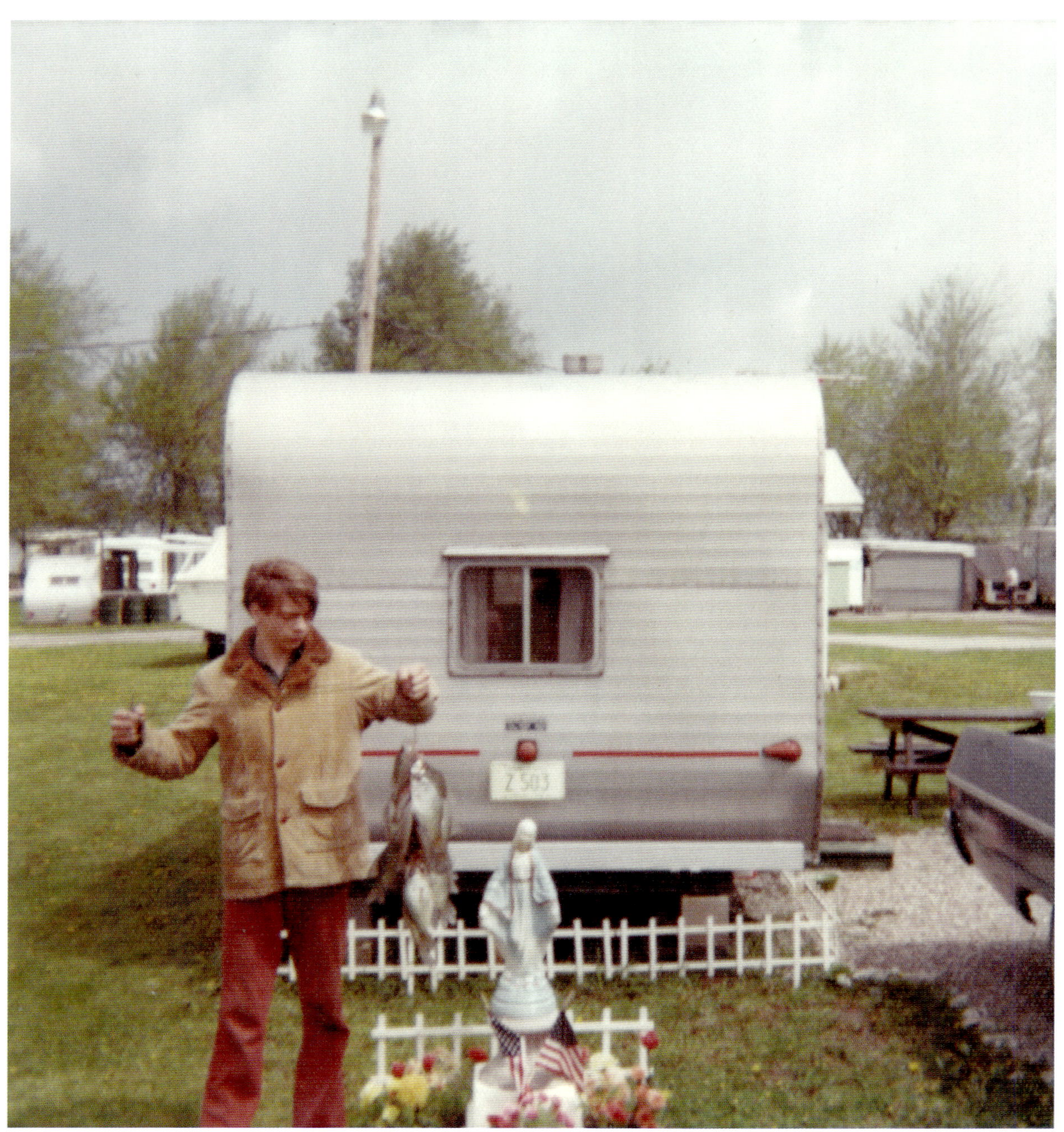

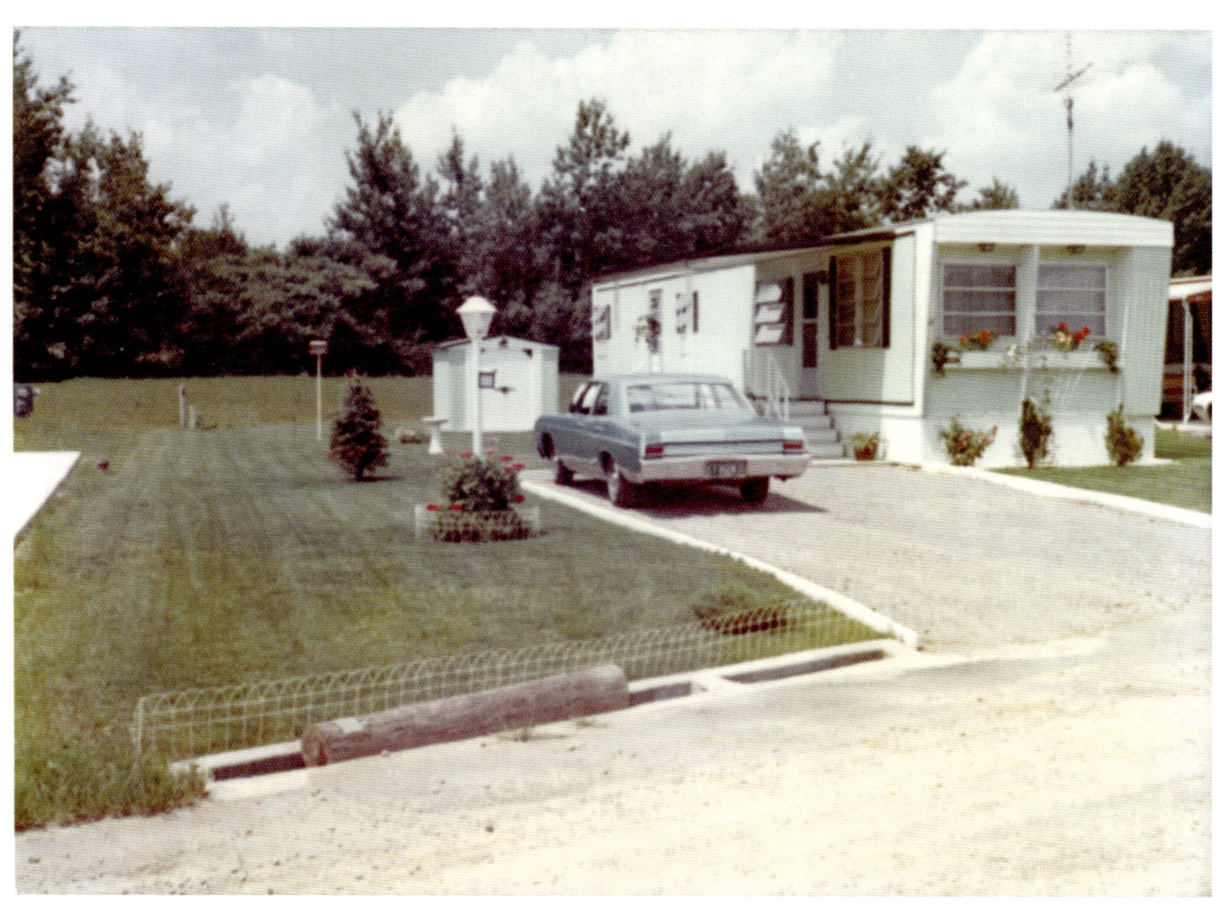

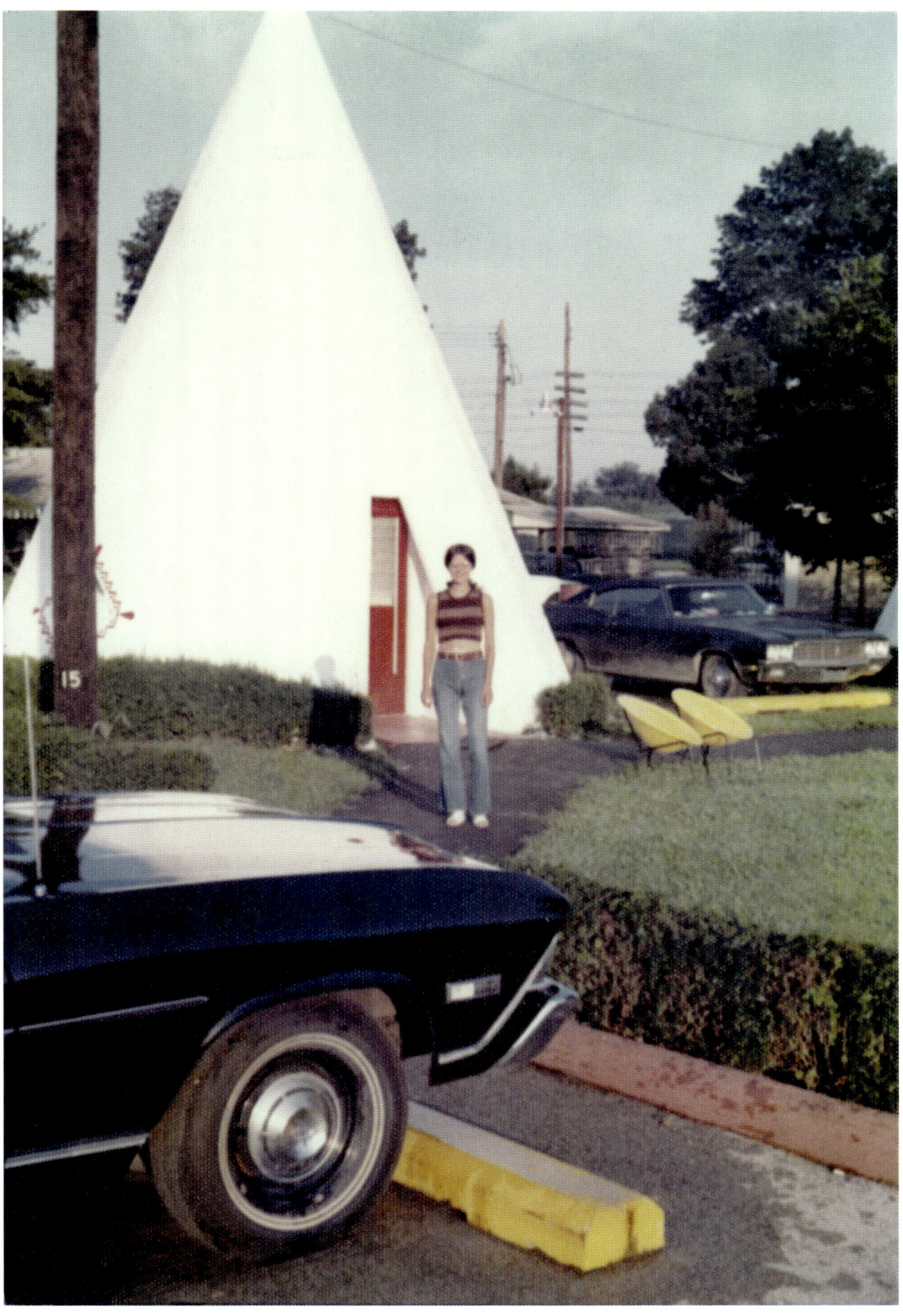
15

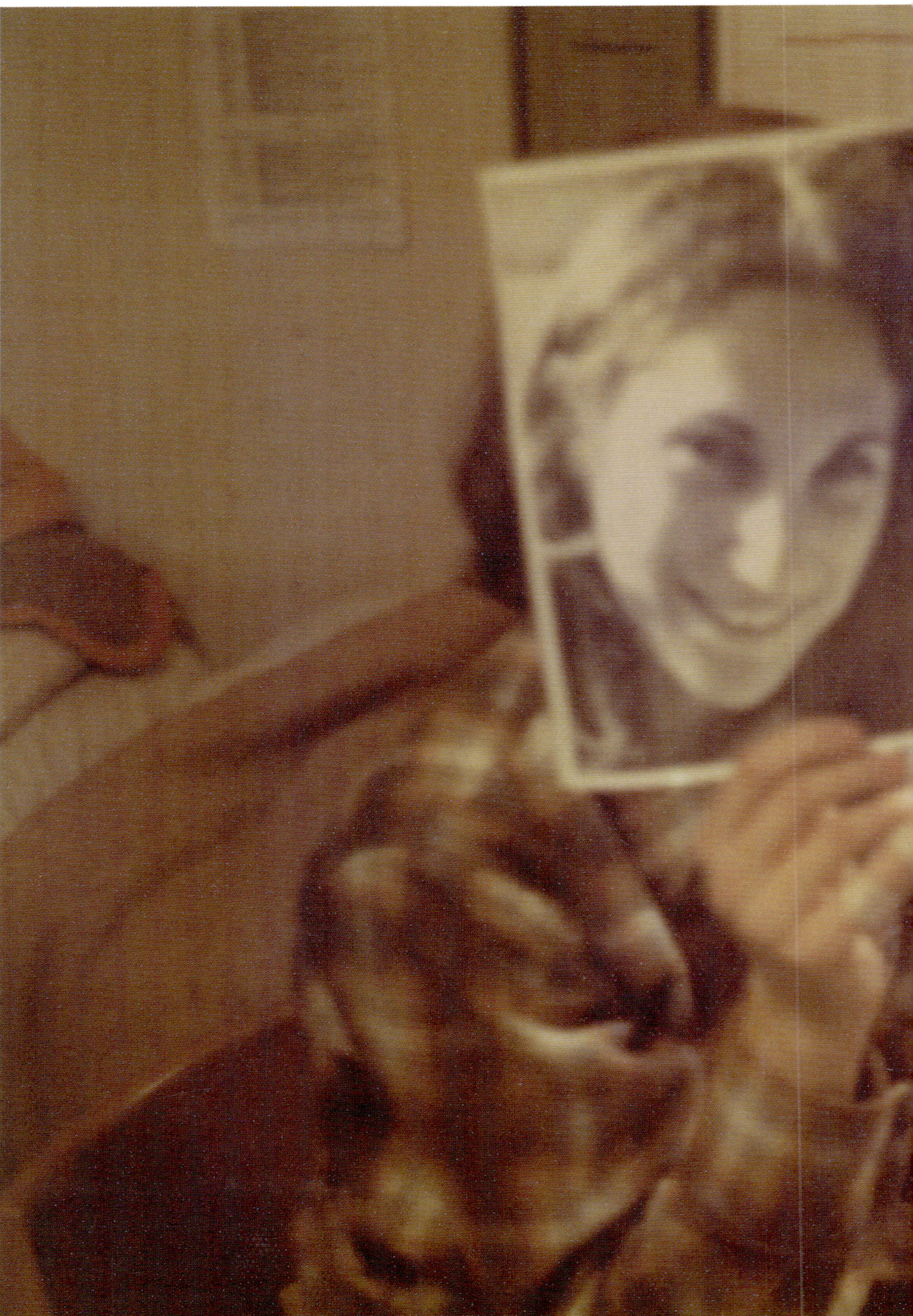

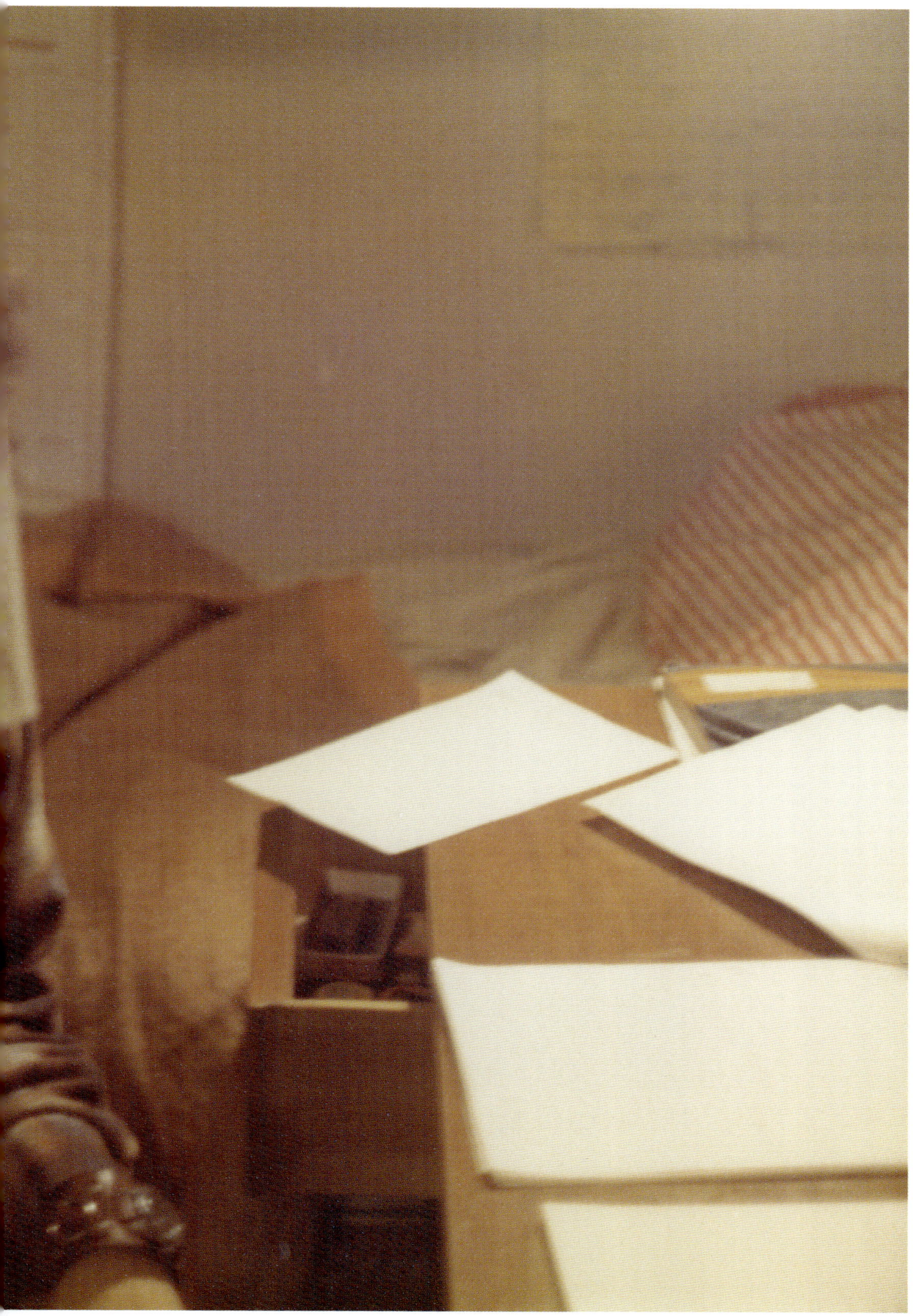

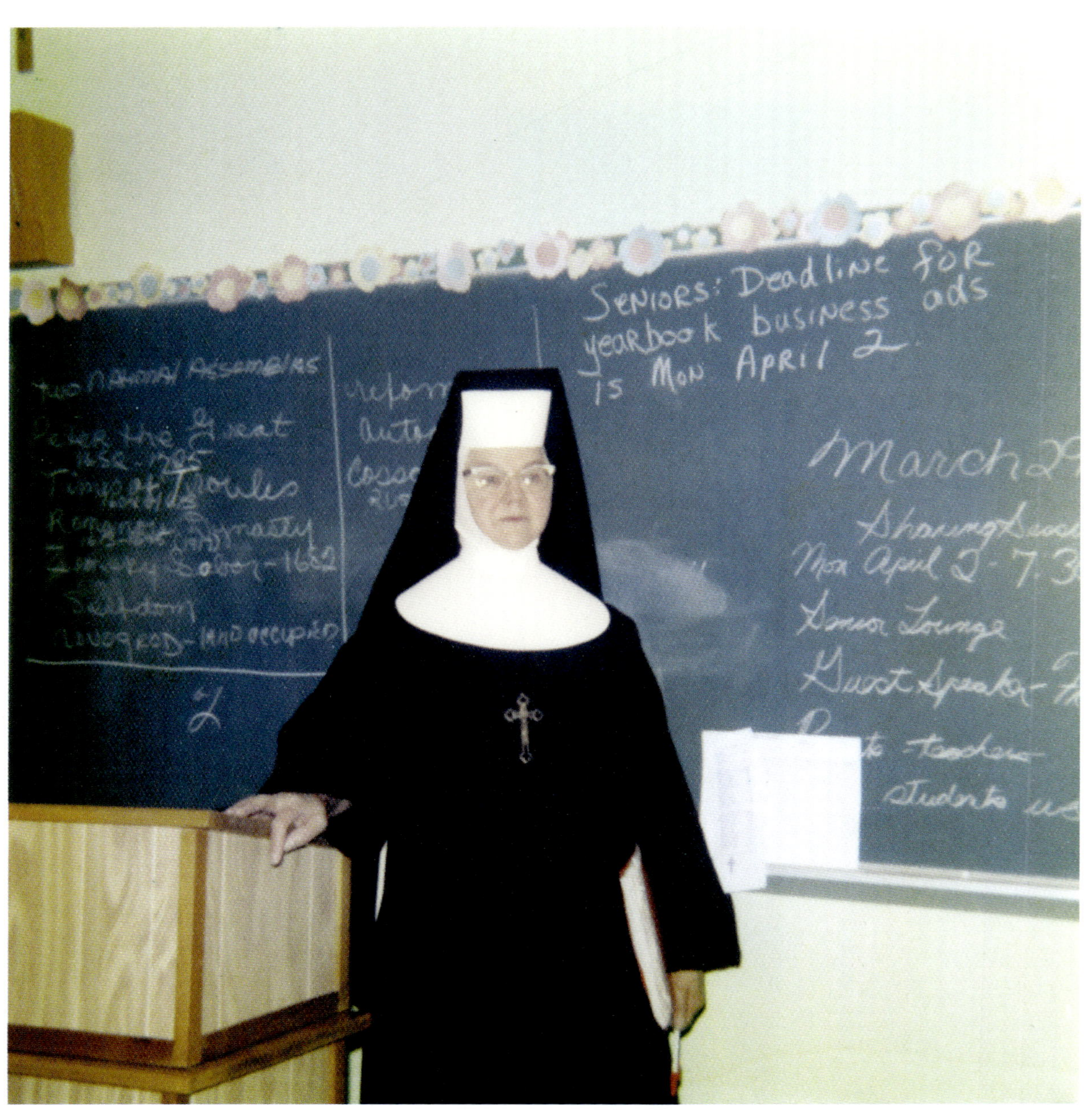

SENIORS: Deadline FOR
yearbook business ads
is Mon April 2
Peter the Great
Senior Lounge

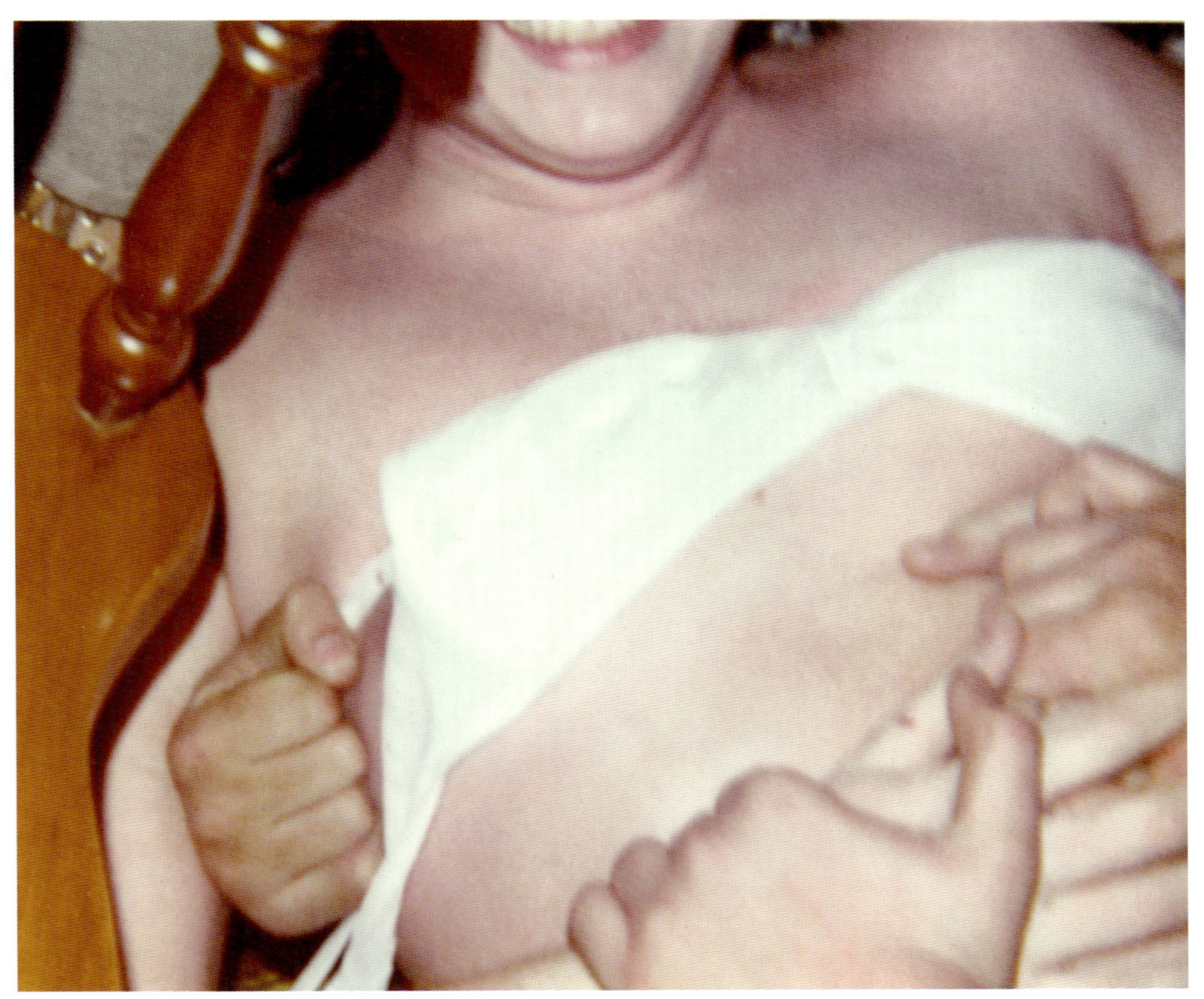

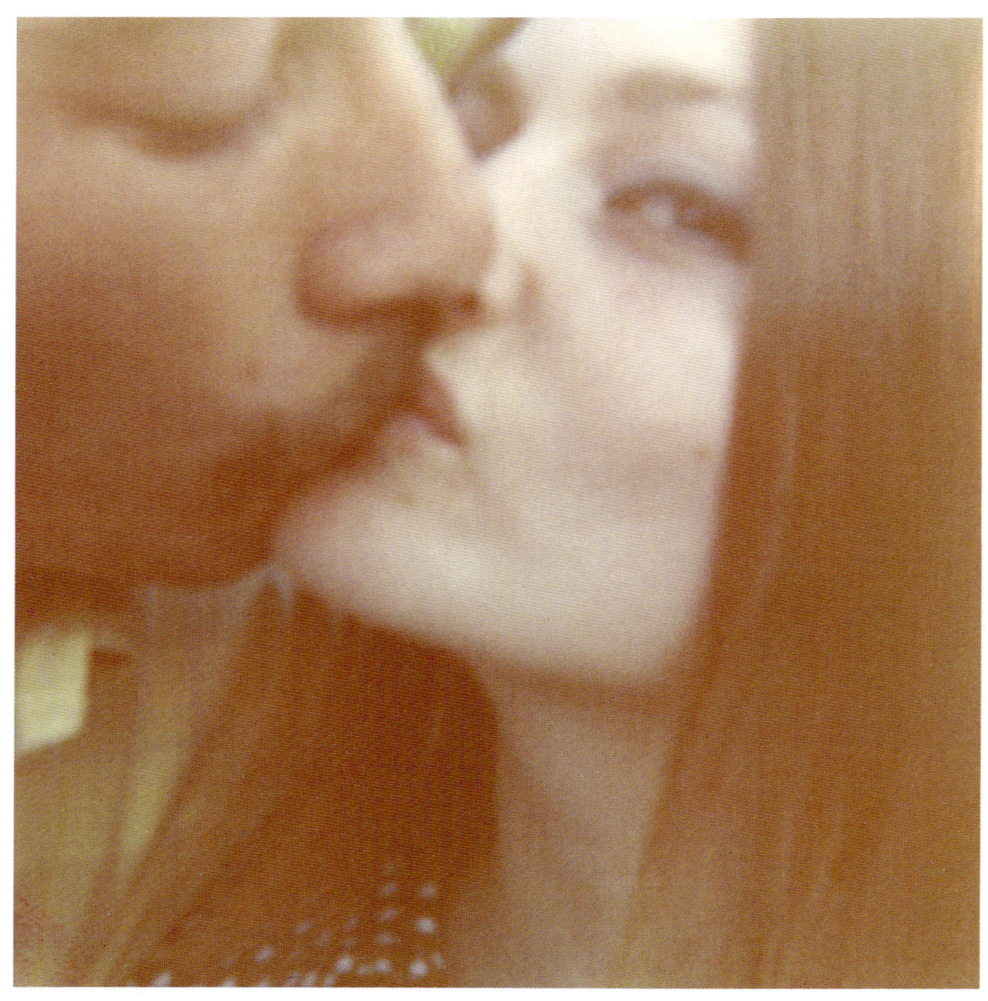

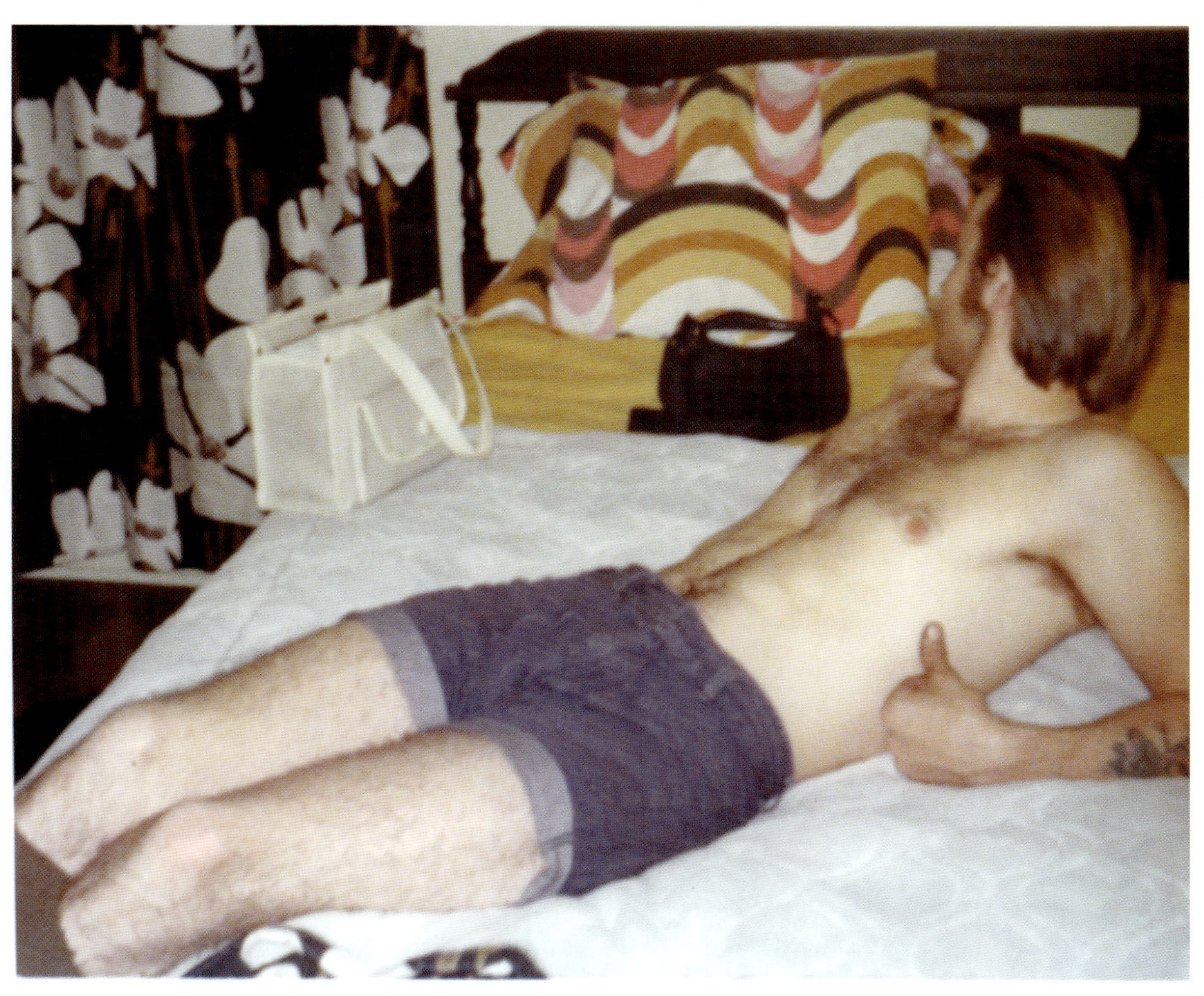

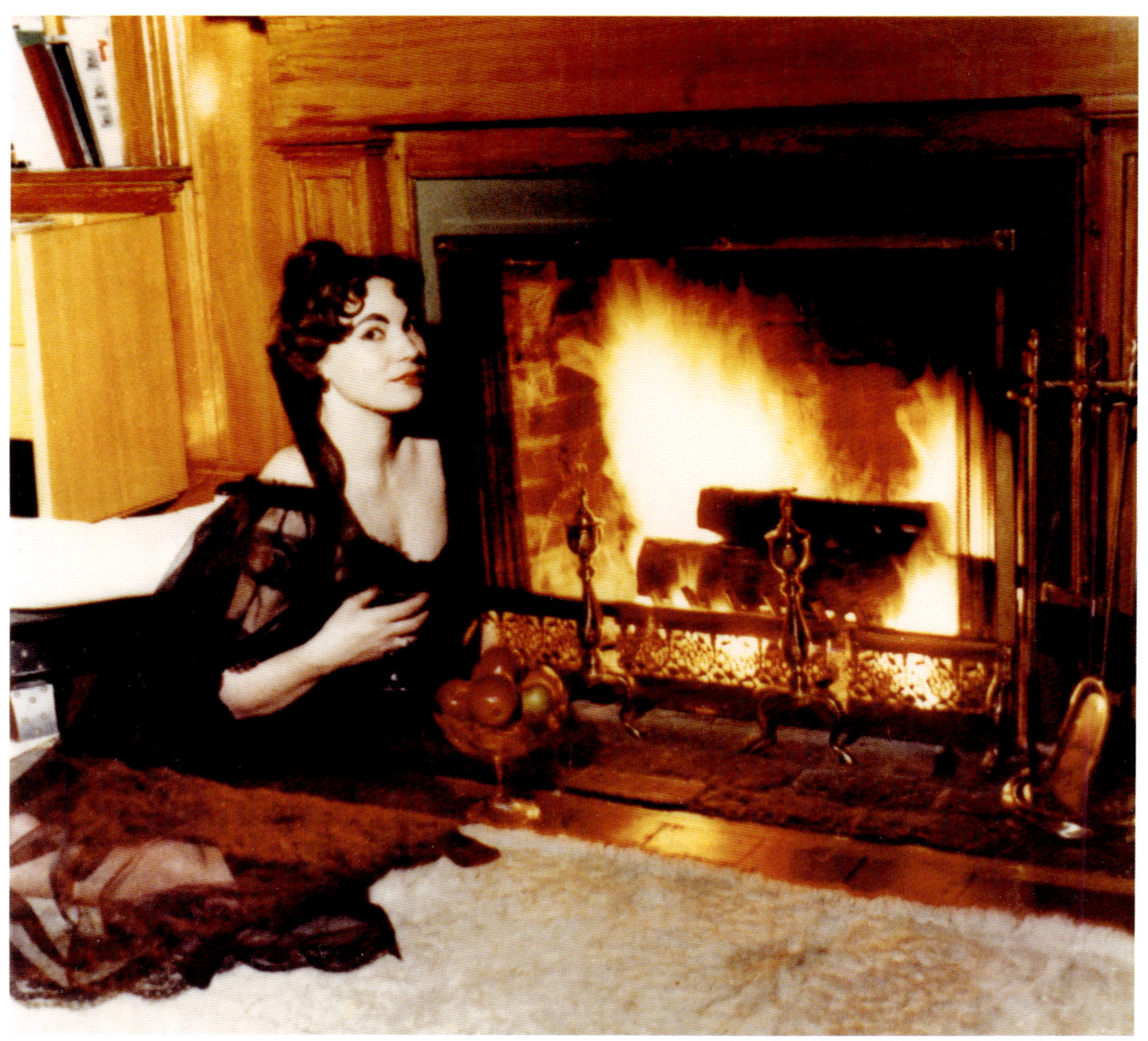

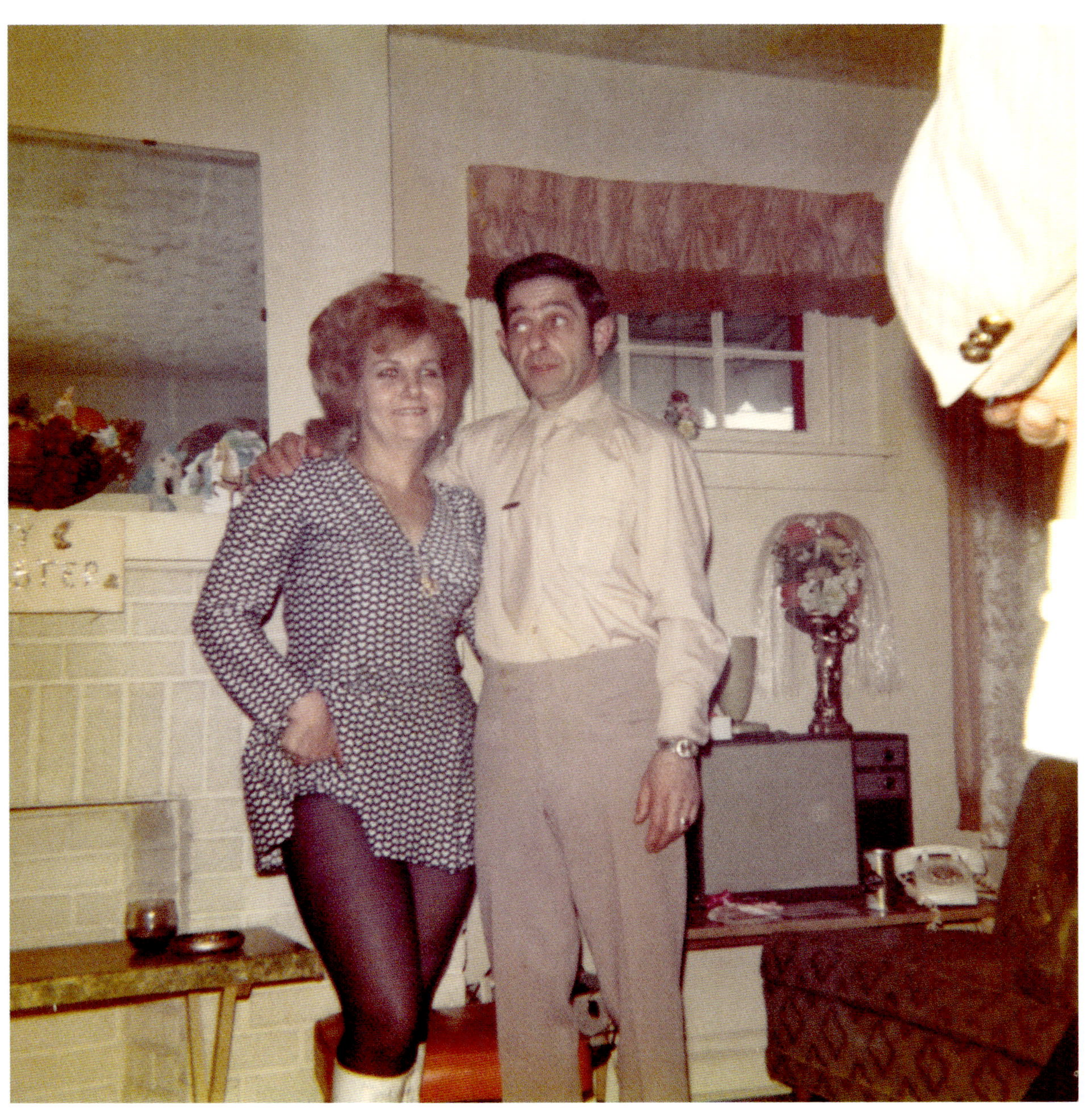

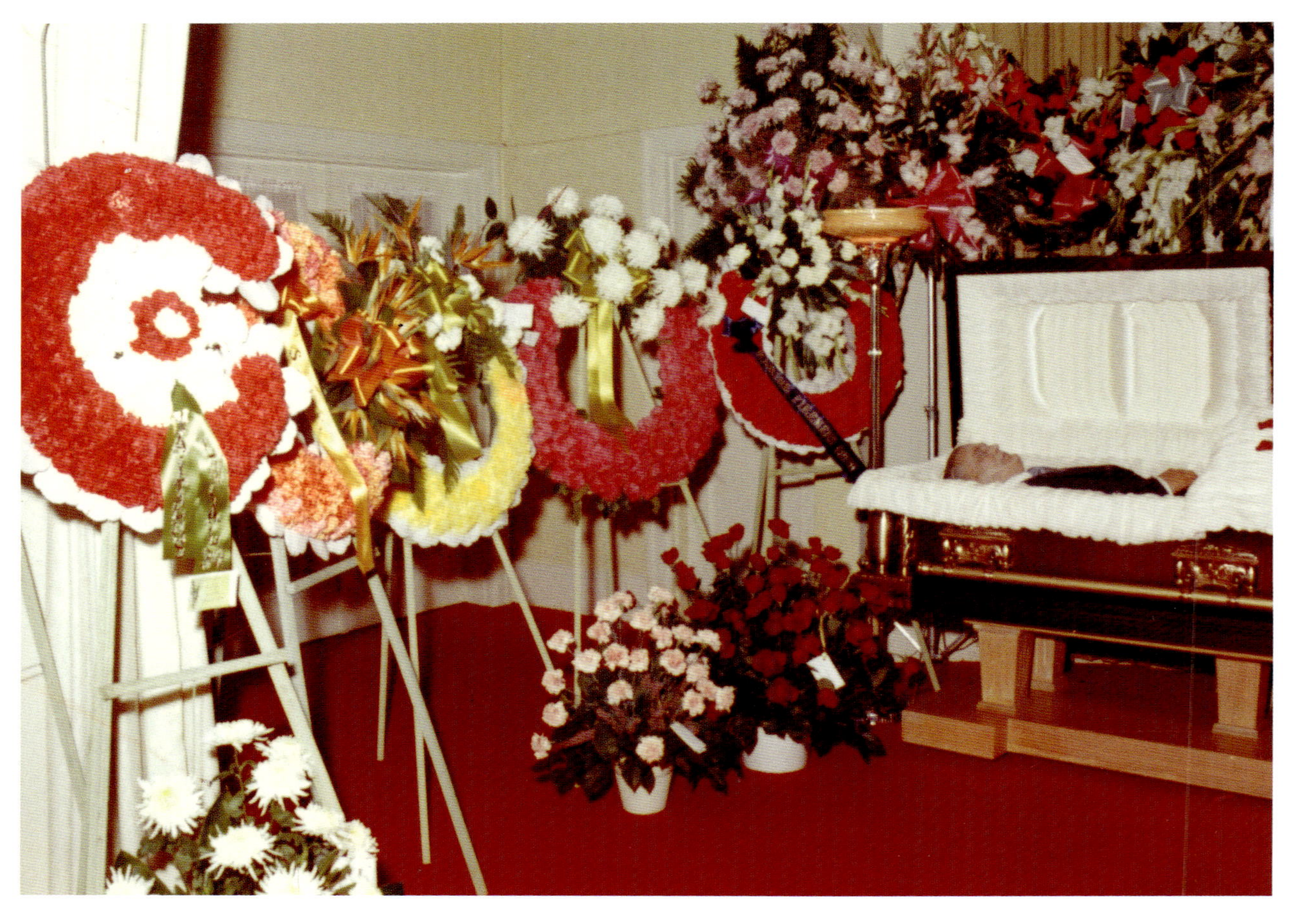

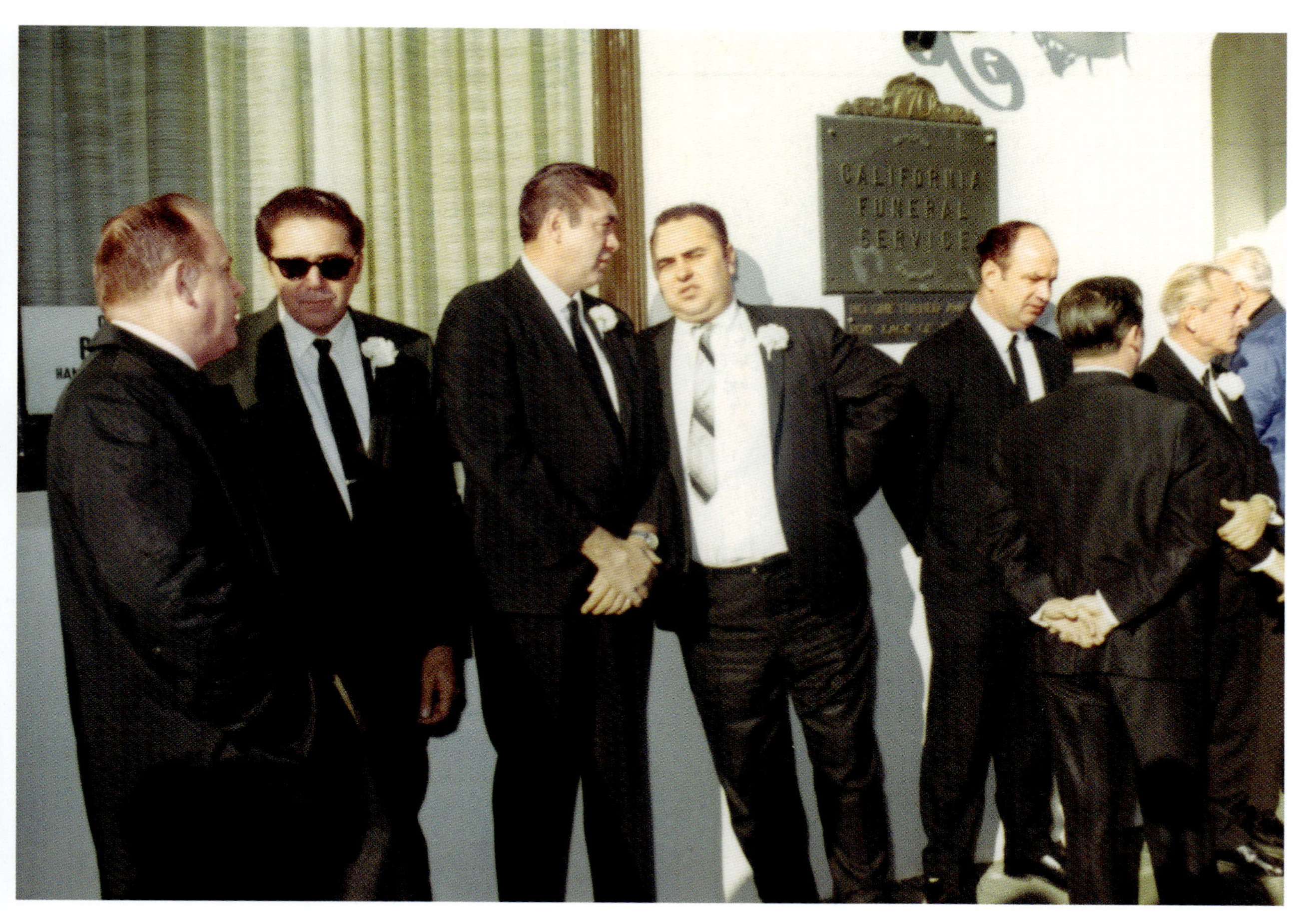
CALIFORNIA
FUNERAL
SERVICE

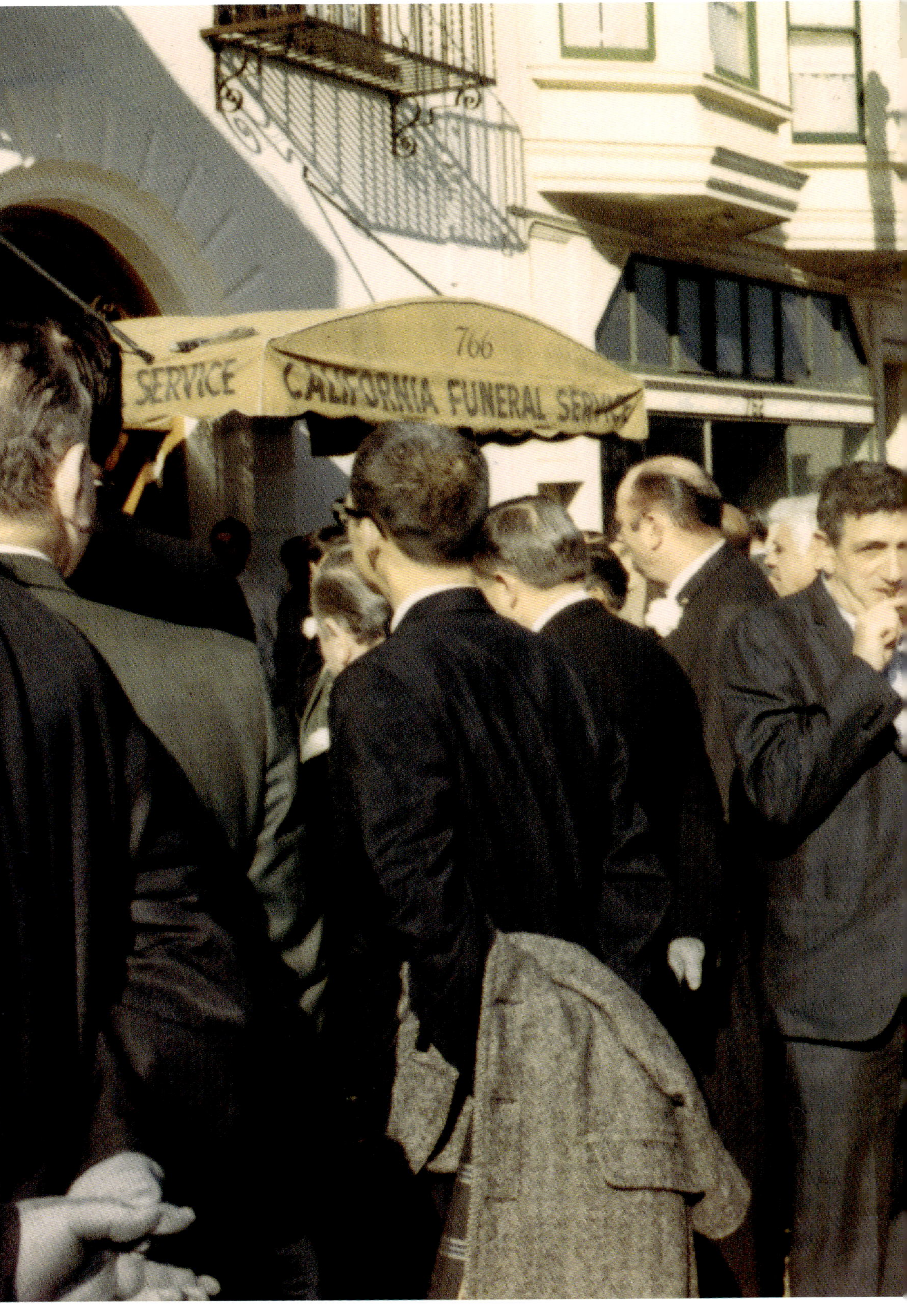
SERVICE
766
CALIFORNIA FUNERAL SERVICE

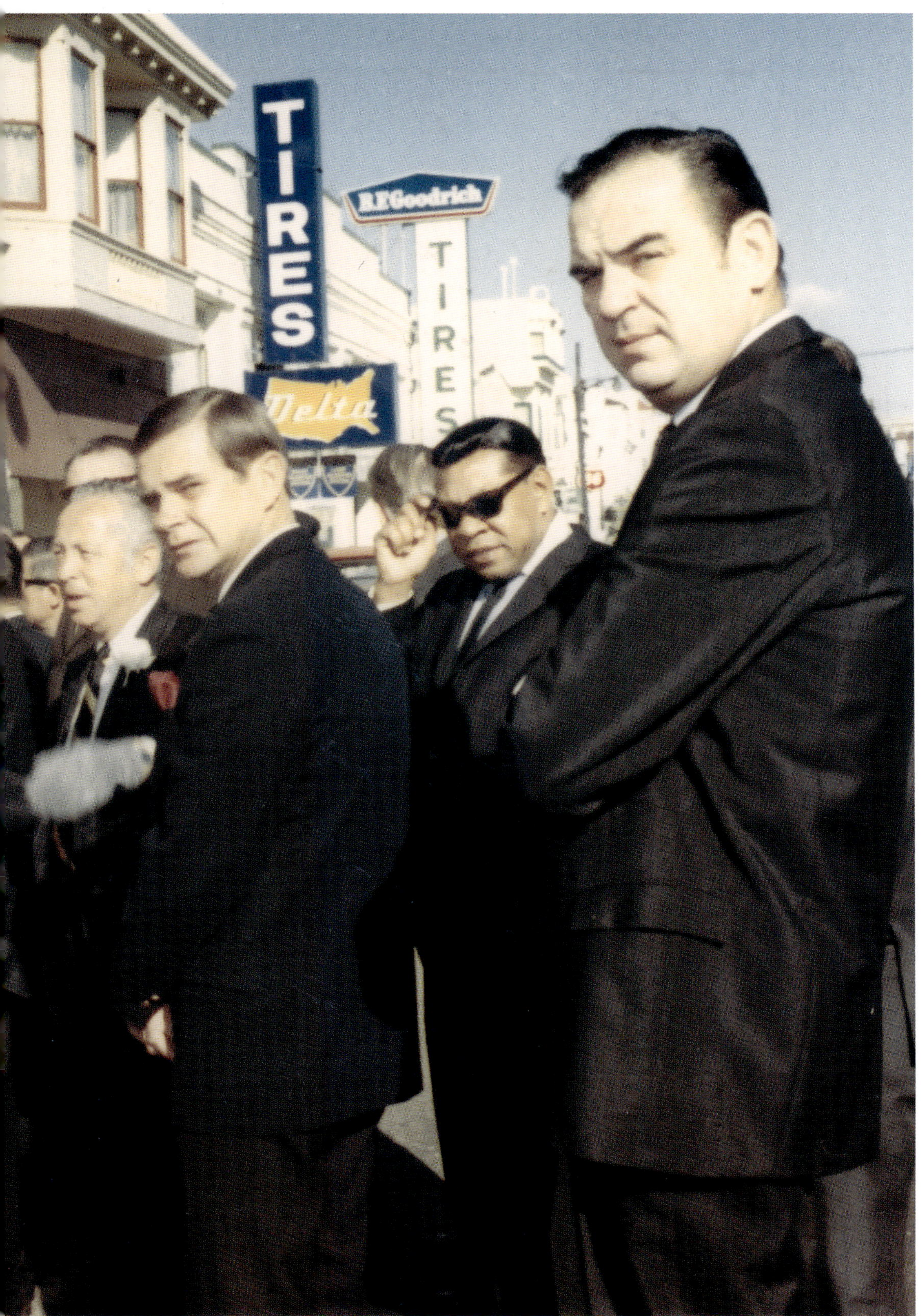
TIRES
B.F.Goodrich
TIRES
Delta

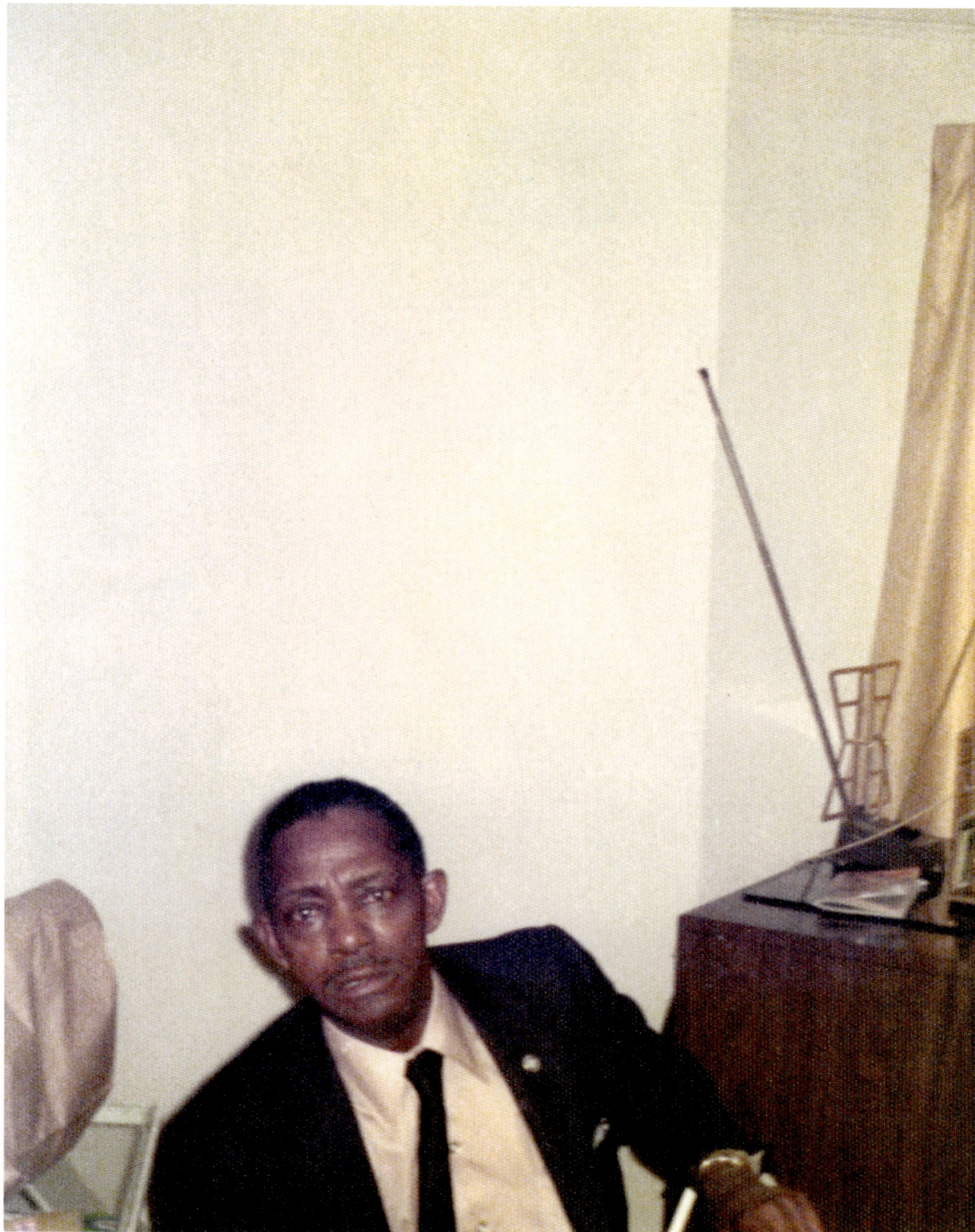

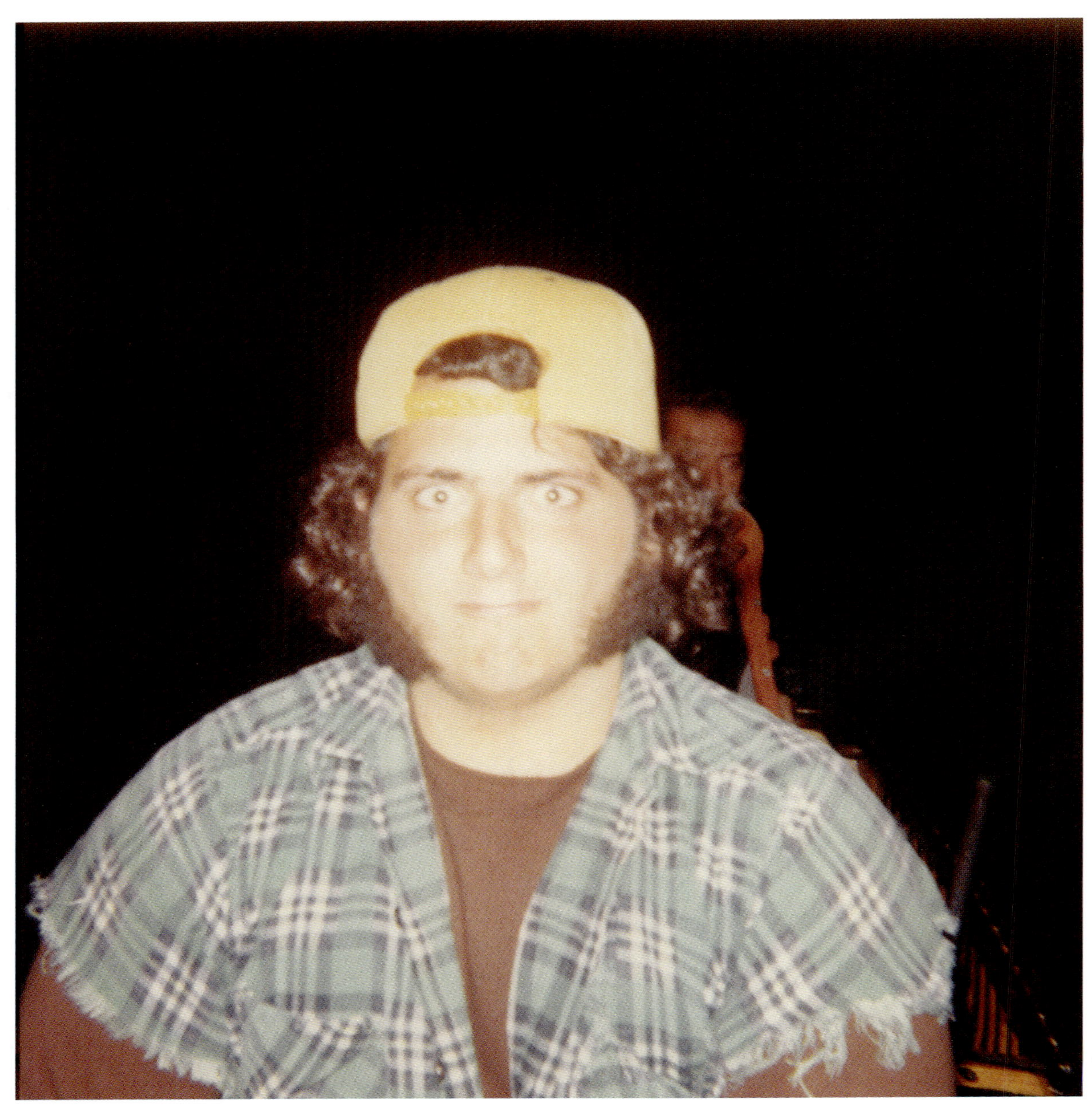

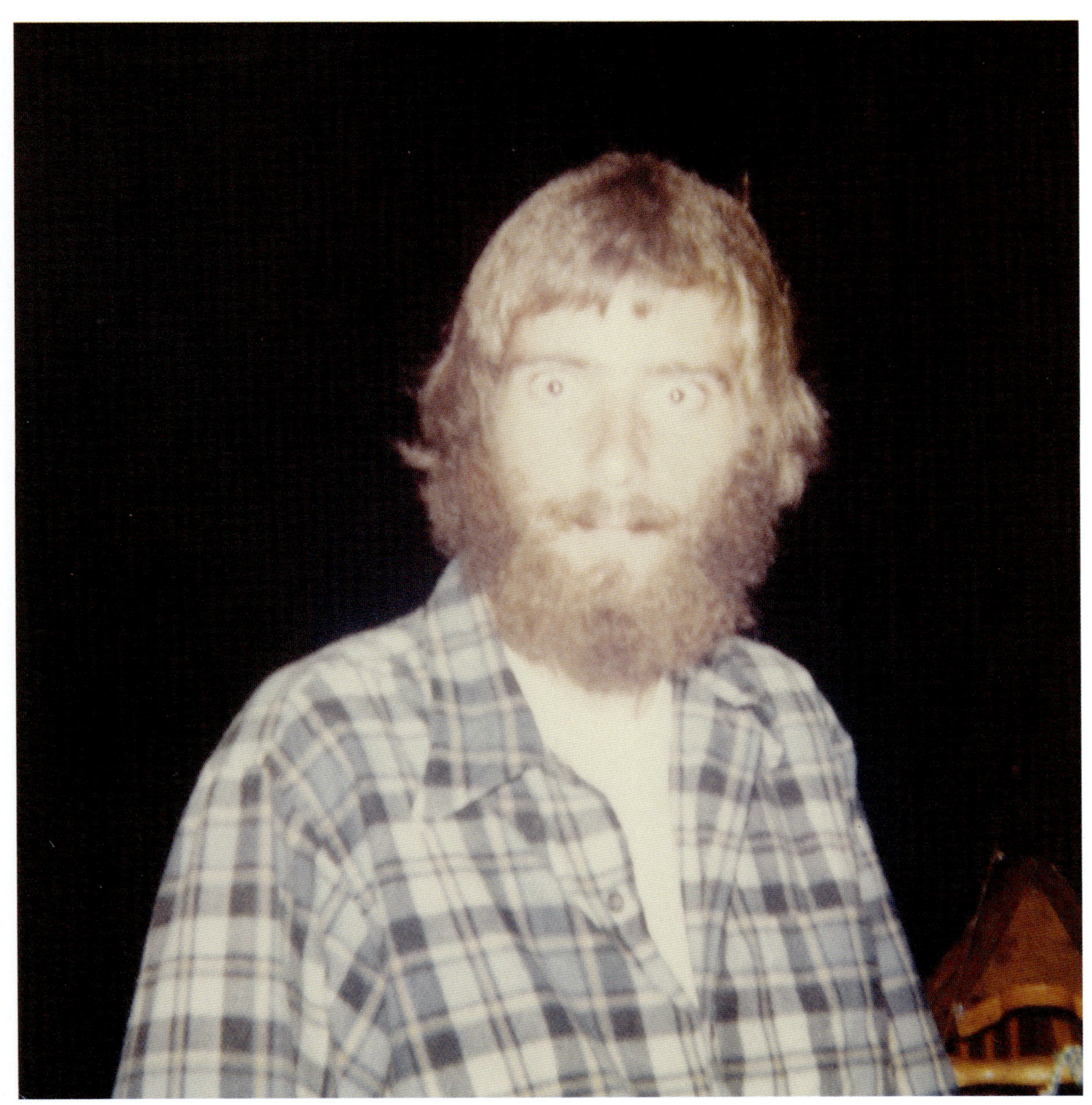

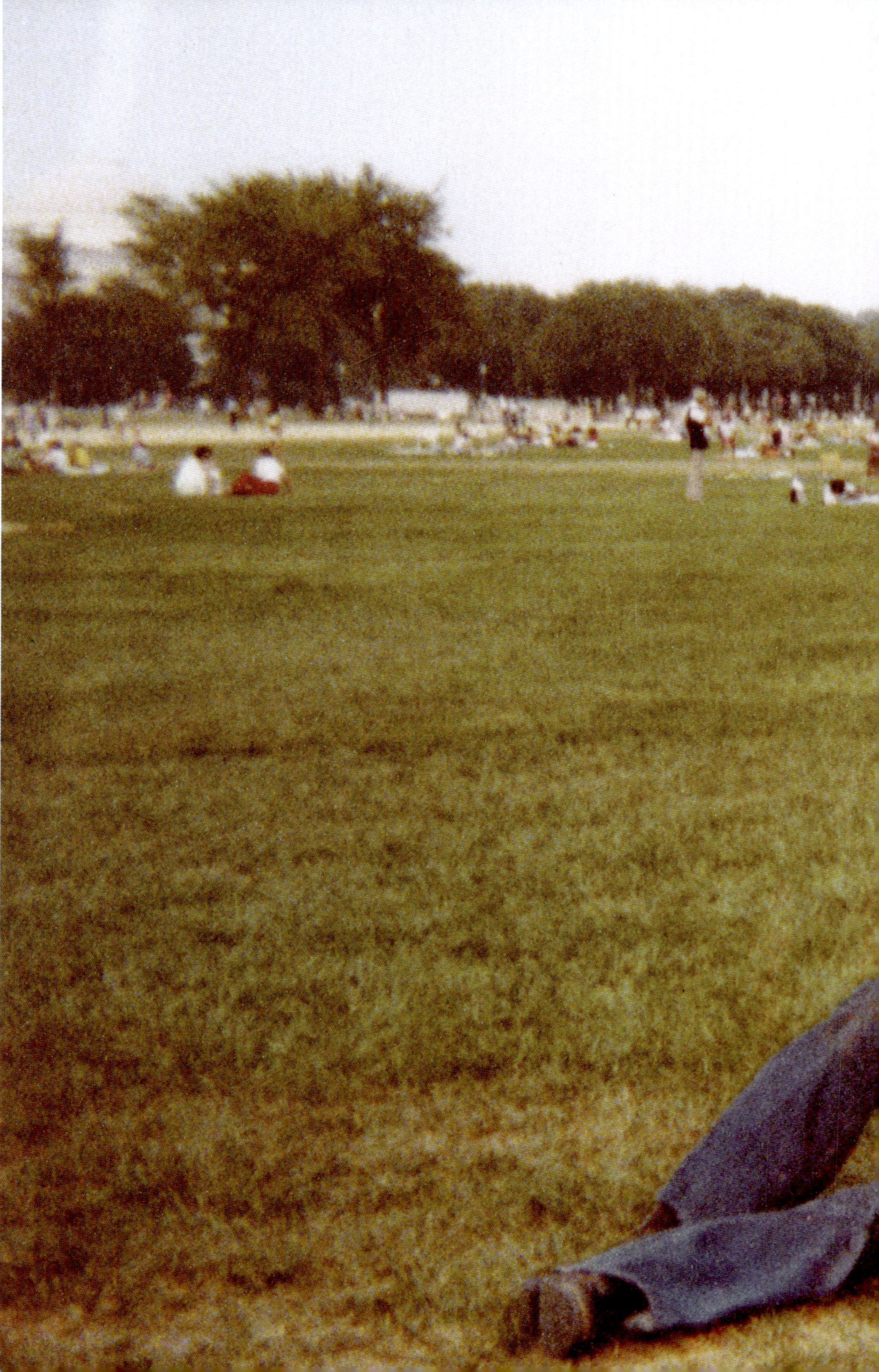

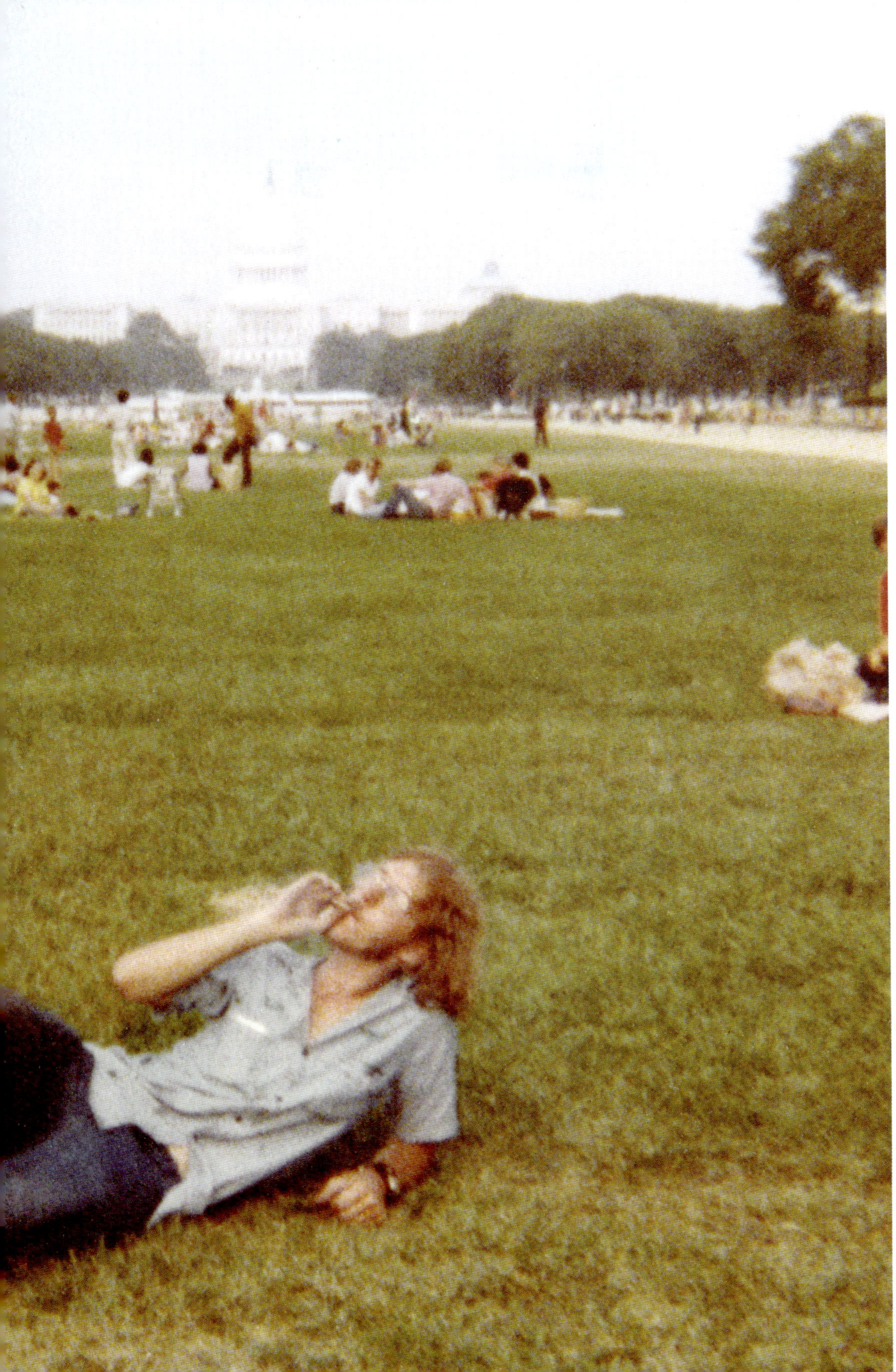

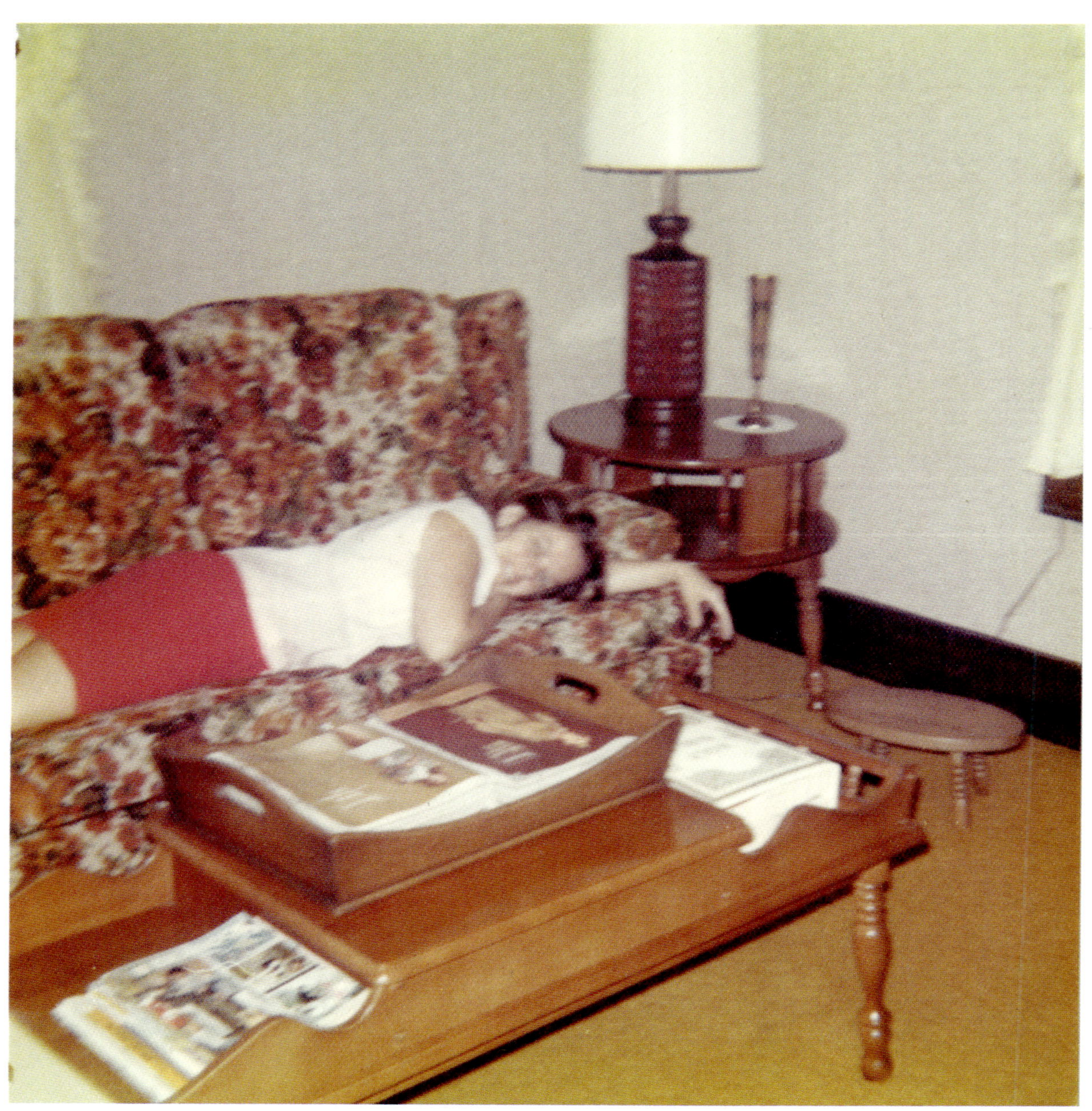

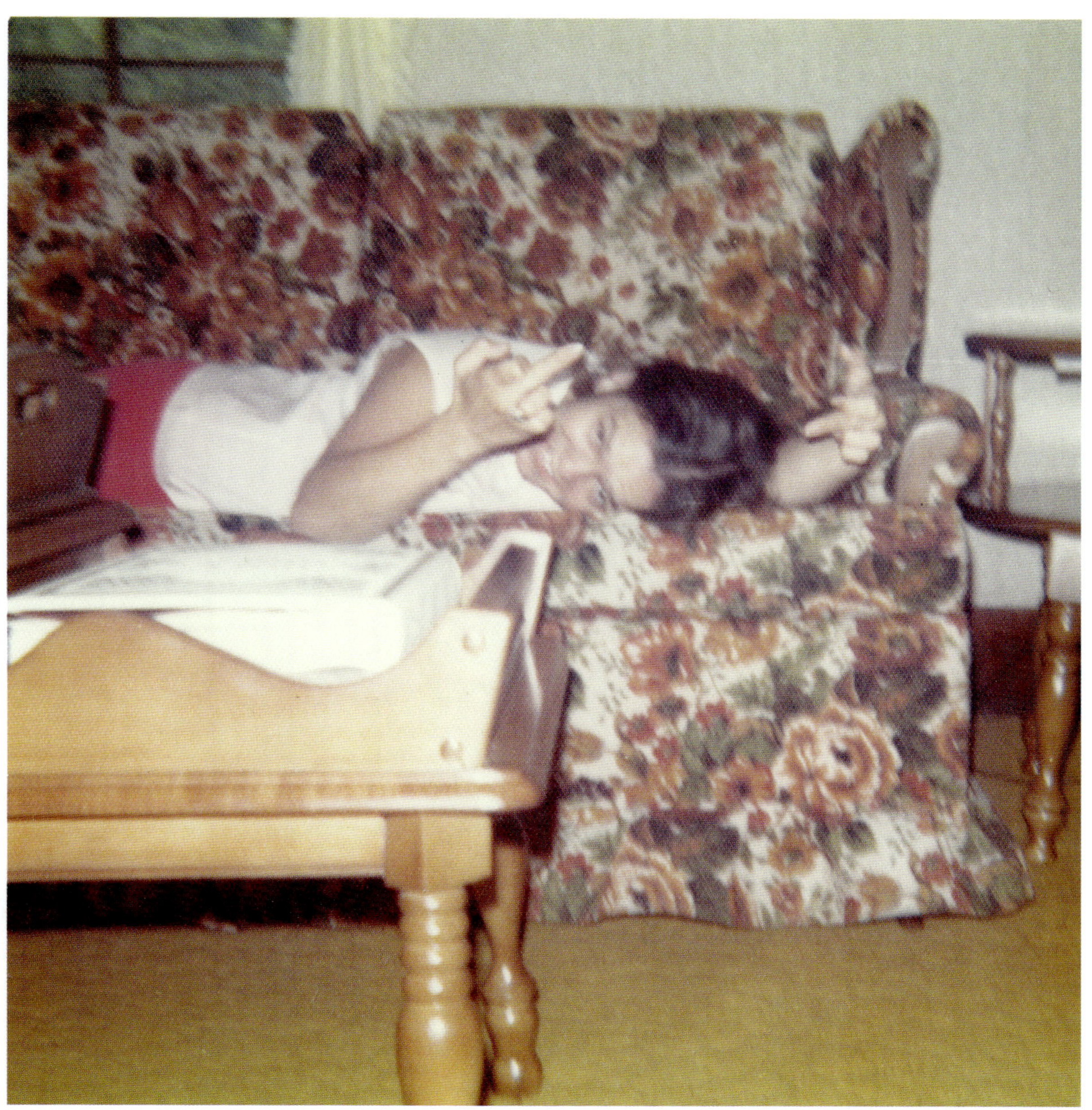

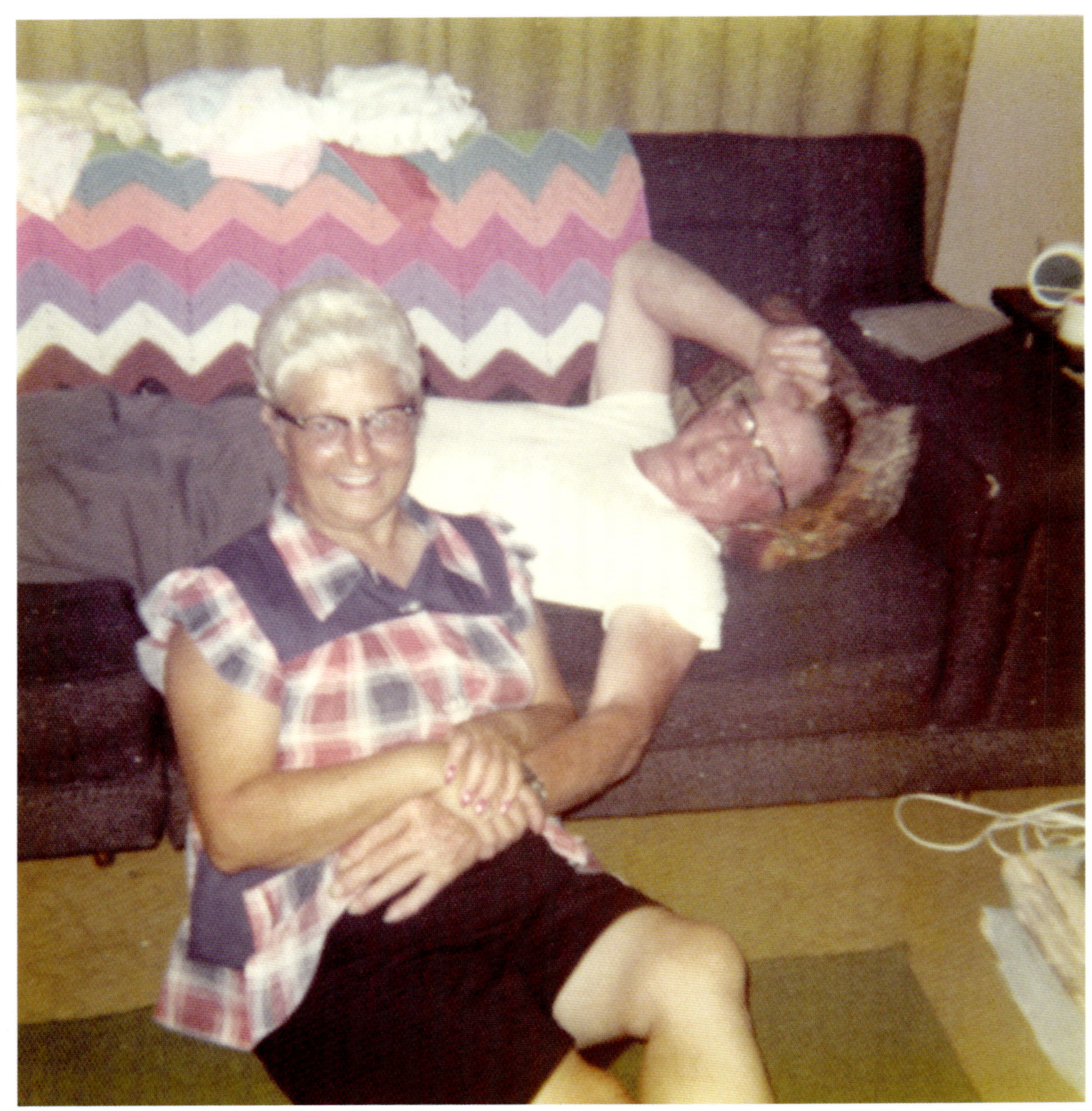

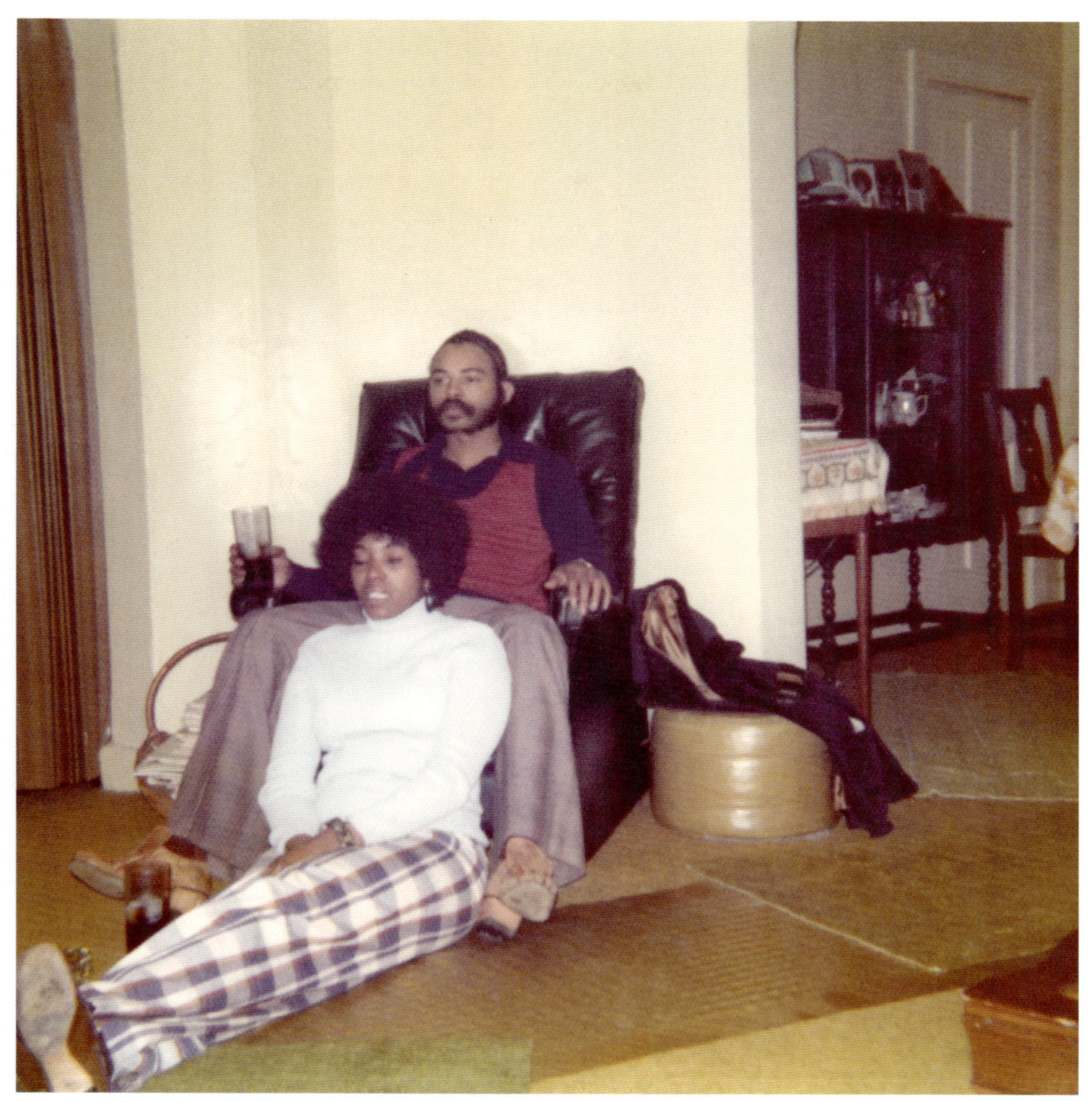

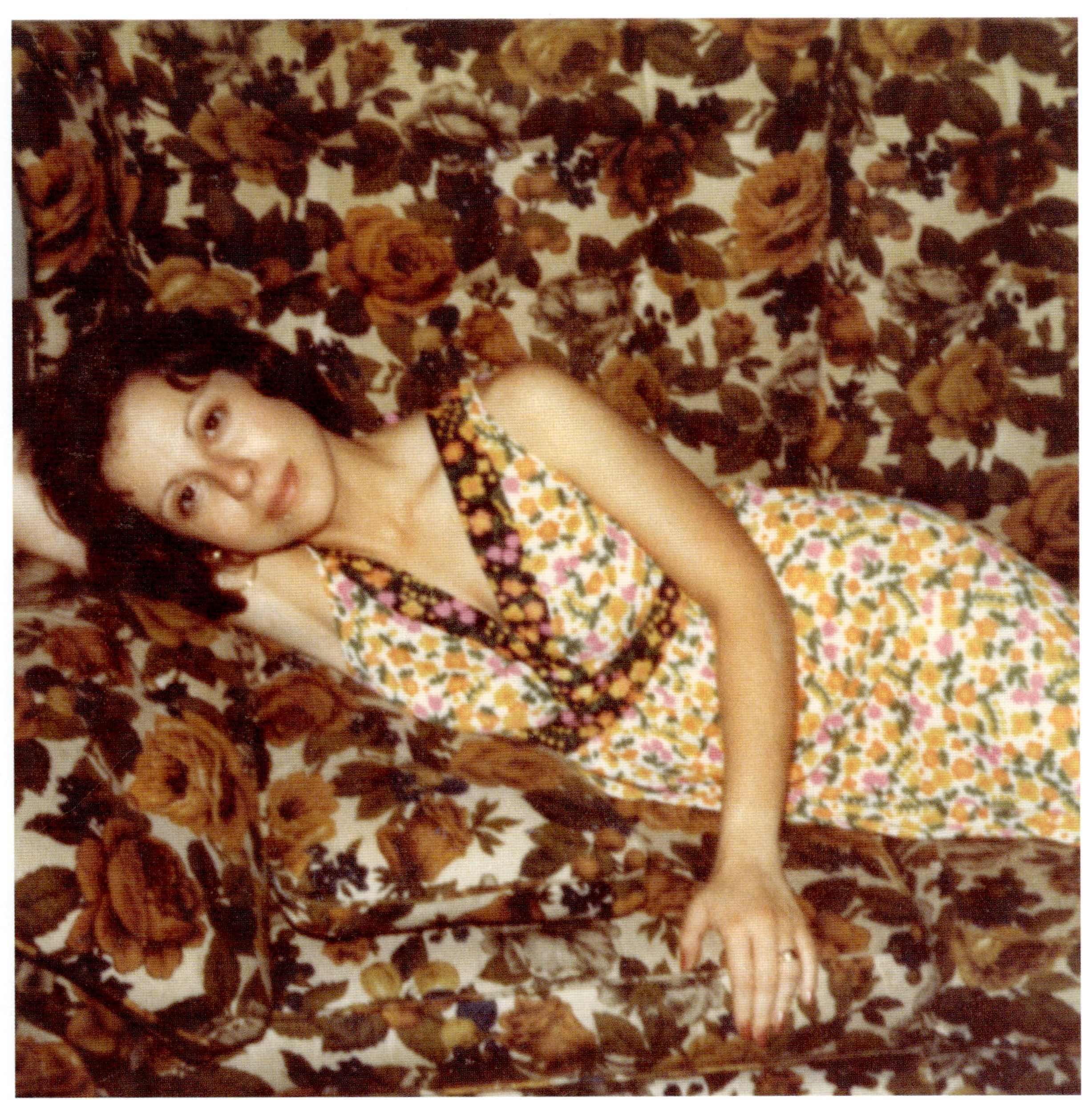

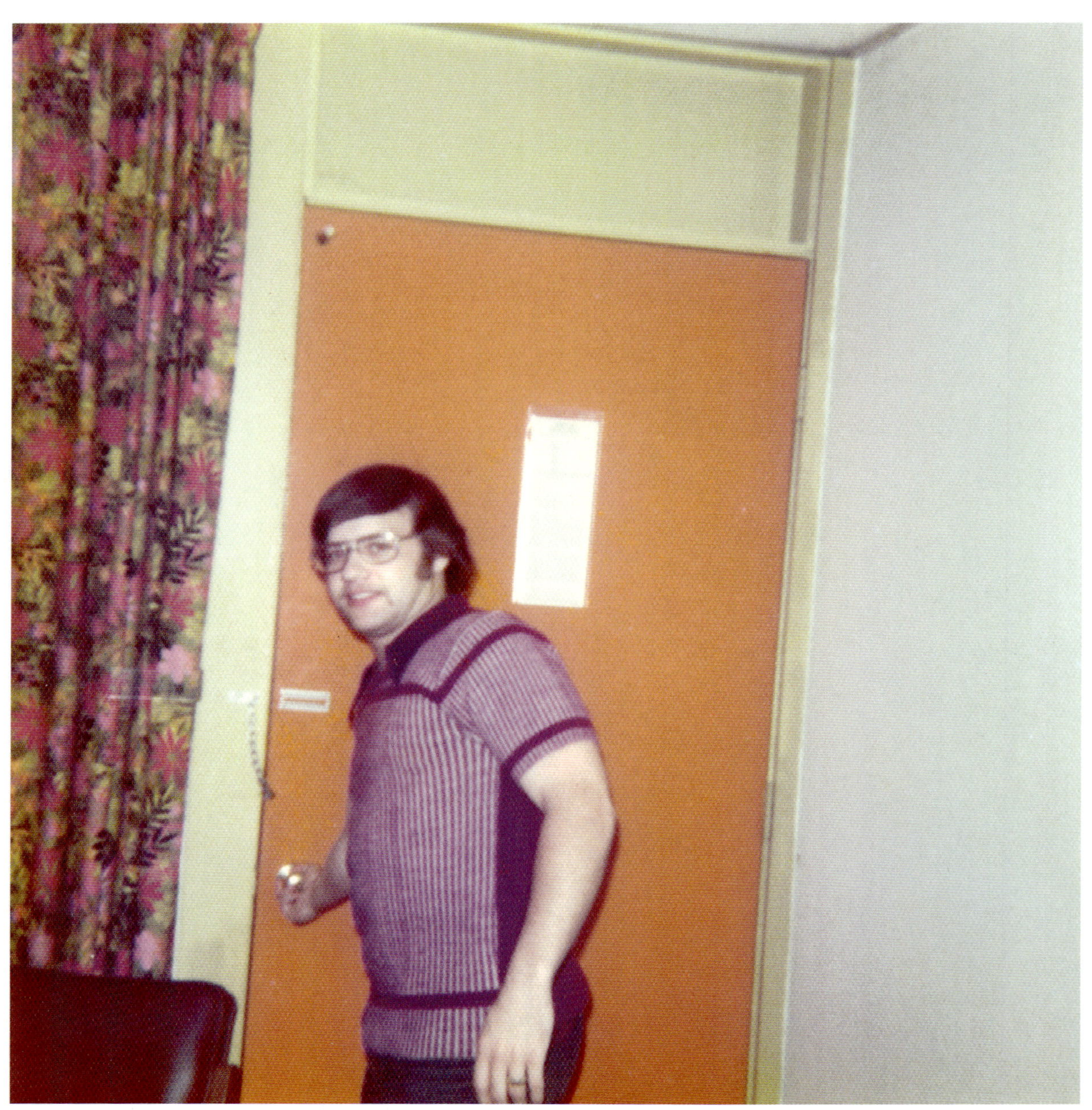

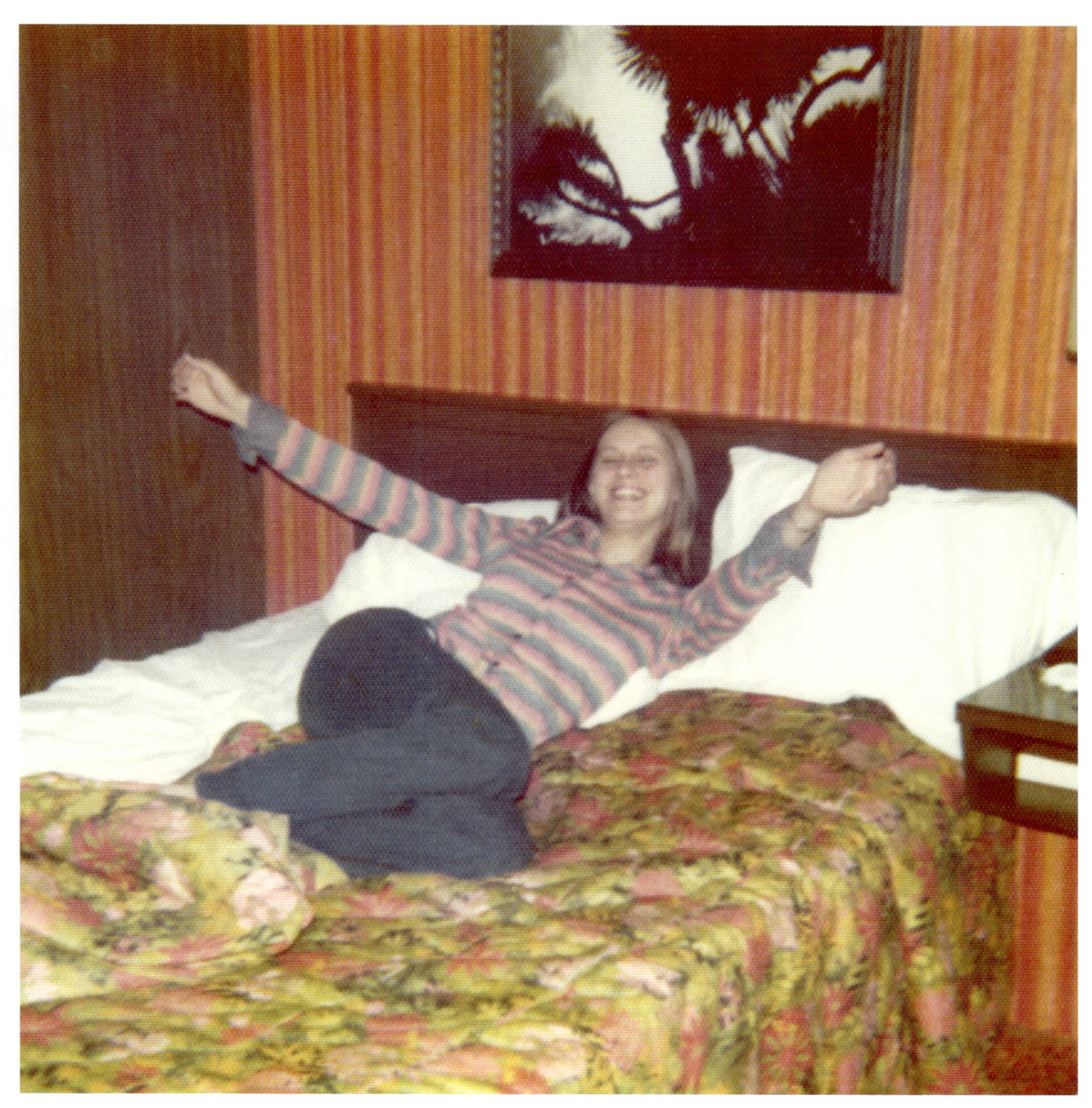

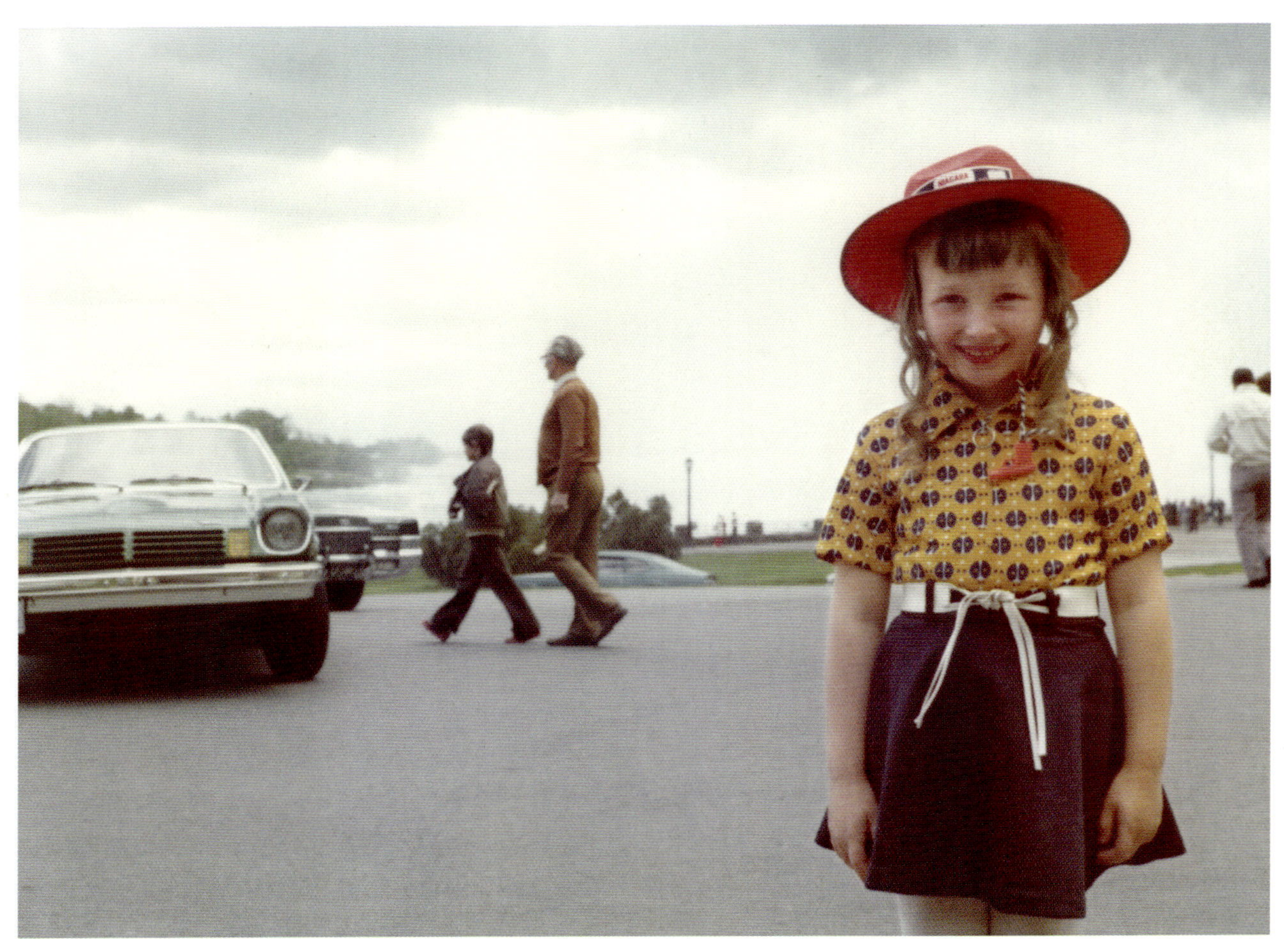

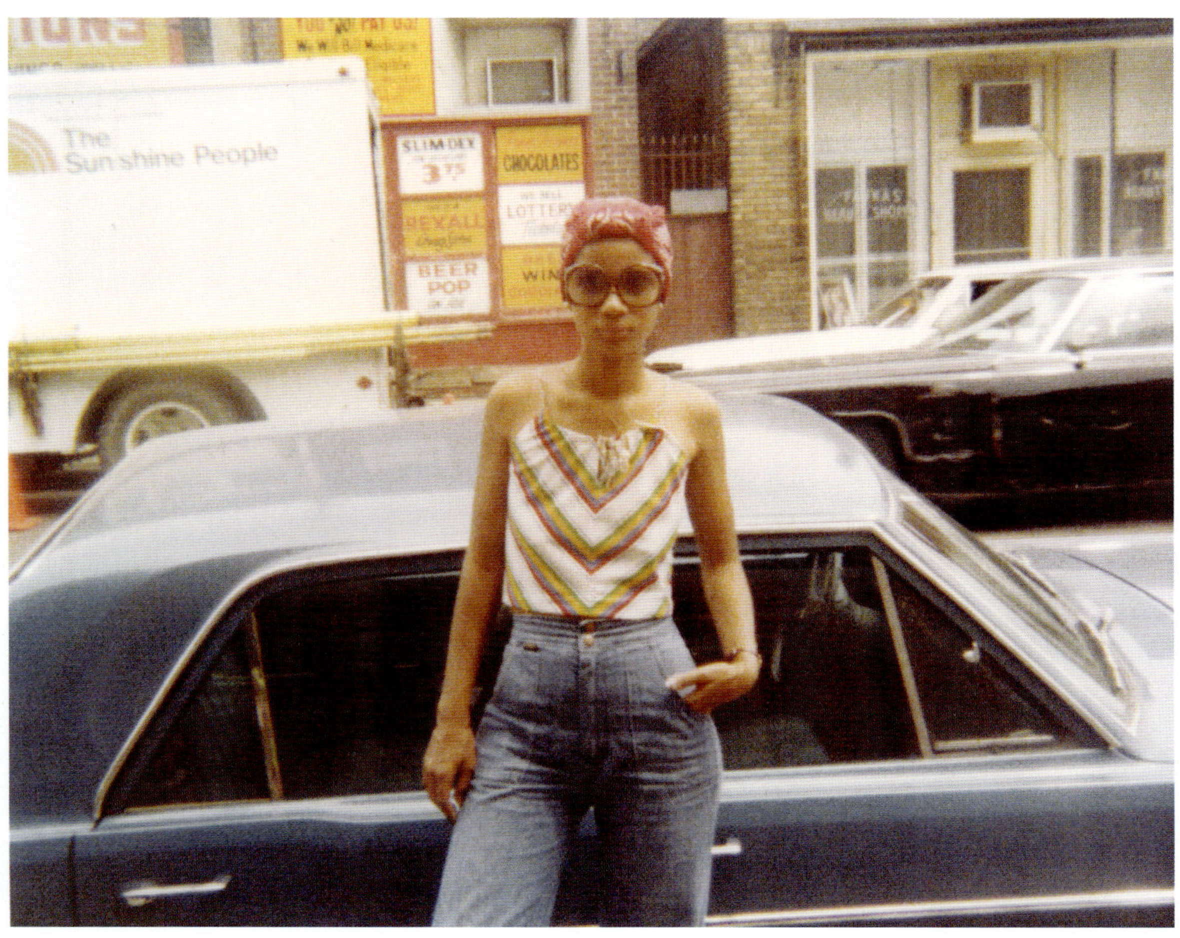
The
Sunshine People
CHOCOLATES
REXALL
BEER
POP

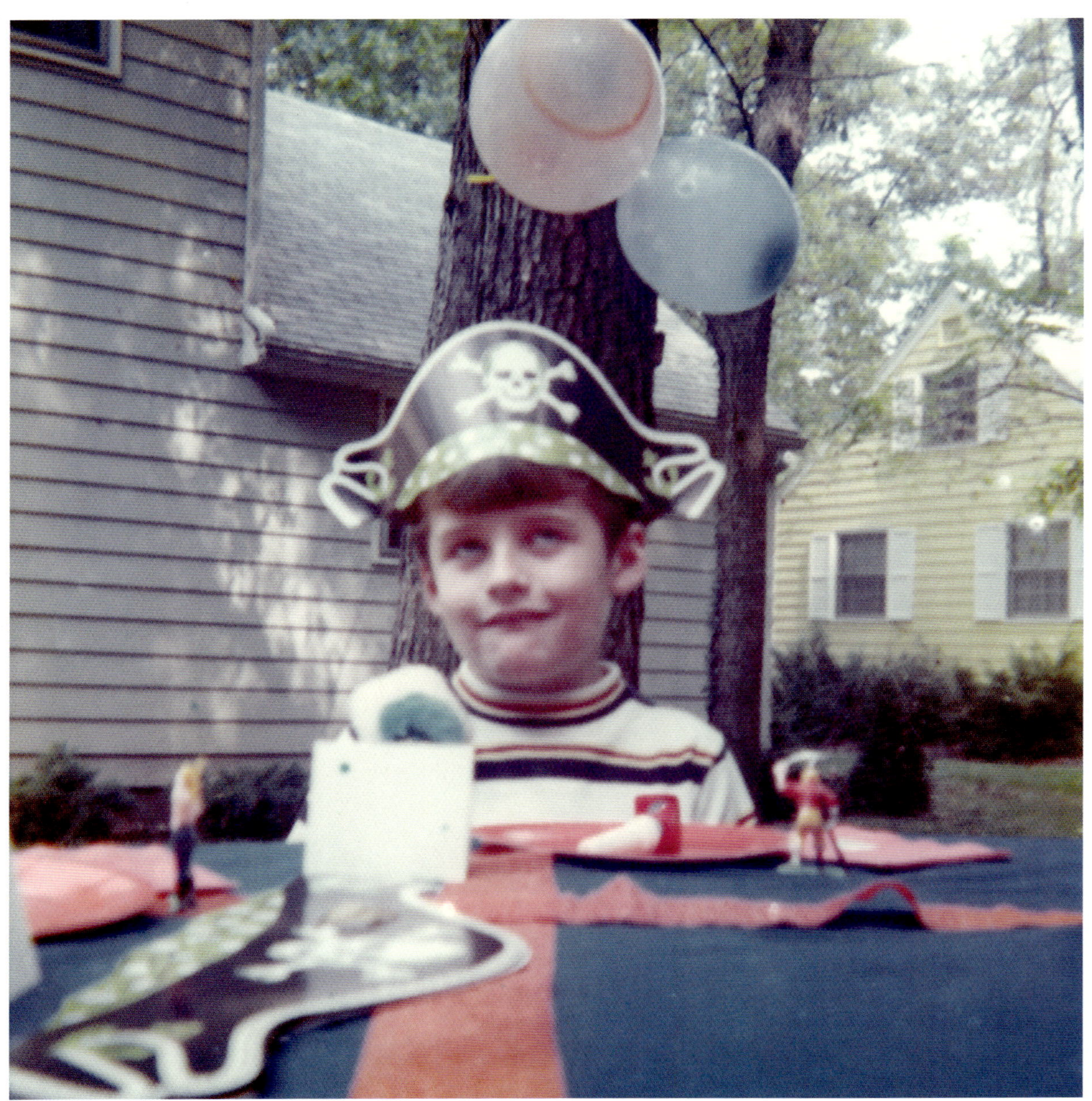

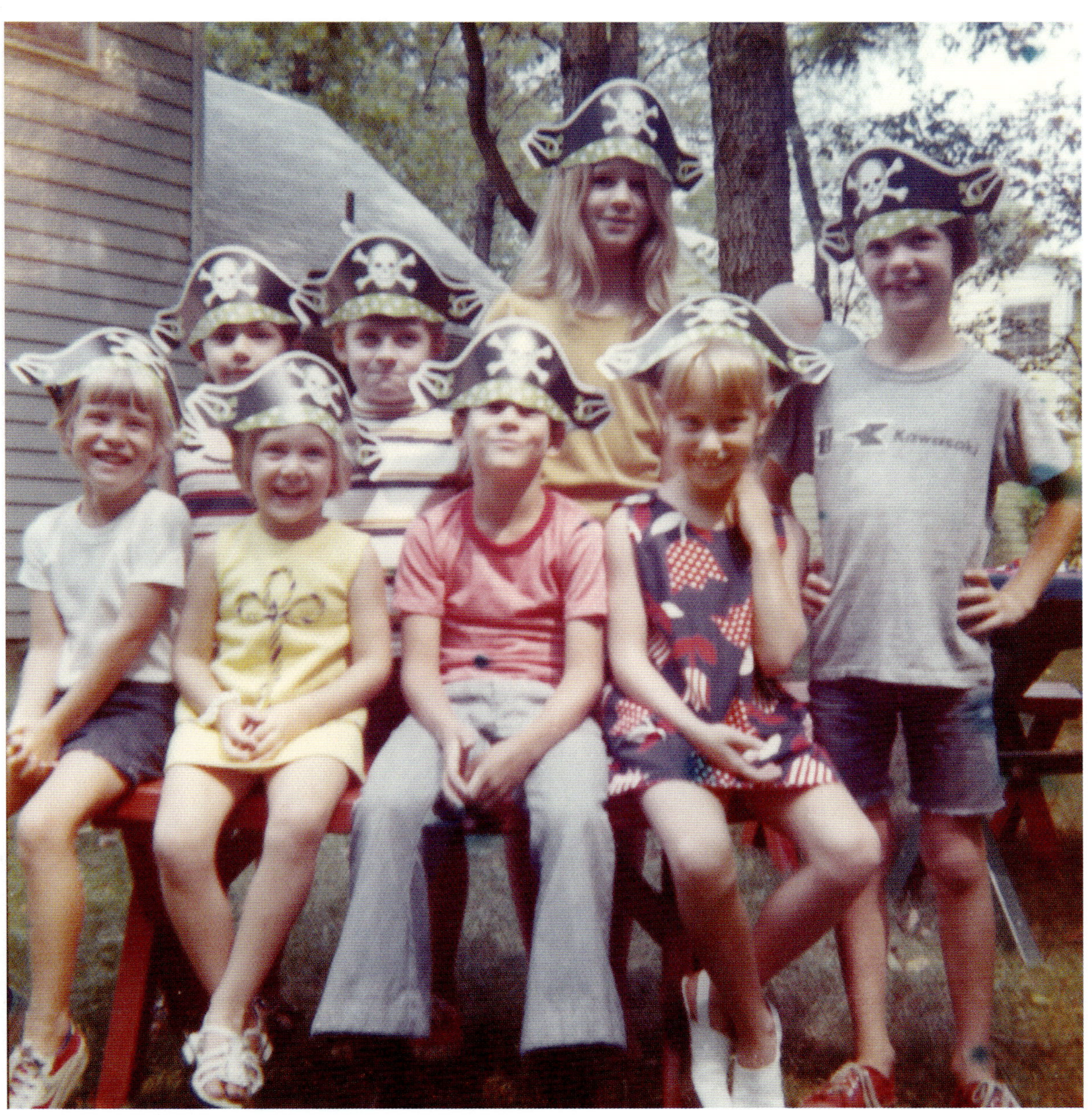
Kawasaki

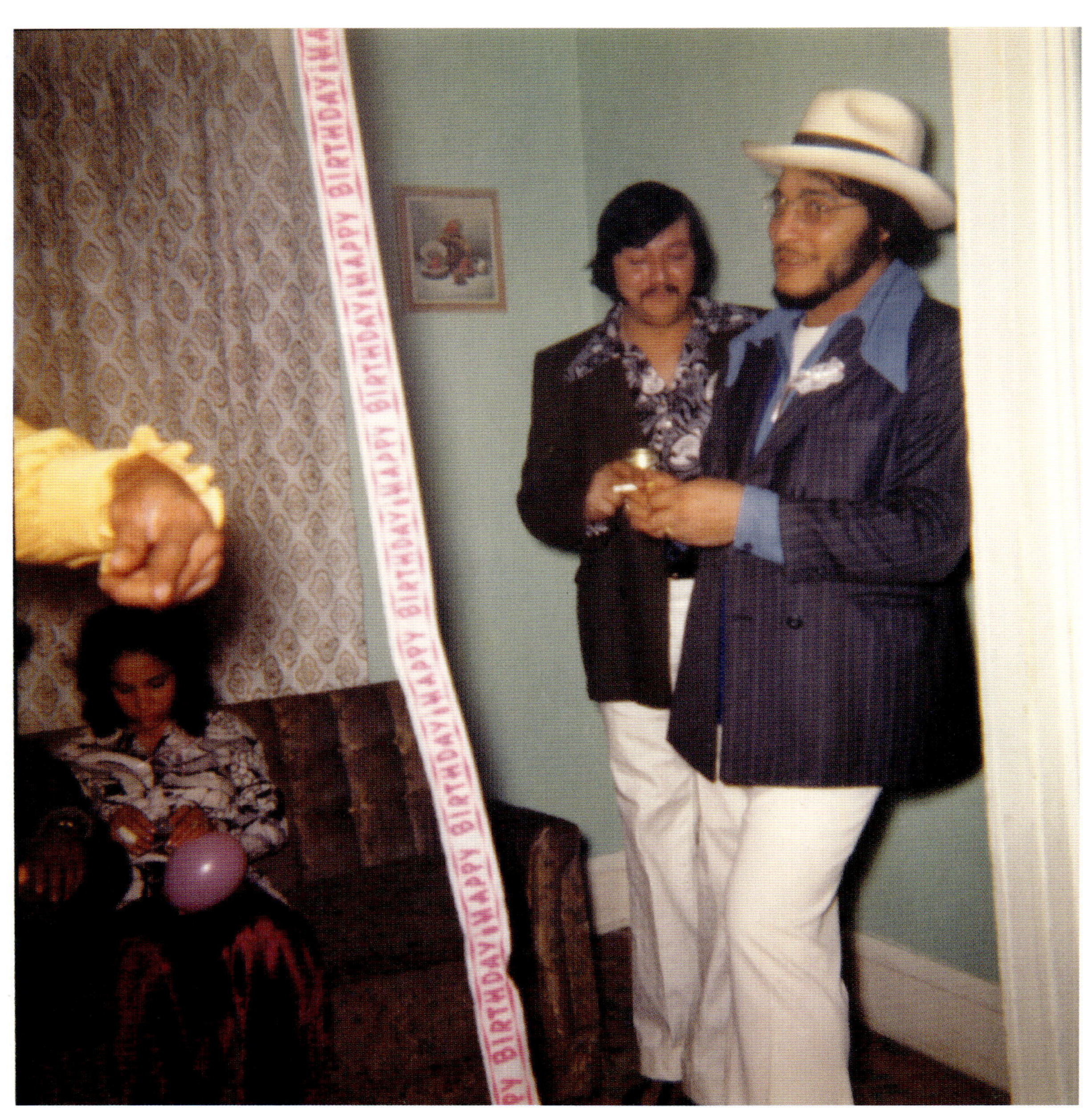
HAPPY BIRTHDAY

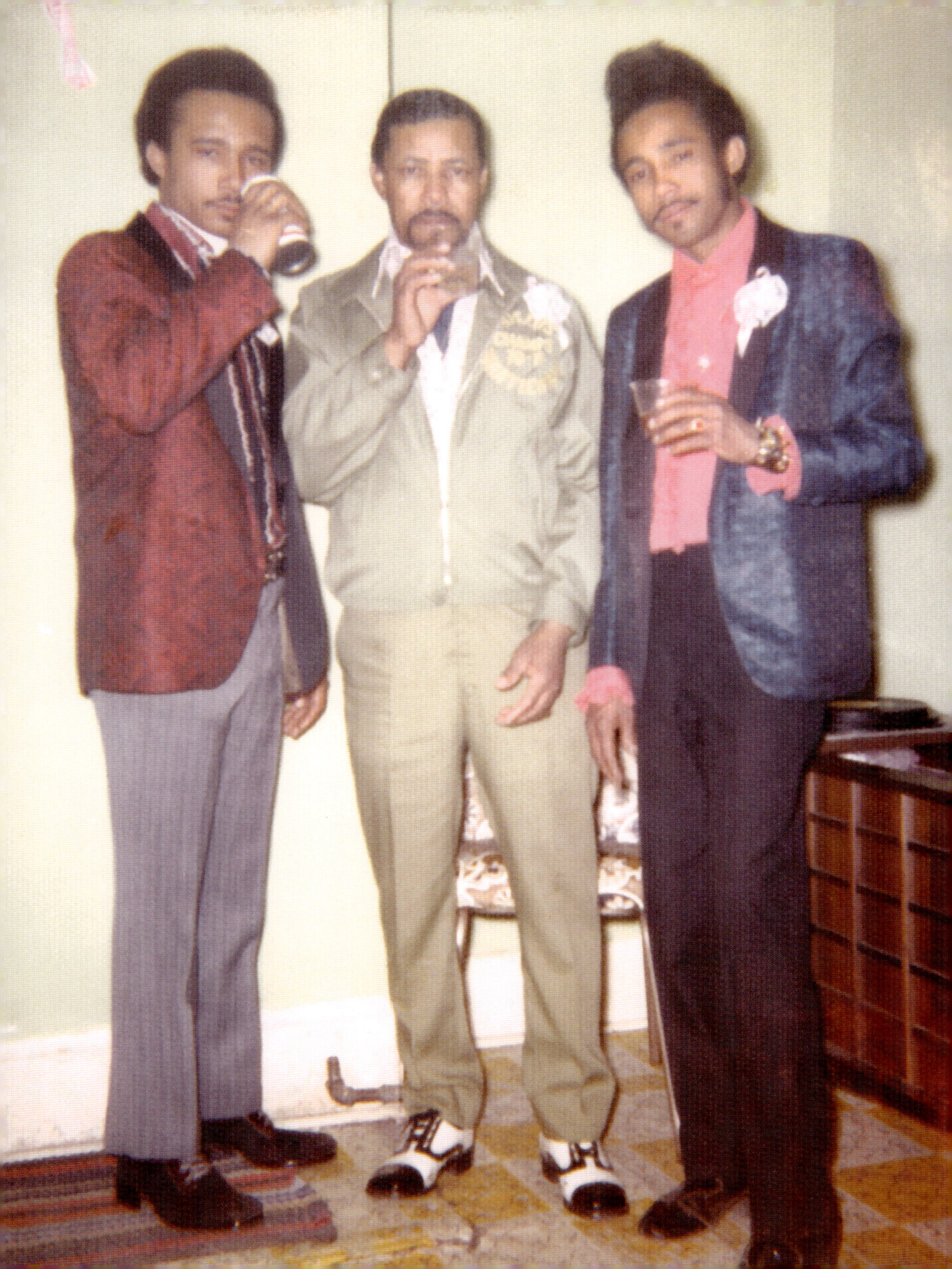

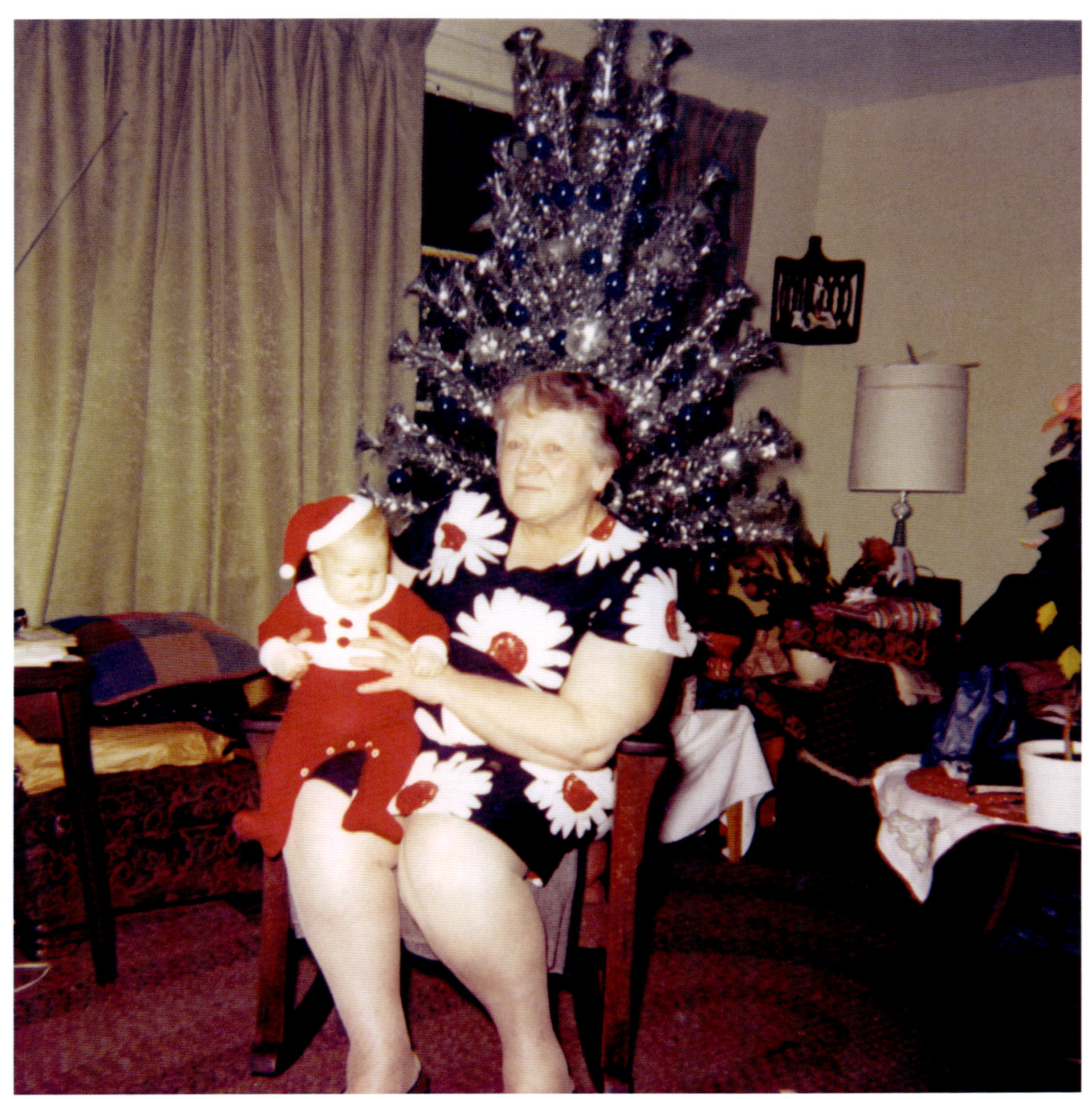

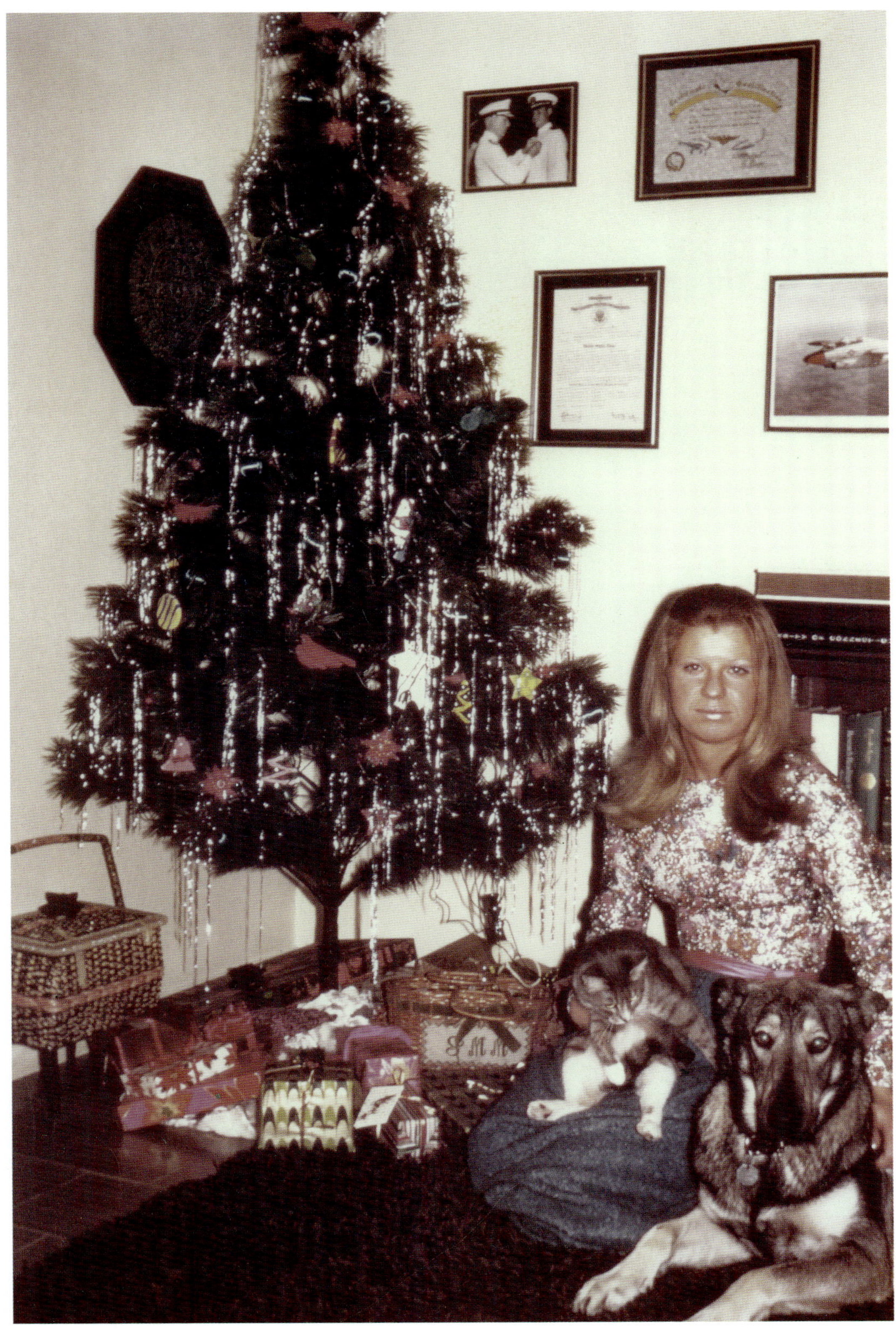

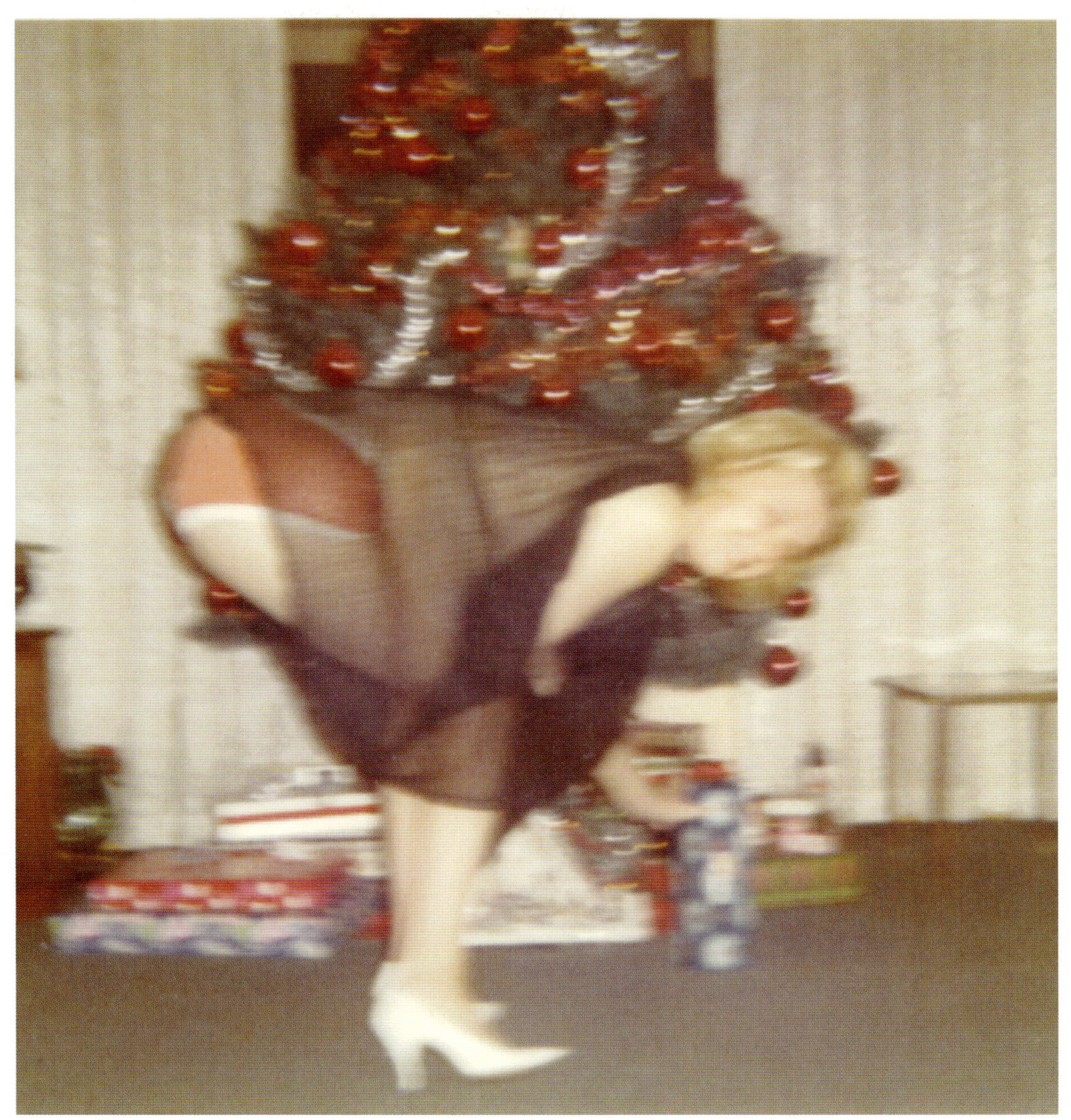

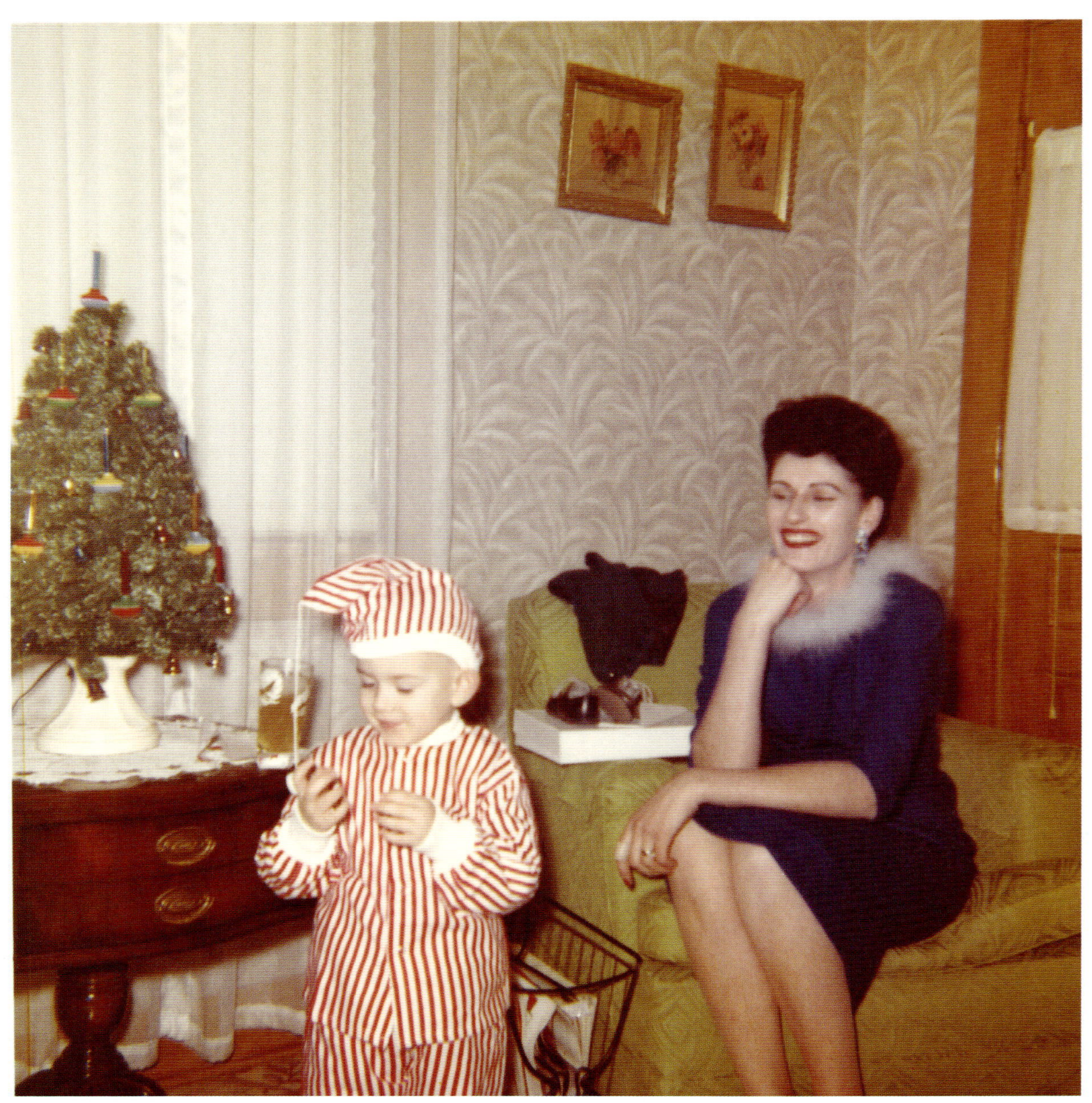

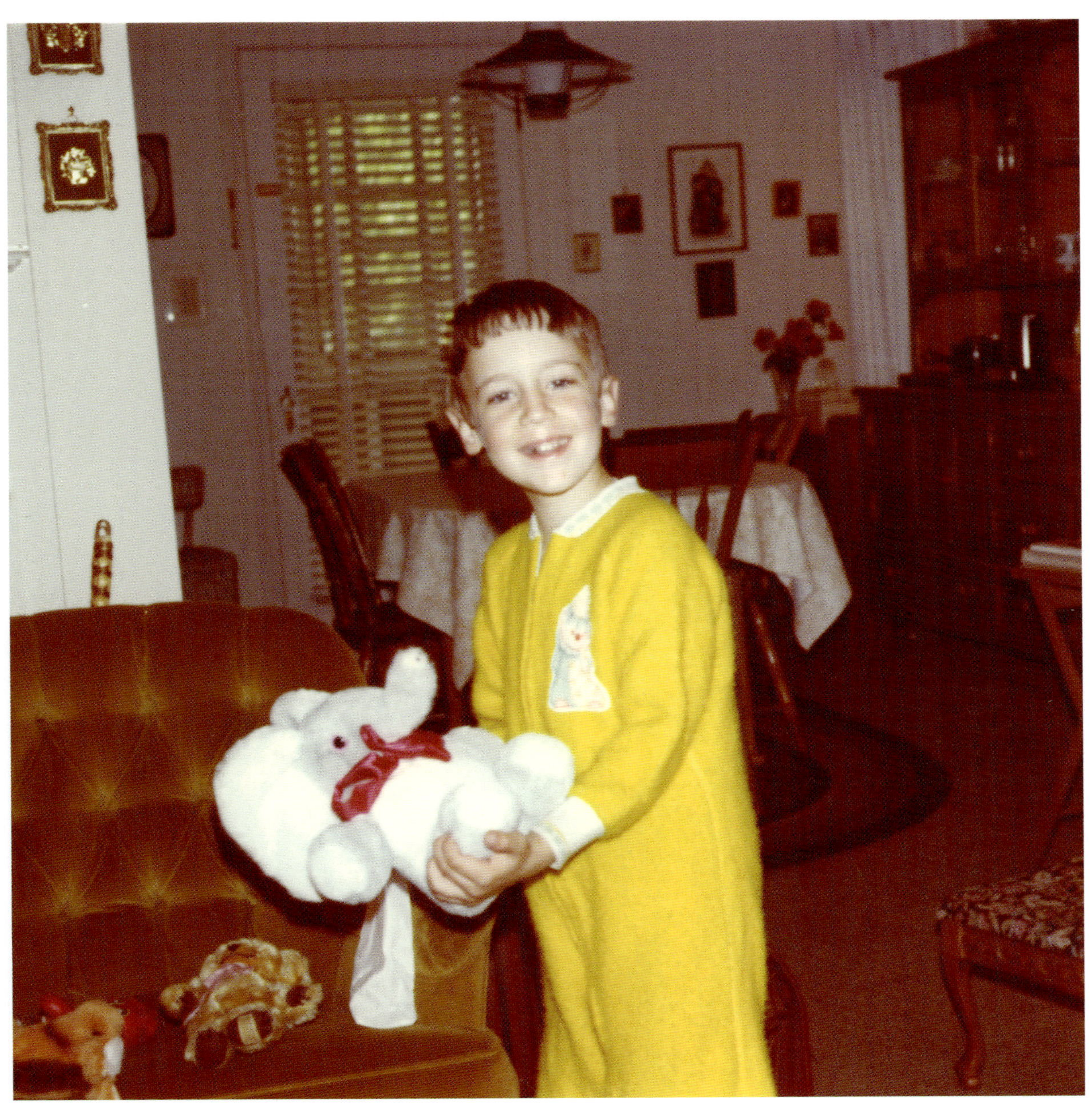

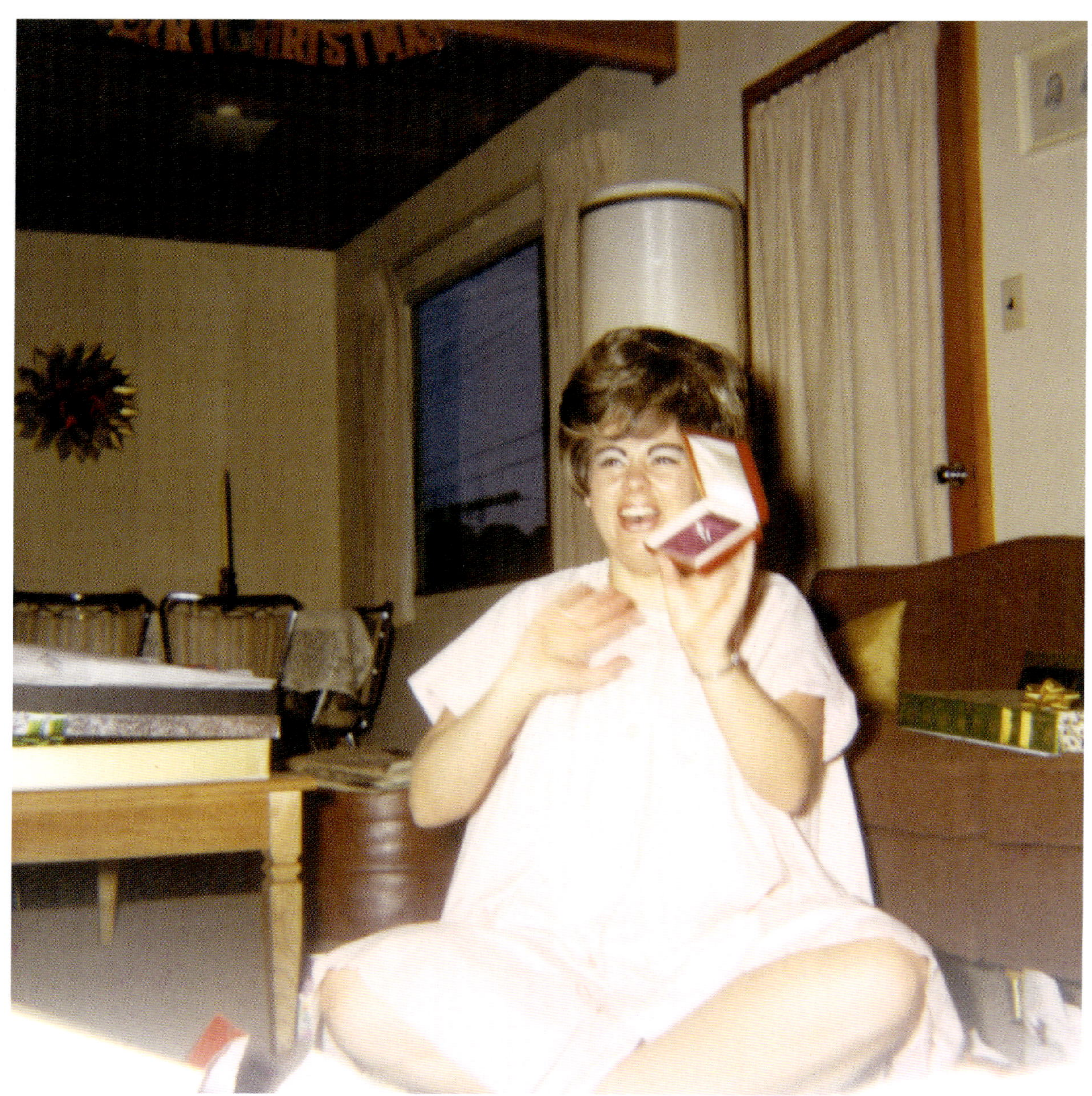

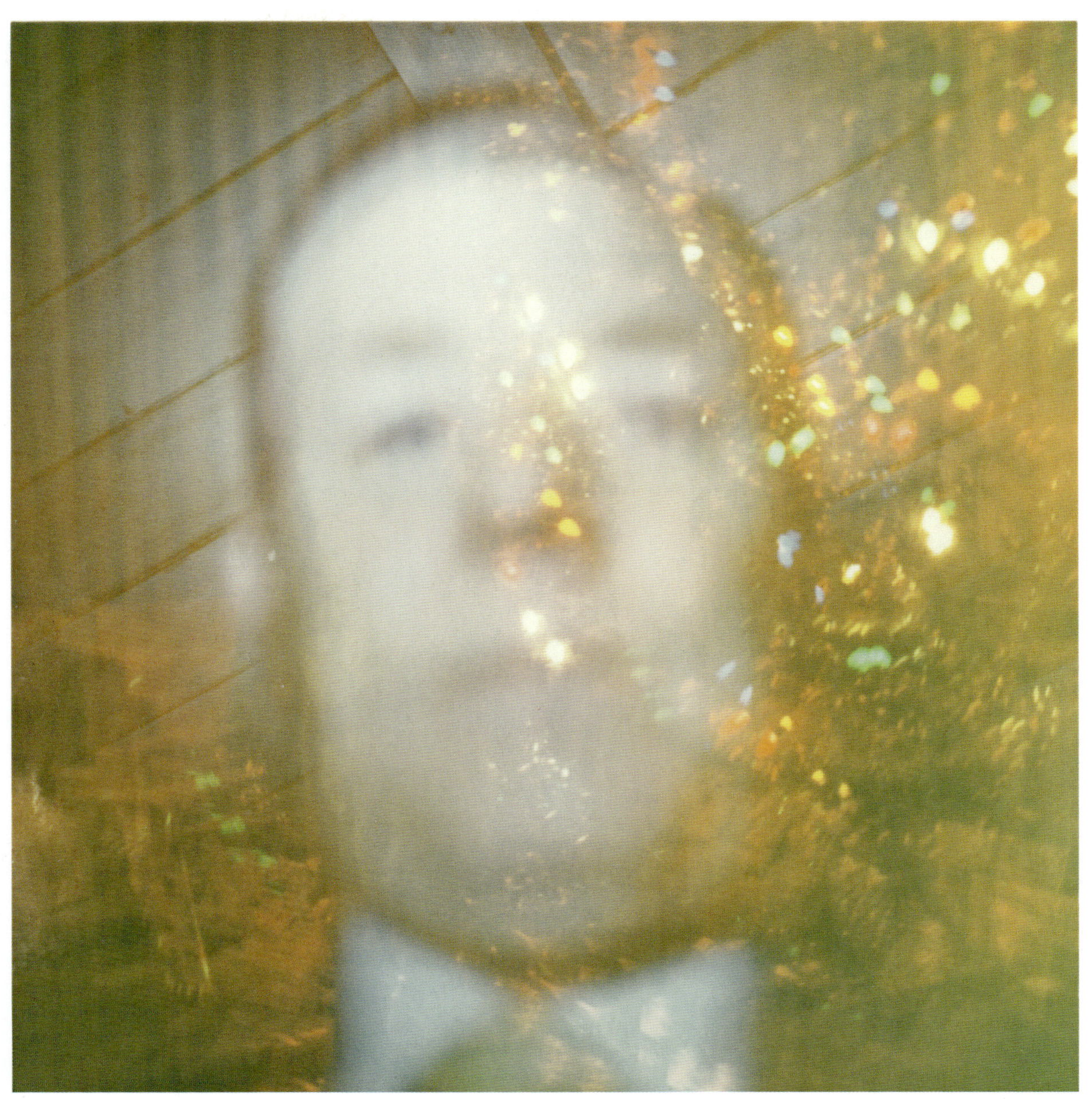

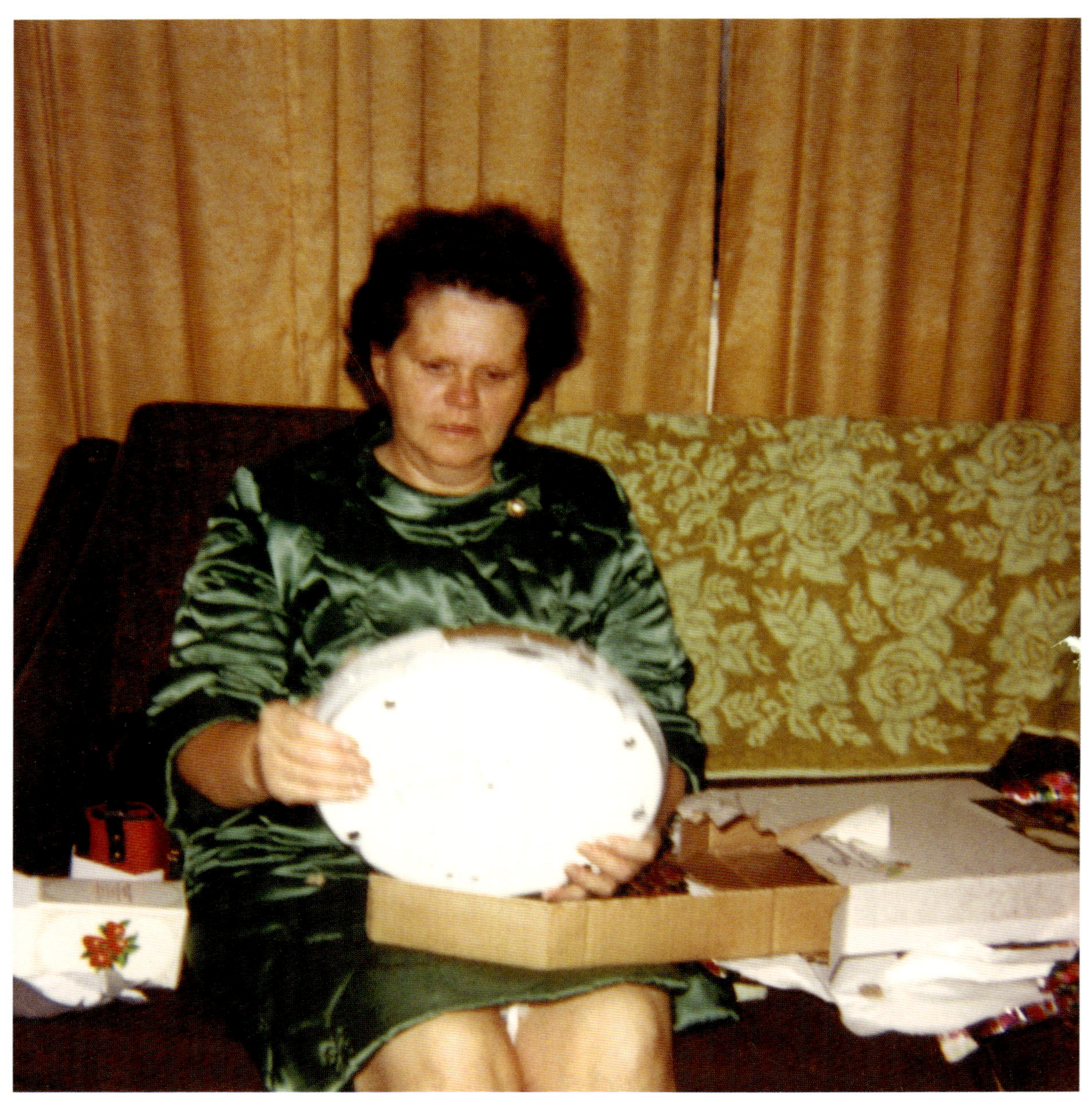

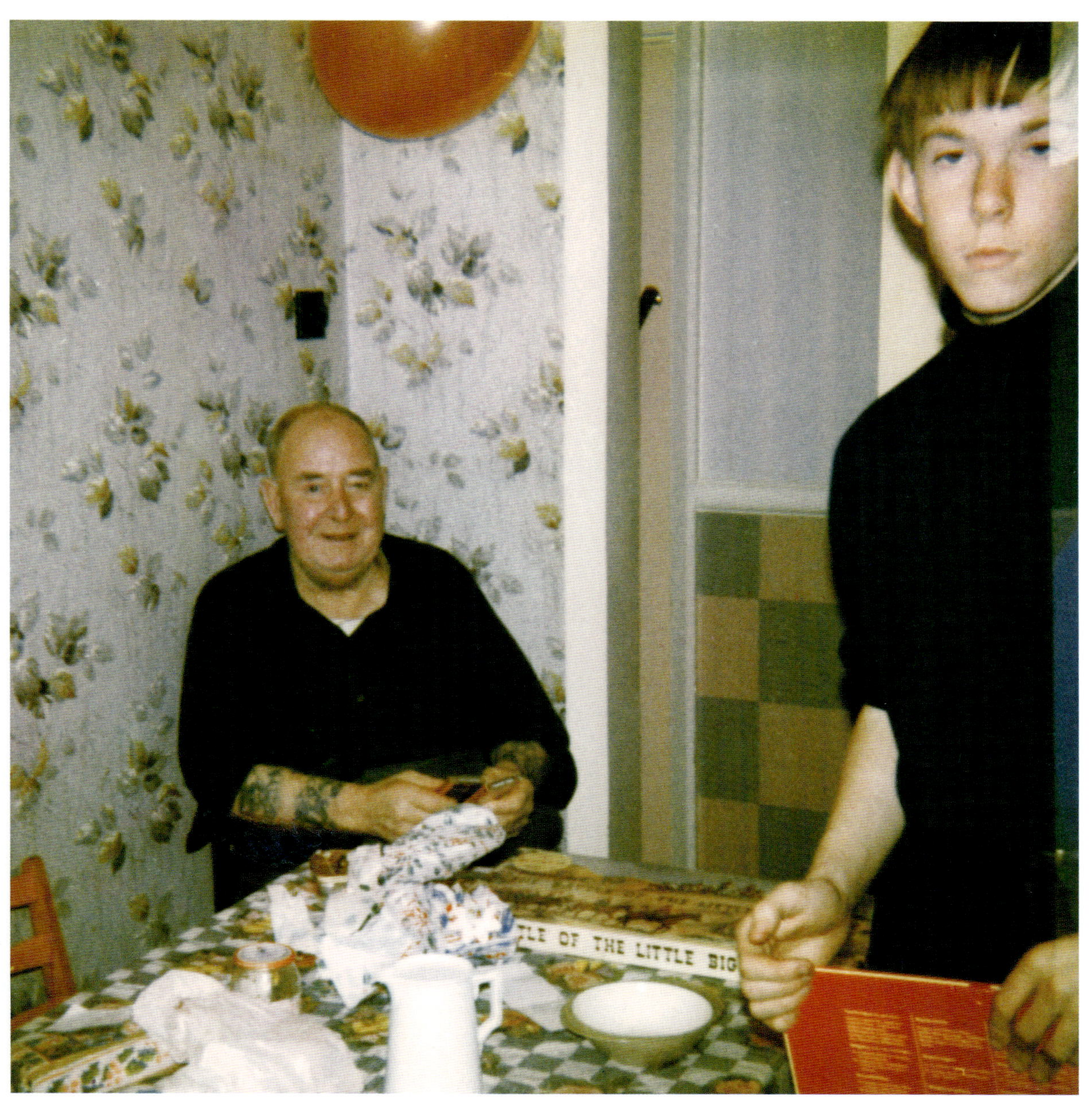
TLE OF THE LITTLE BIG

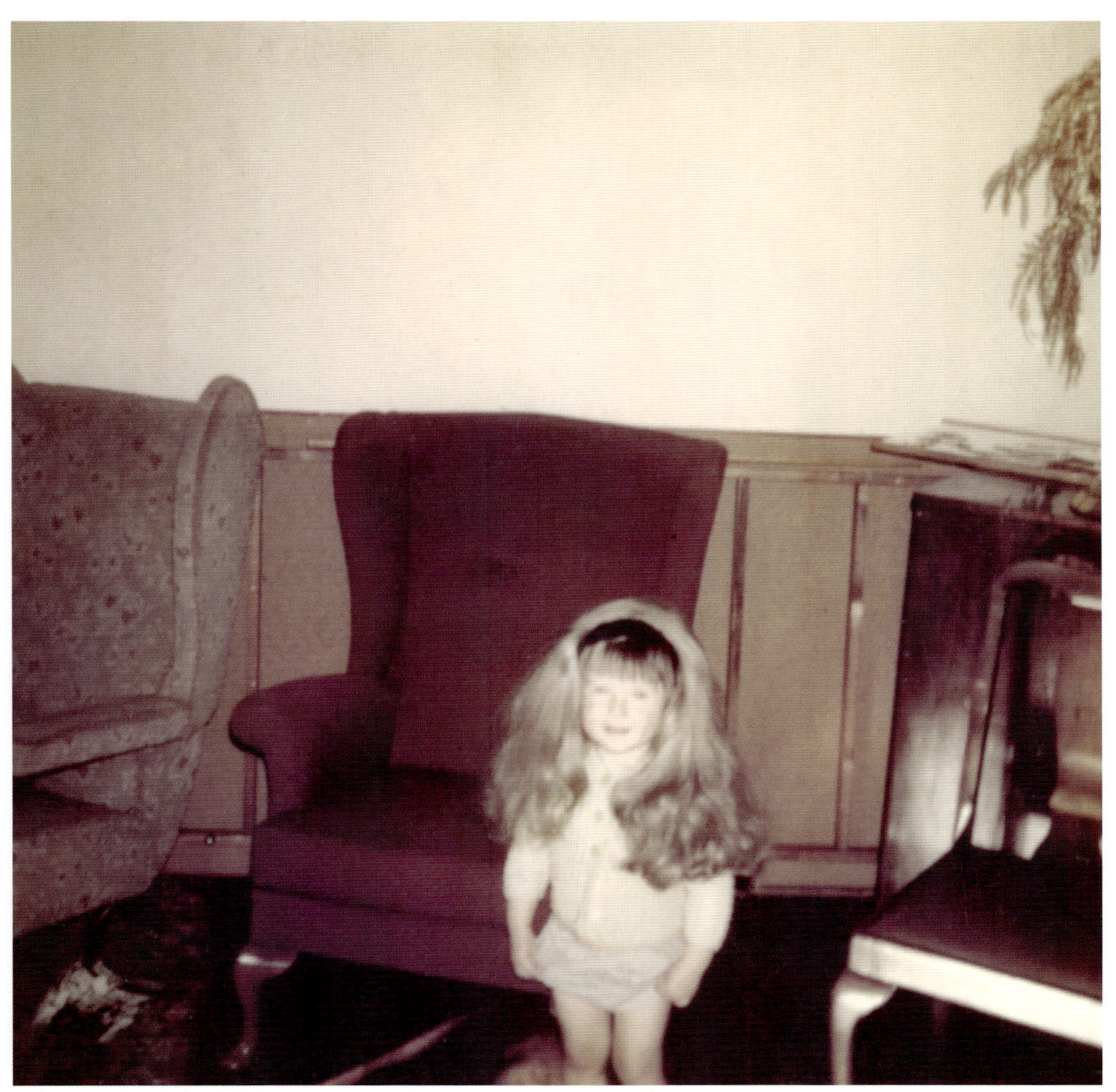

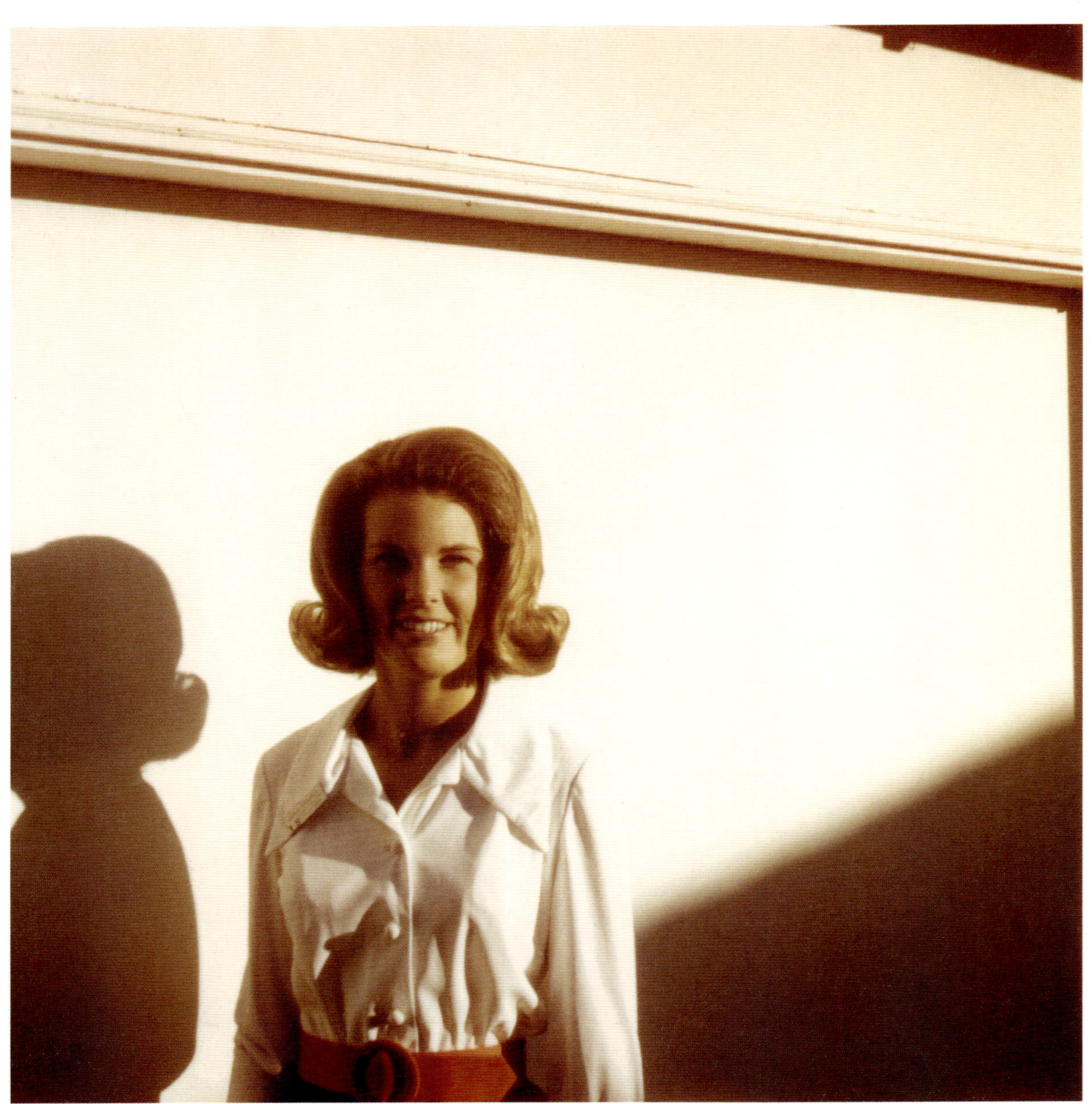

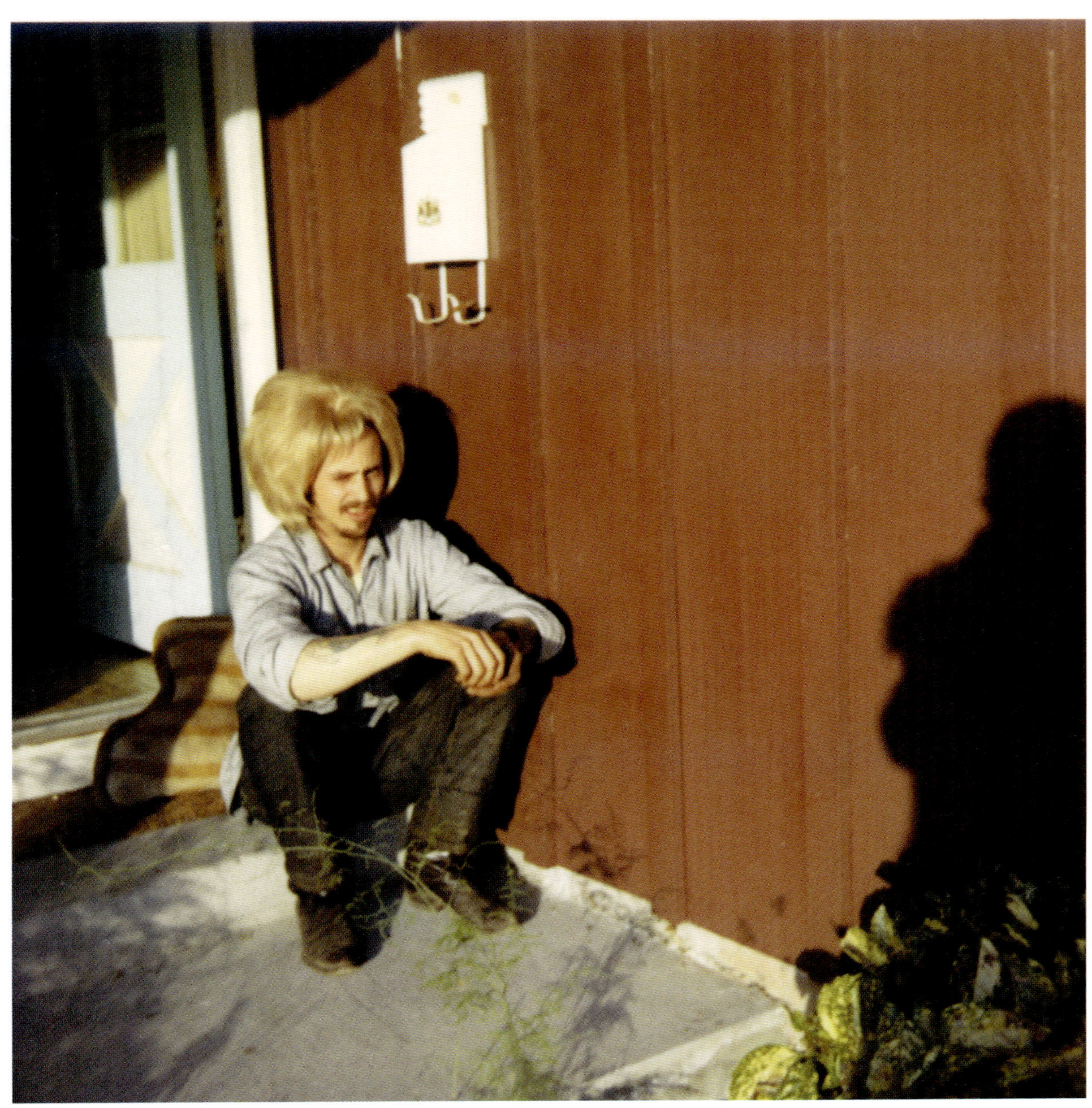

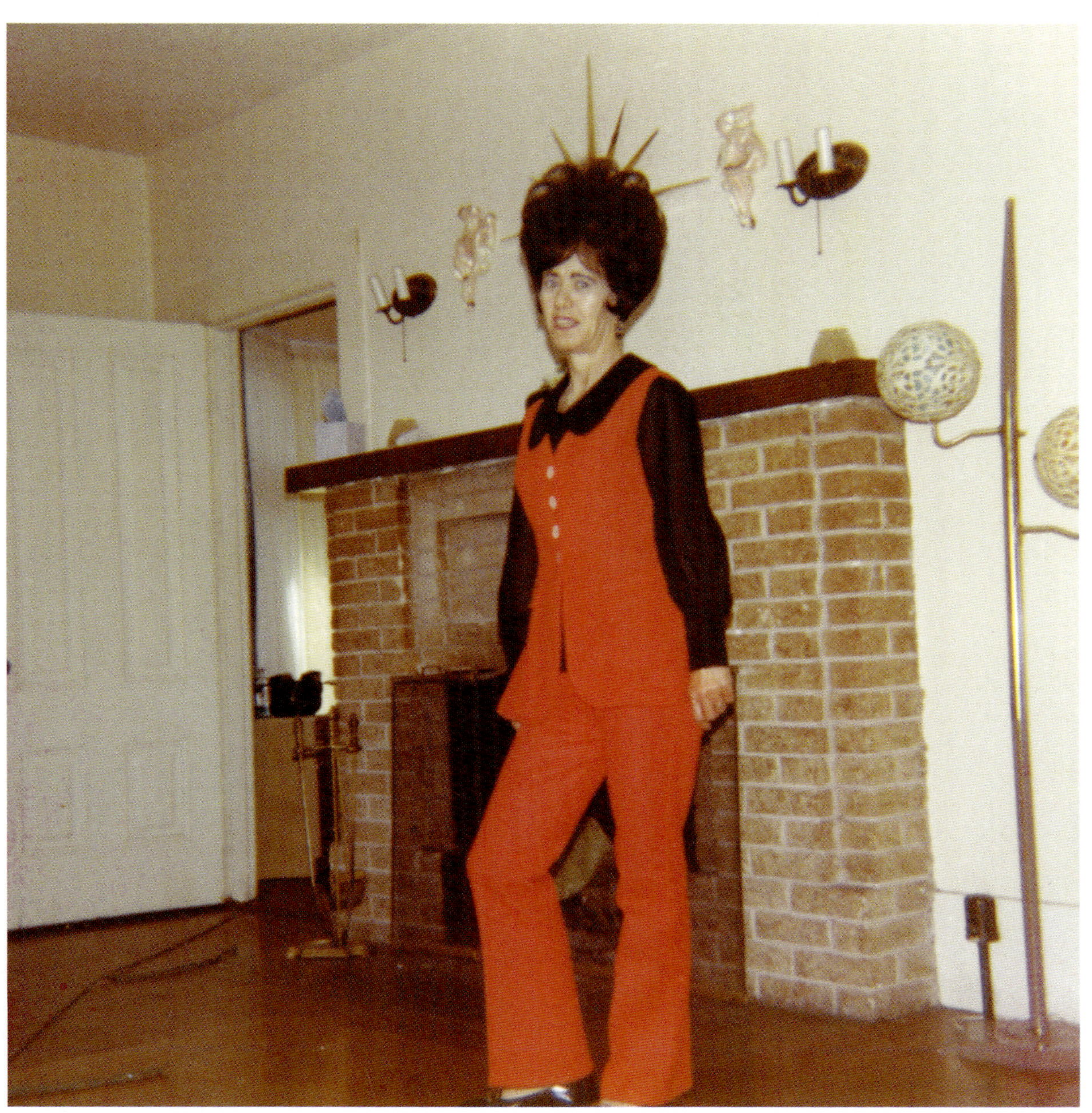

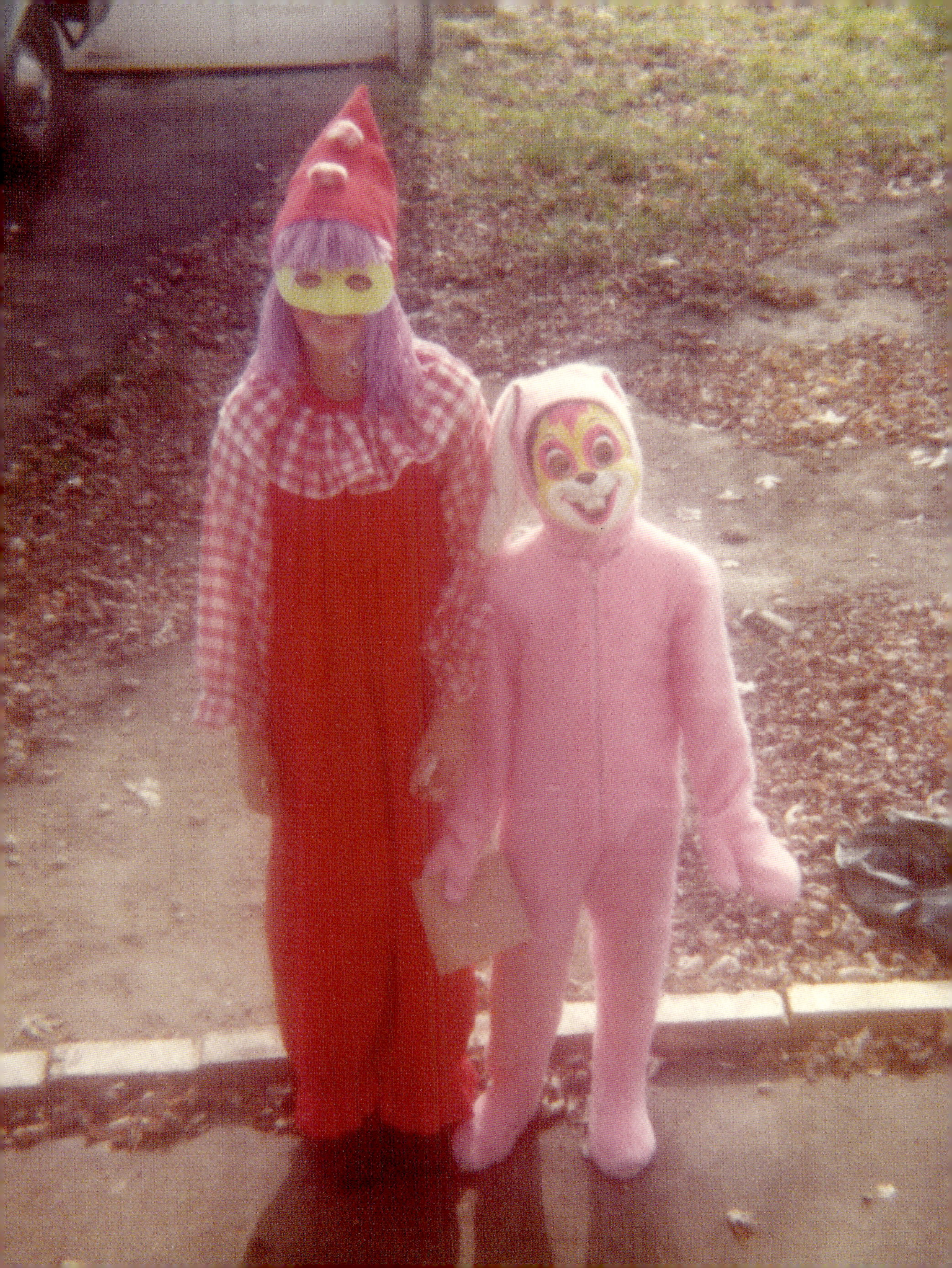

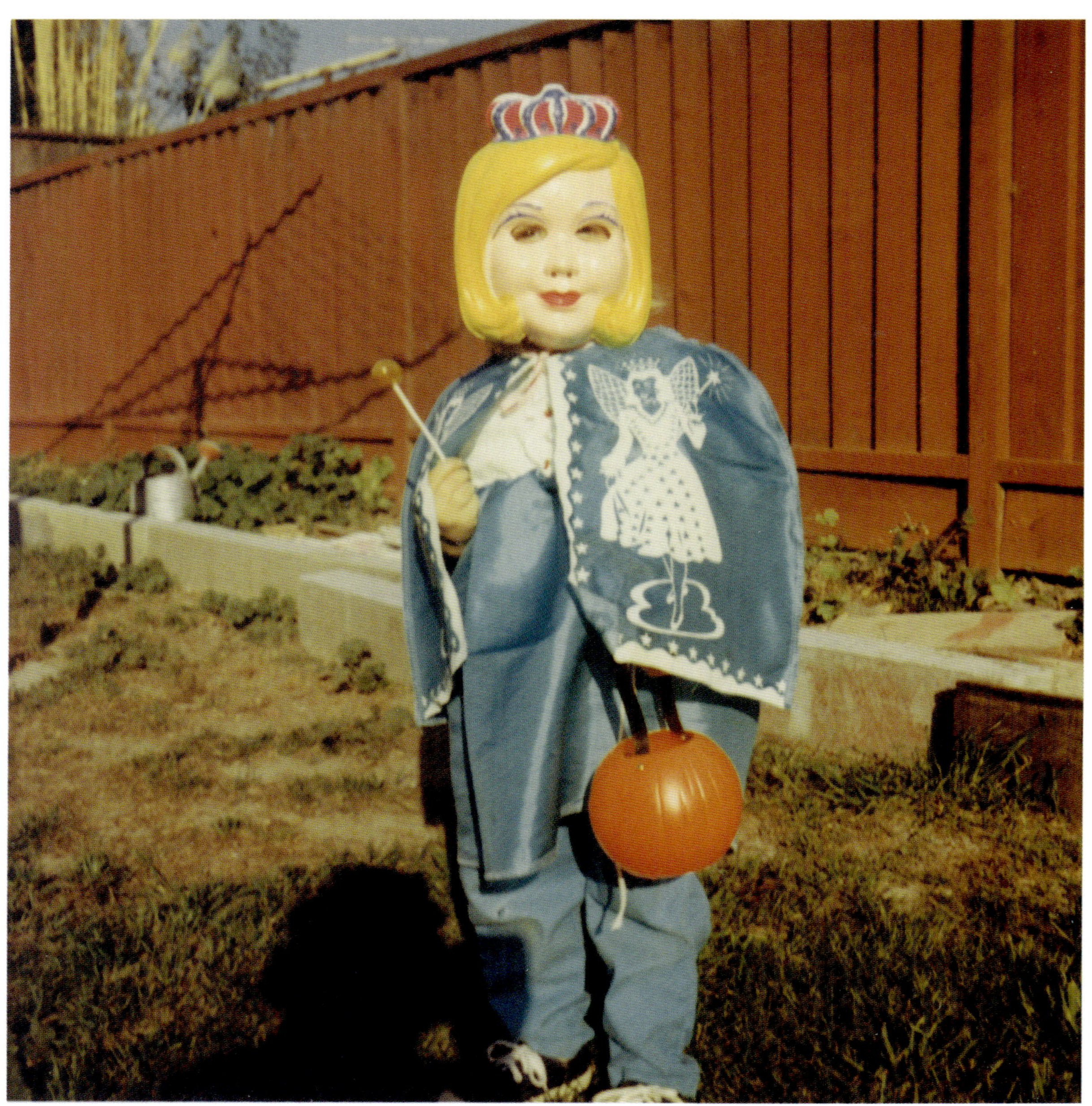

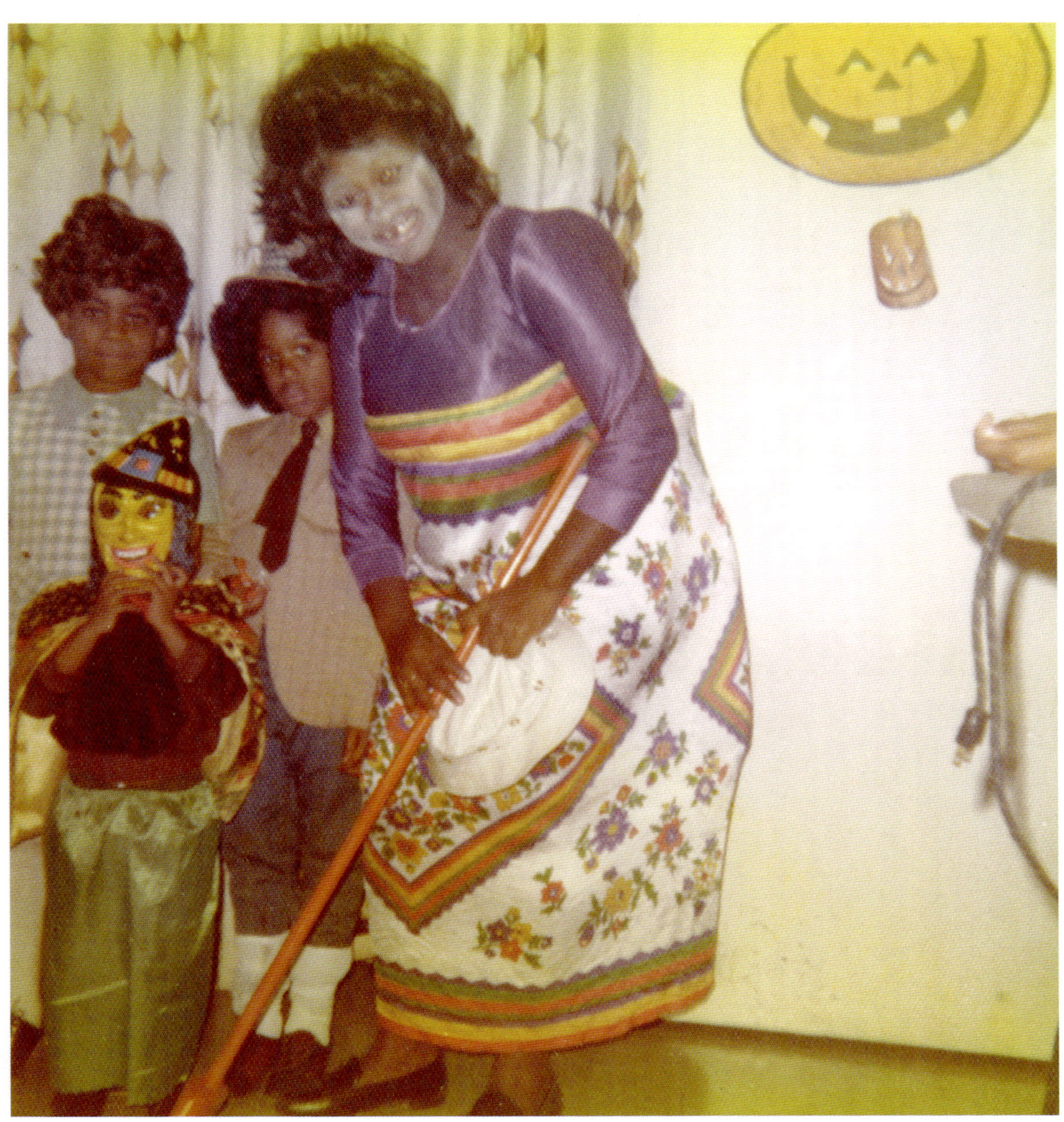

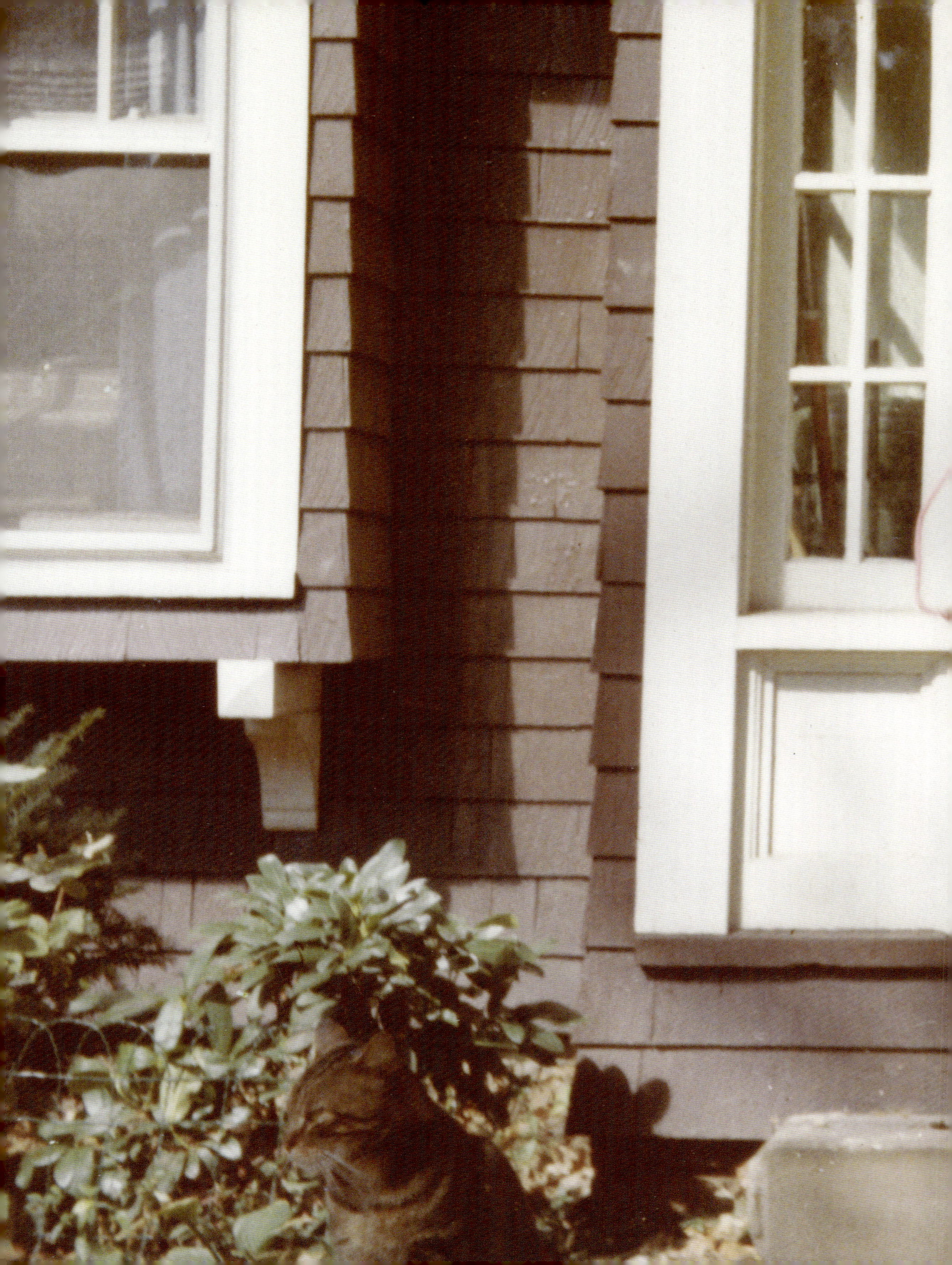

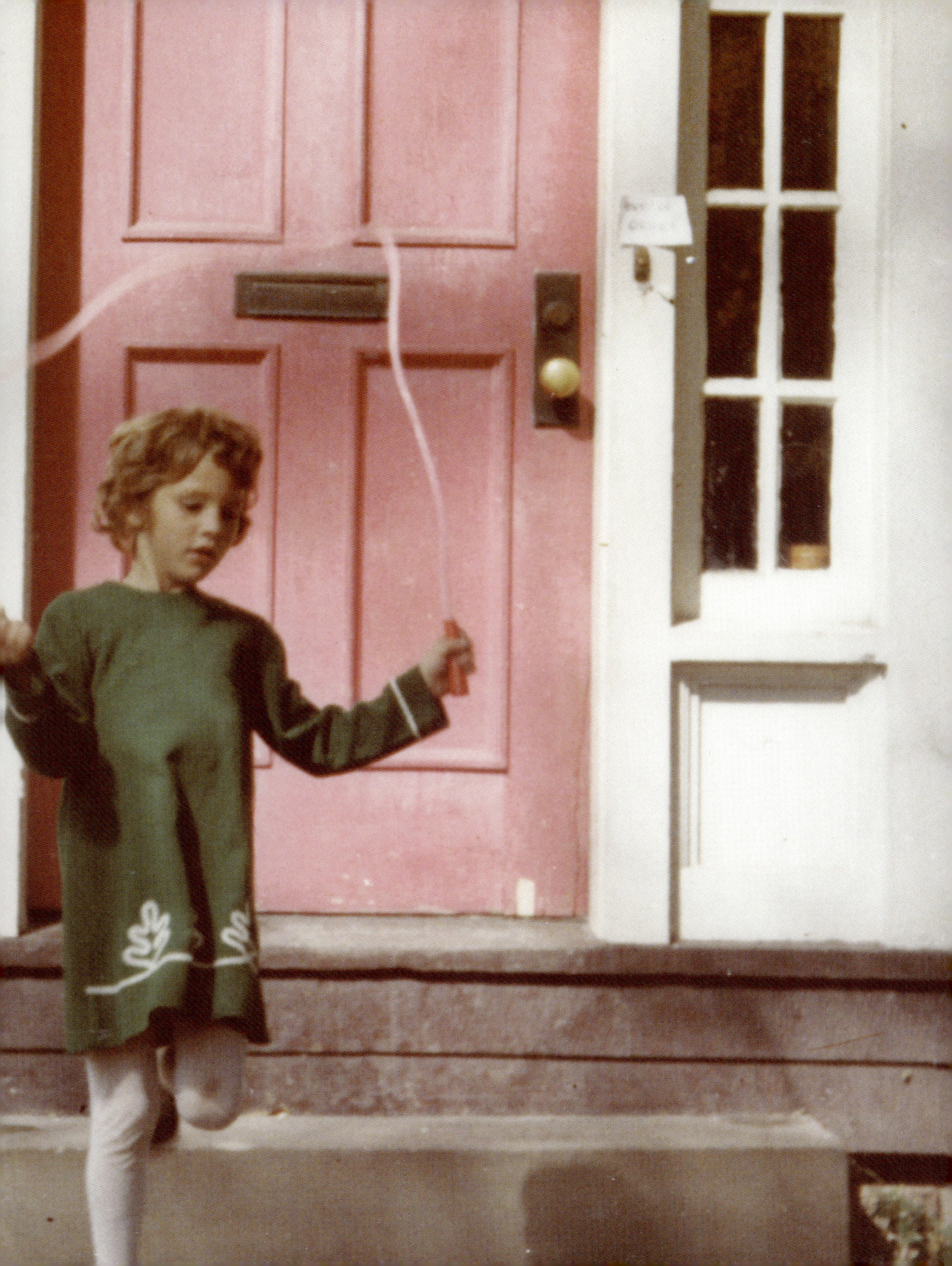

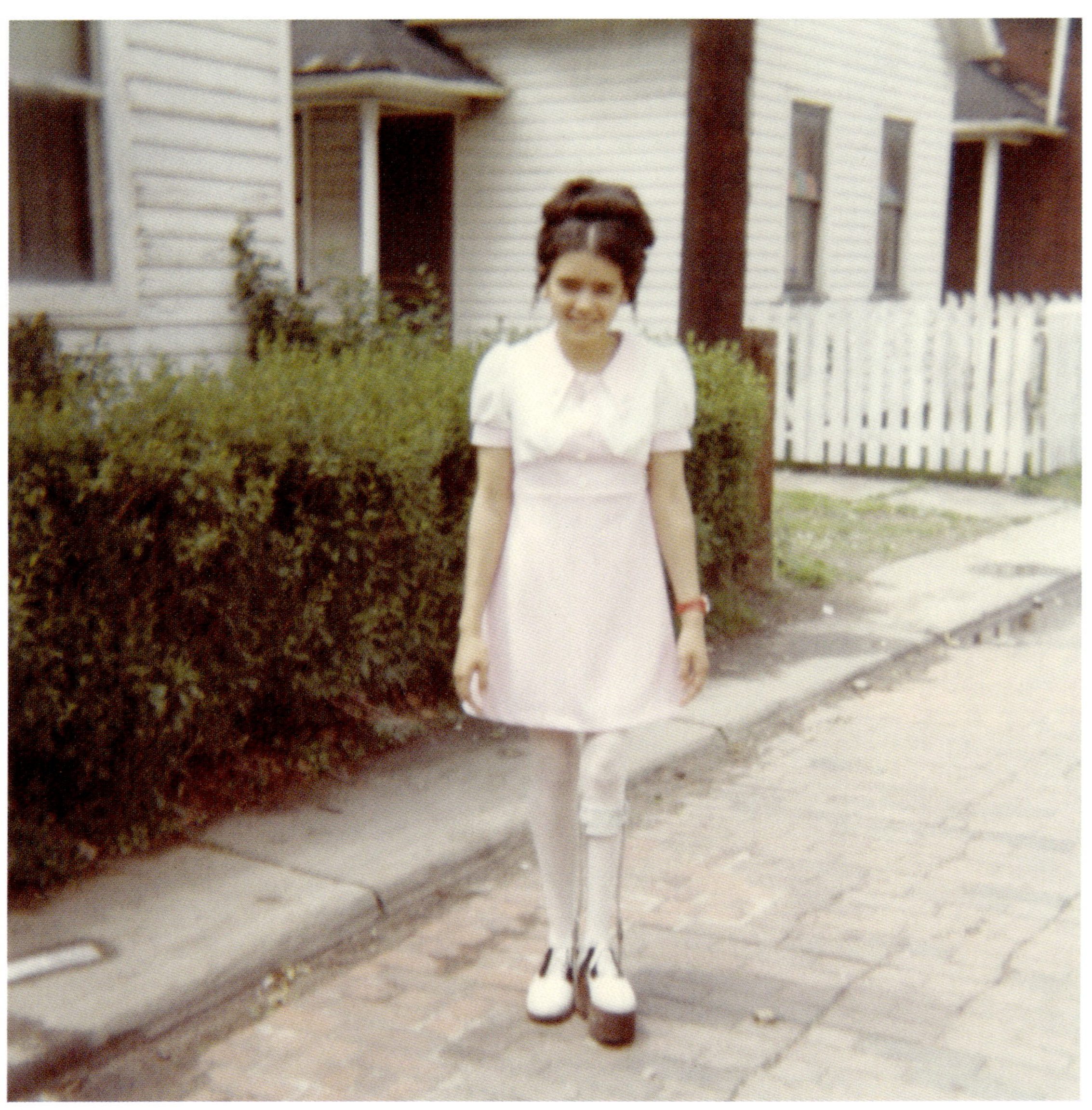

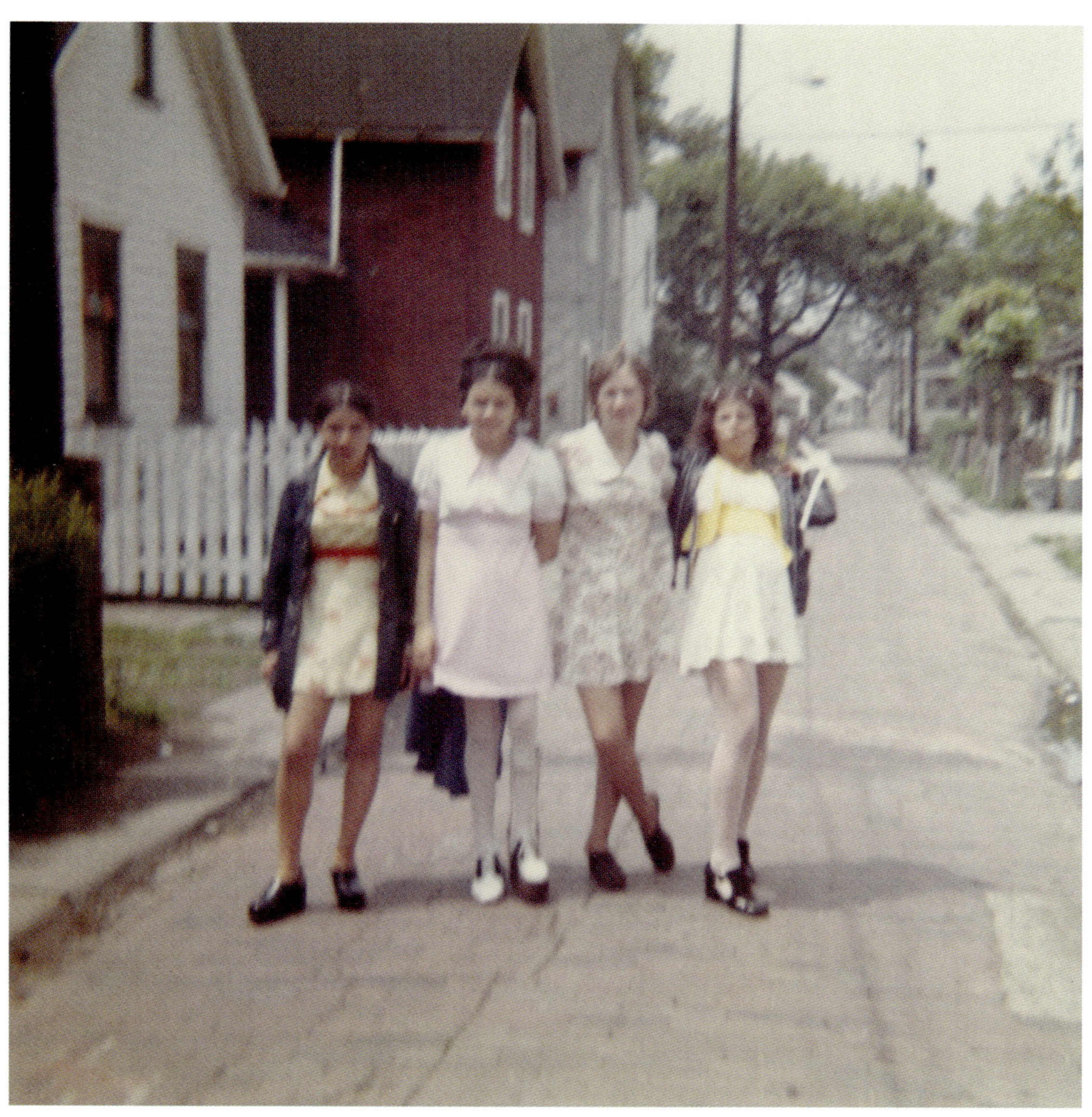

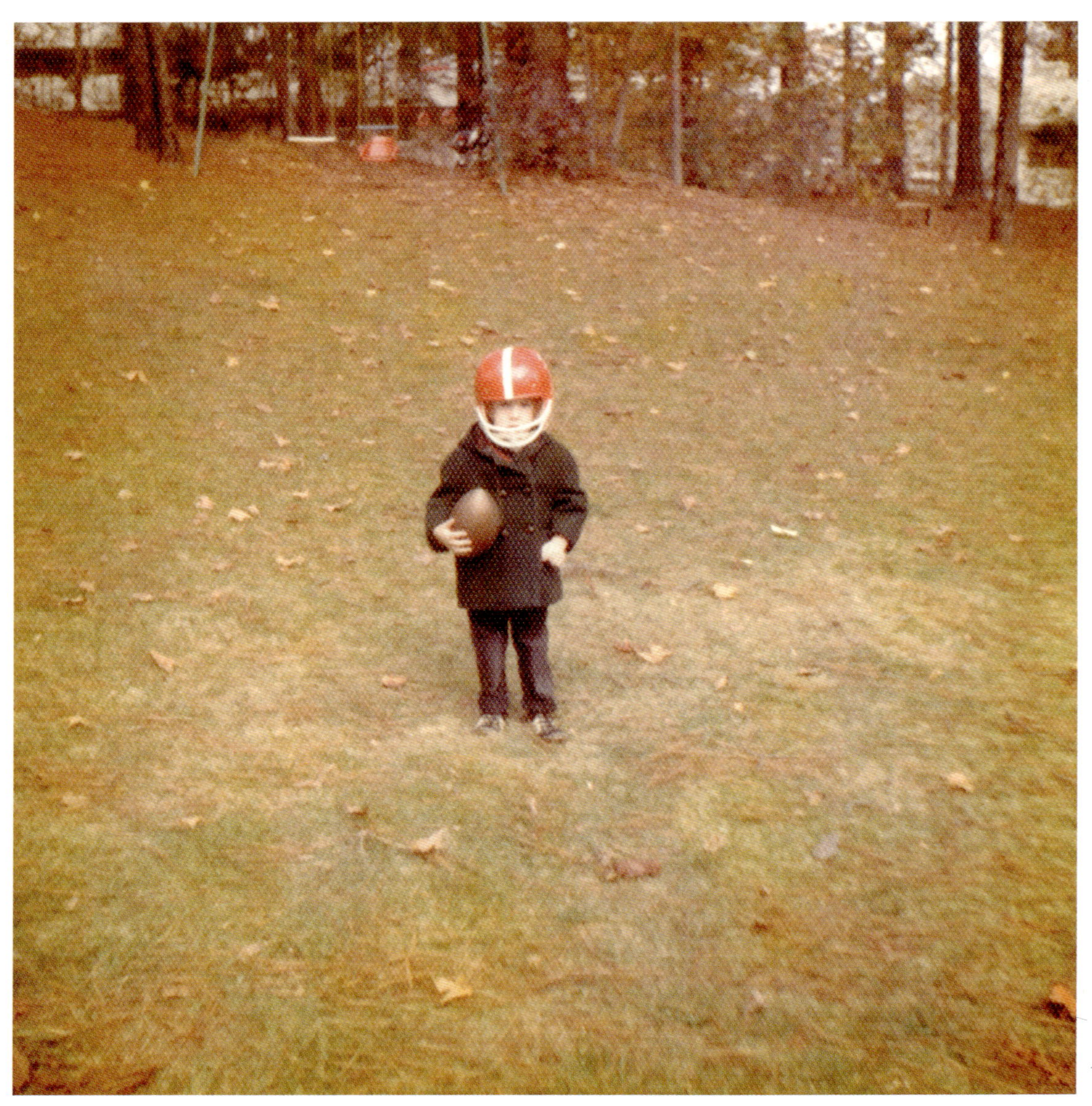

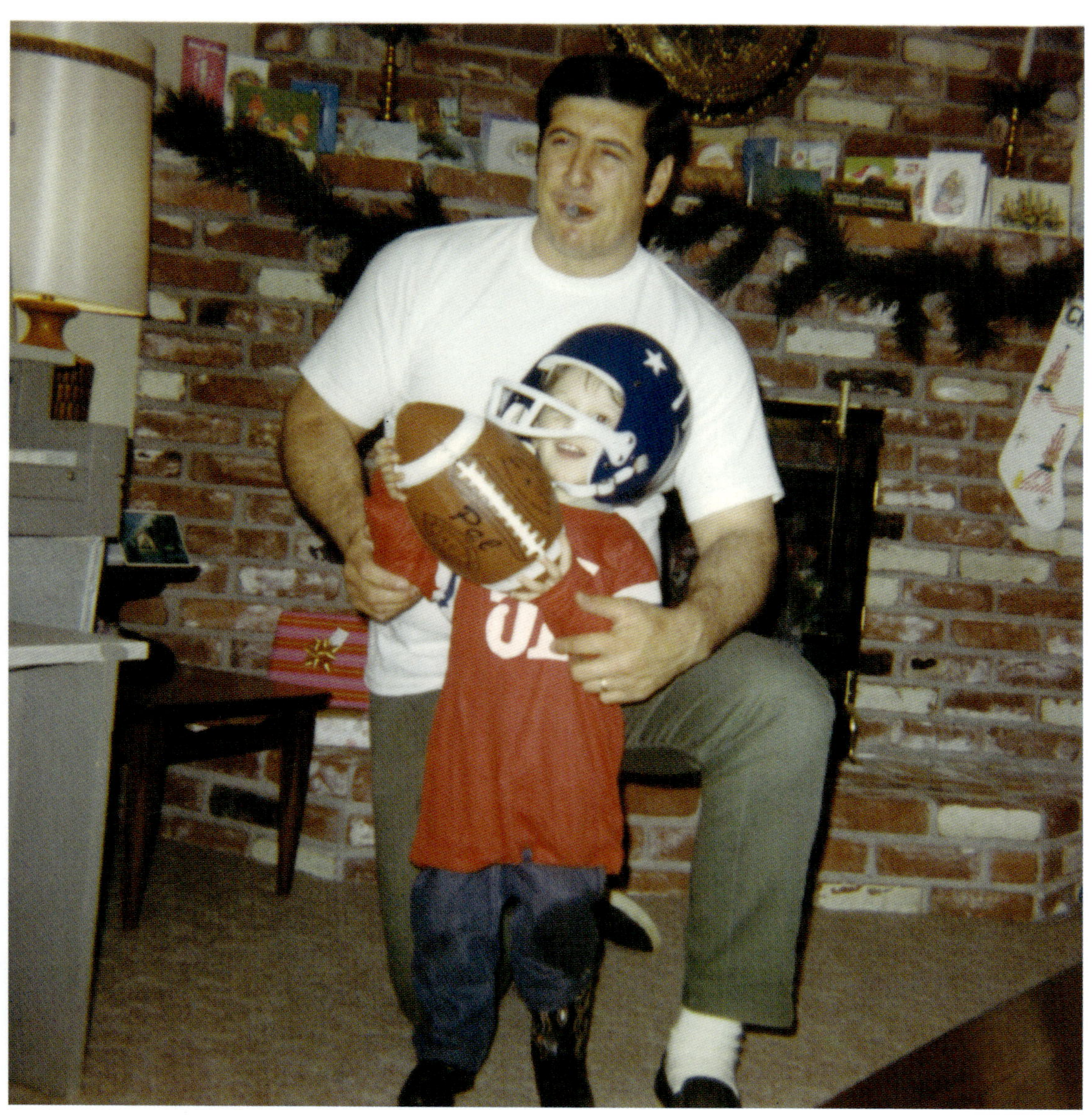

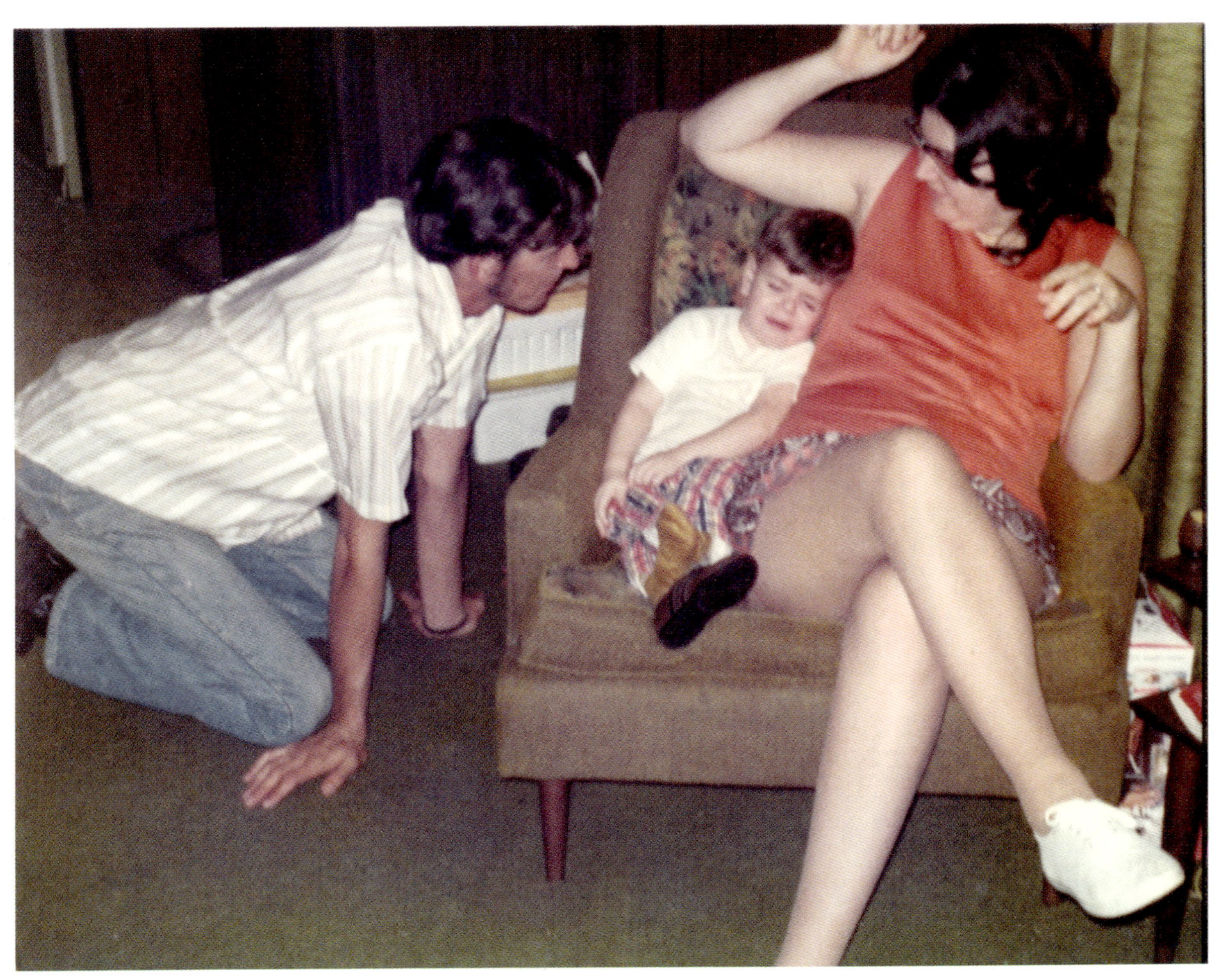

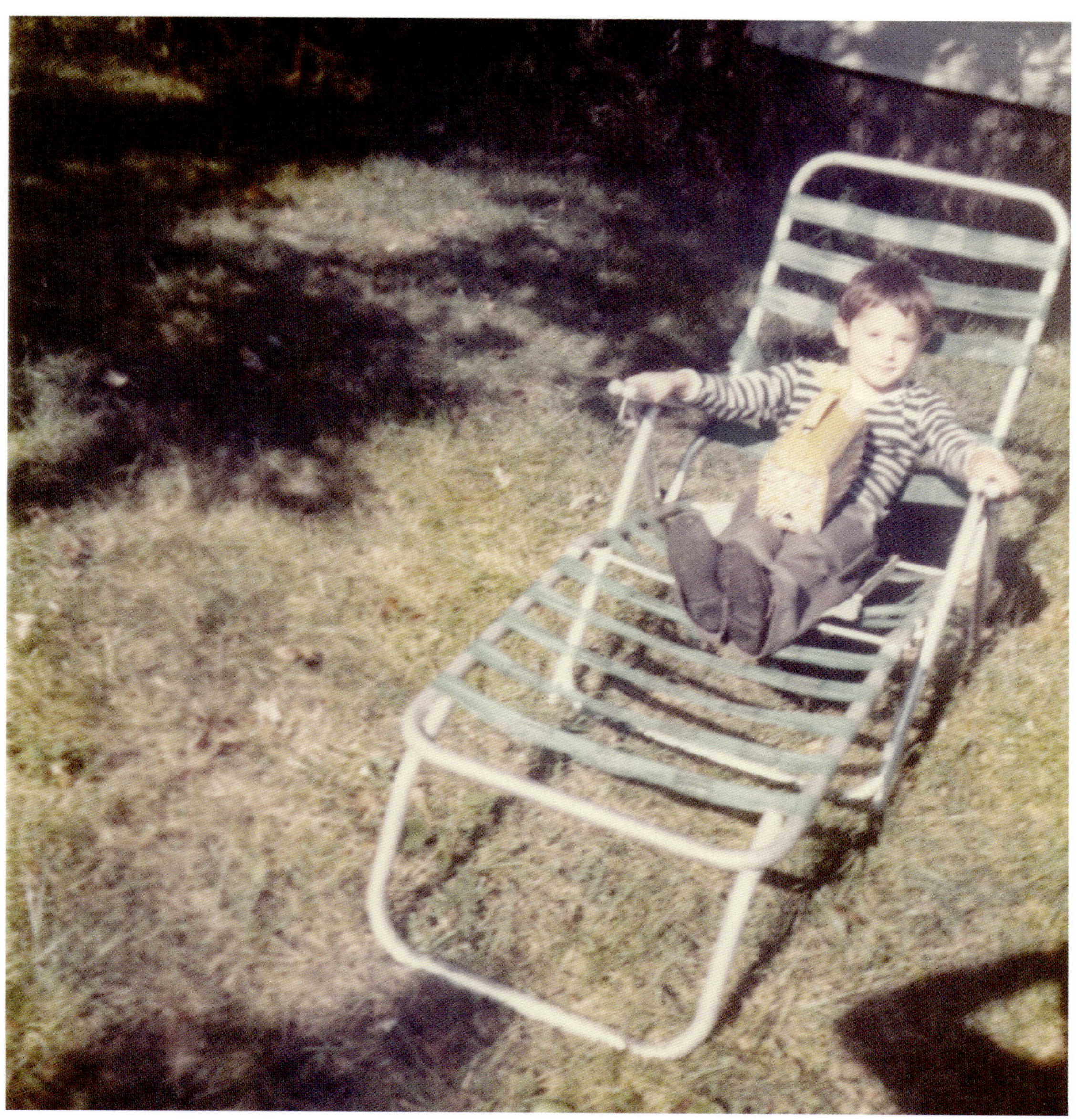

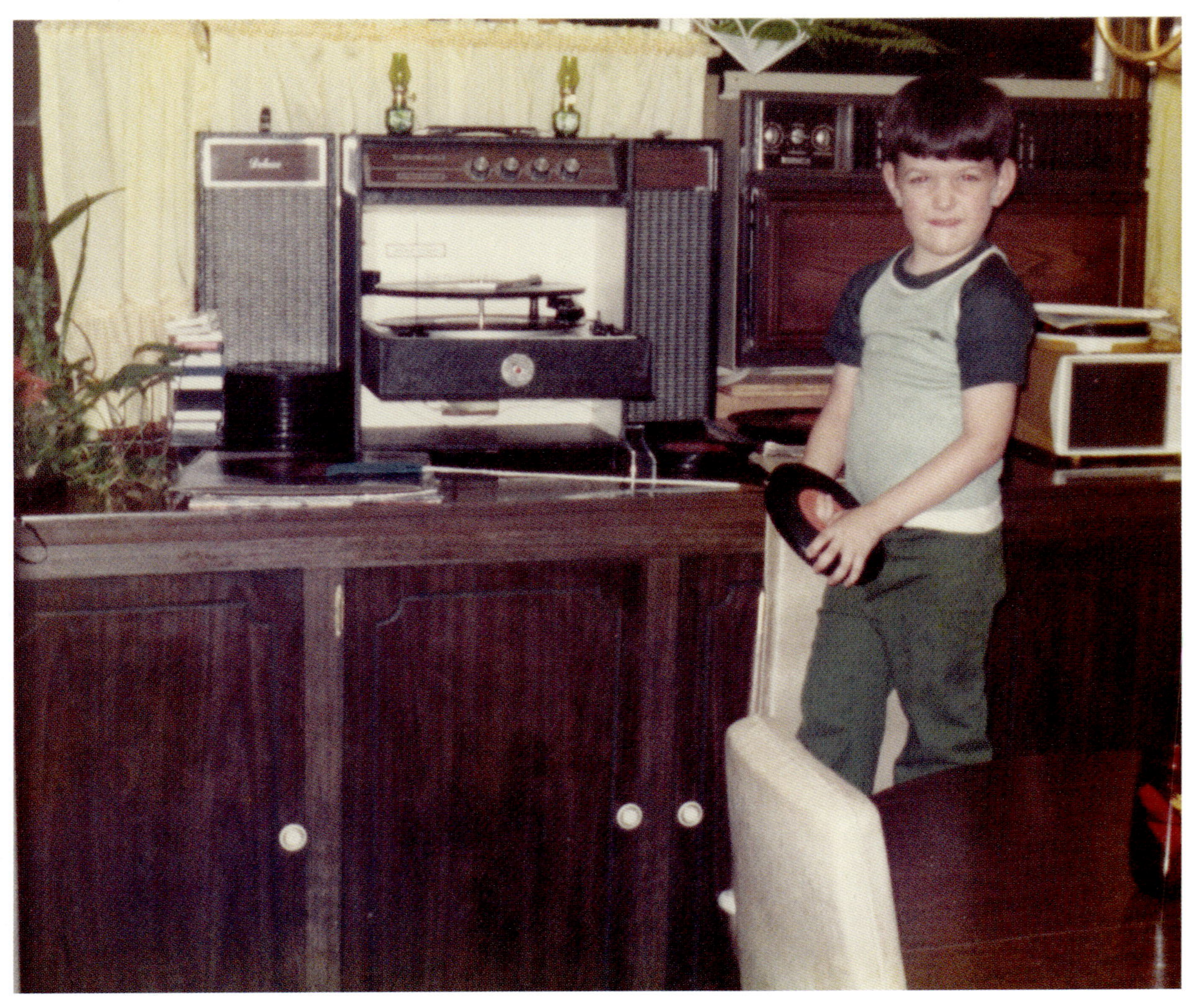

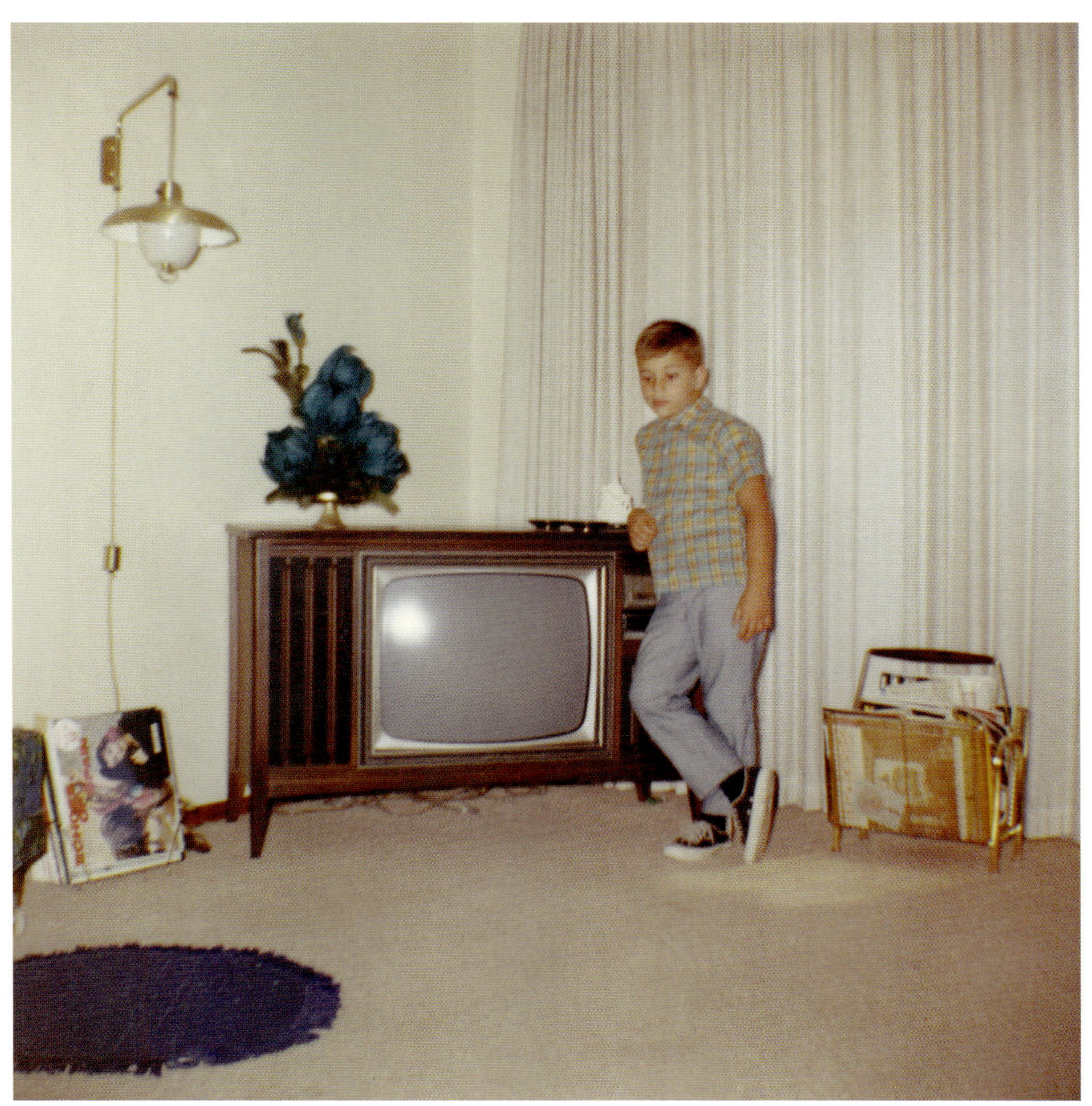

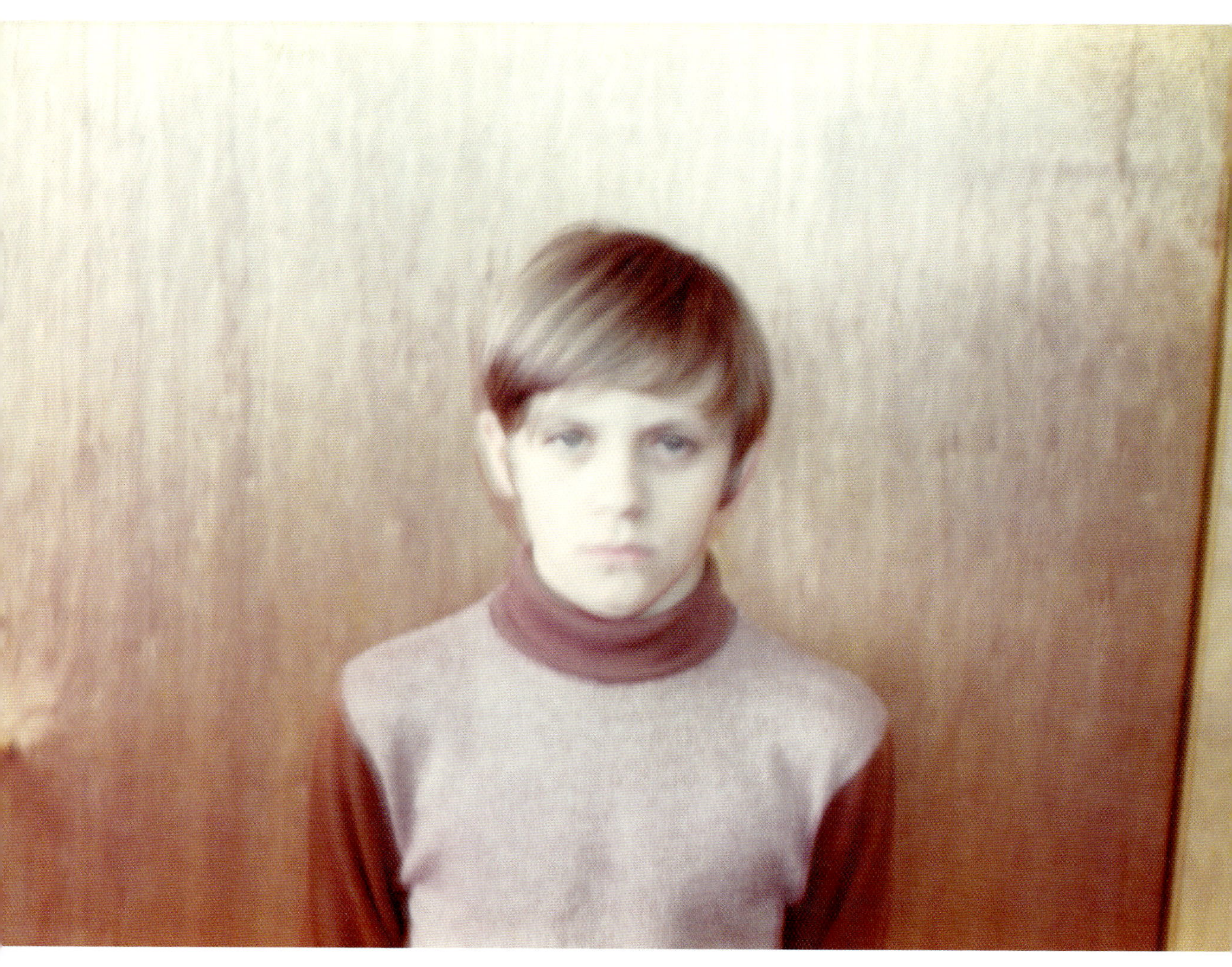

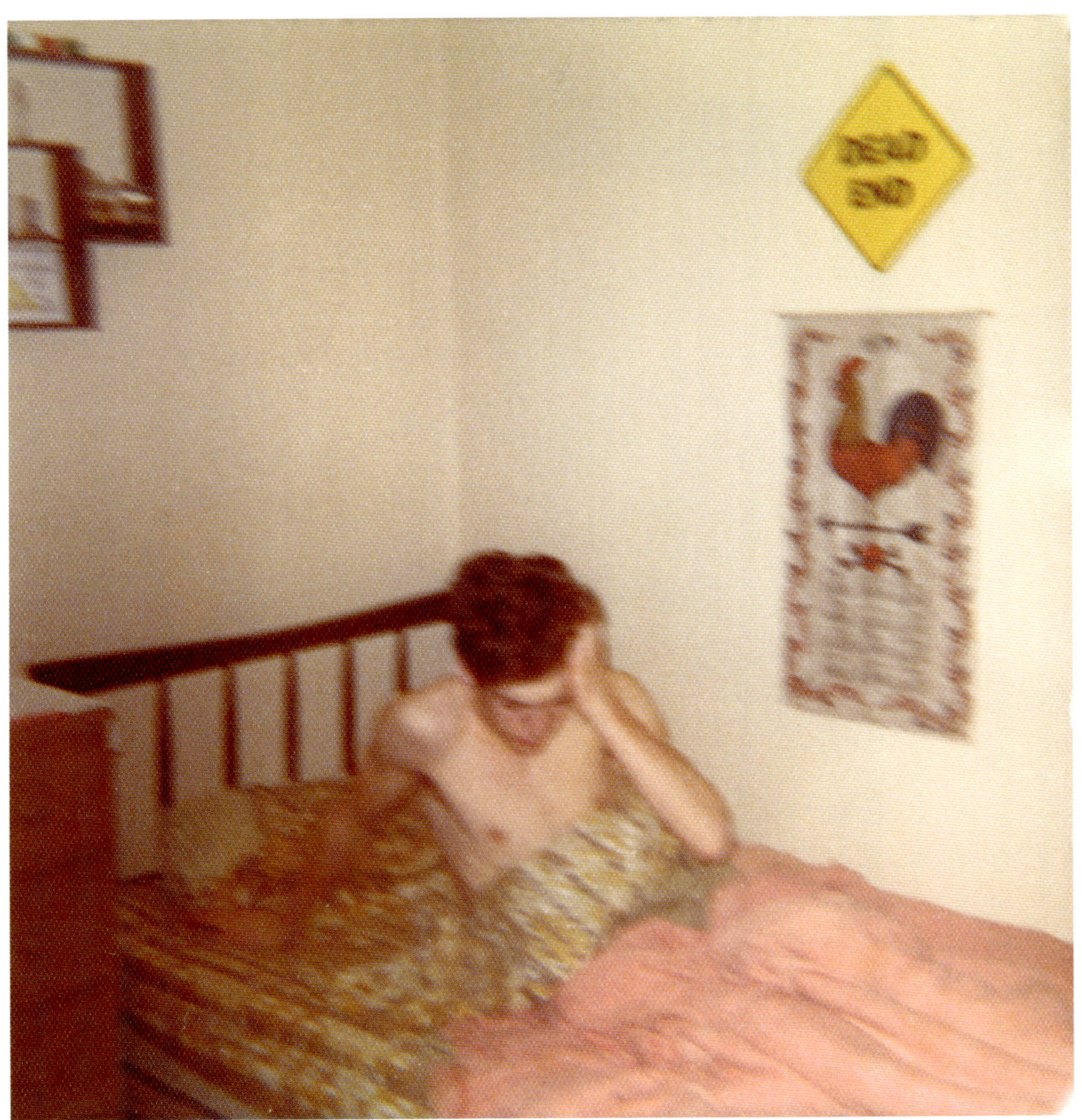

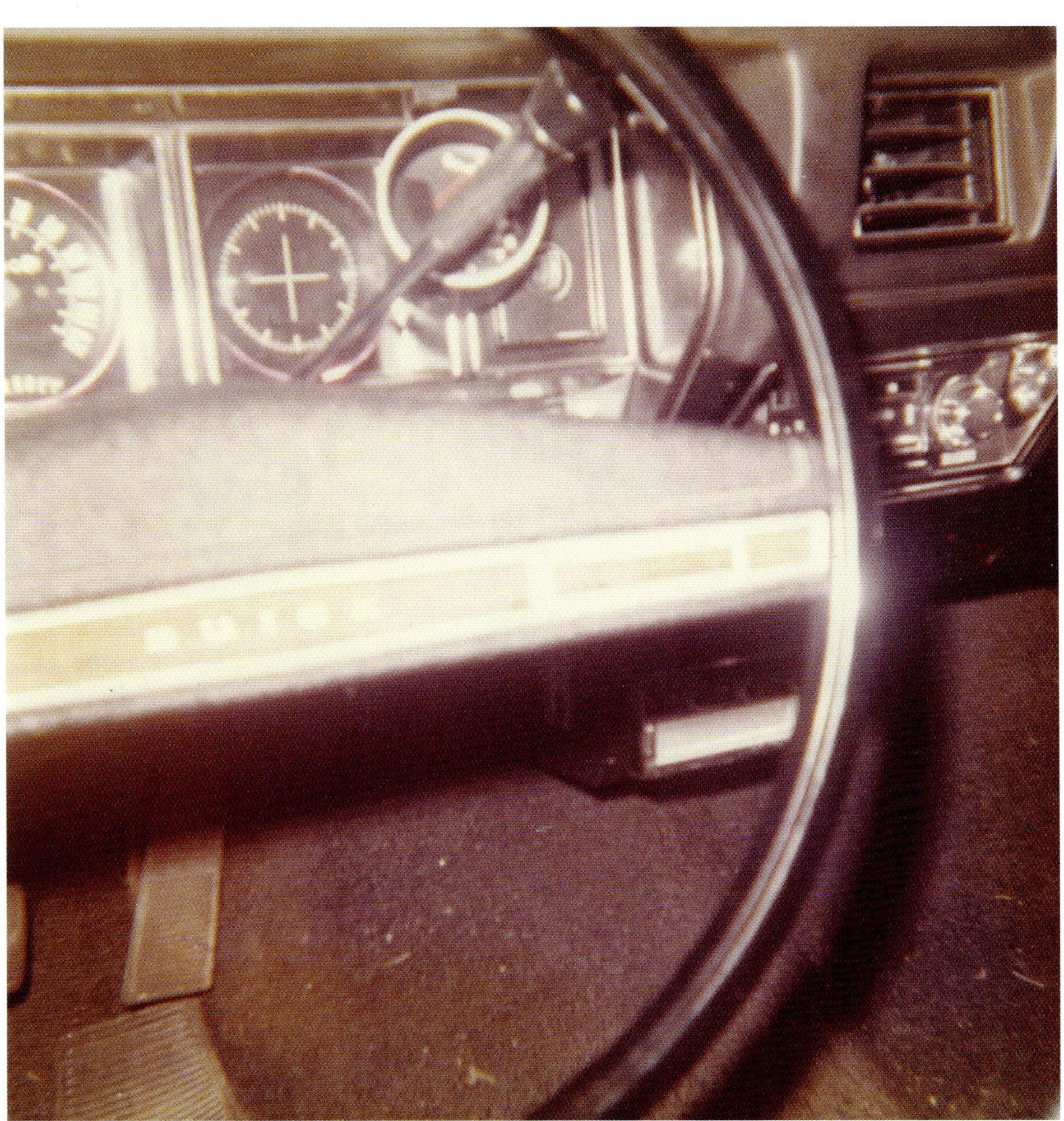

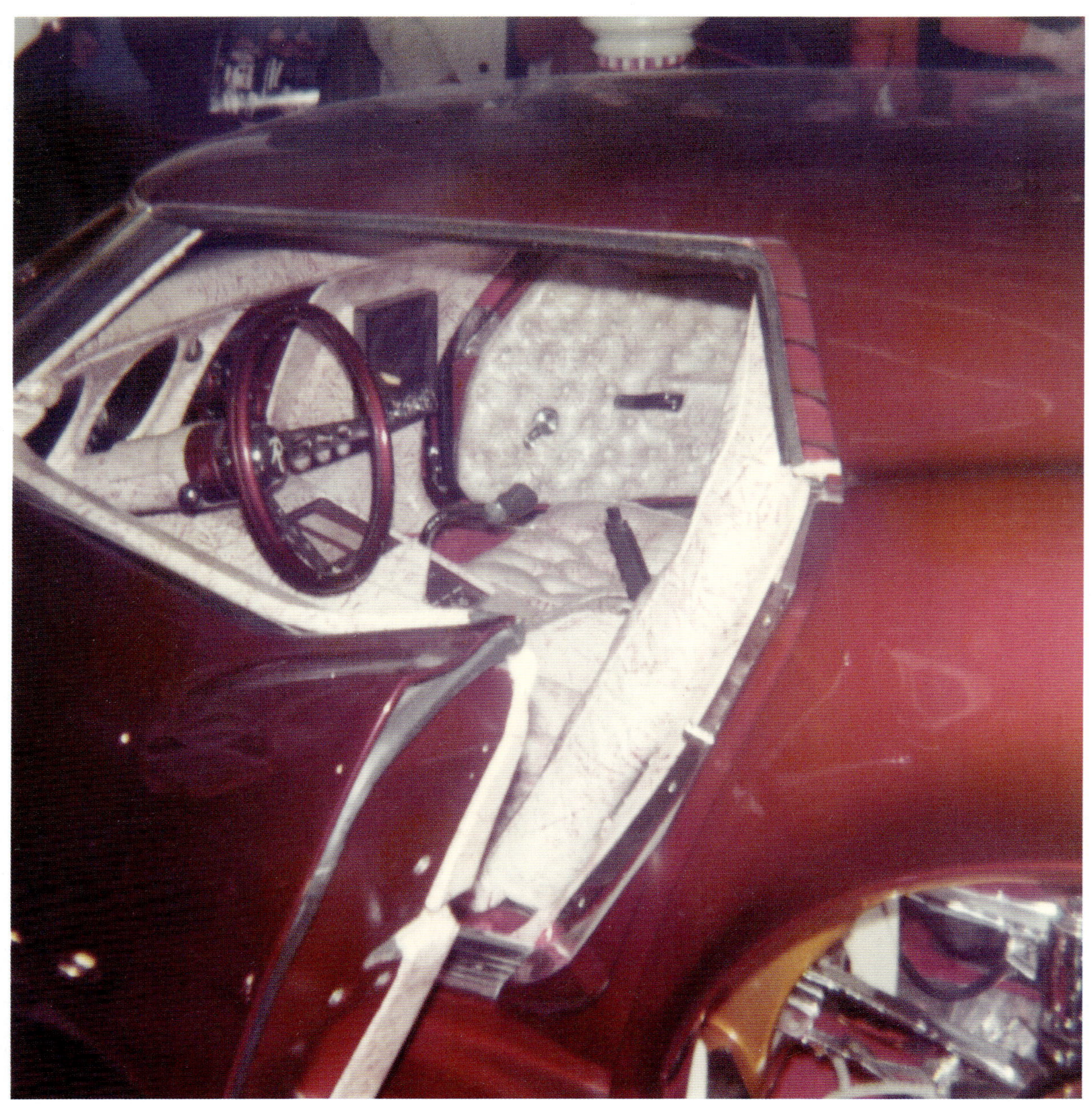

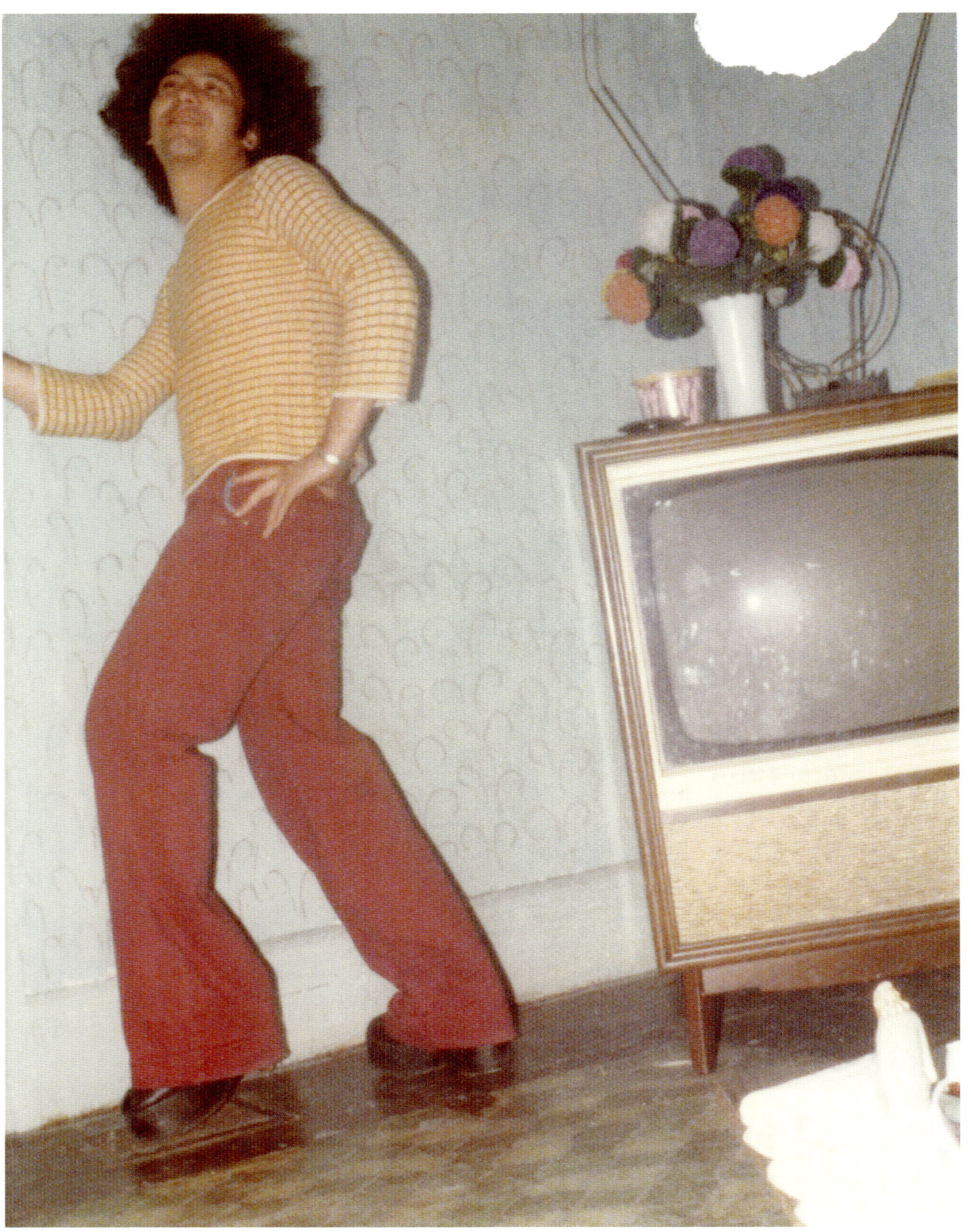

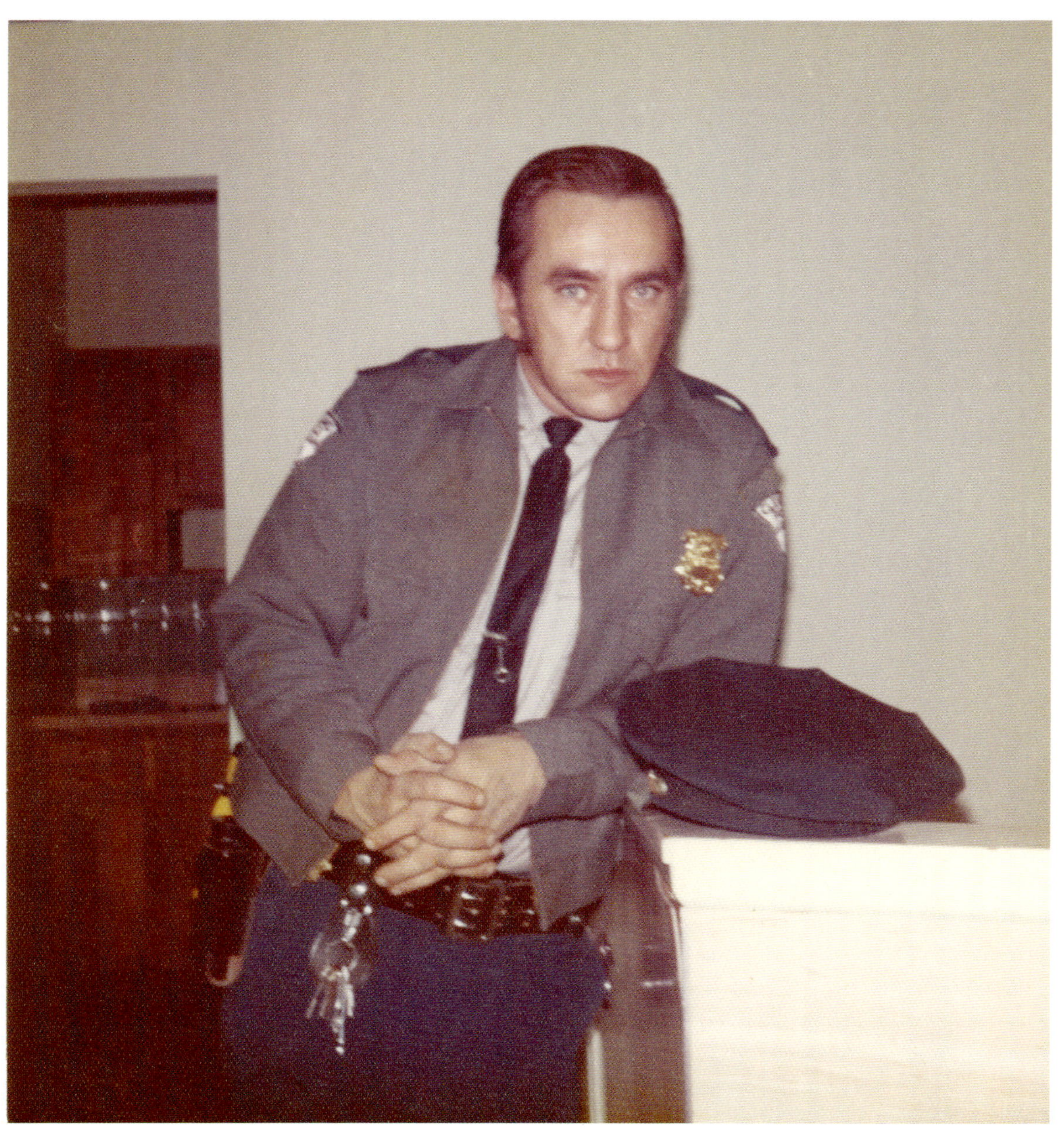

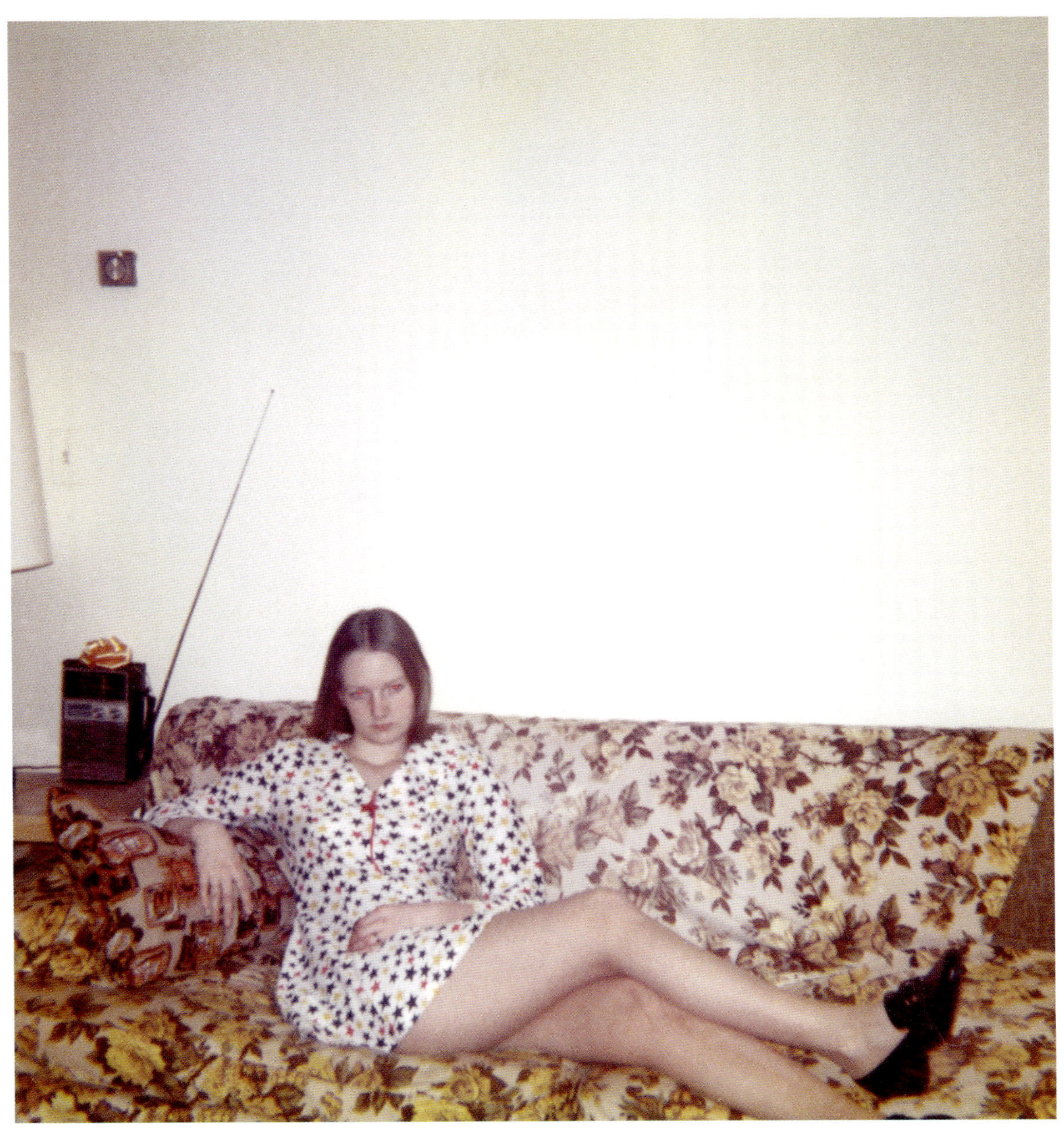

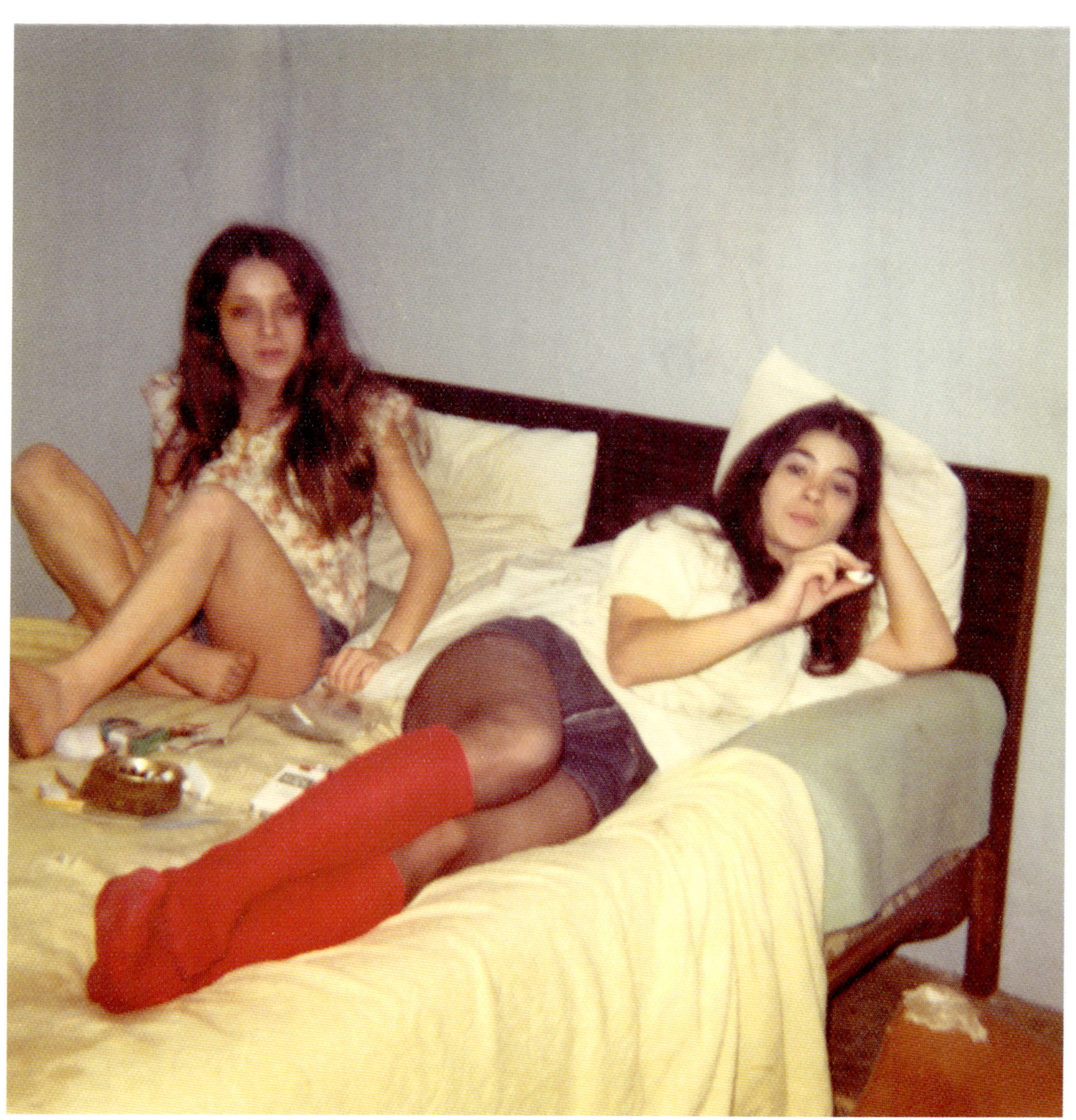

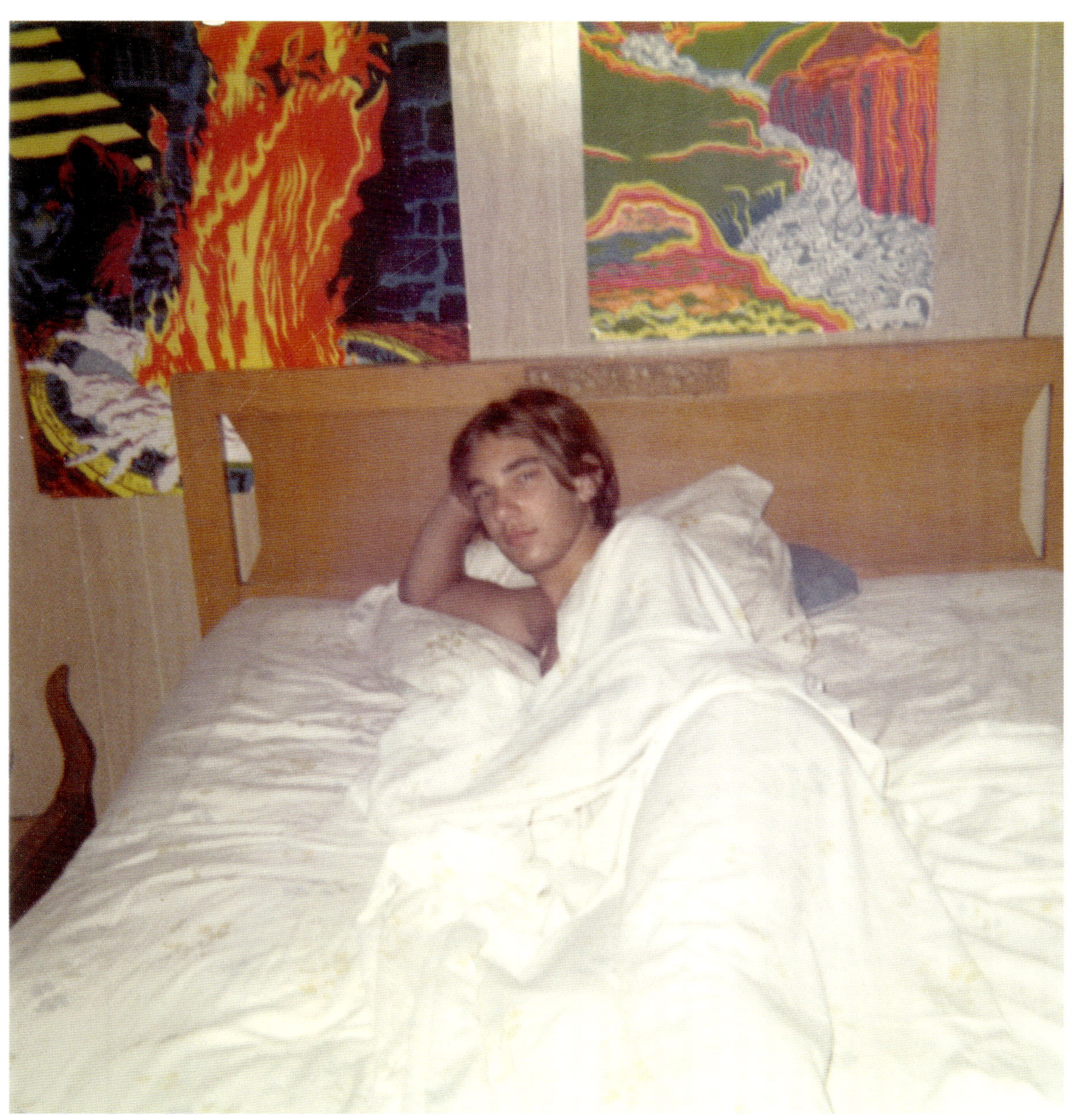

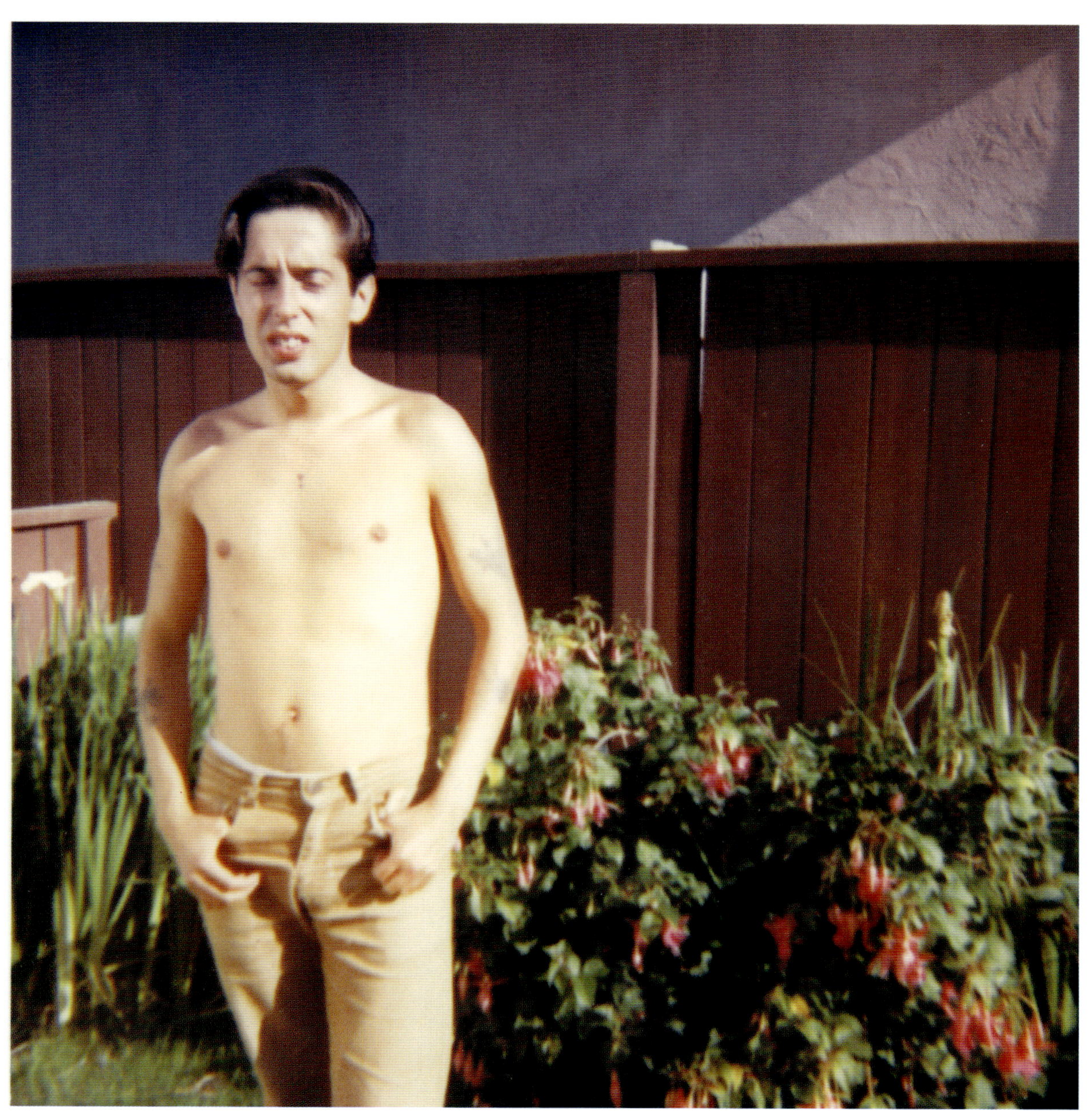

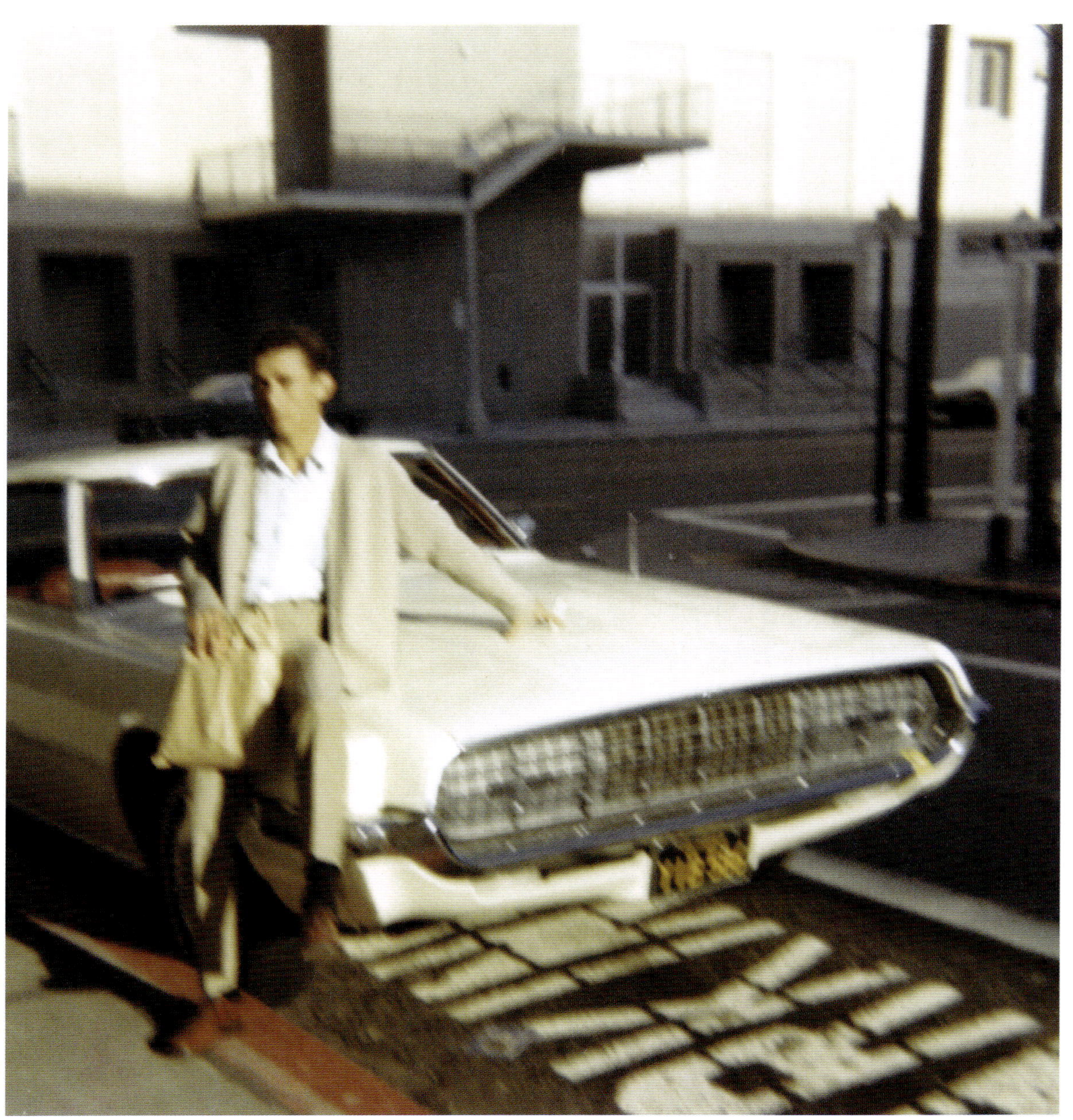

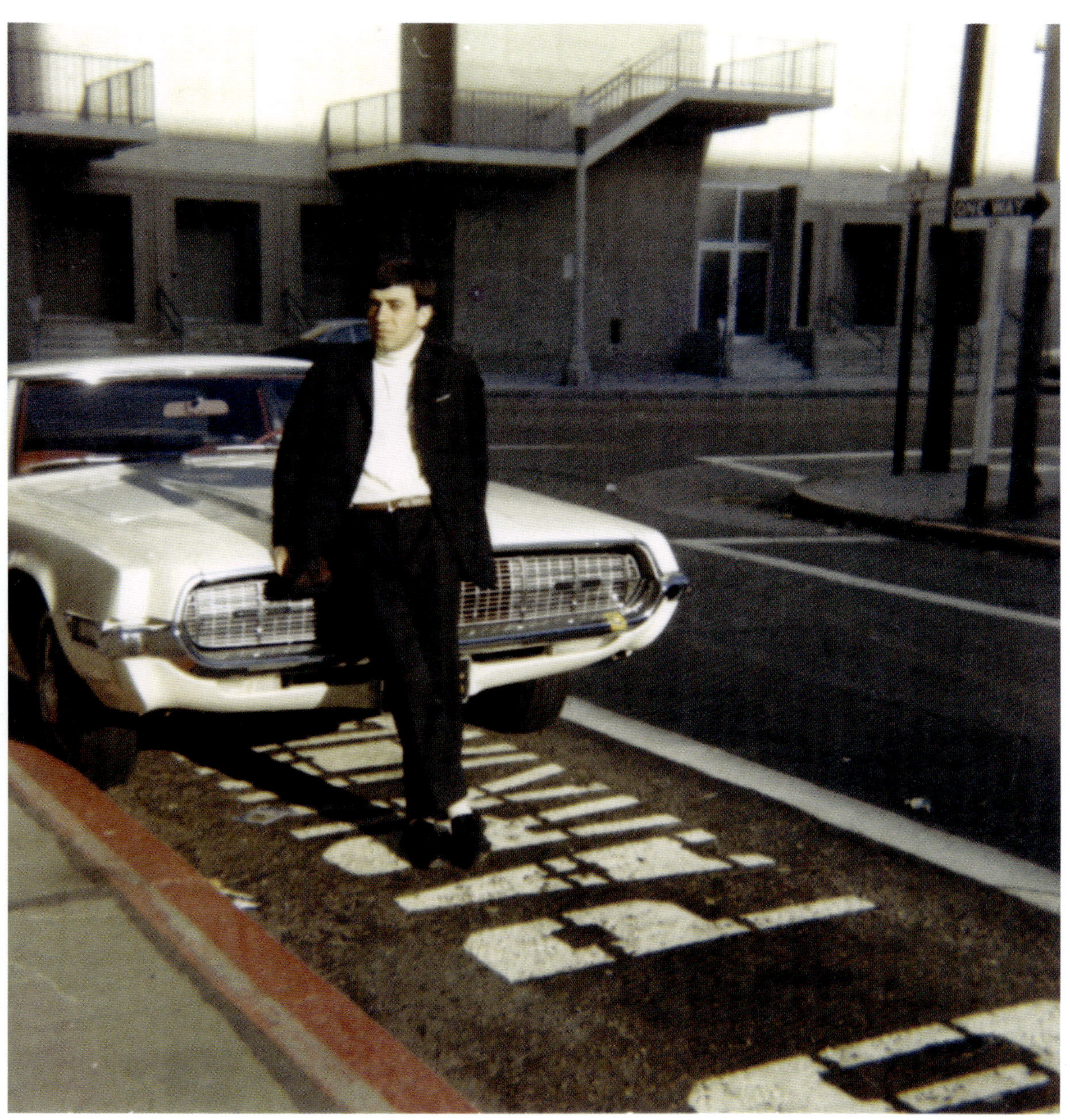
ONE WAY

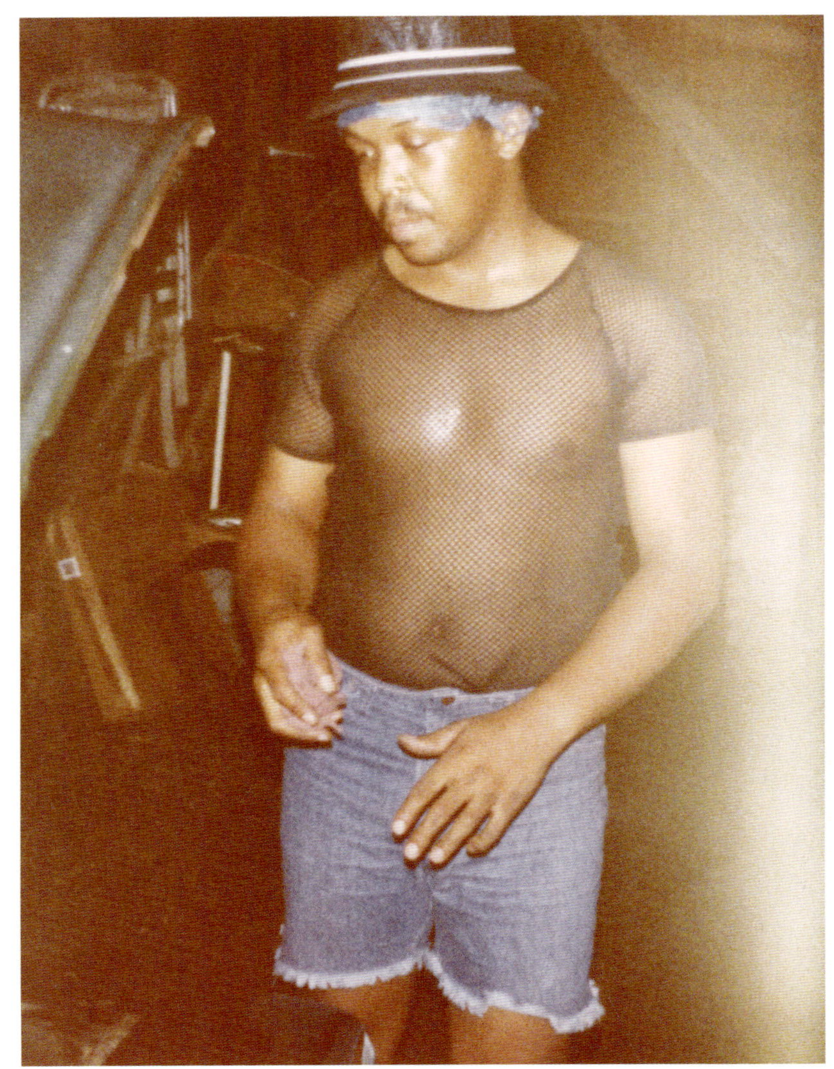

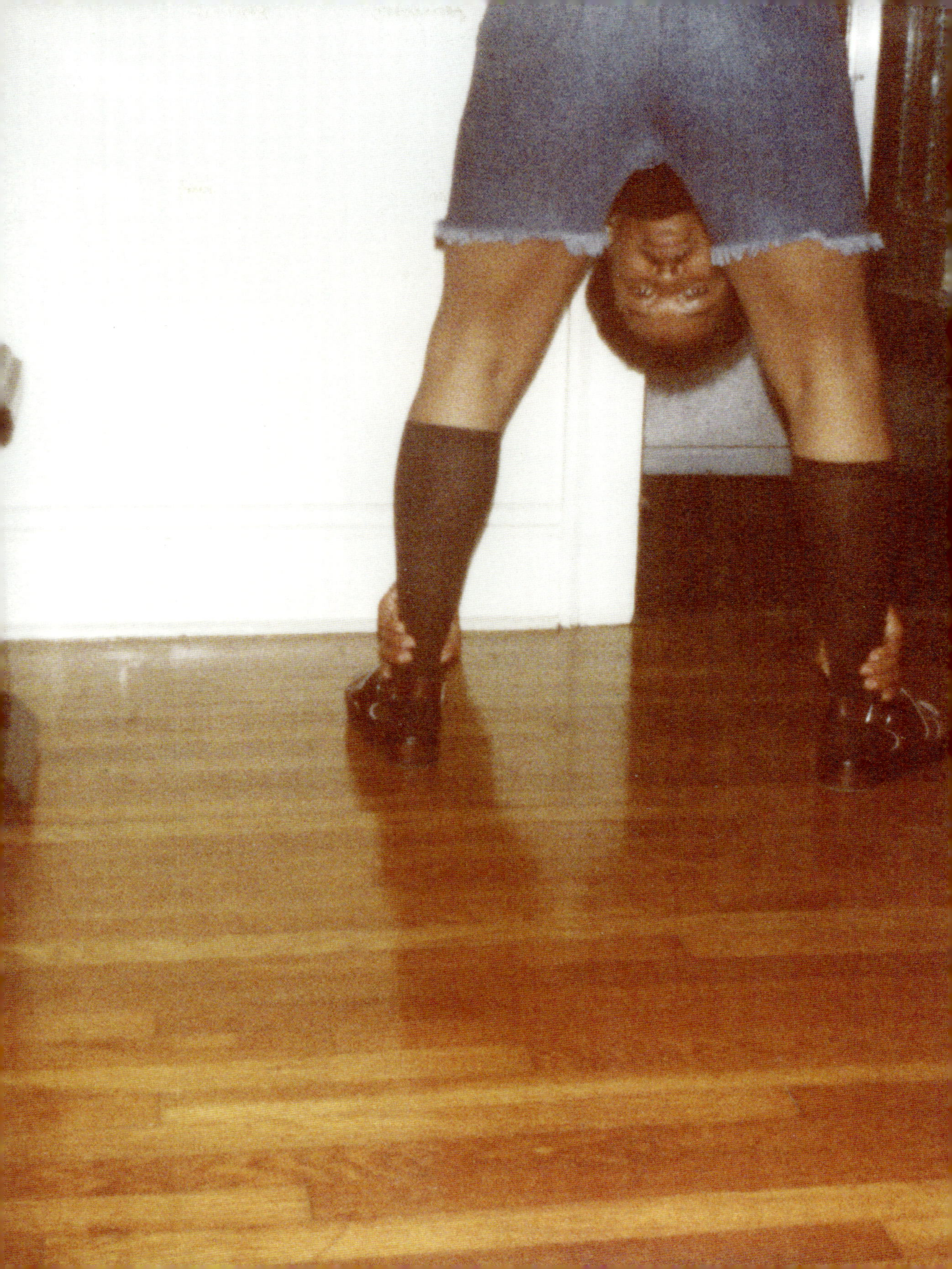

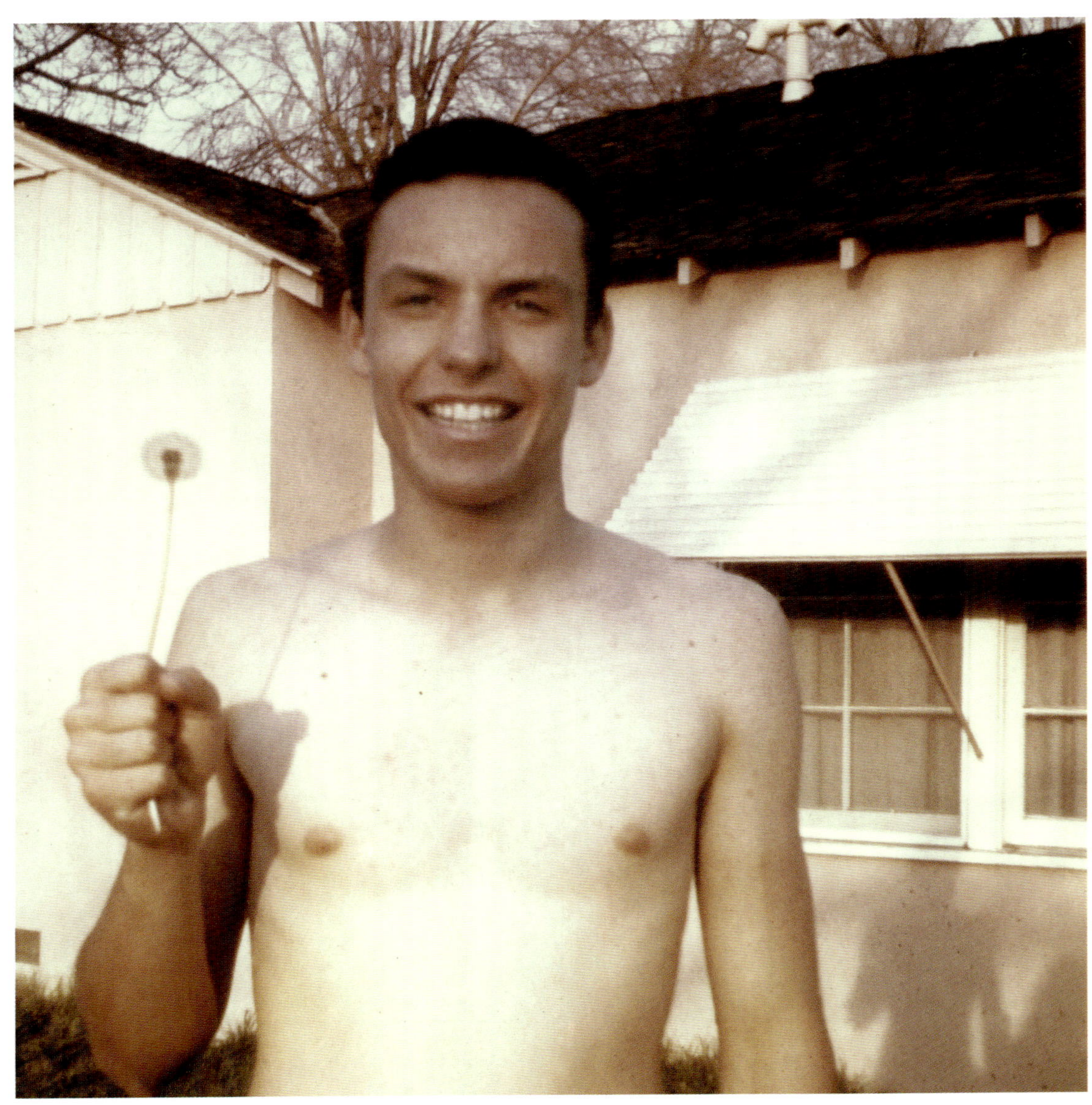

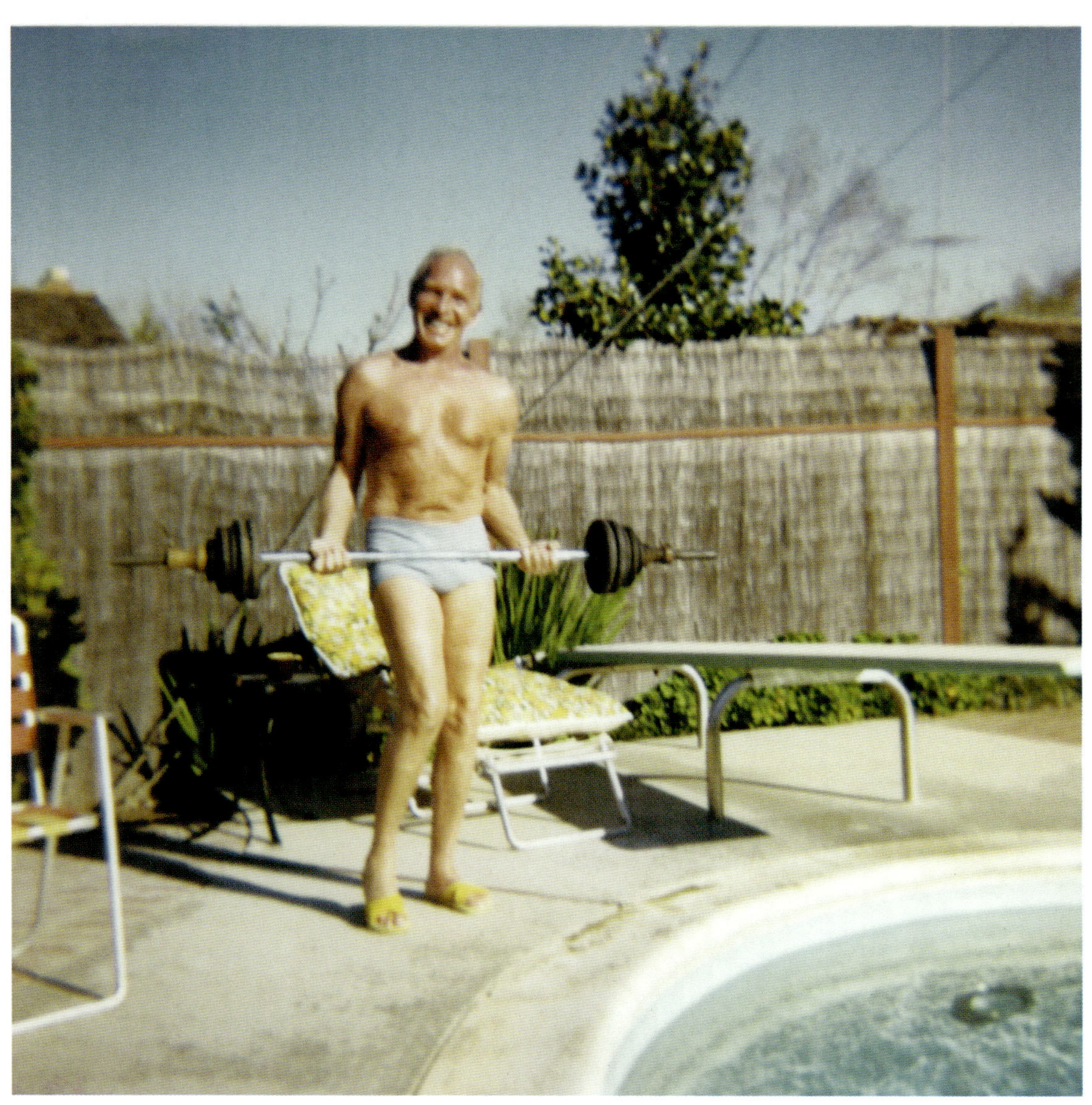

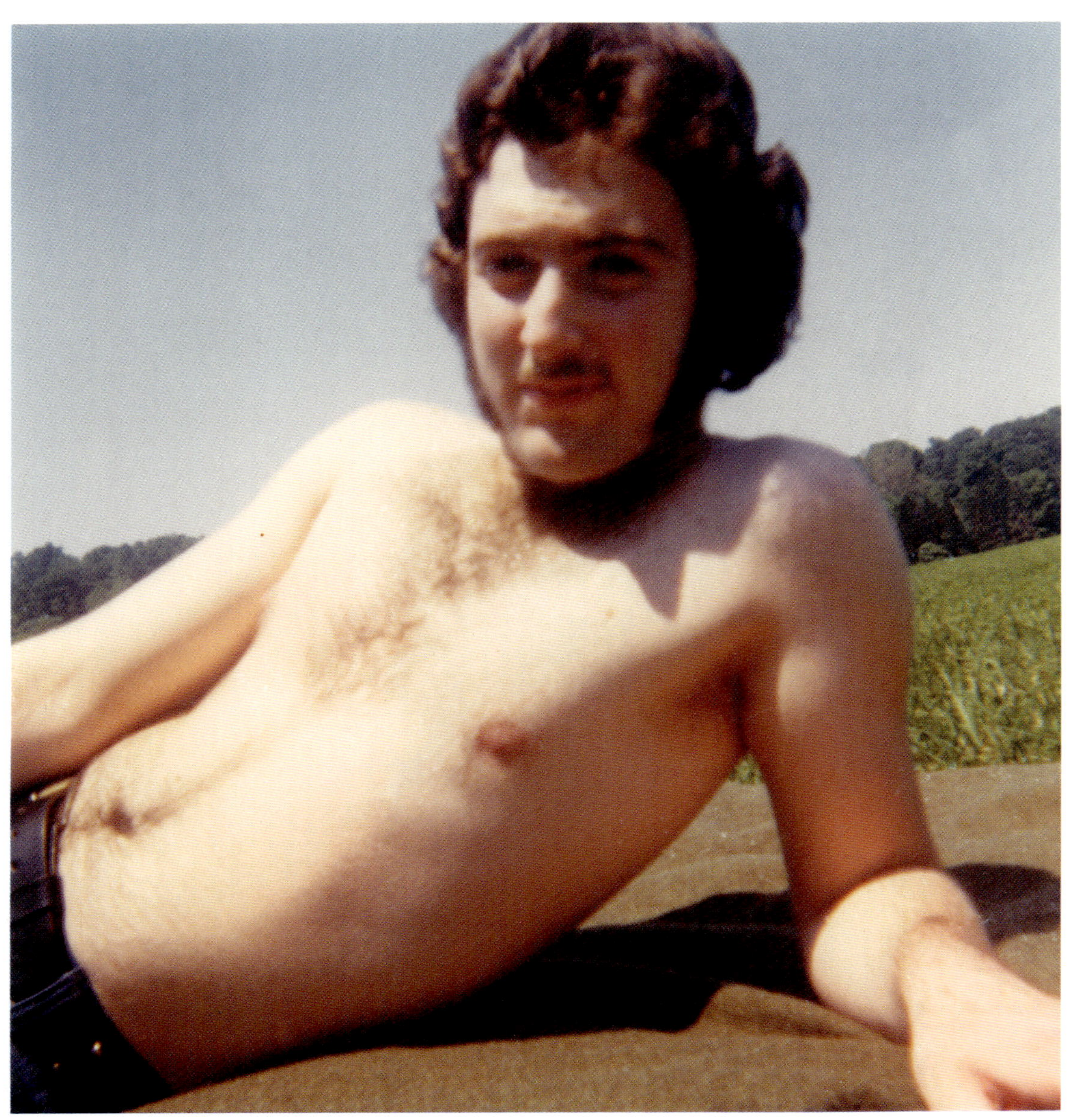

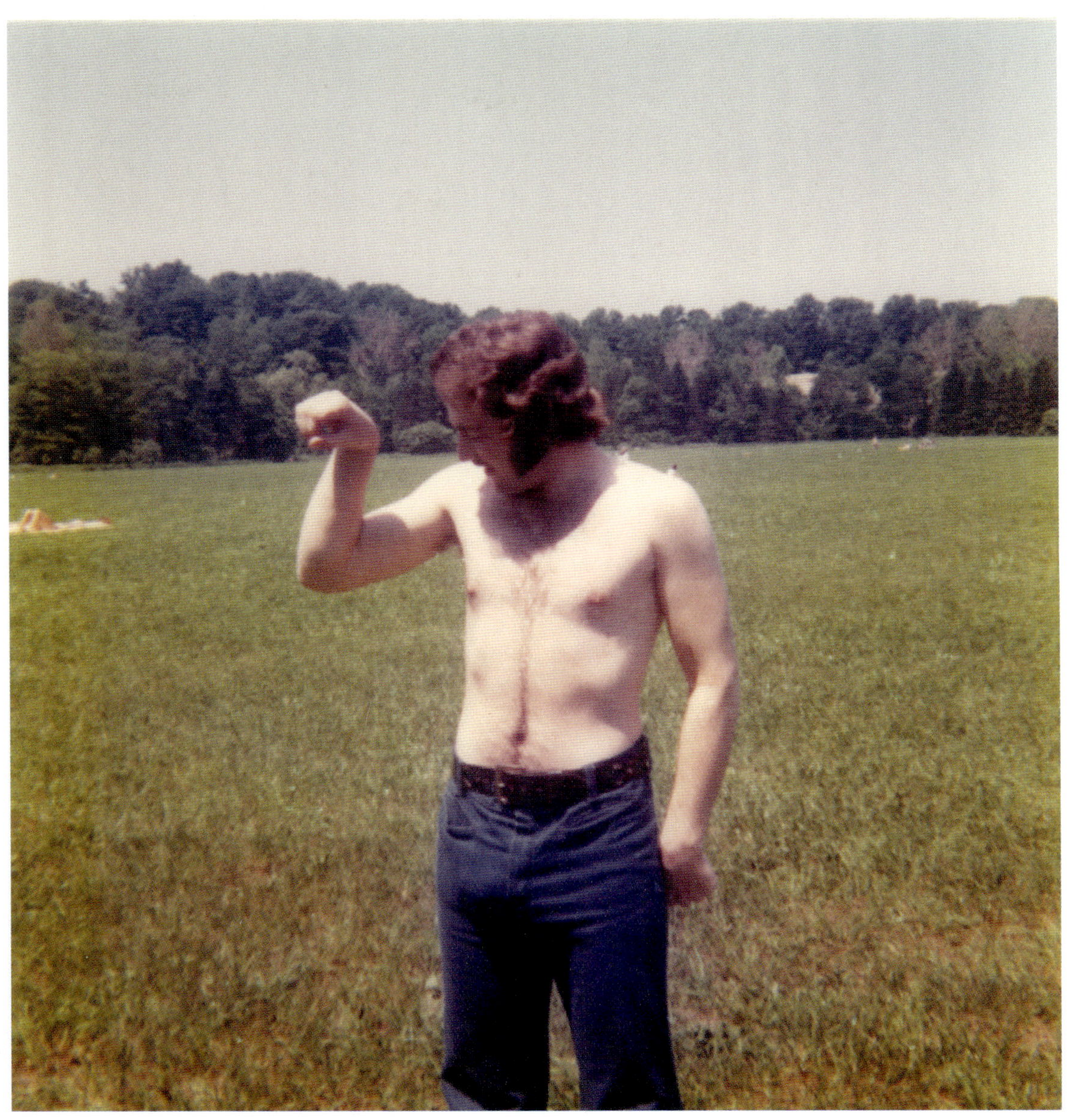

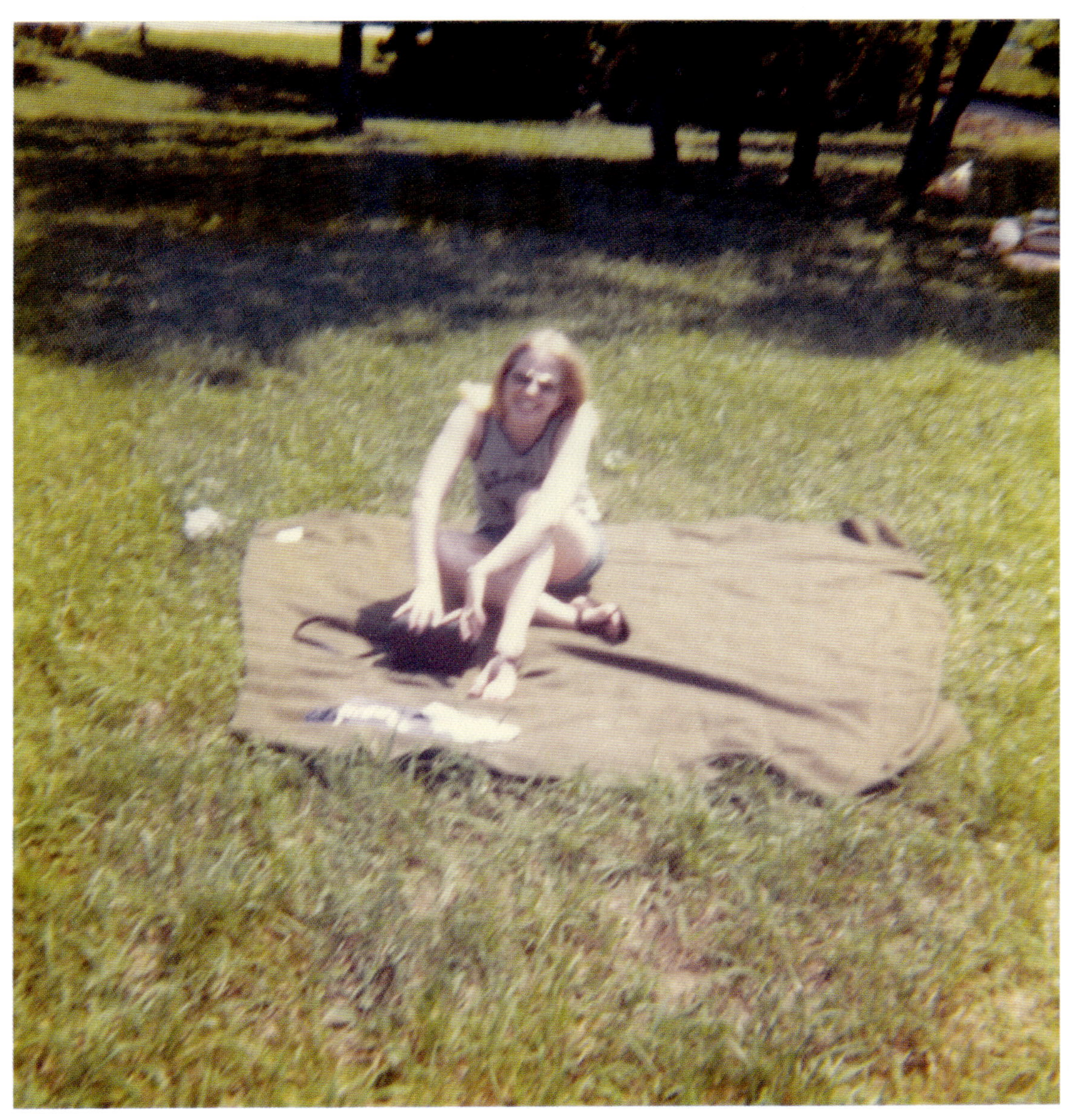

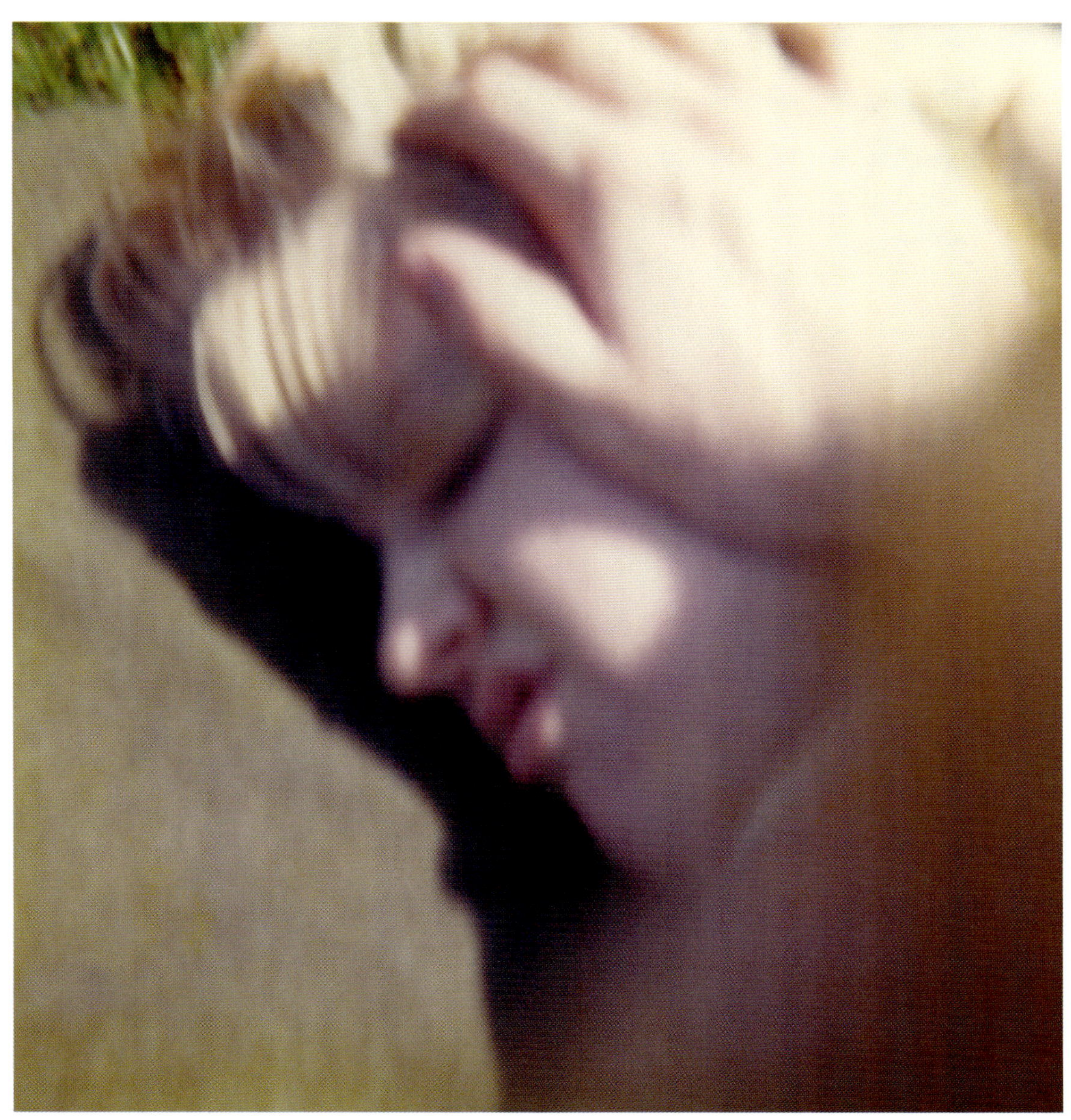

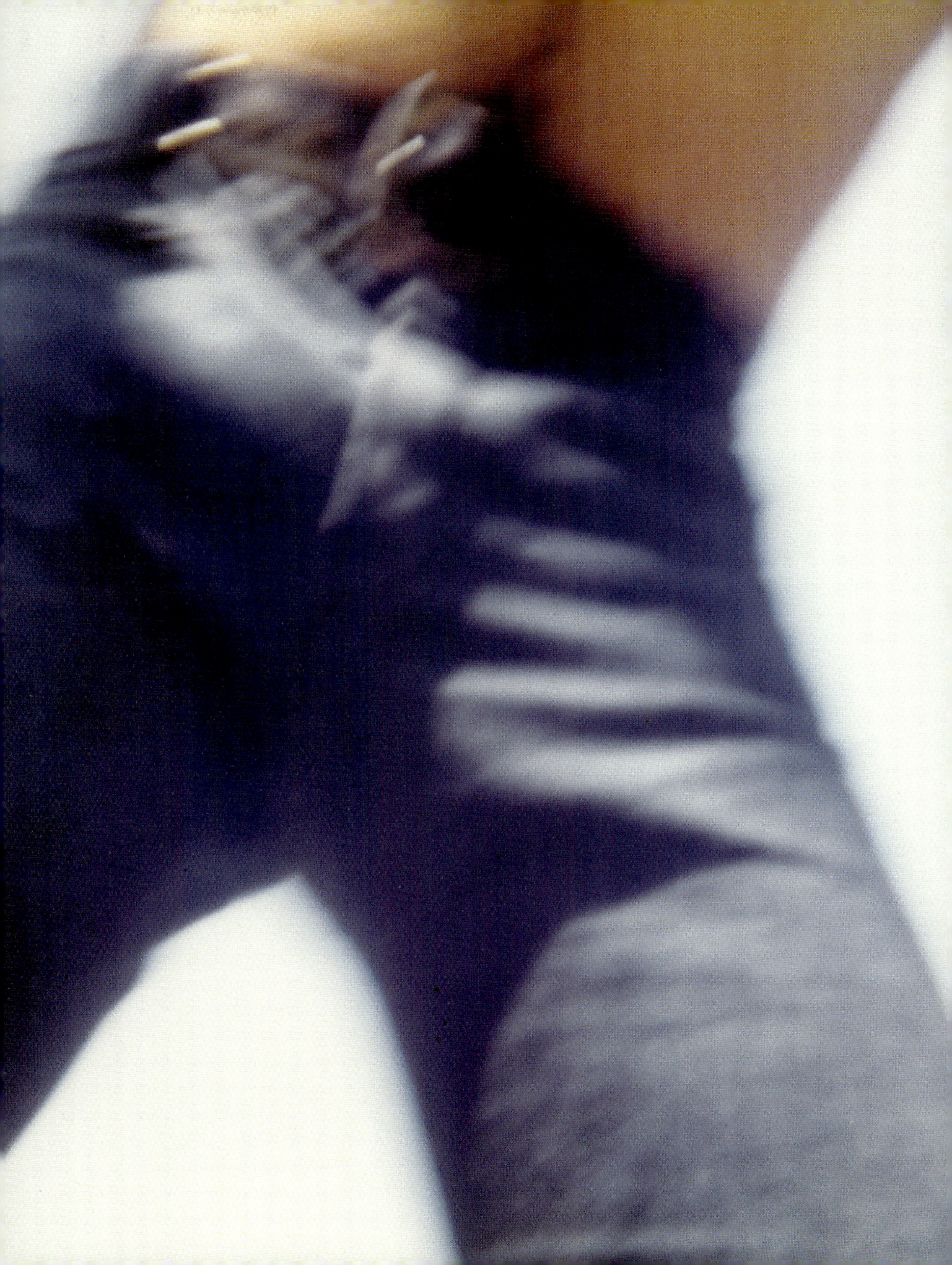

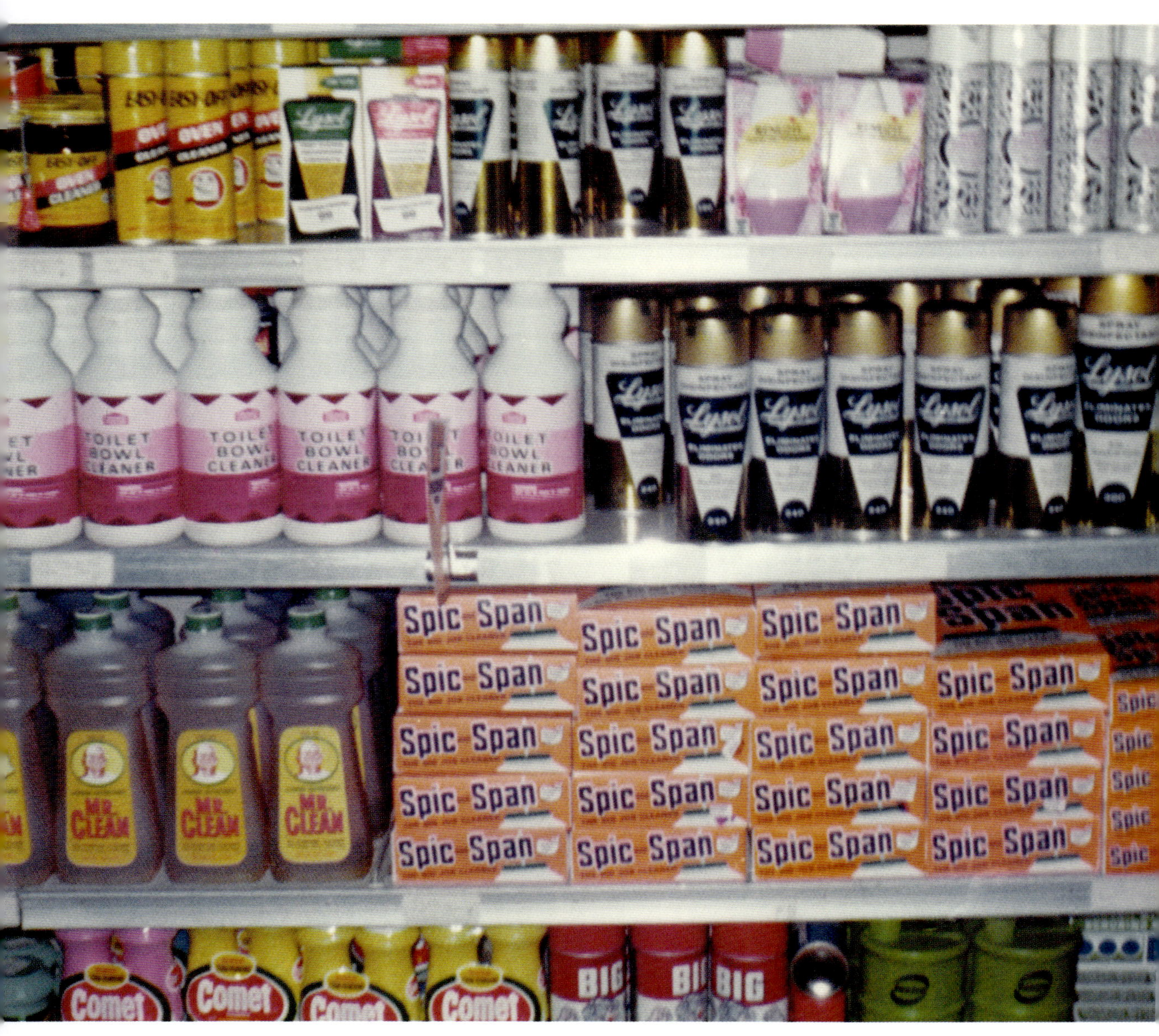
EASY-OFF
OVEN CLEANER
Lysol
TOILET BOWL CLEANER
Lysol
MR. CLEAN
Spic Span
Comet
BIG

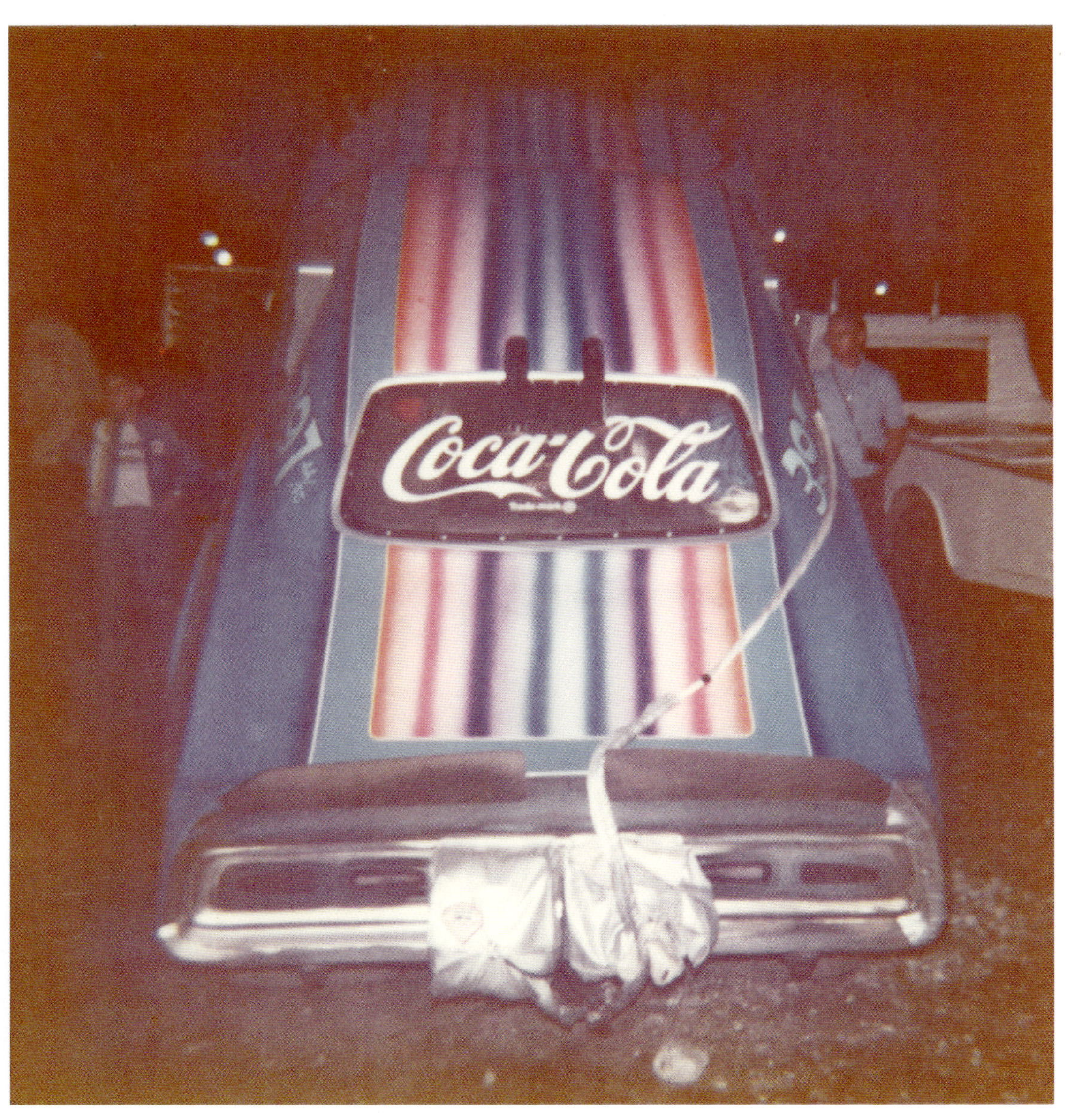
Coca-Cola

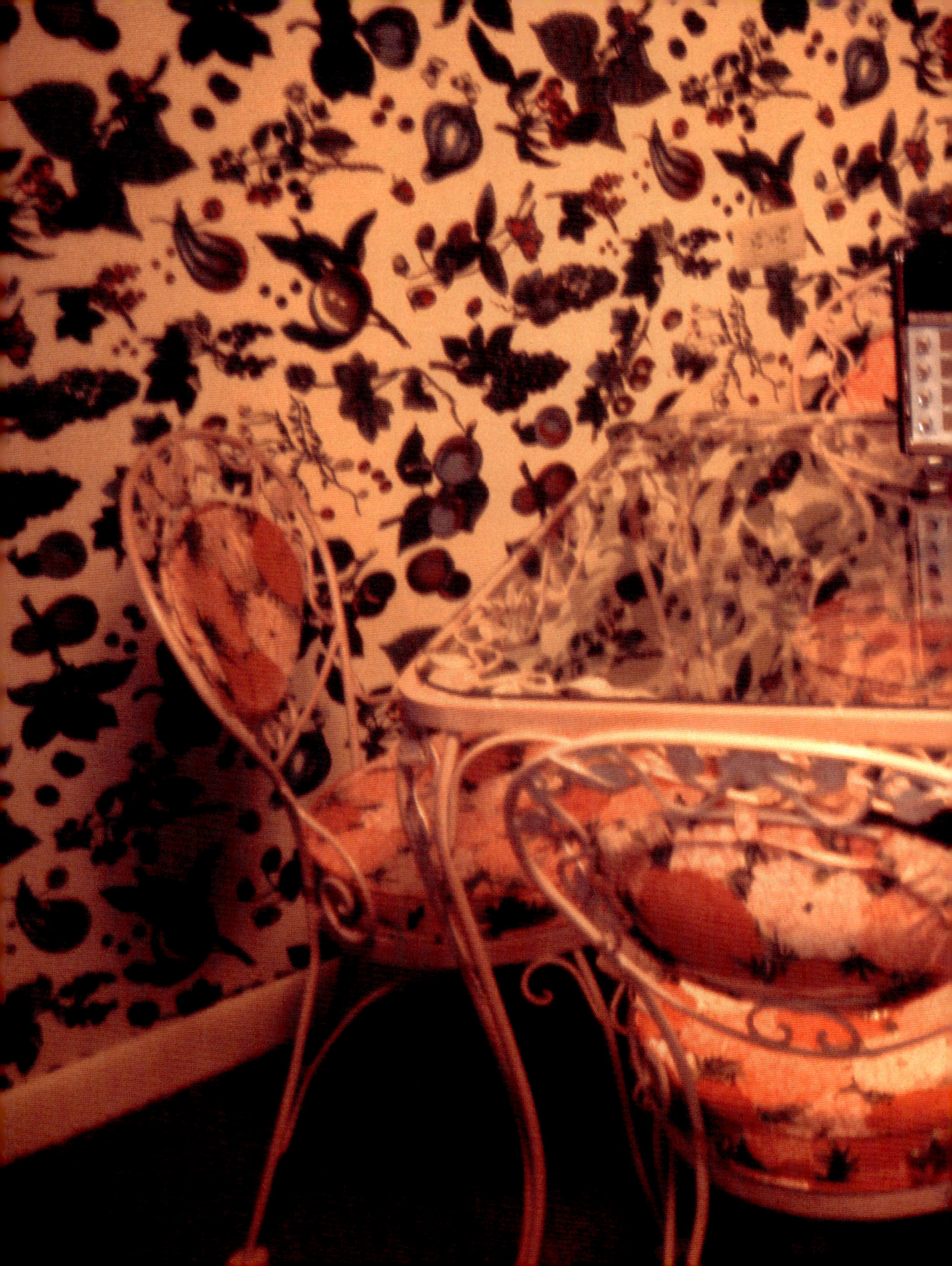

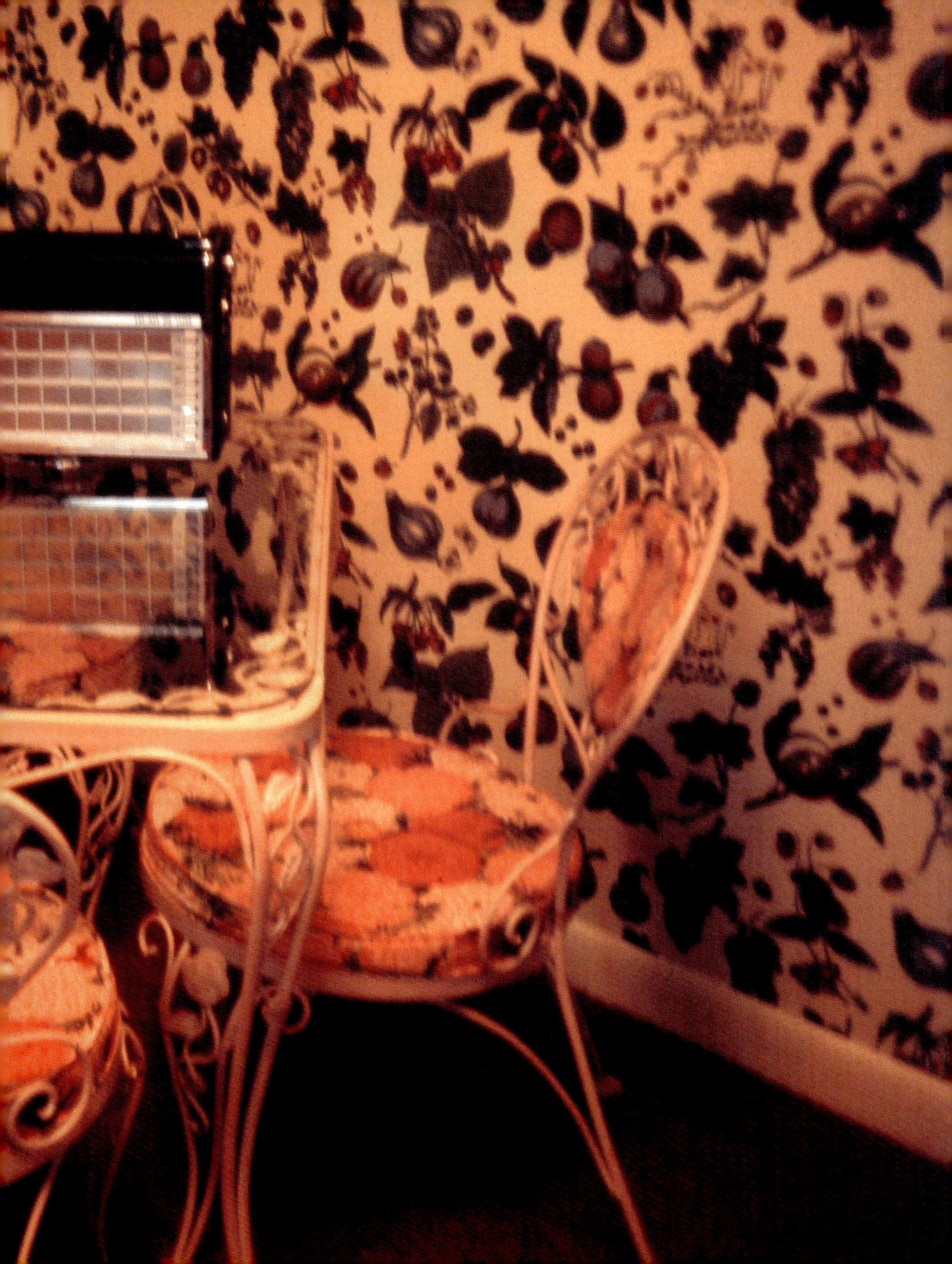

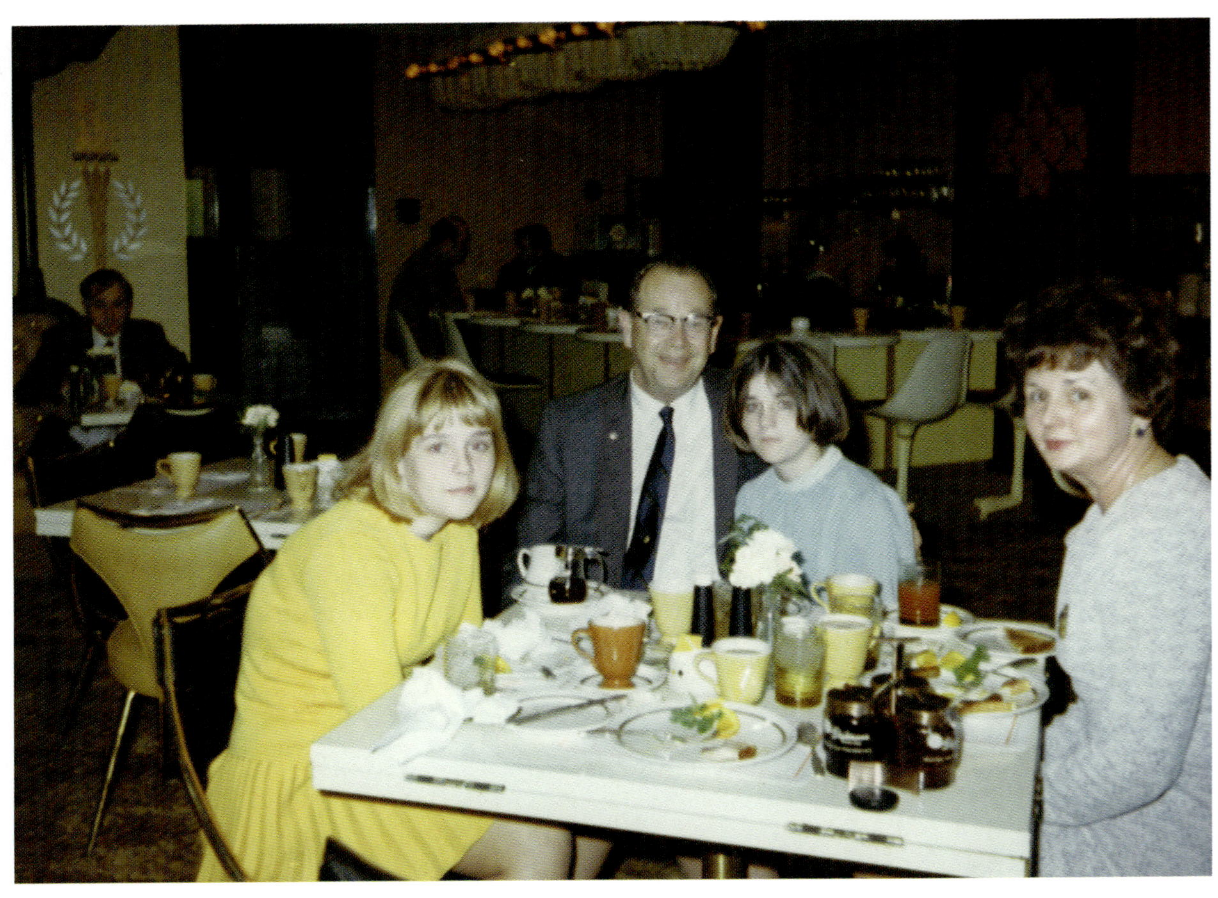

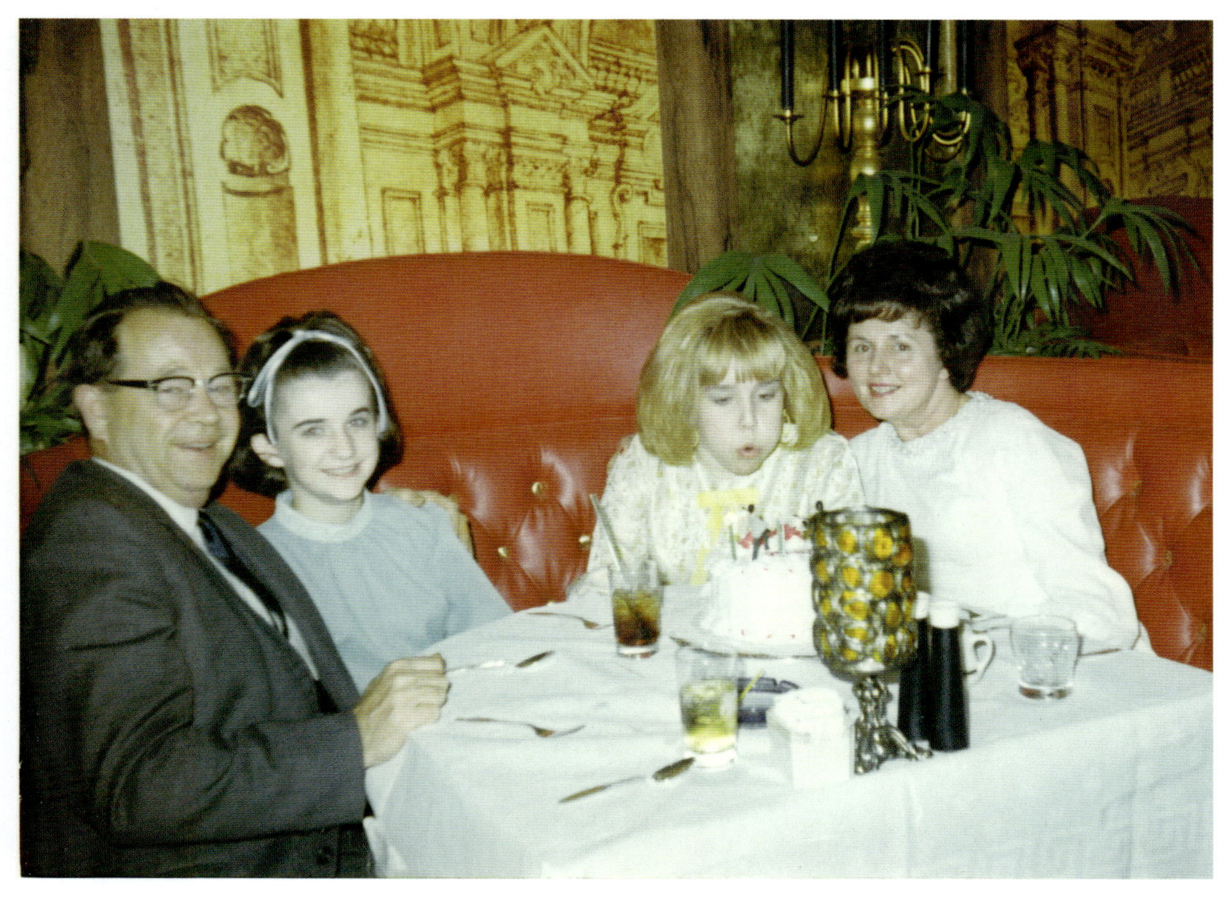

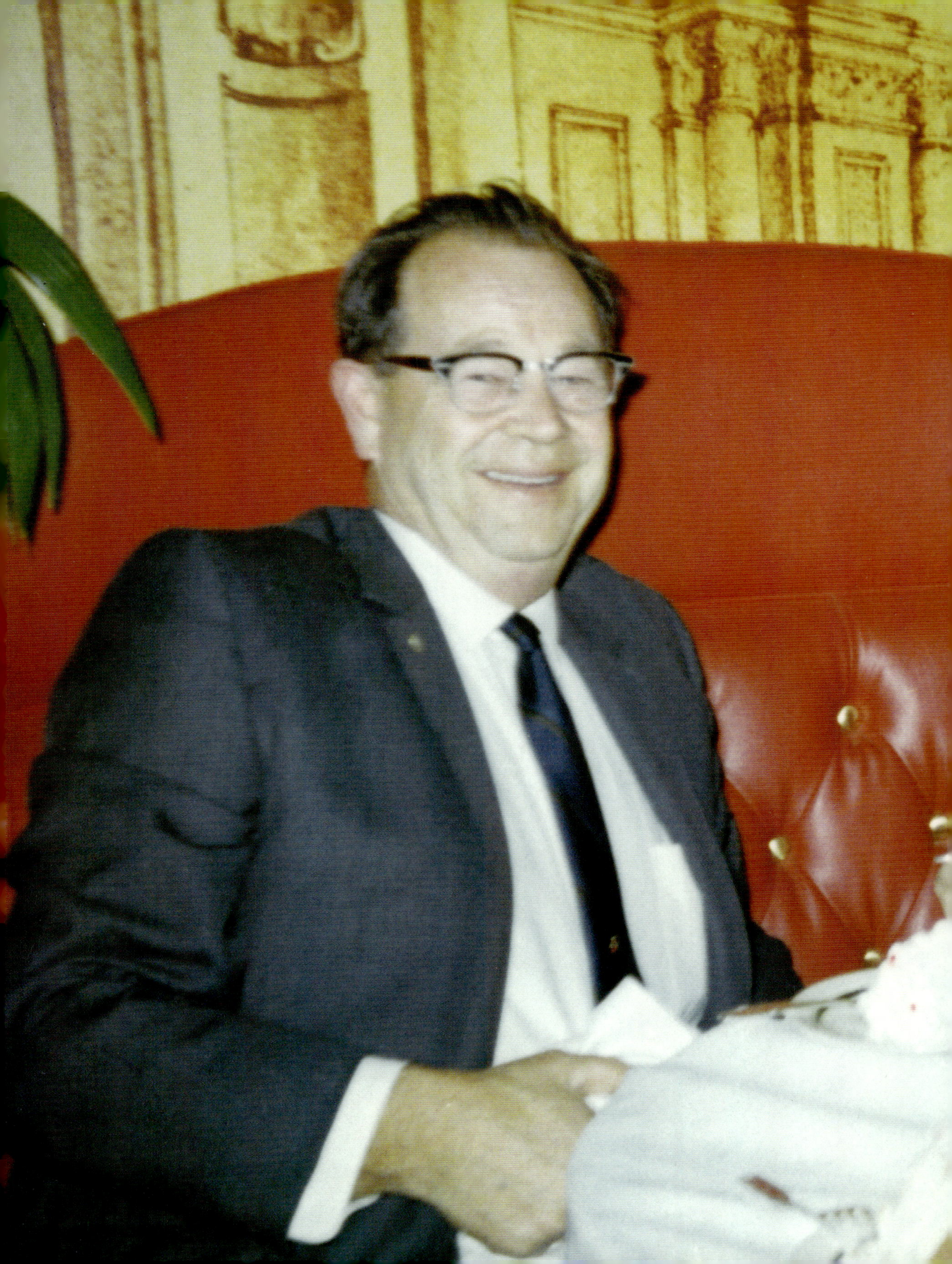

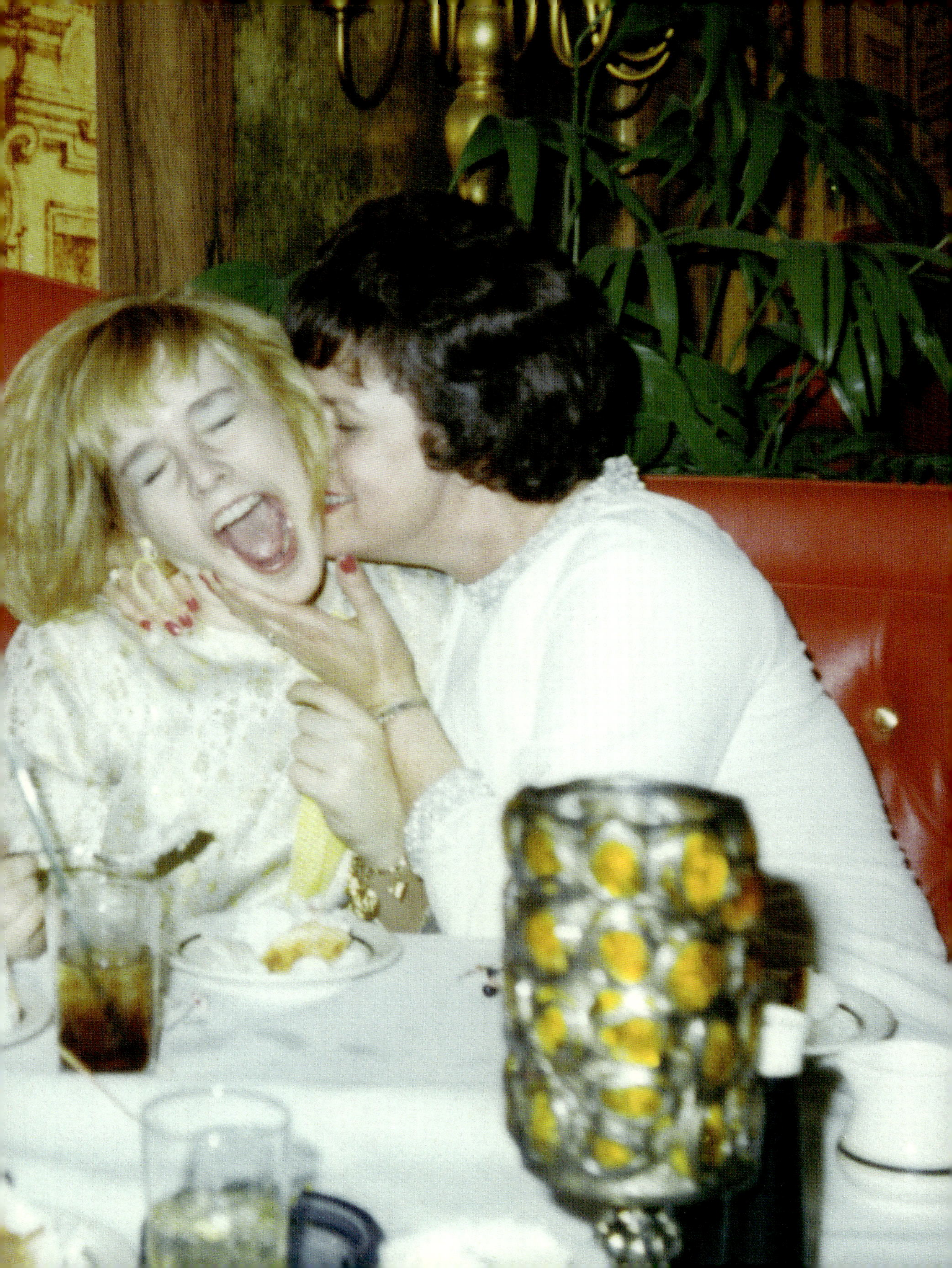

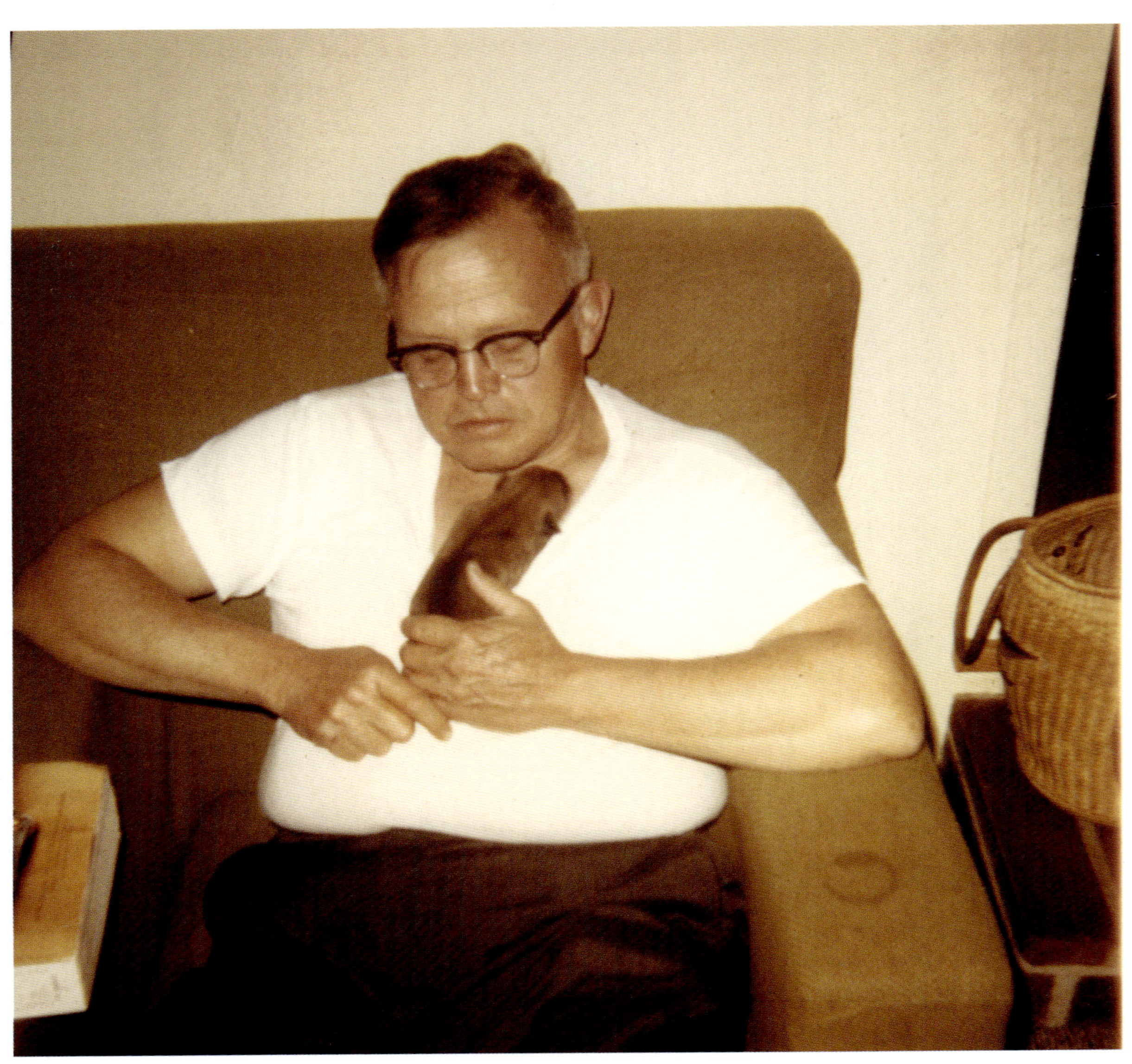

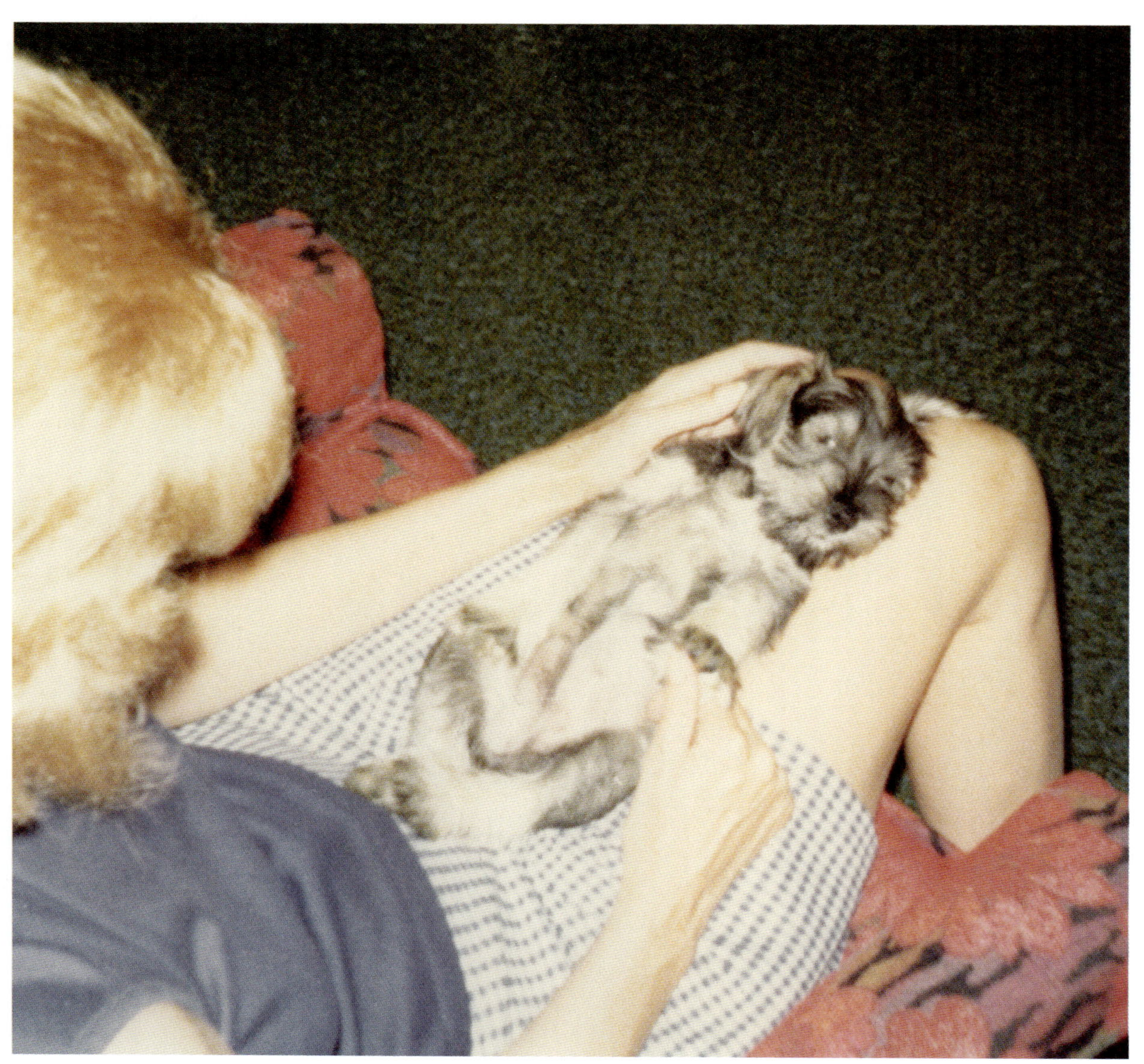

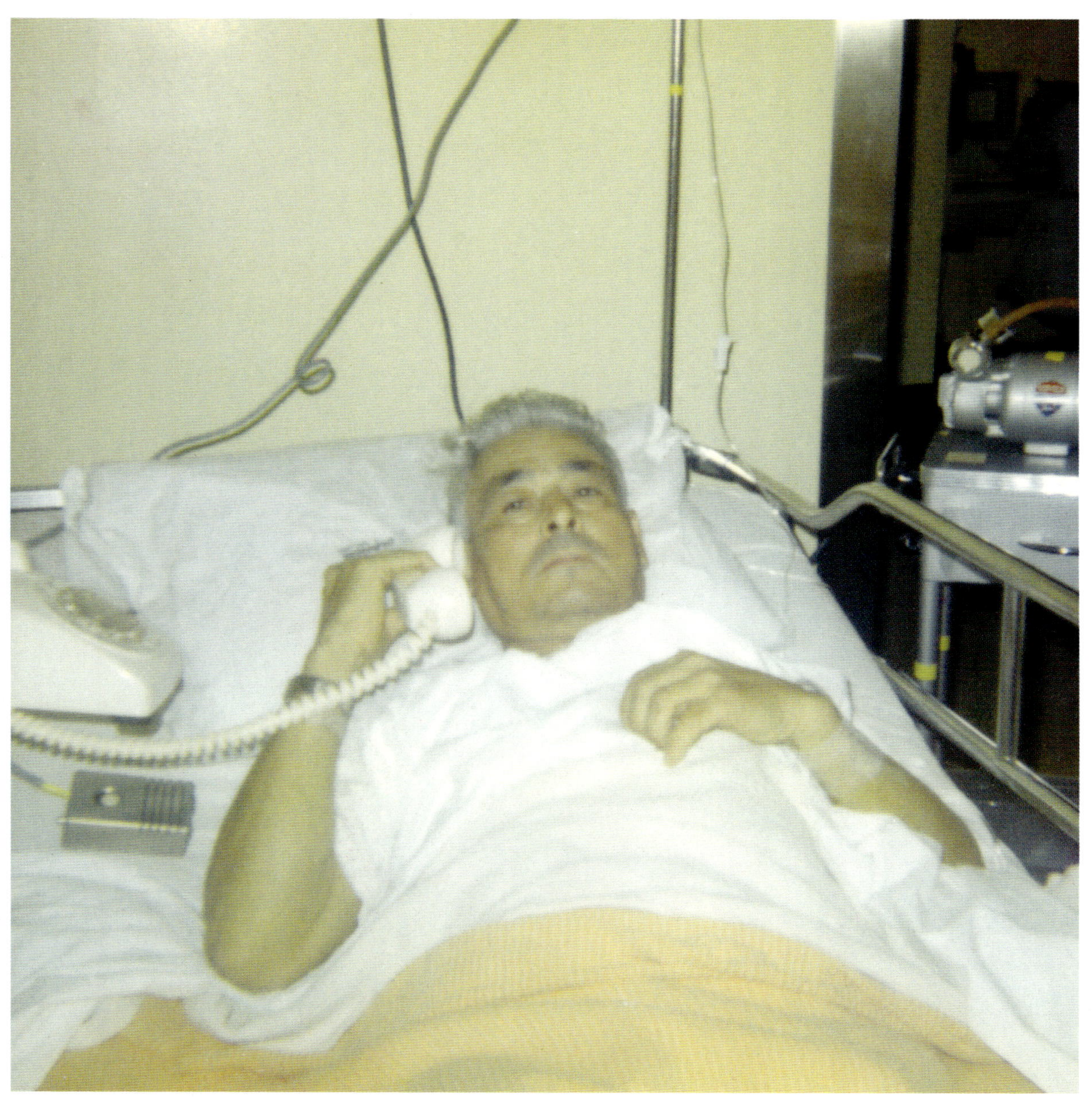

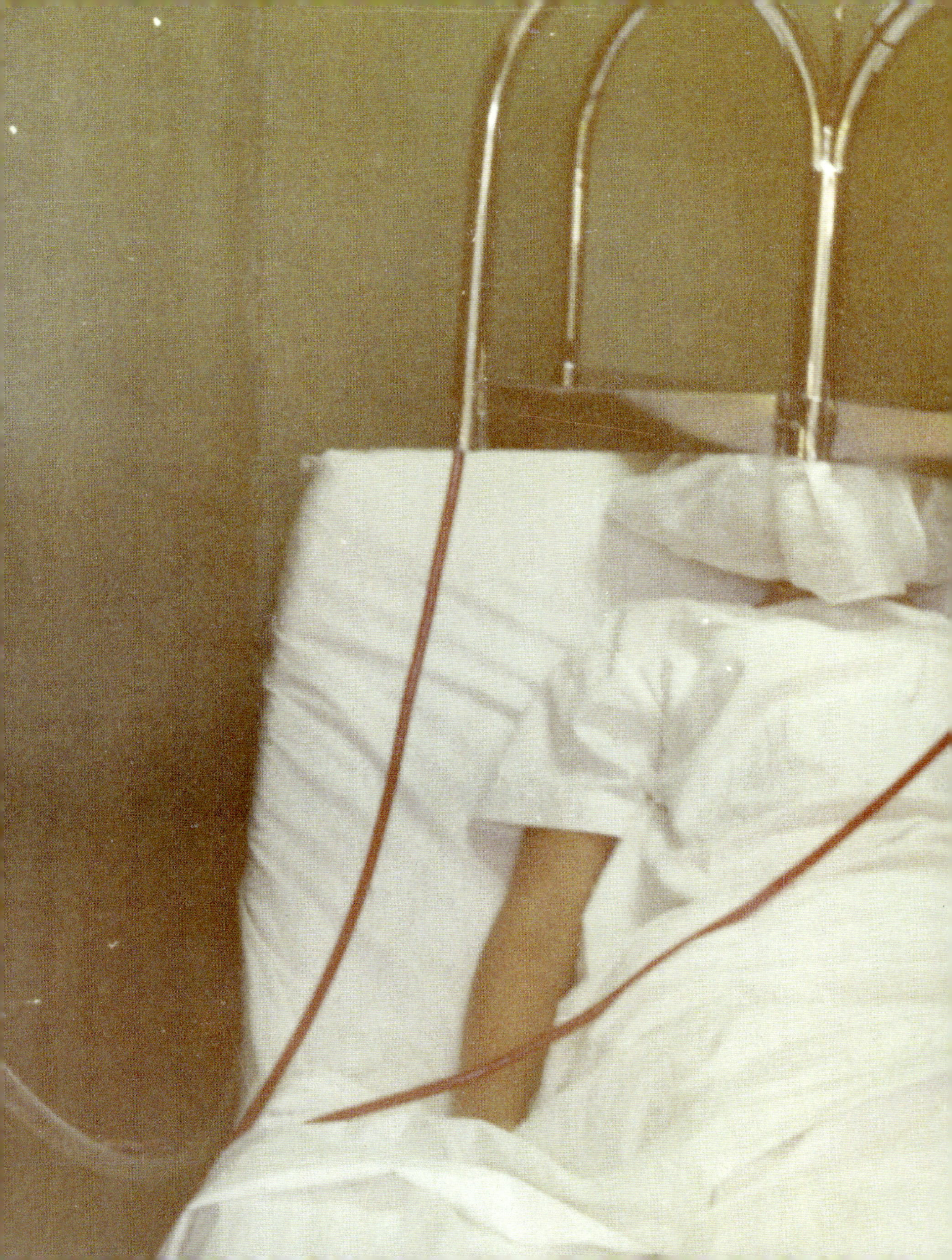

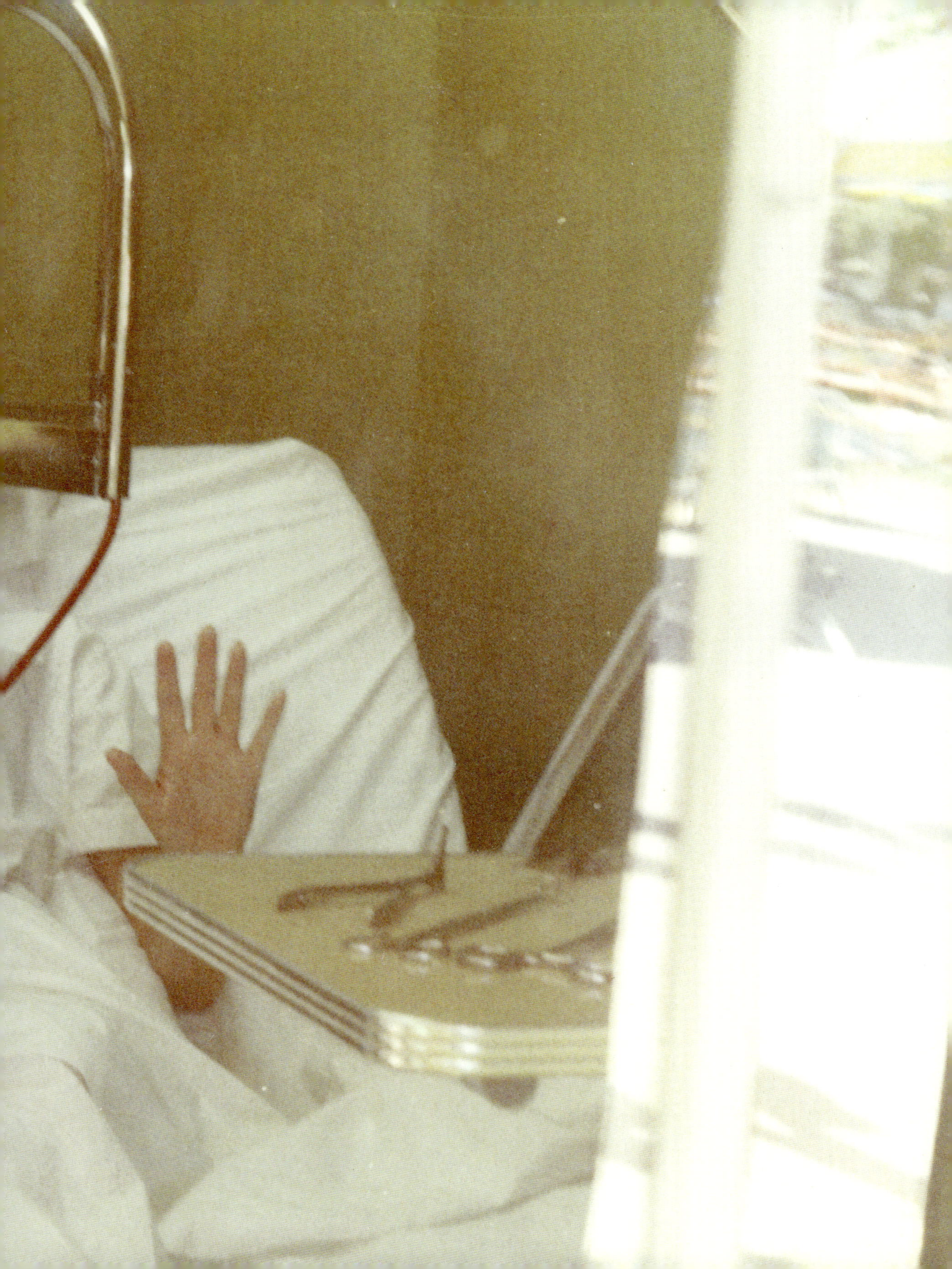

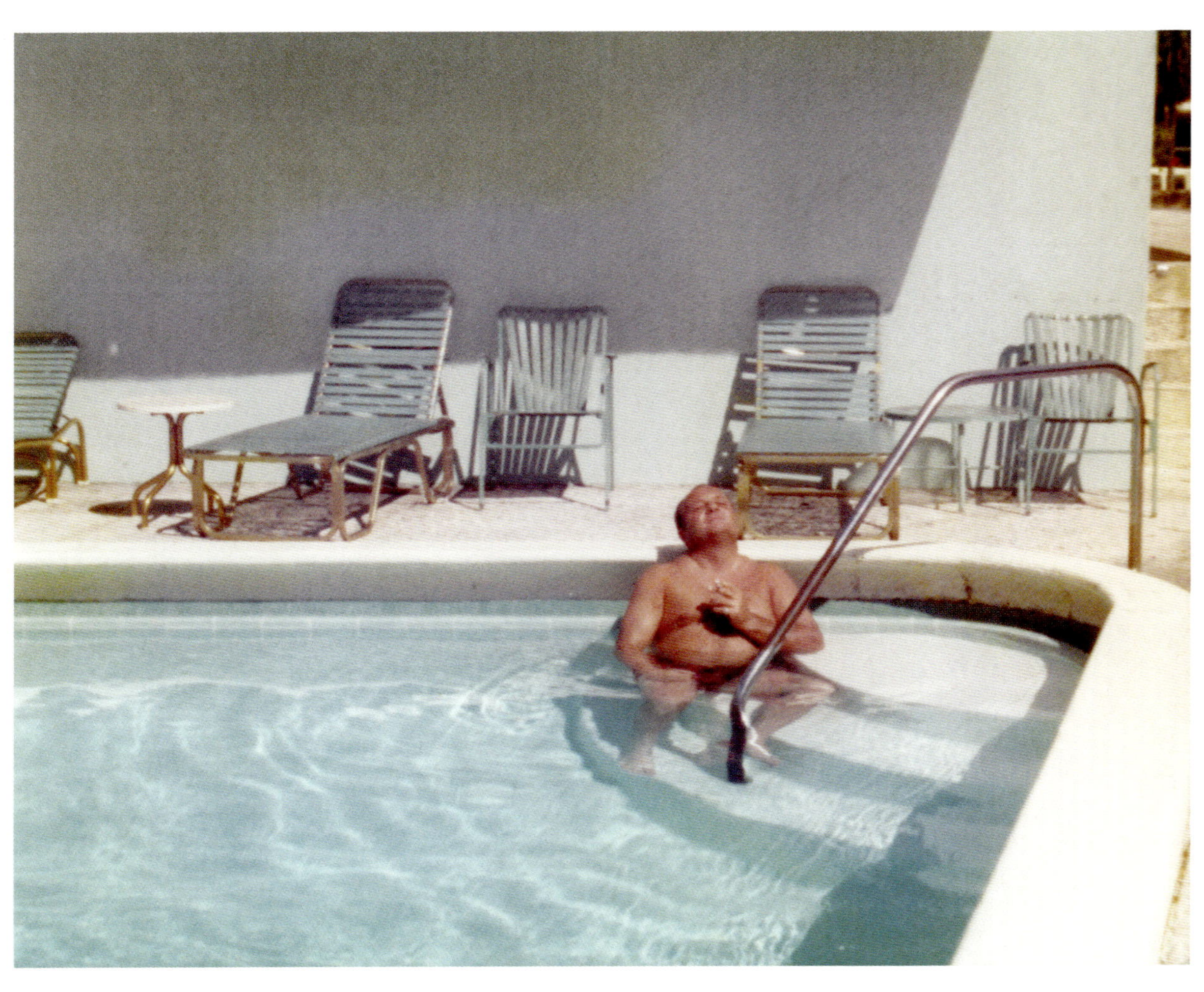

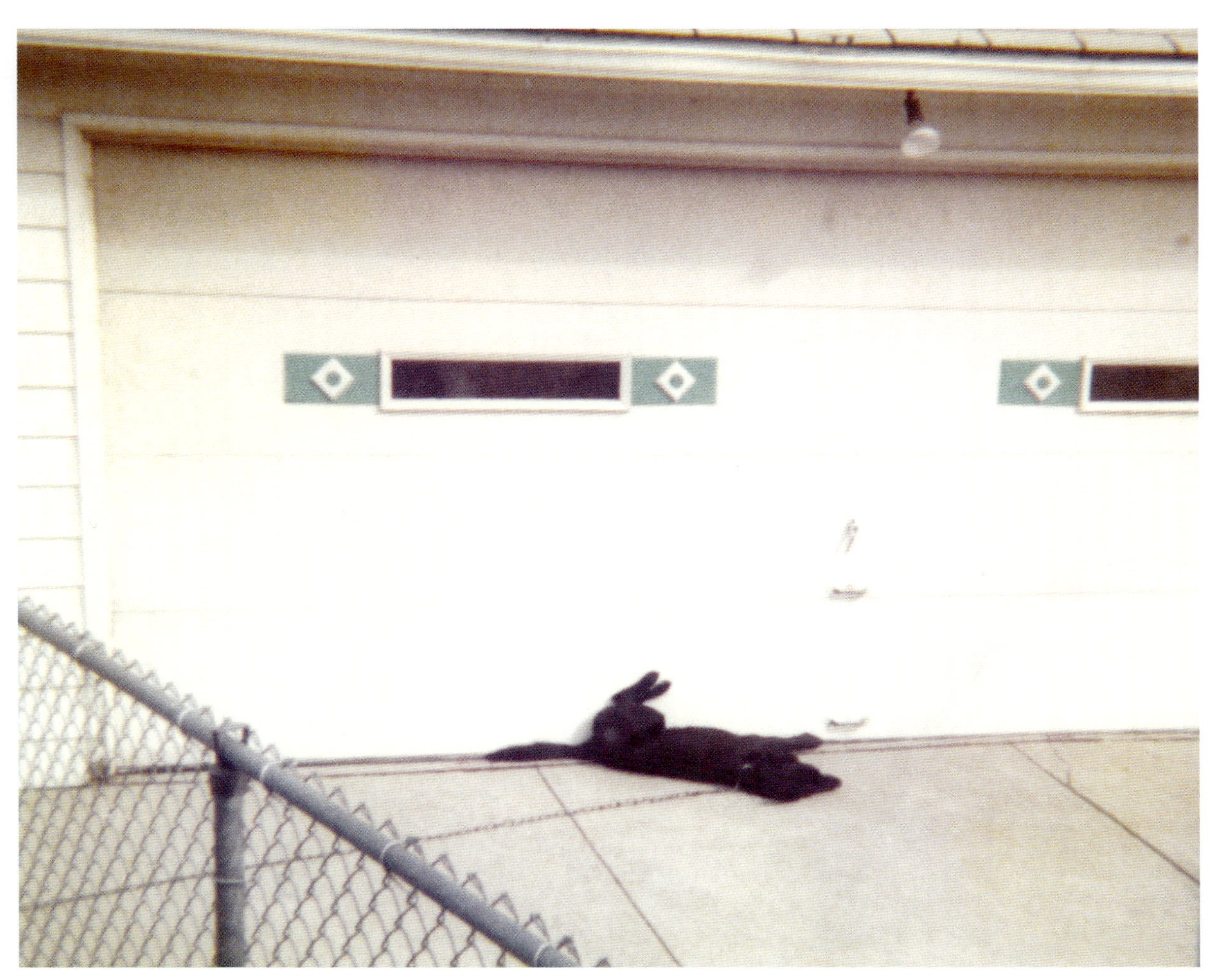

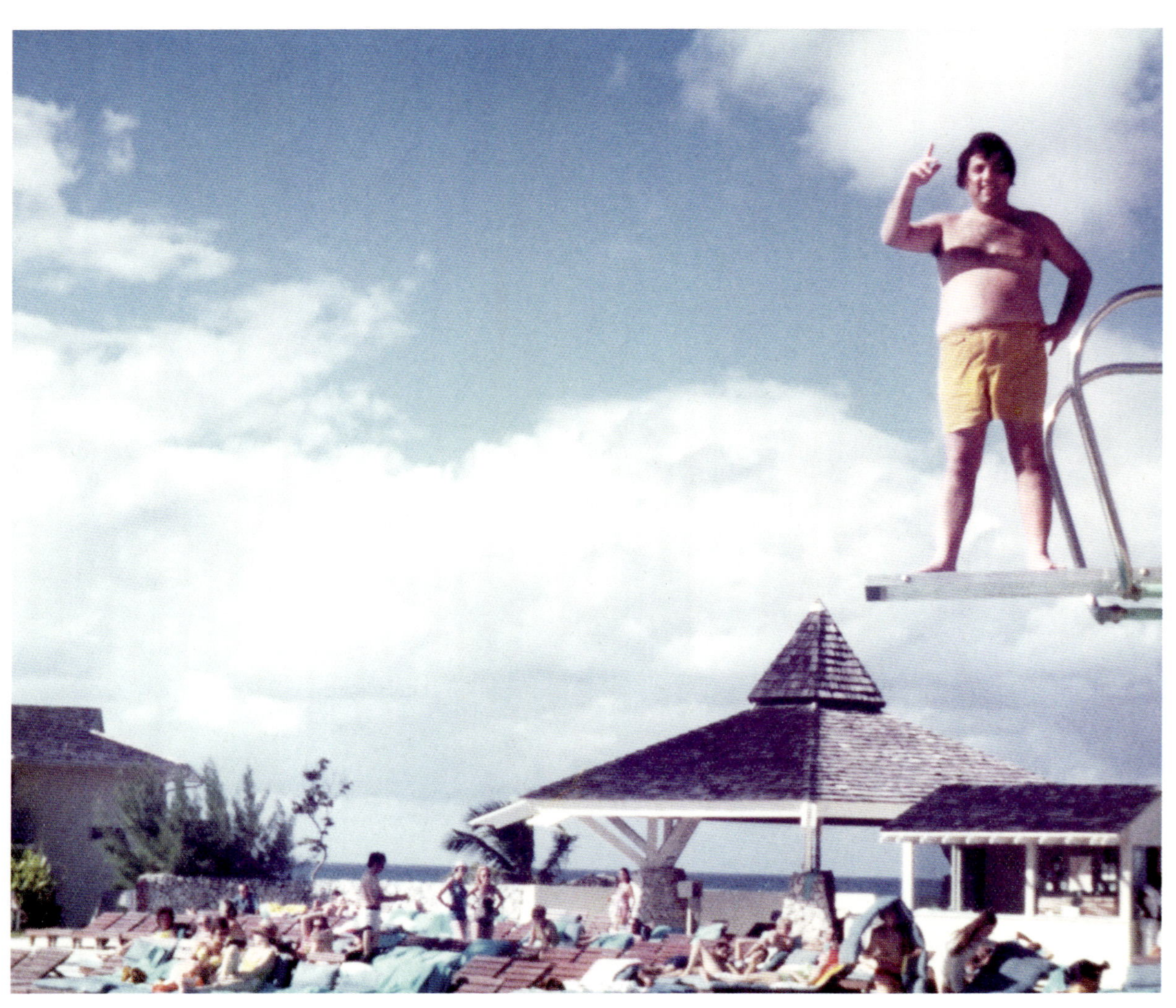

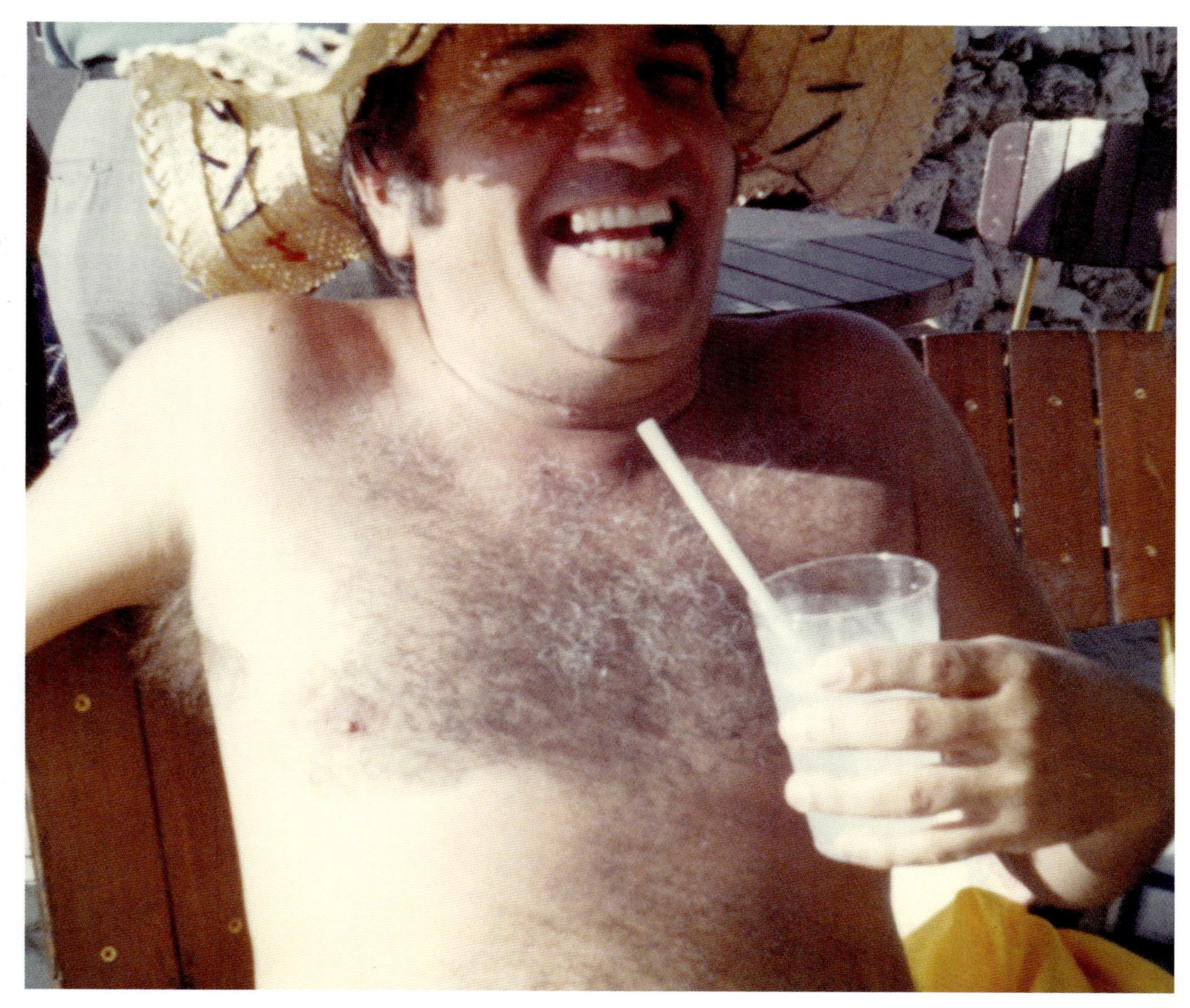

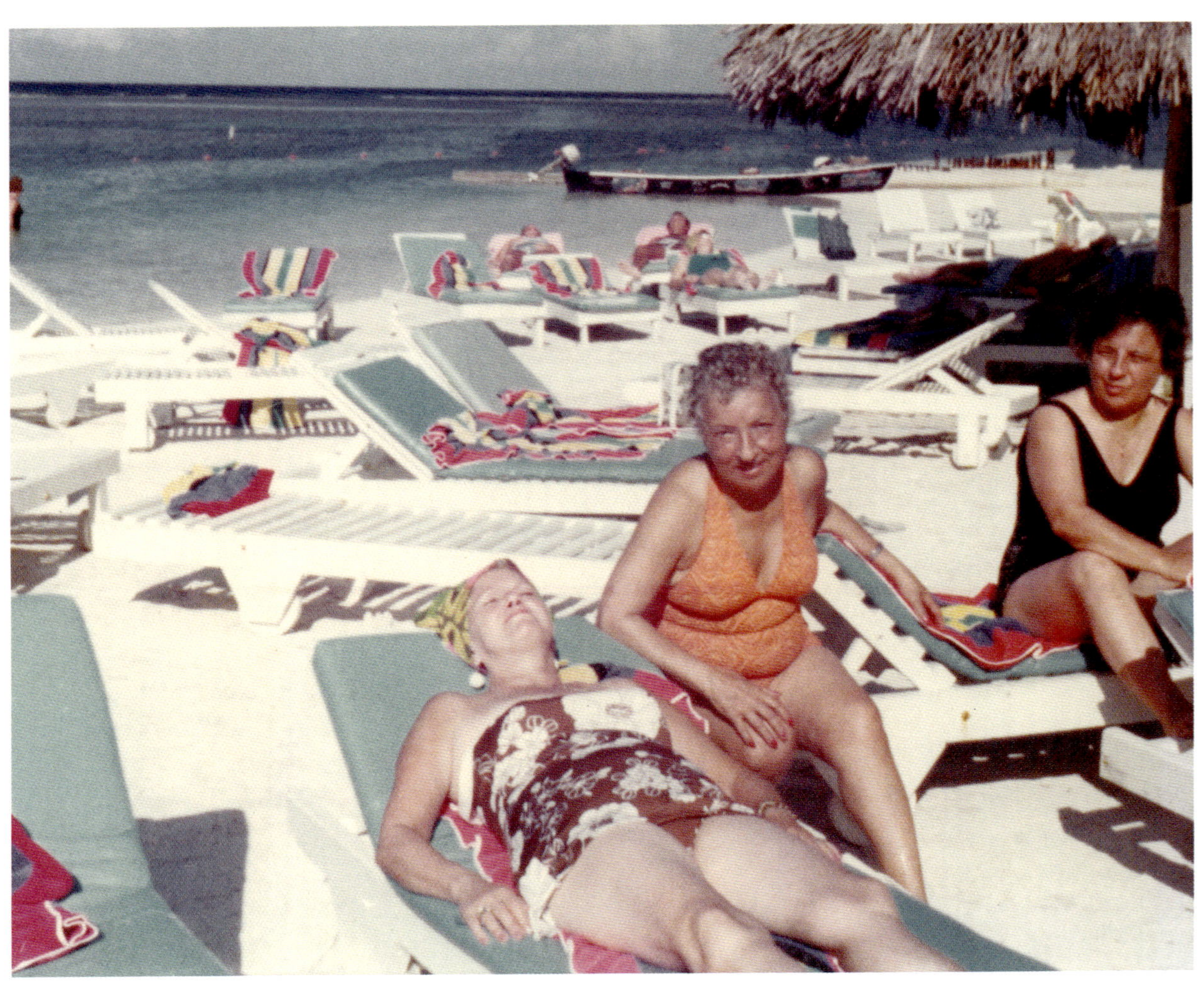

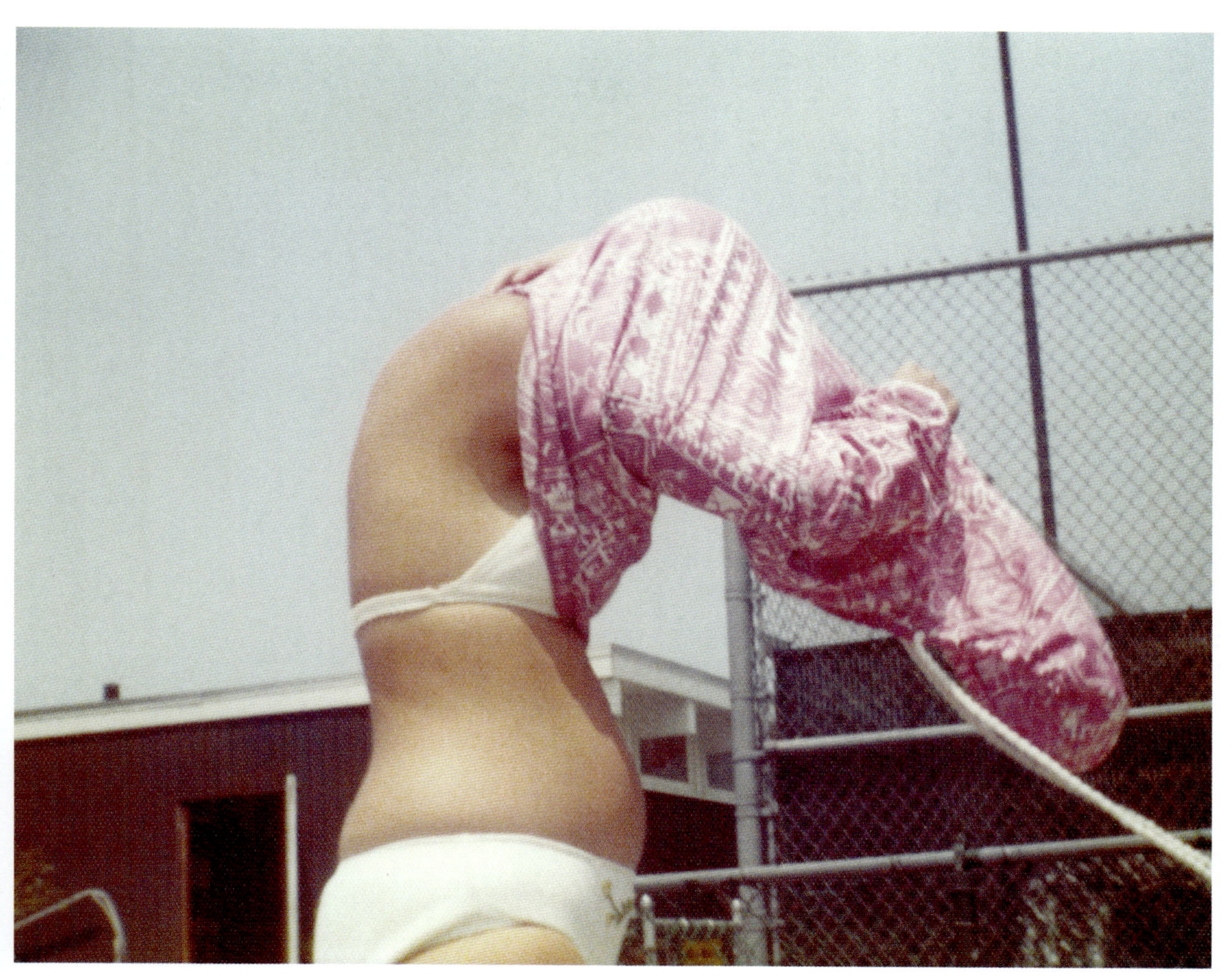

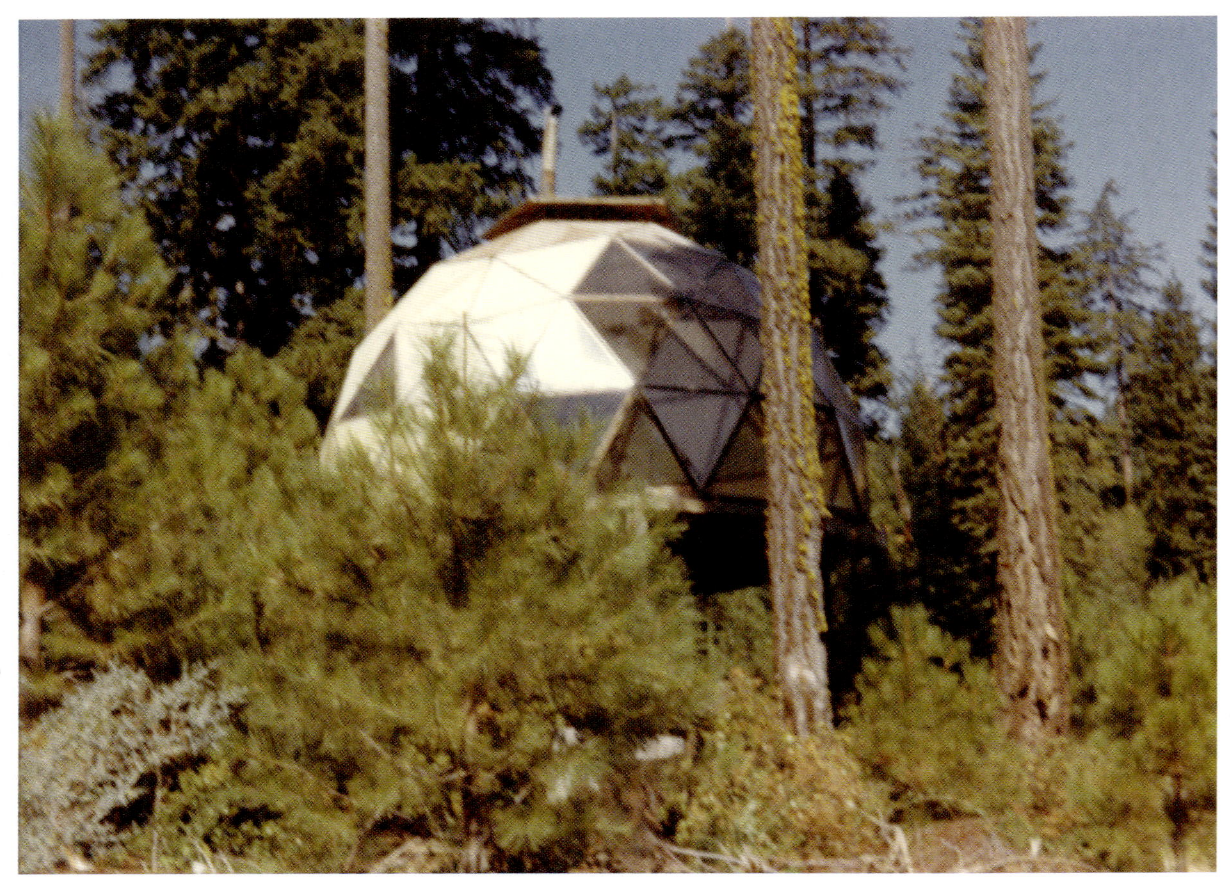

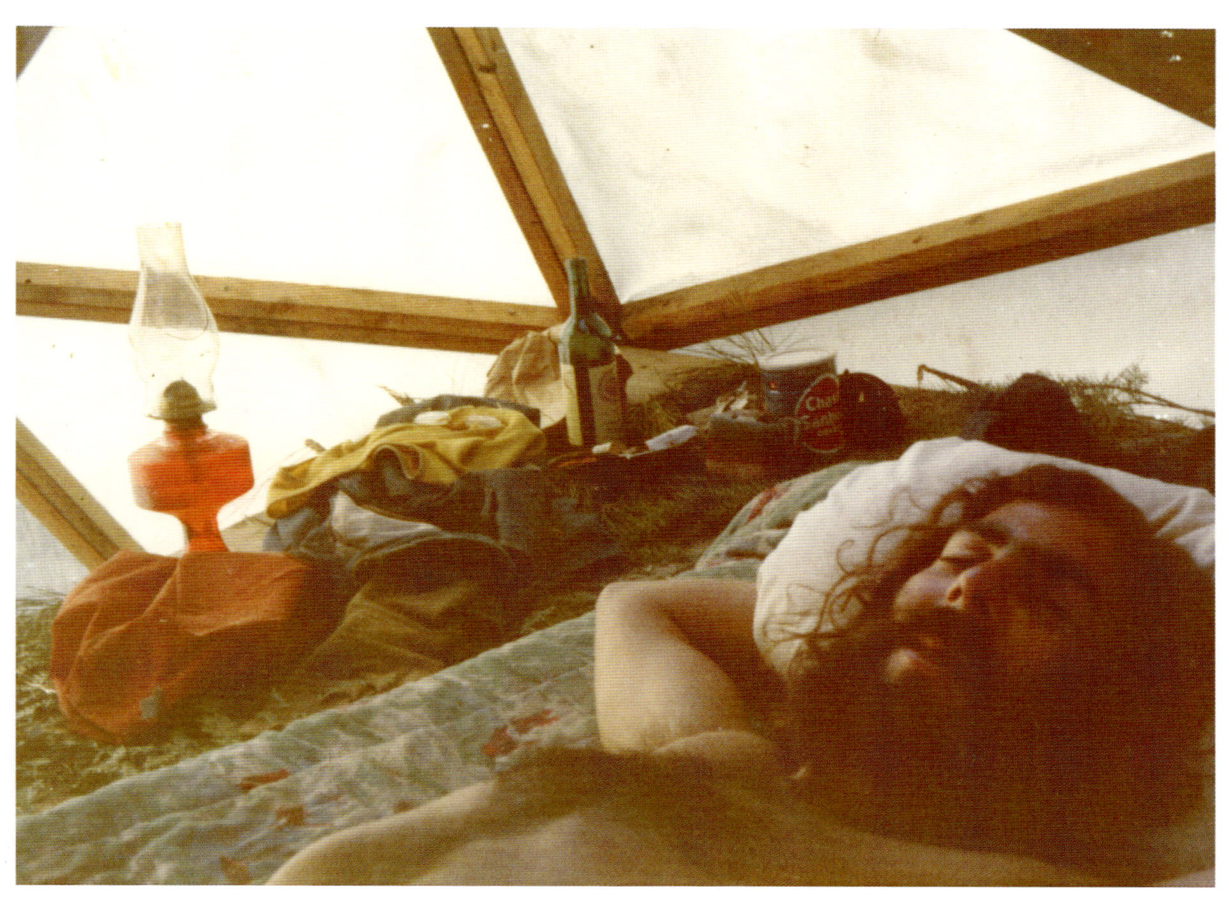

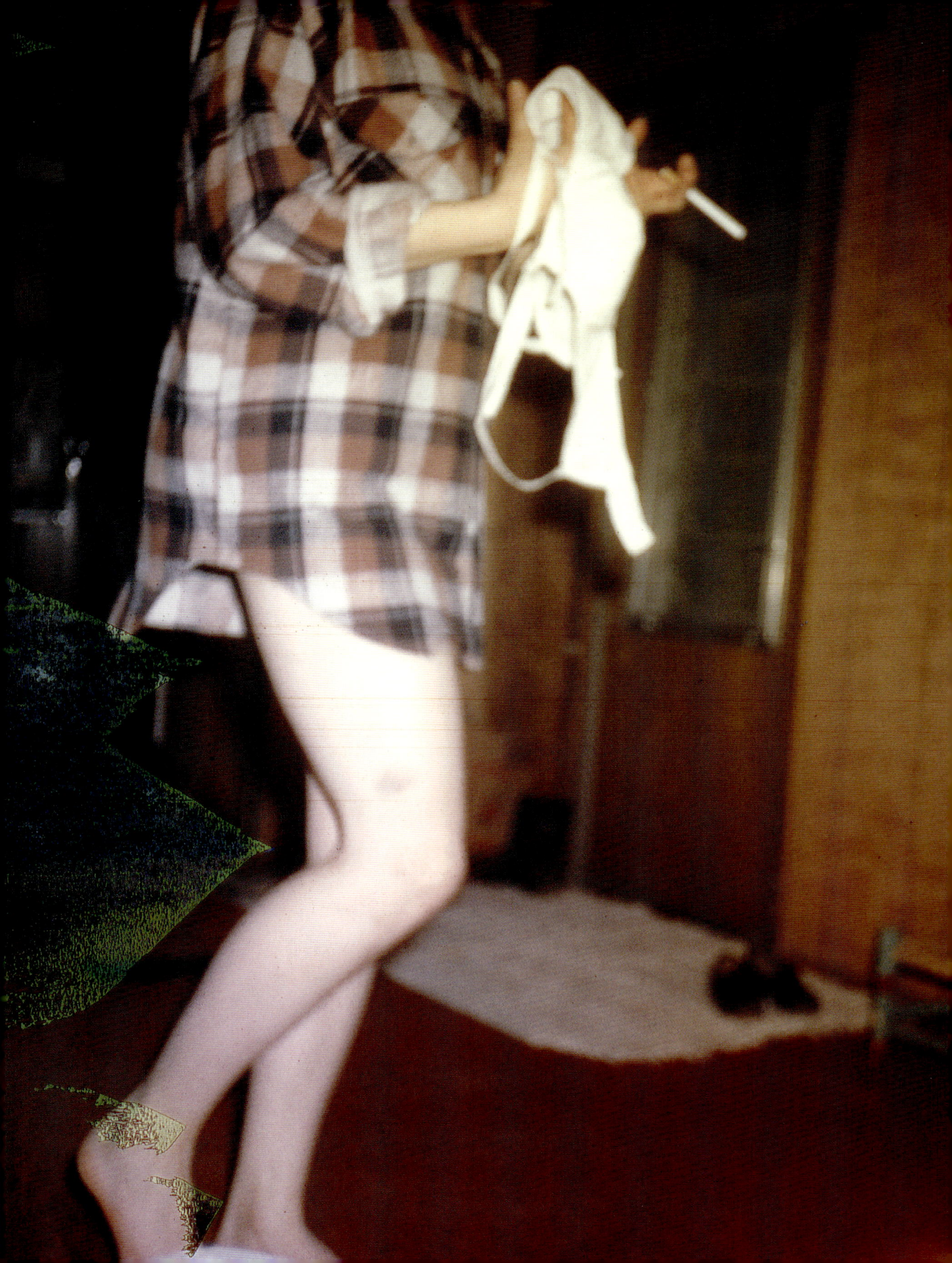

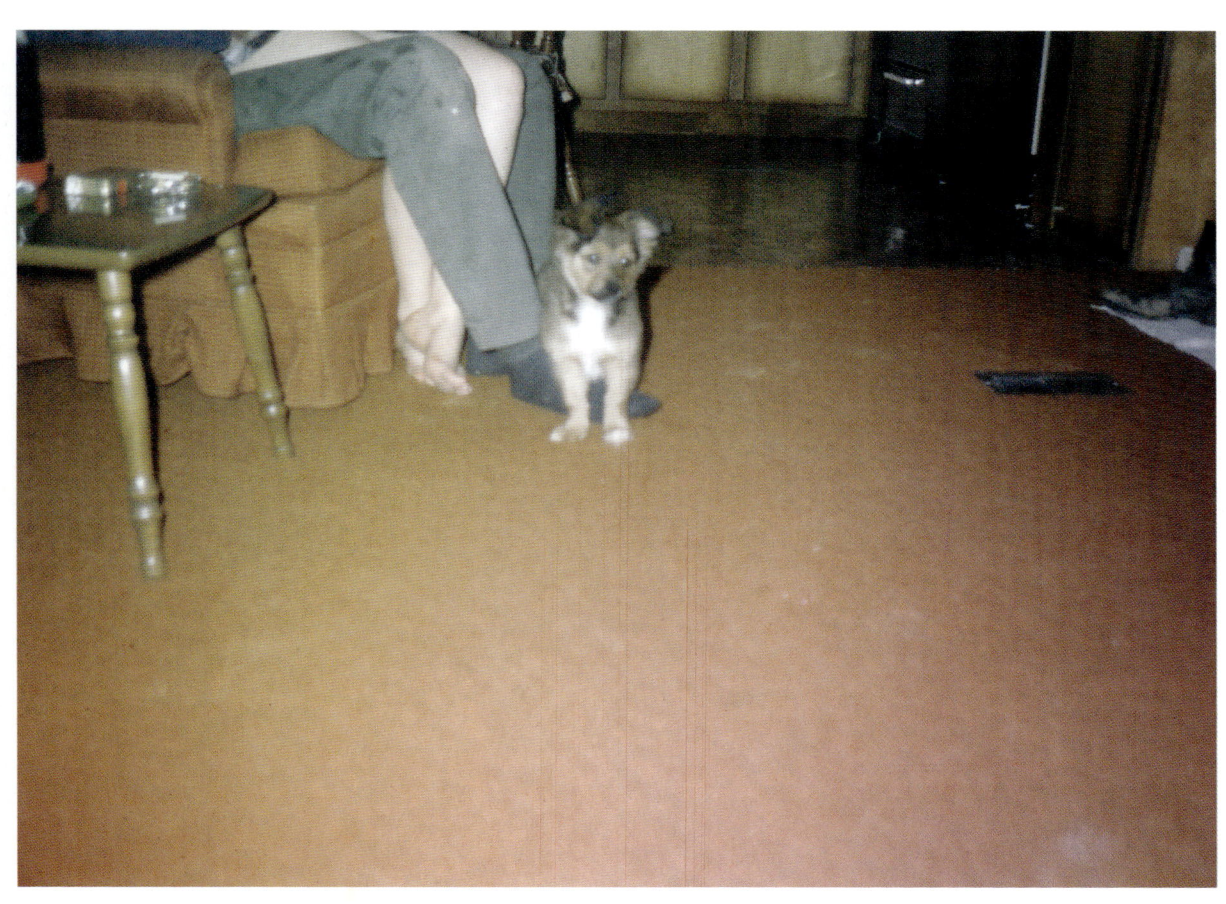

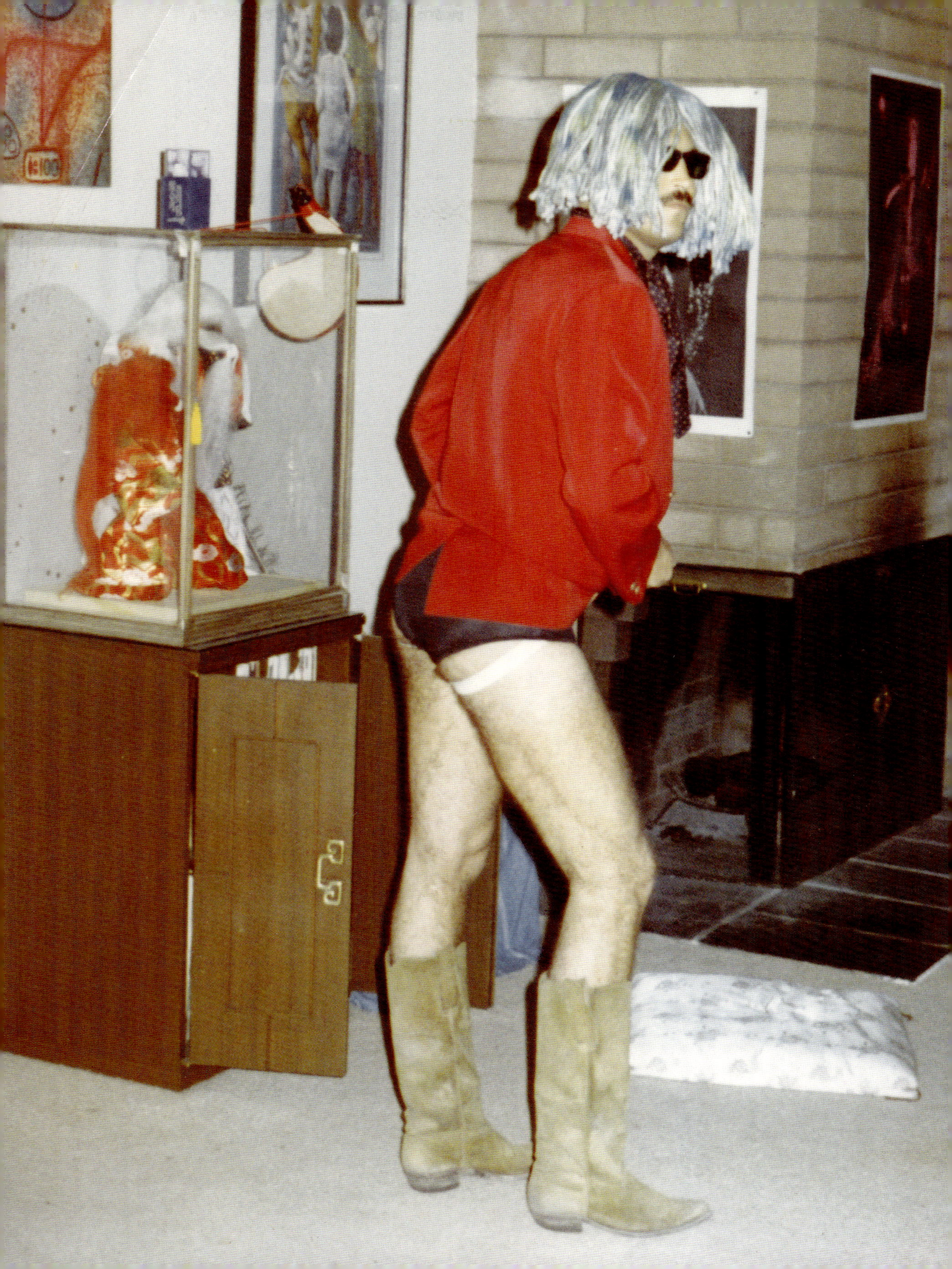

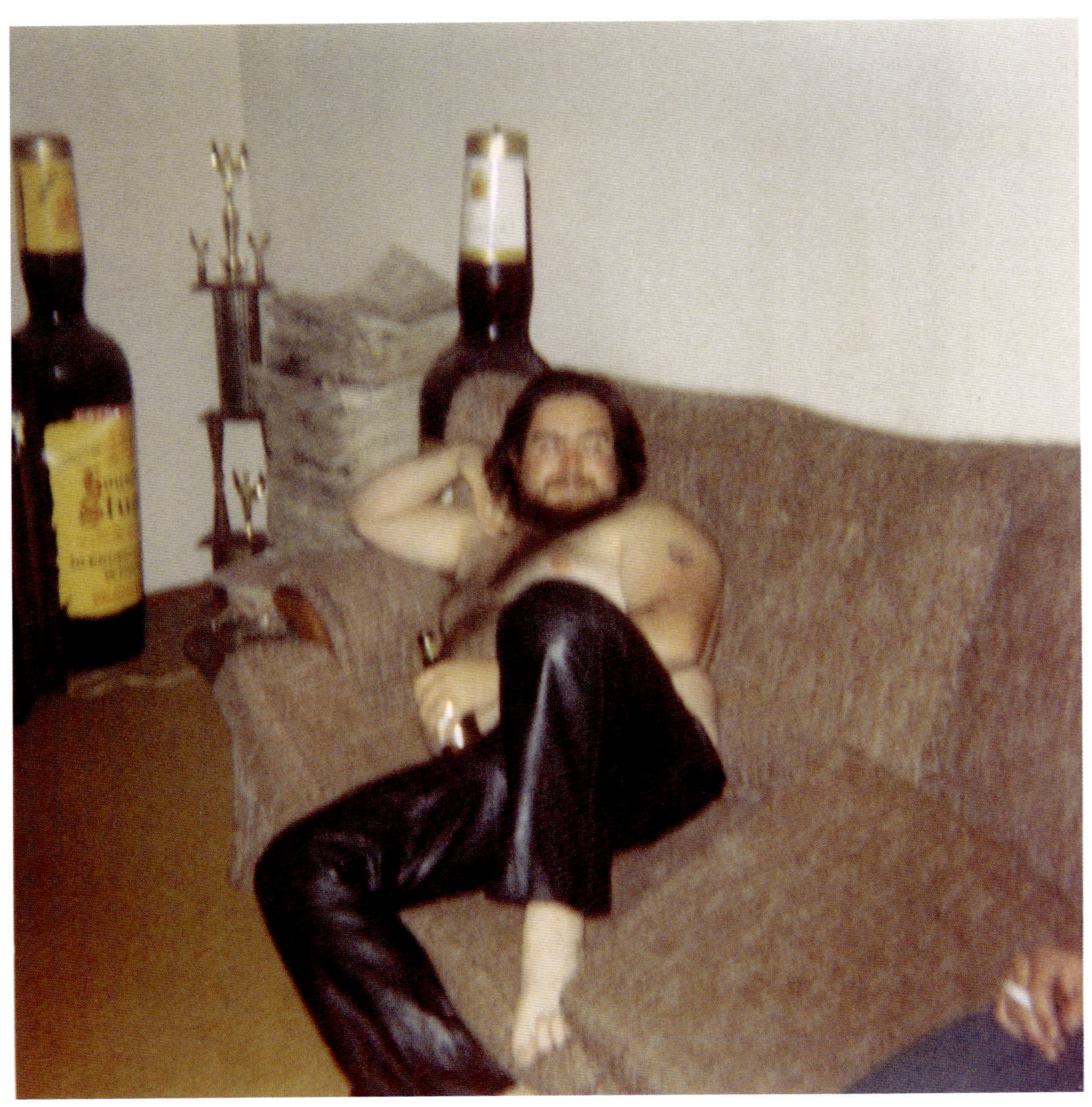

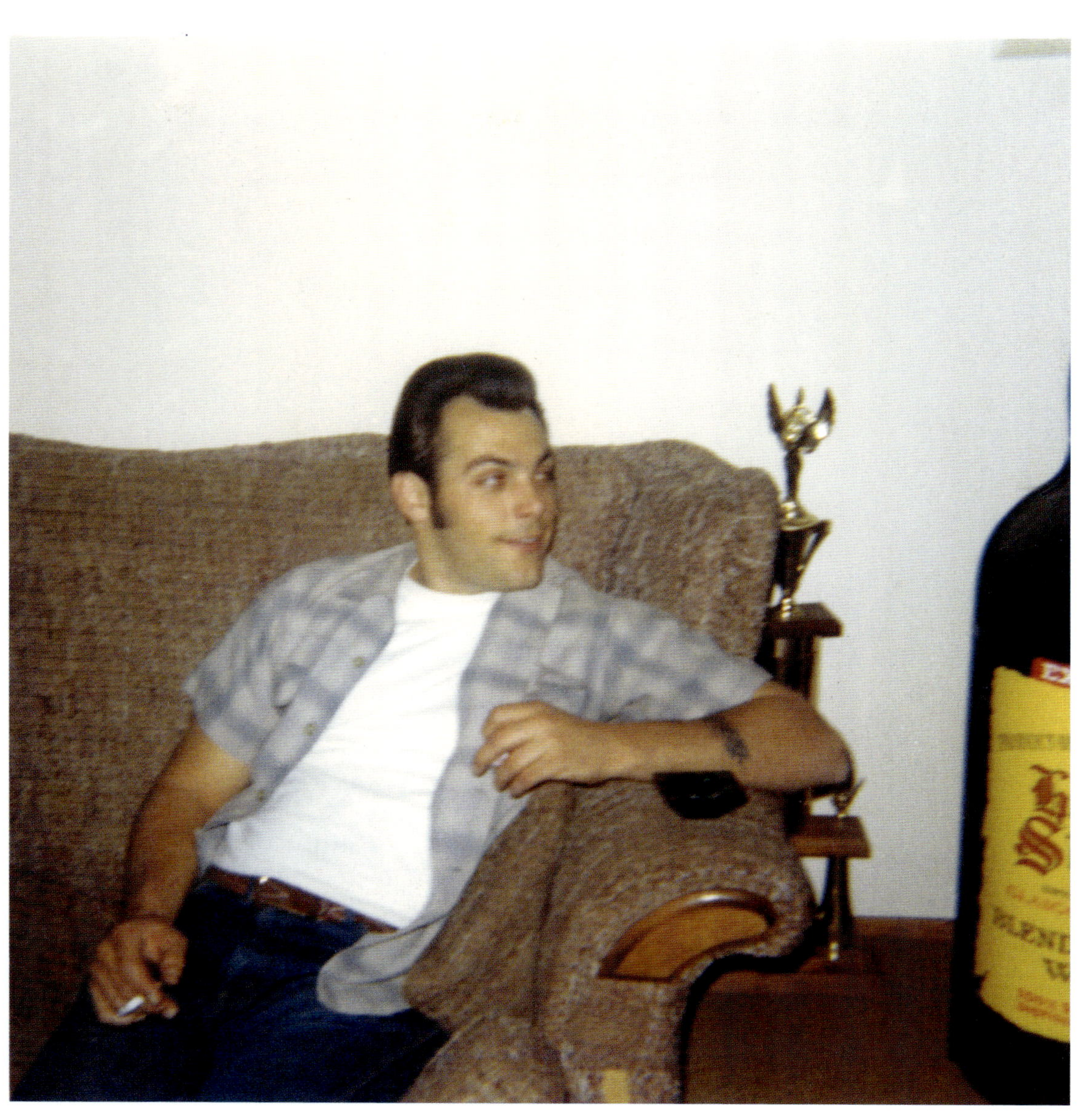

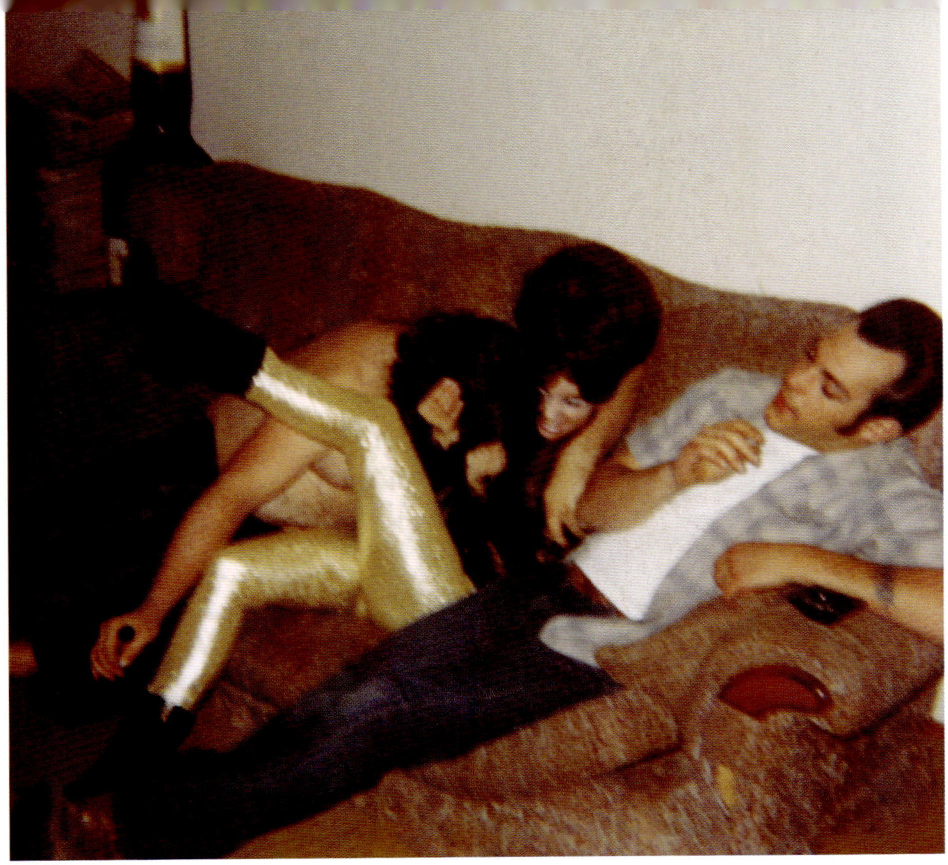

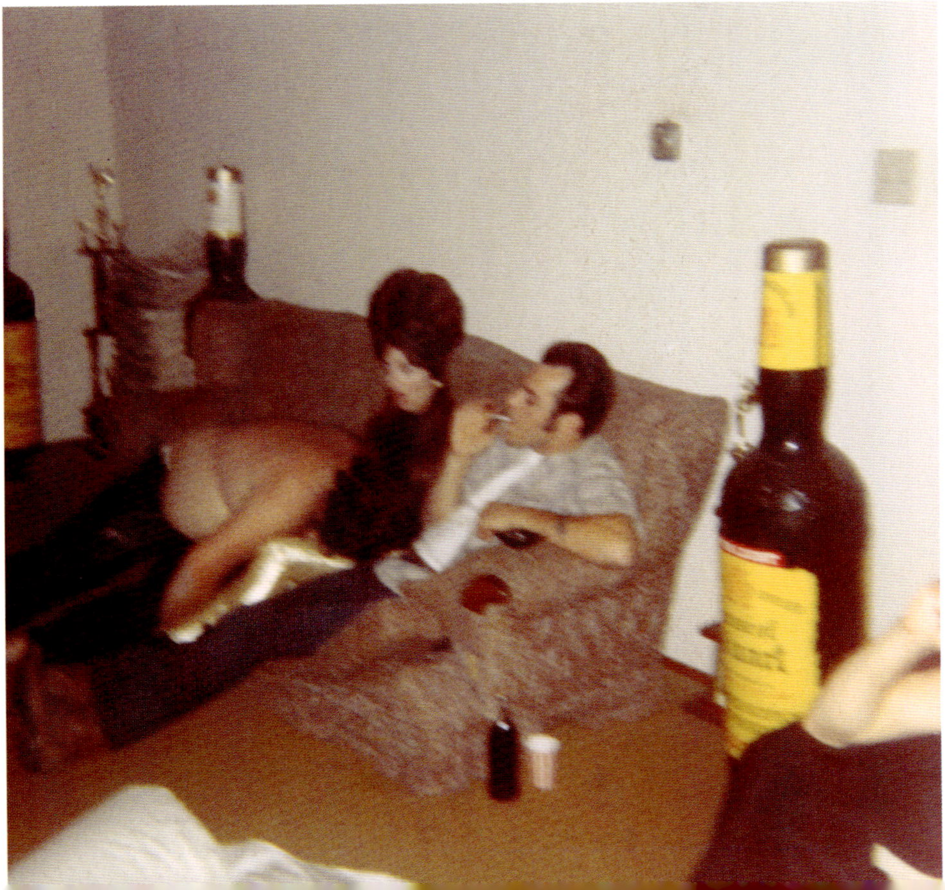

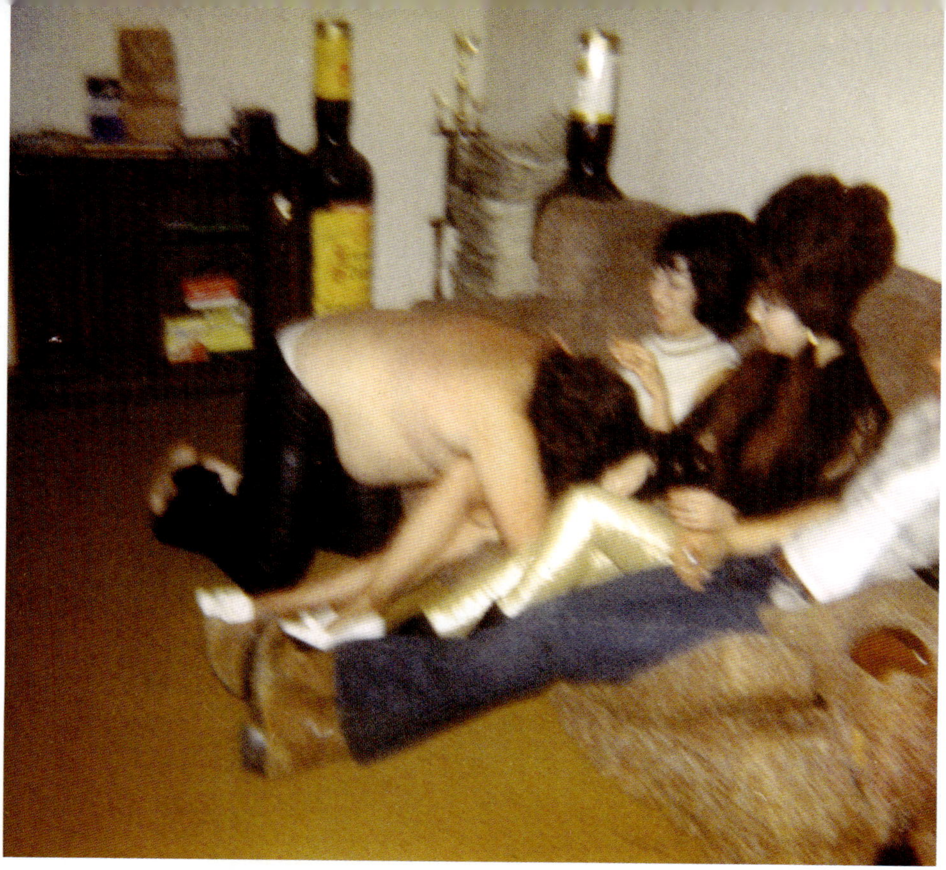

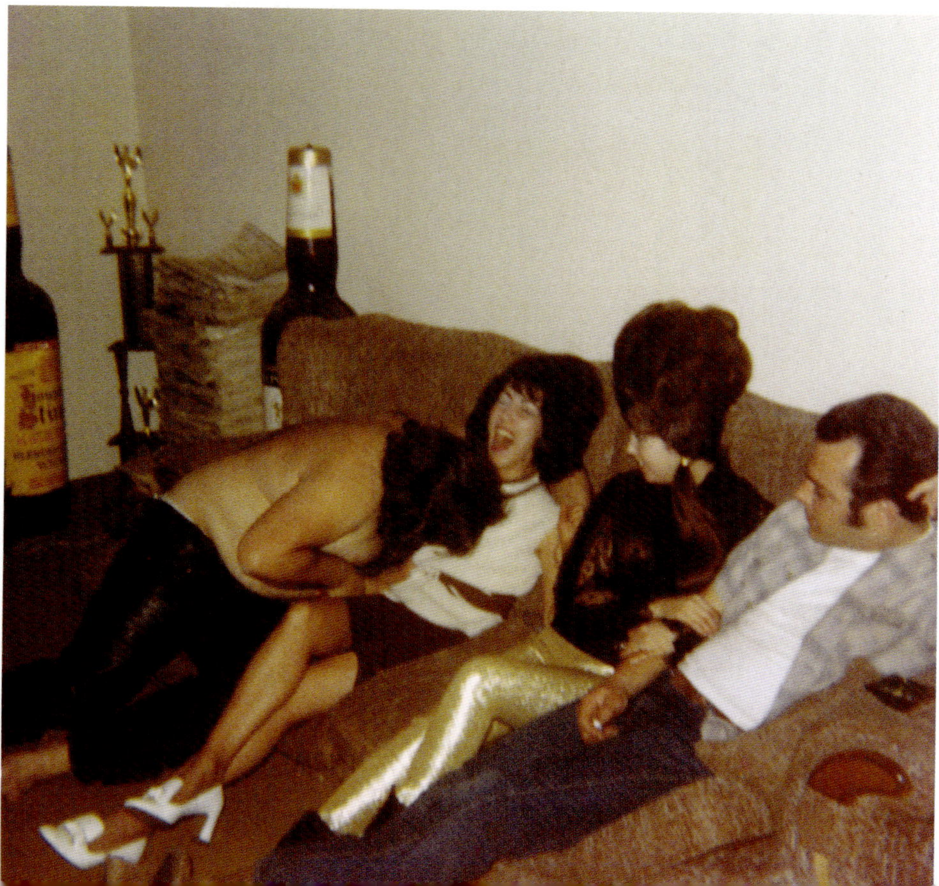

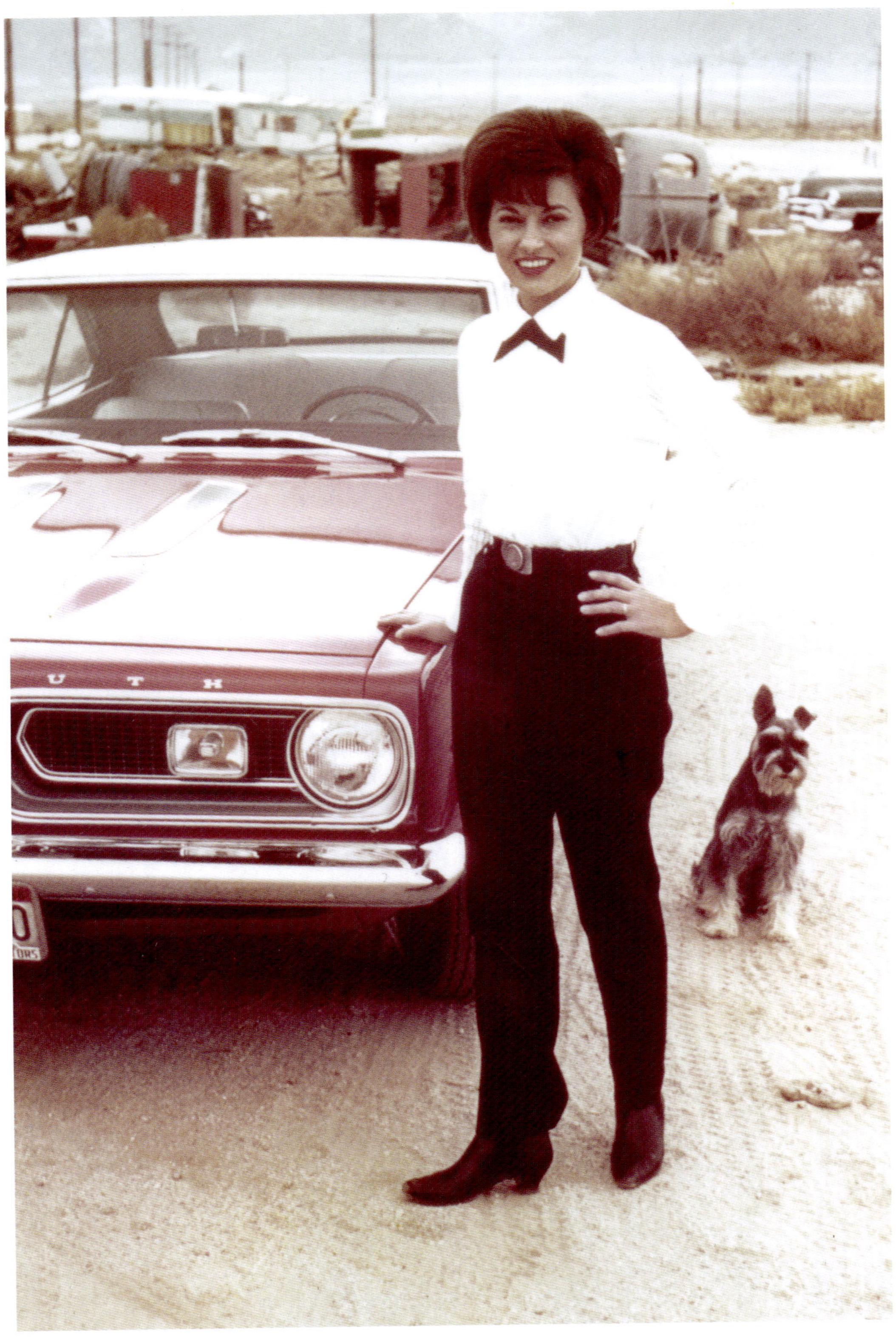

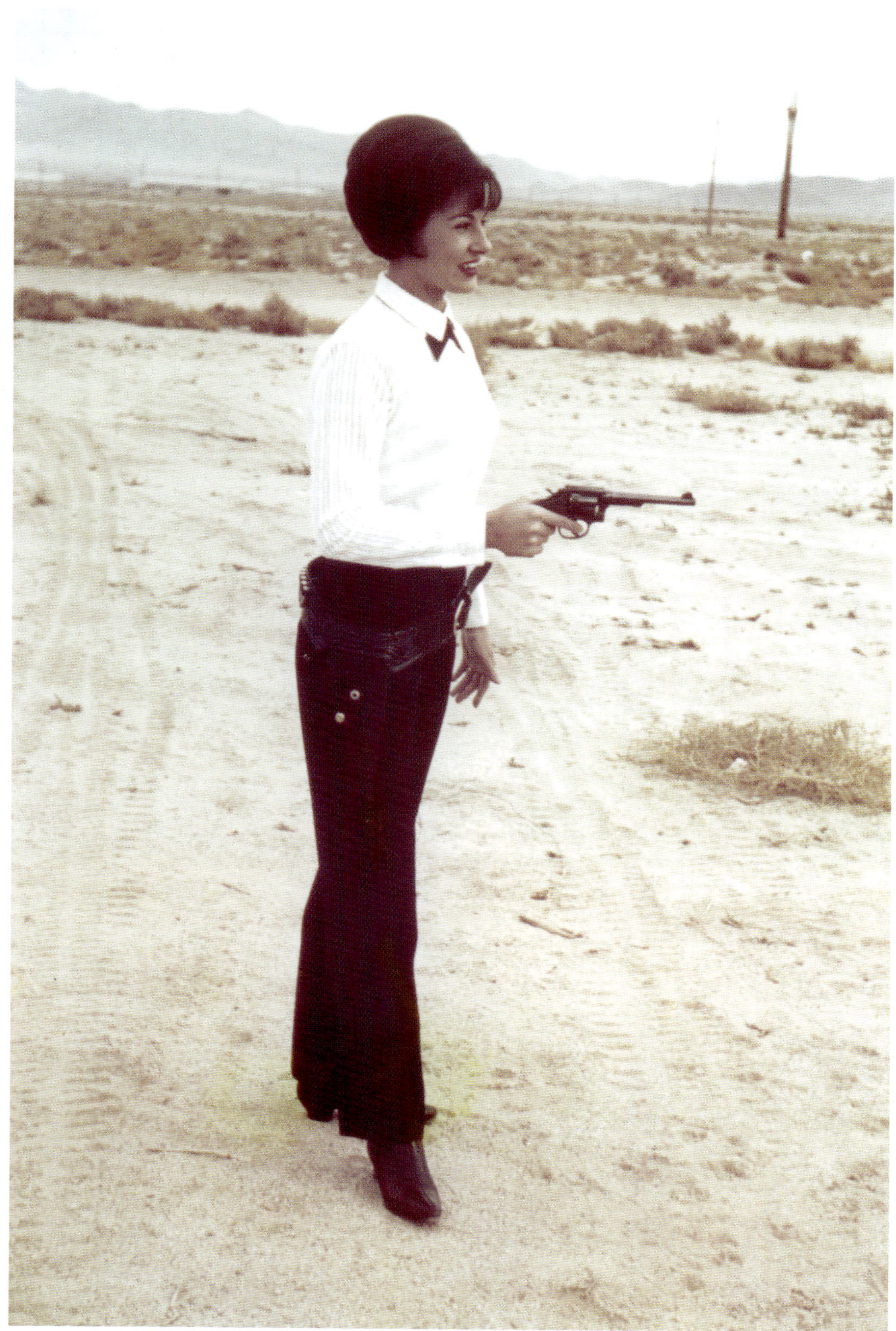

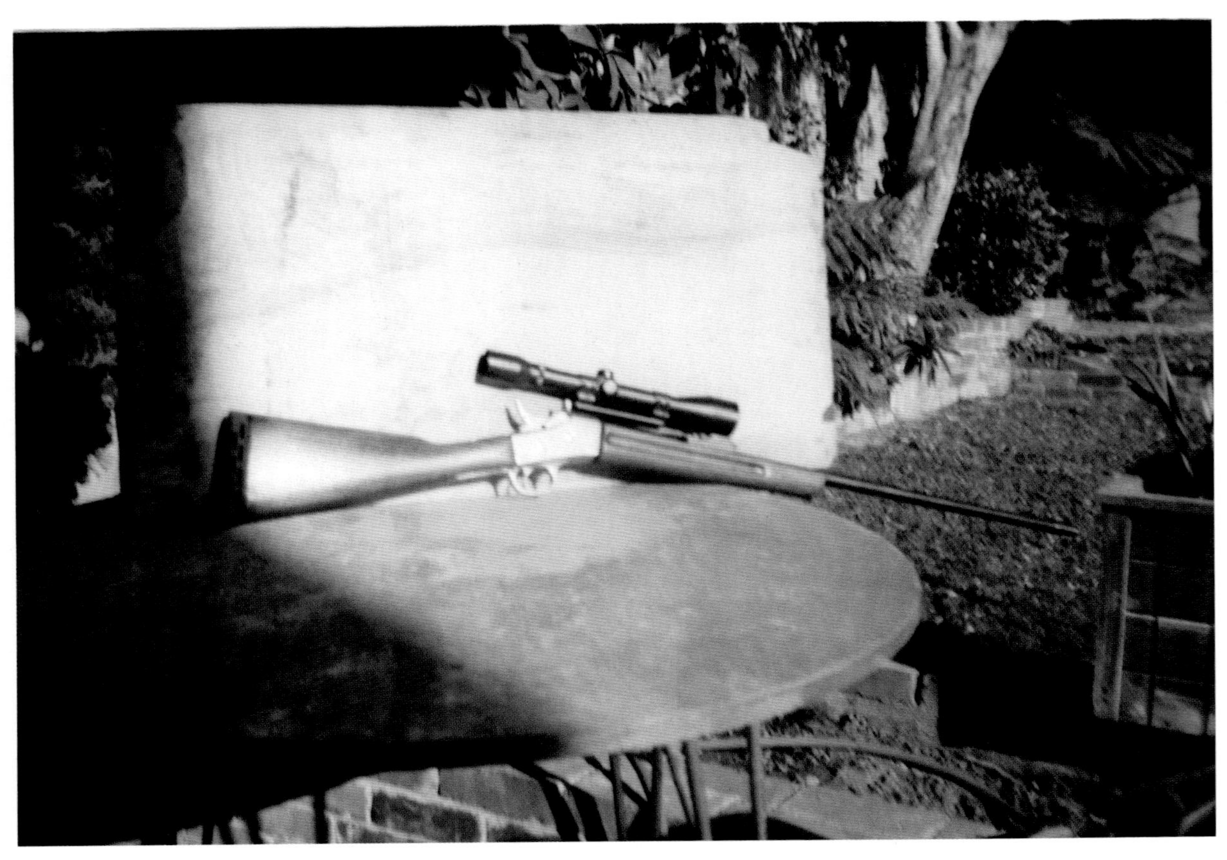

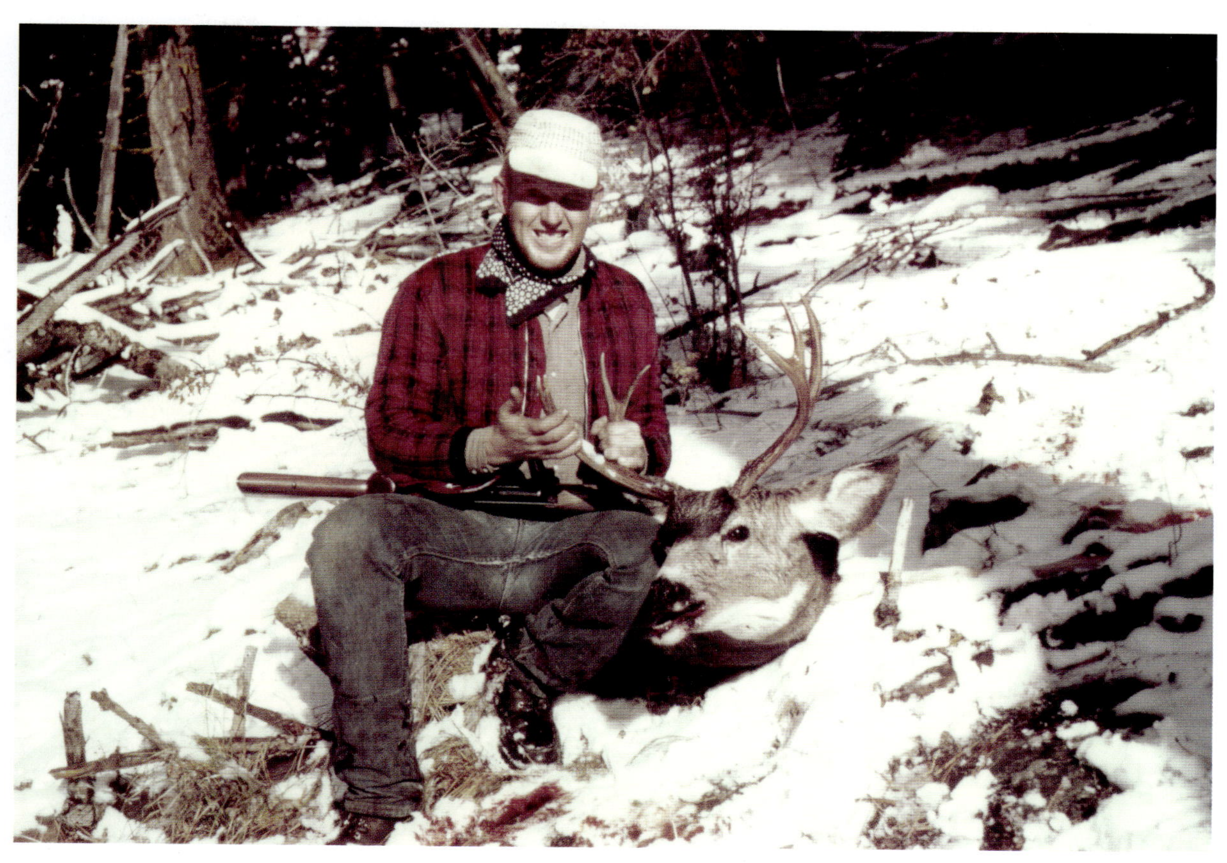

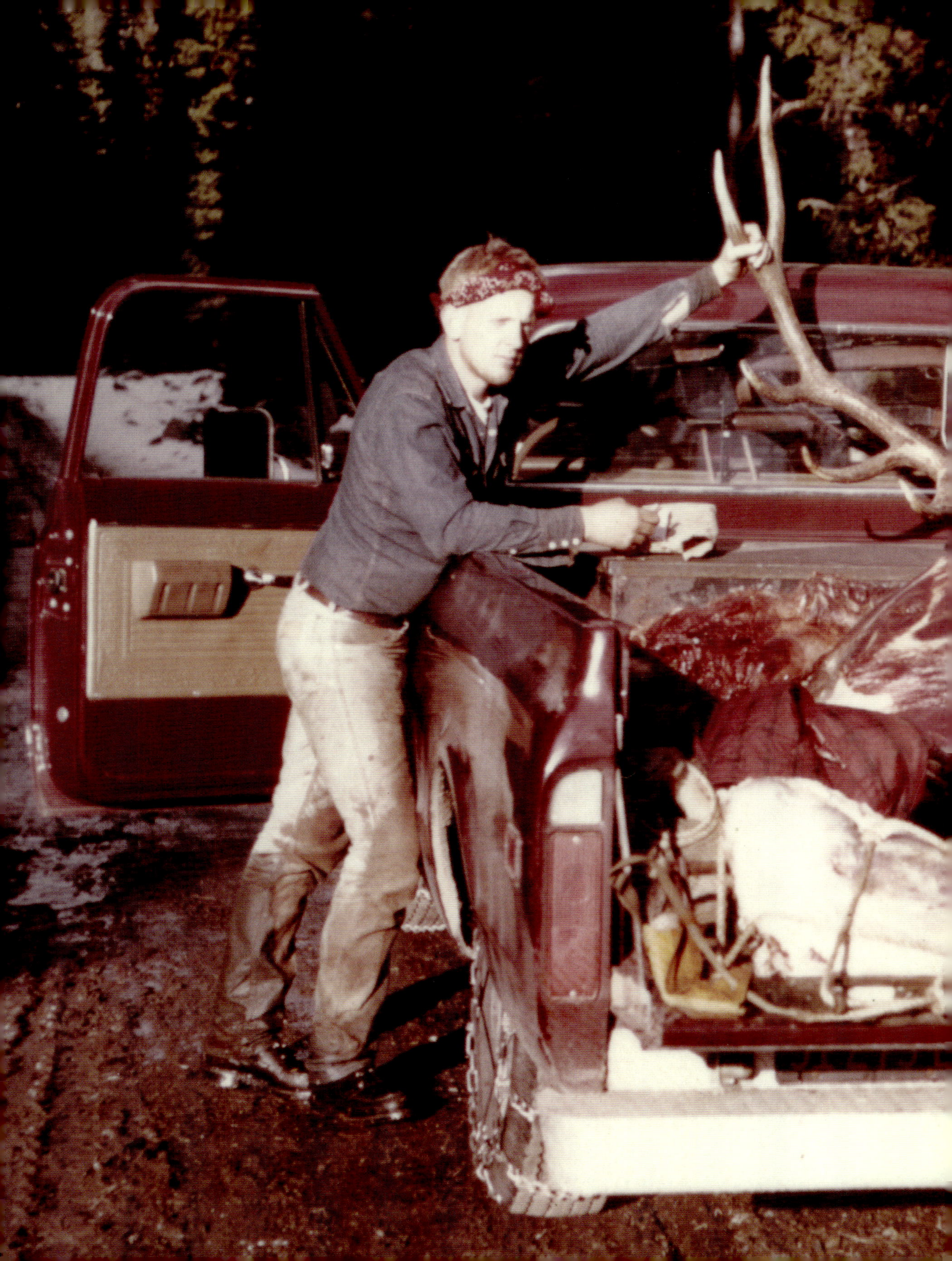

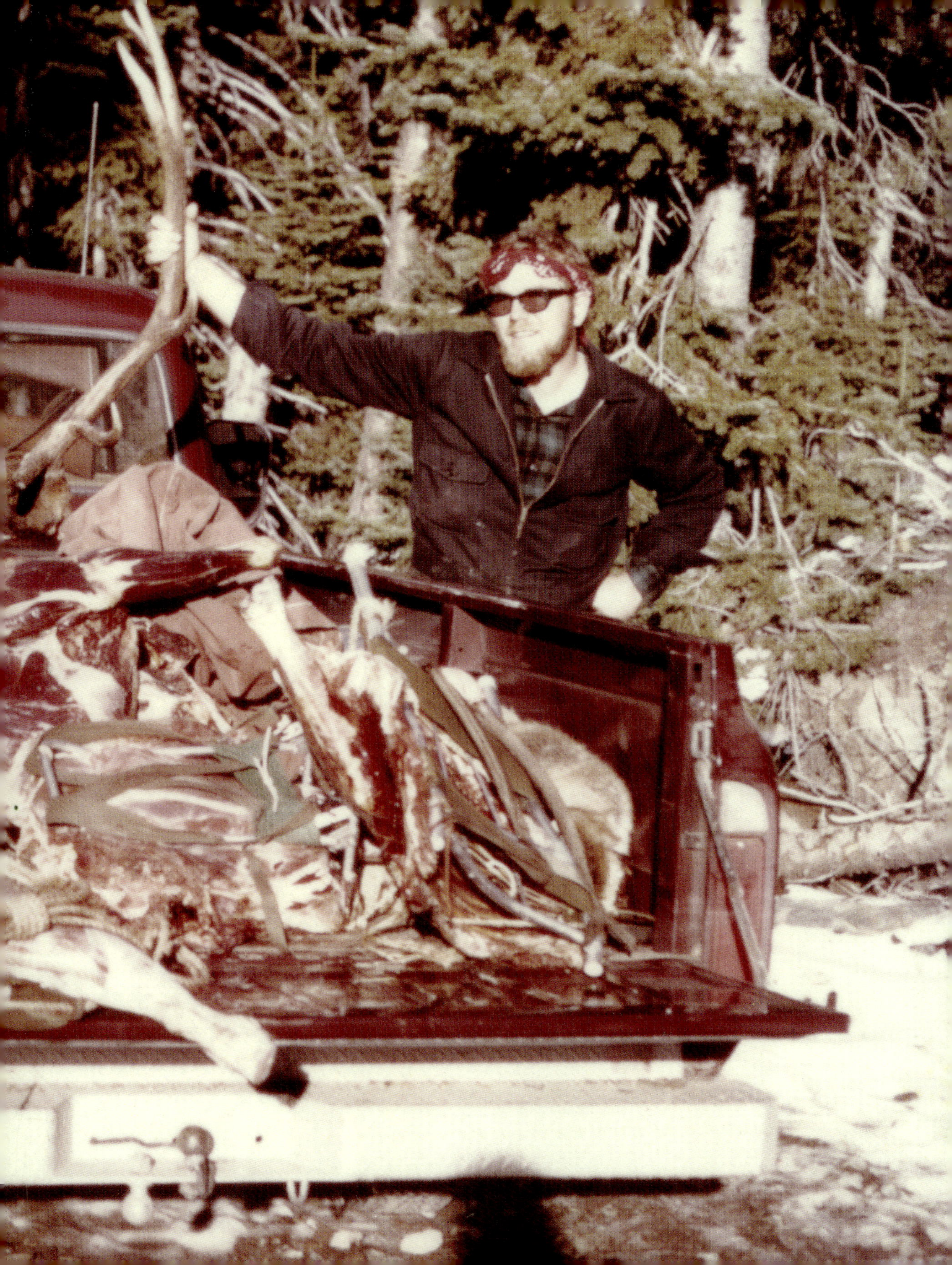

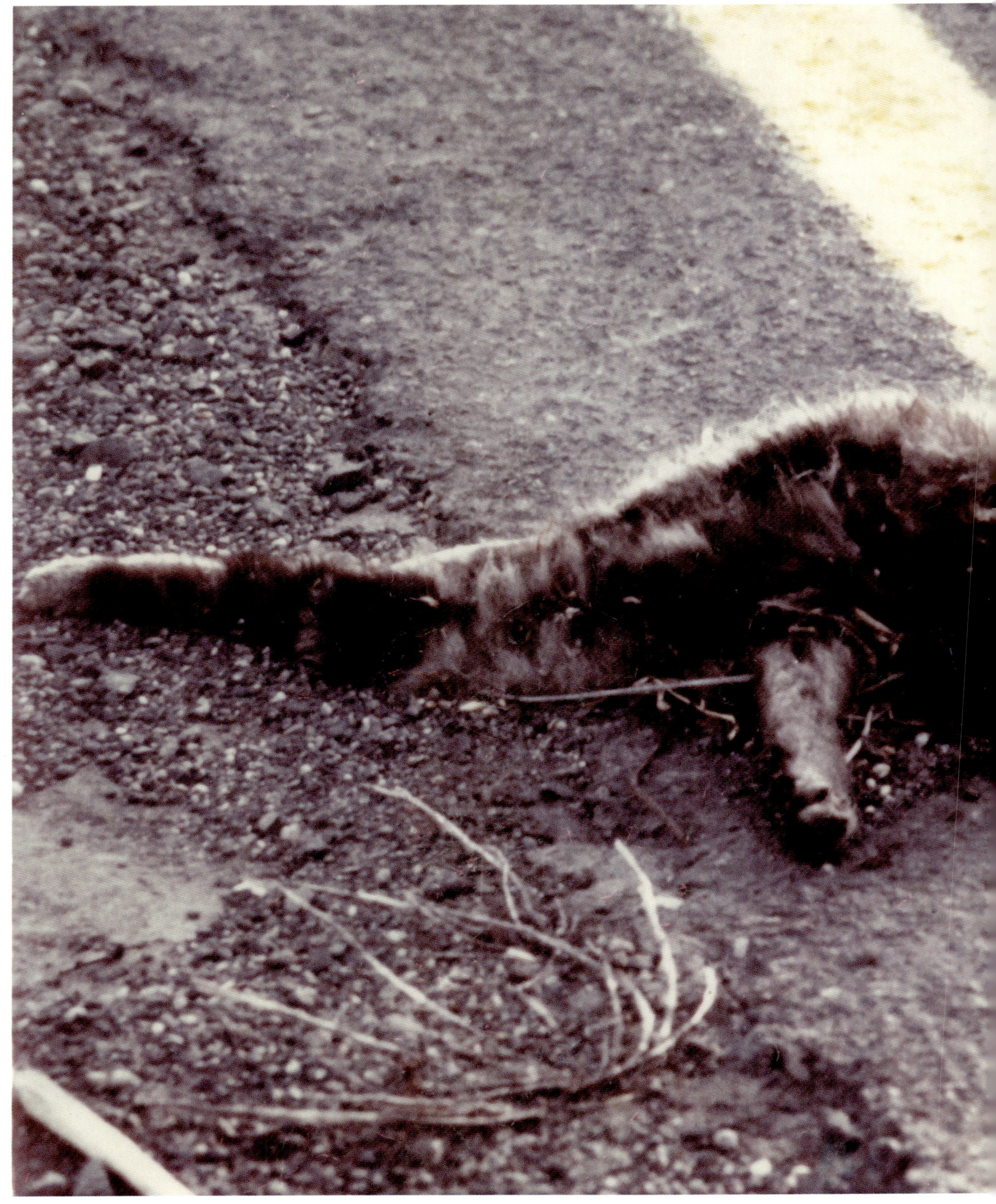

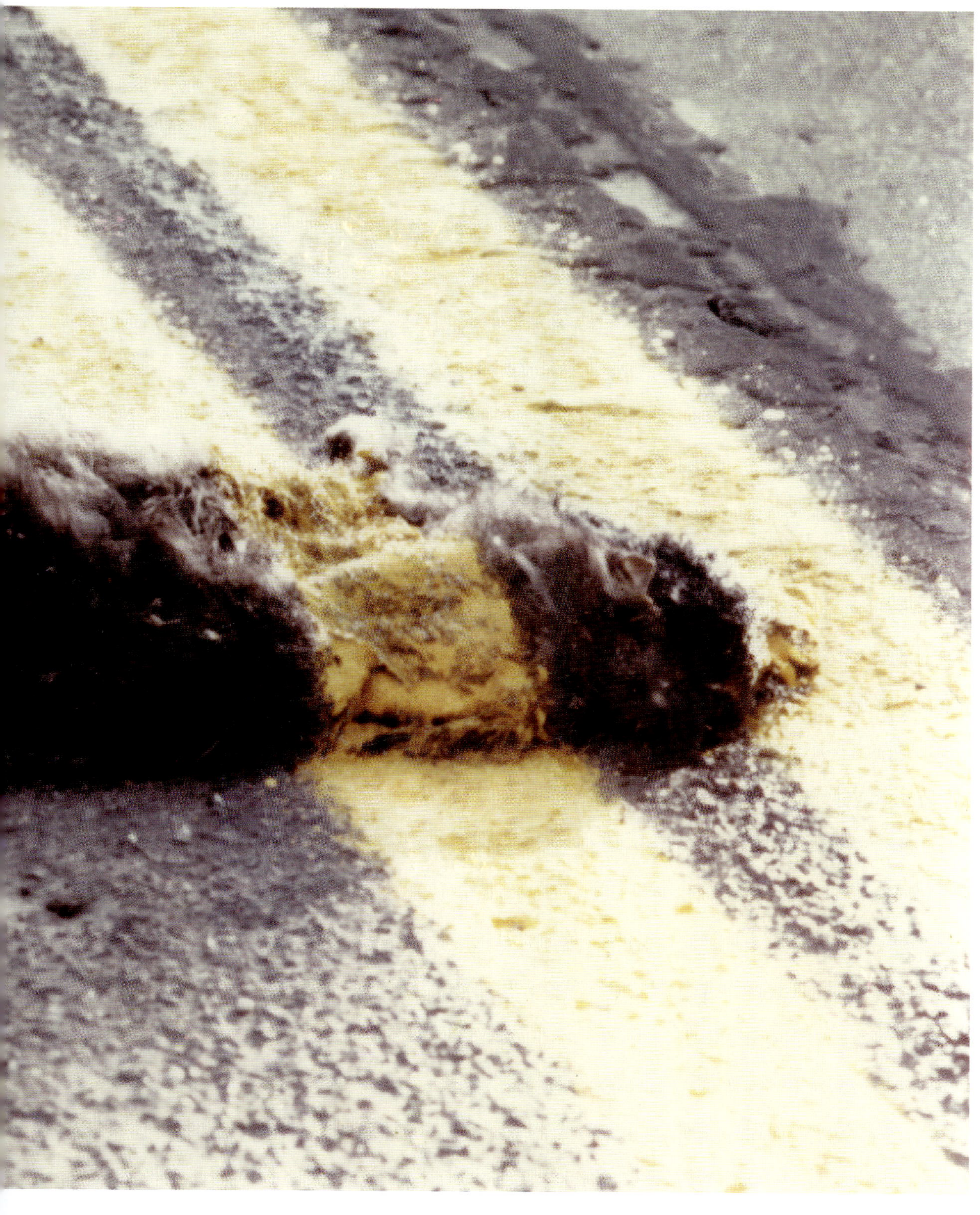

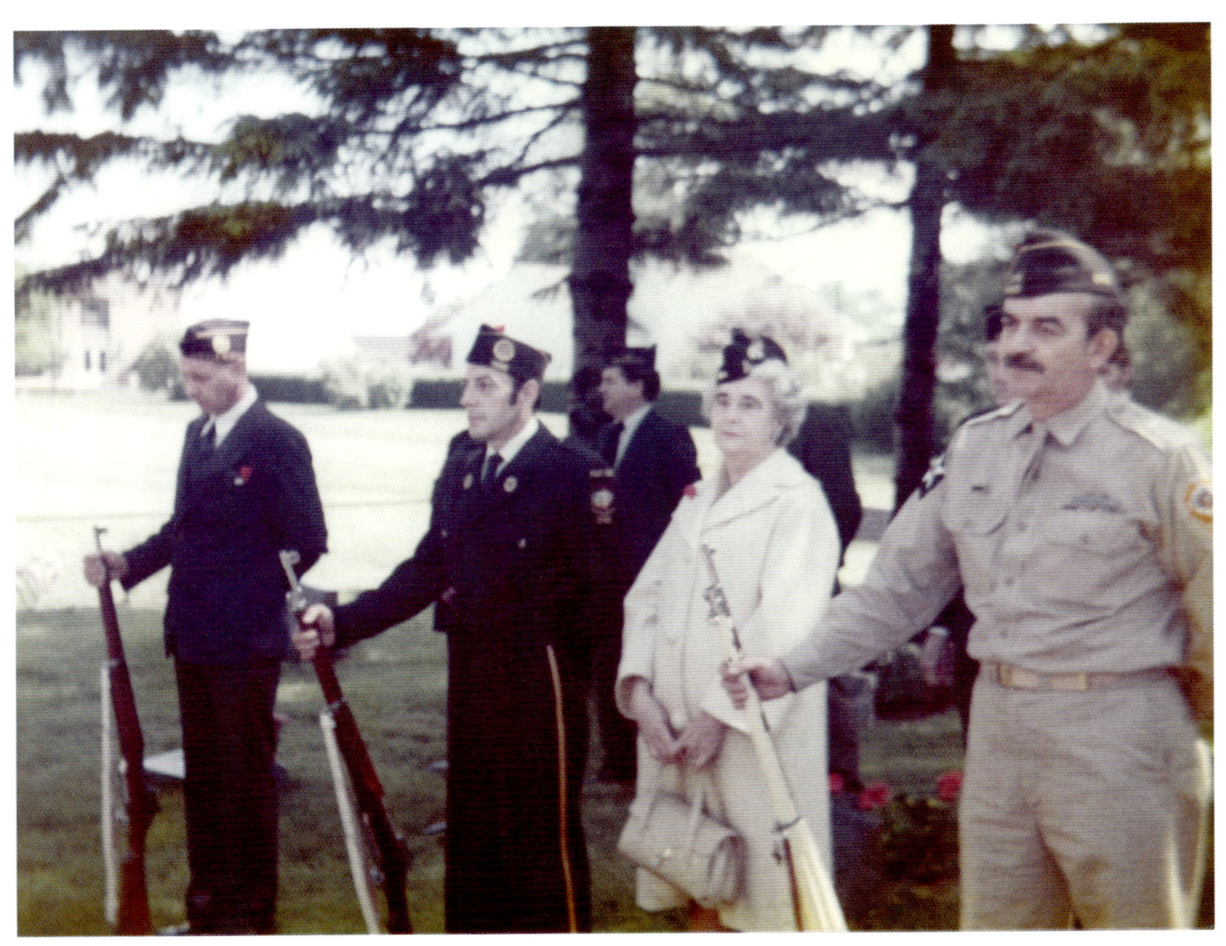

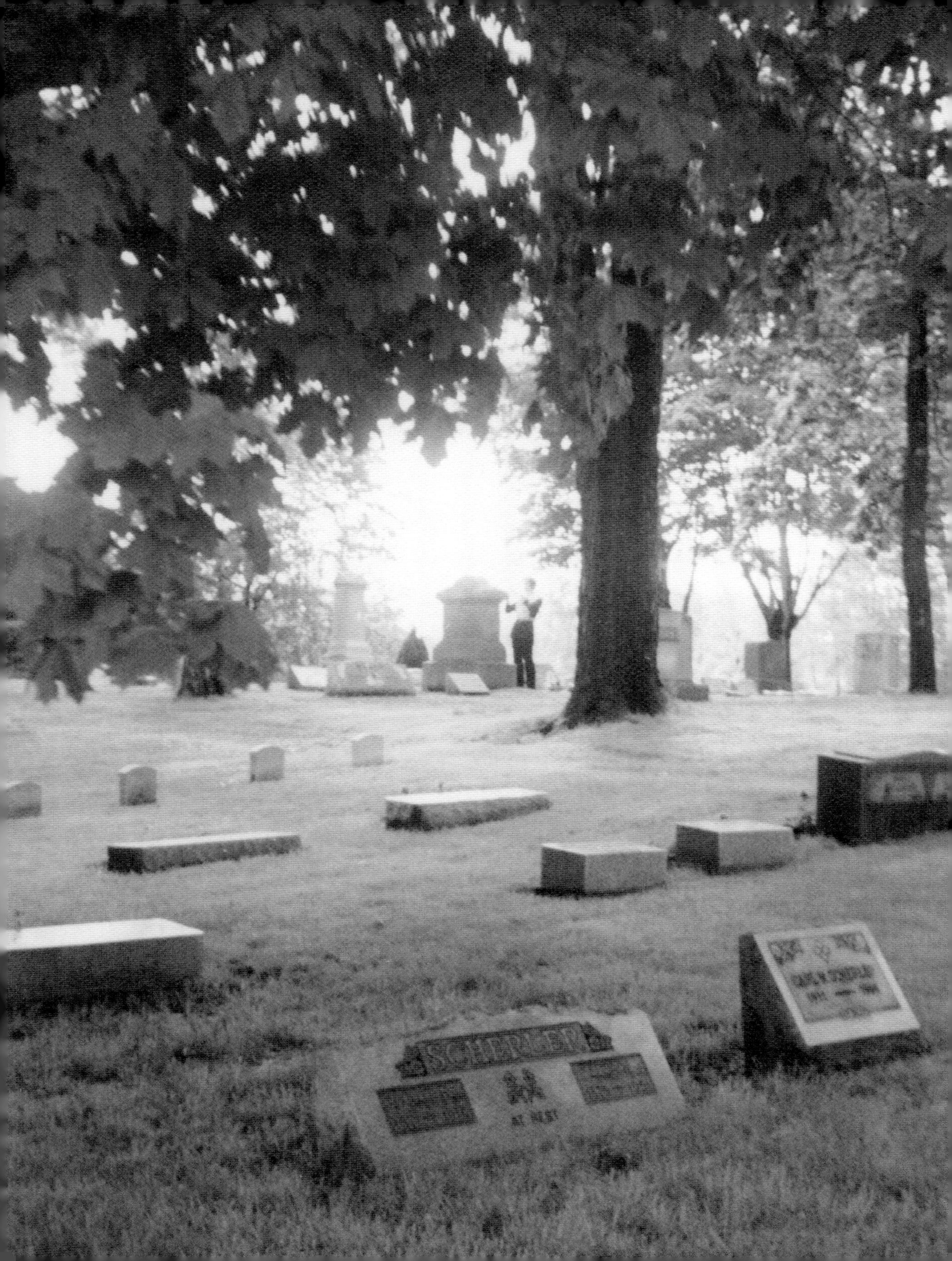
SCHERLER
AT REST

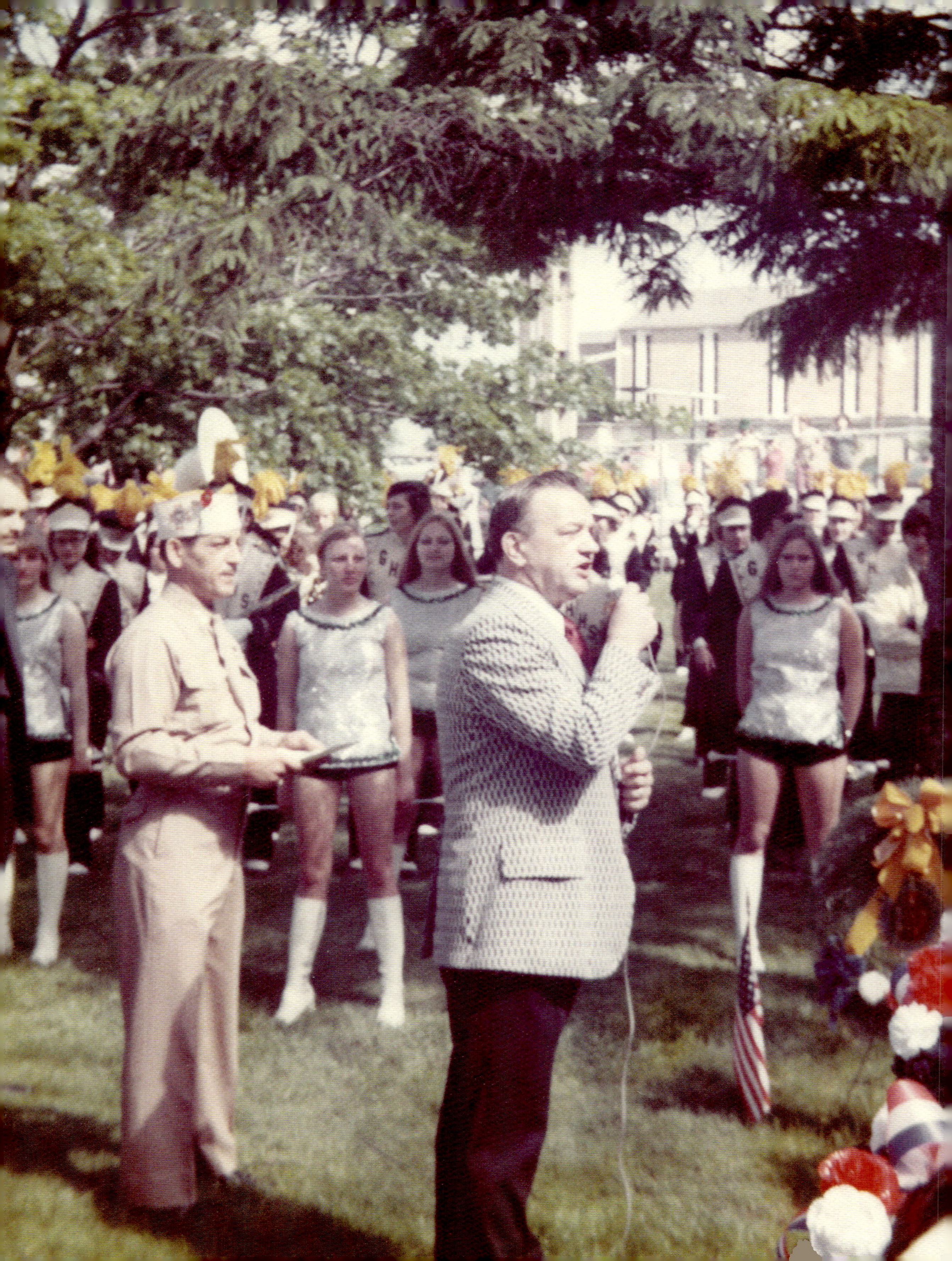

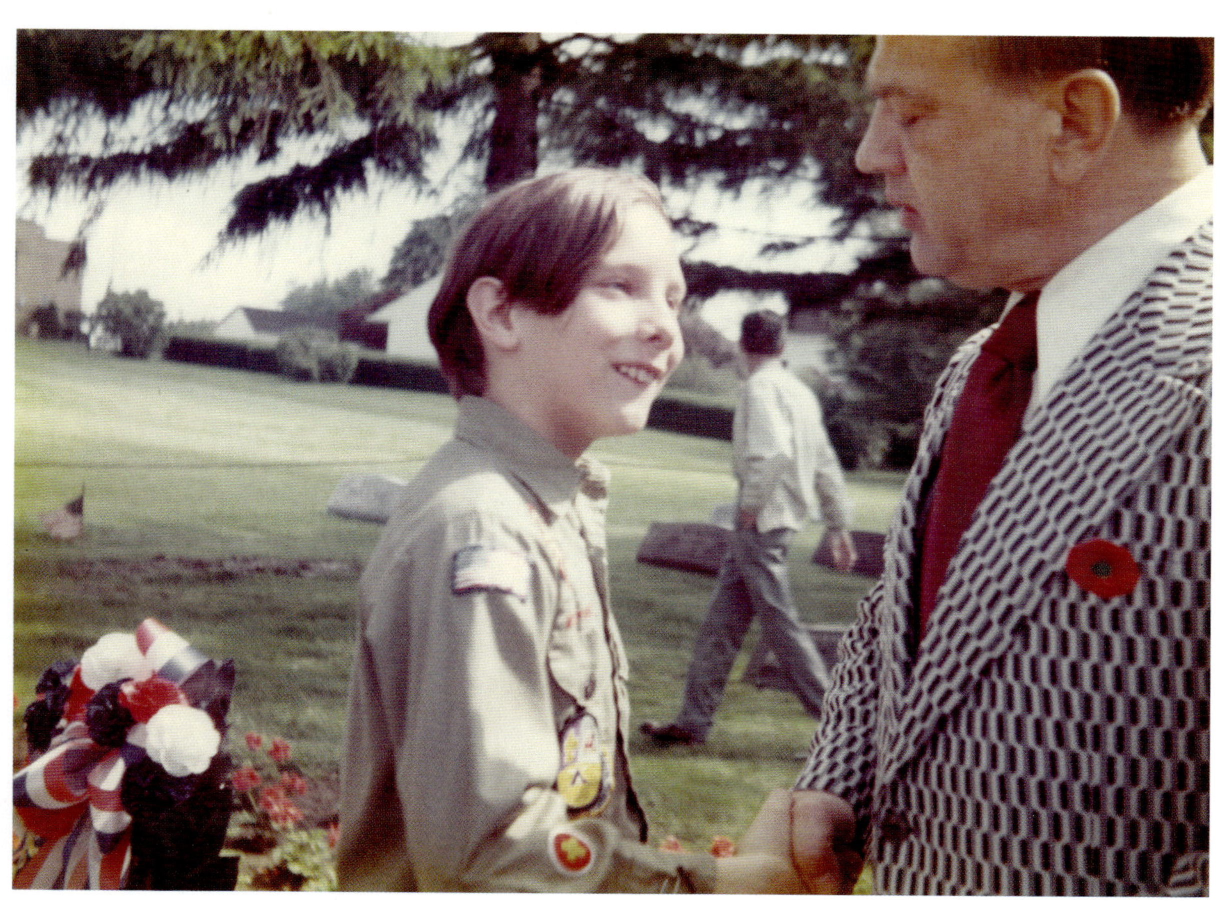

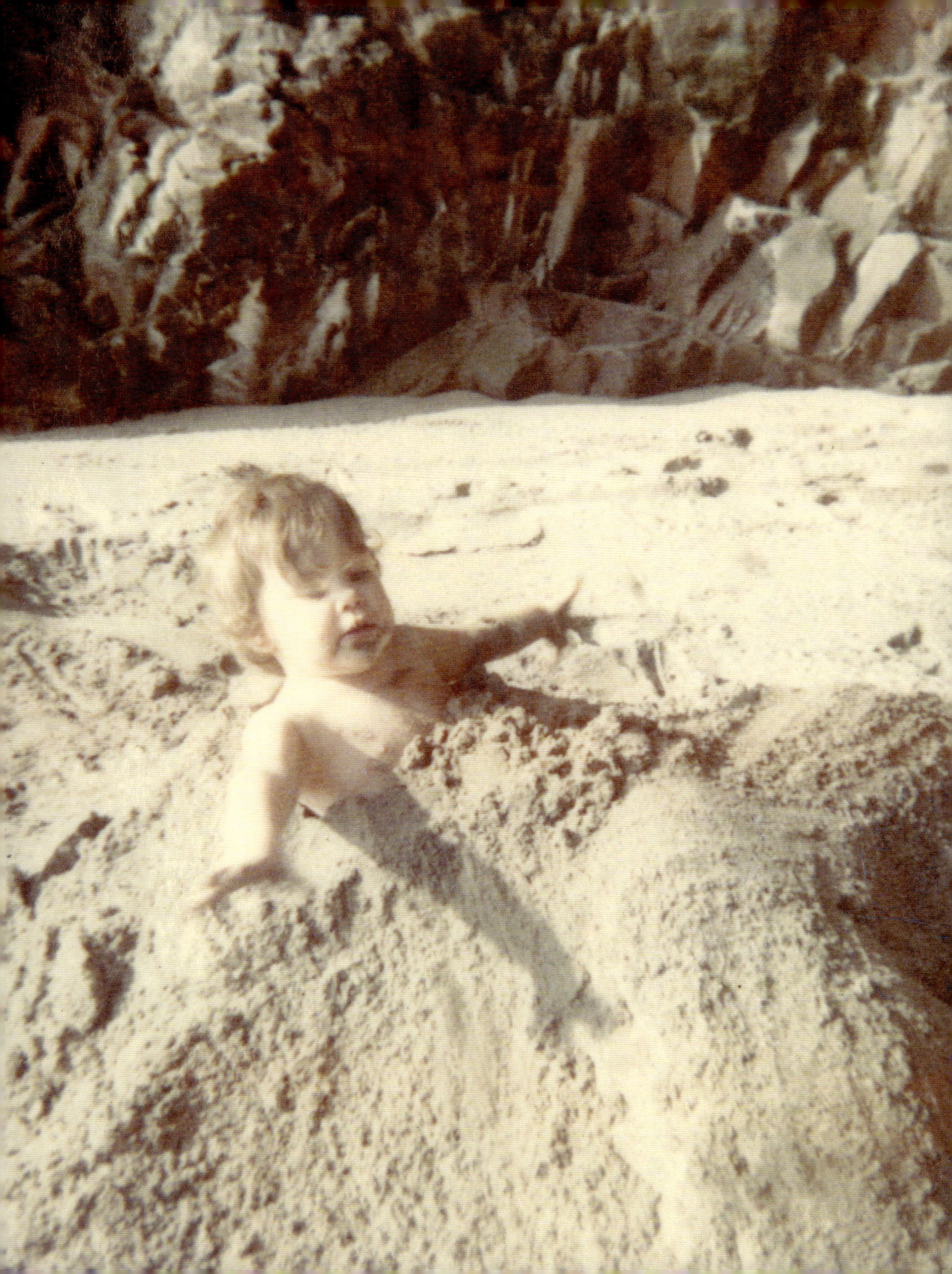